The Fatal Breath

For Romy and Francesca

THE FATAL BREATH

Covid-19 and Society in Britain

David Vincent

polity

First published in 2023 by Polity Press

Polity Press
65 Bridge Street
Cambridge CB2 1UR, UK

Polity Press
111 River Street
Hoboken, NJ 07030, USA

ISBN-13: 978-1-5095-5167-5

A catalogue record for this book is available from the British Library.

Library of Congress Control Number: 2023931012

Typeset in 11.5 on 14pt Adobe Garamond Pro by
Cheshire Typesetting Ltd, Cuddington, Cheshire
Printed and bound in the UK by CPI Group (UK) Ltd, Croydon

The publisher has used its best endeavours to ensure that the URLs for external websites referred to in this book are correct and active at the time of going to press. However, the publisher has no responsibility for the websites and can make no guarantee that a site will remain live or that the content is or will remain appropriate.

Every effort has been made to trace all copyright holders, but if any have been overlooked the publisher will be pleased to include any necessary credits in any subsequent reprint or edition.

For further information on Polity, visit our website: politybooks.com

Contents

Preface

Anyone setting down an account of a lethal pandemic through which they have just lived should begin by giving thanks for their survival. So far, mine has been a lucky Covid-19. Locked down and shielded in a small Shropshire village, needing to make no journeys for work or almost any other purpose over a two-year period, I am one of the diminishing minority in Britain who have escaped infection altogether, as has my wife, who shared my isolation. No fewer than six vaccinations over eighteen months have proved their worth. Children, grandchildren, and other relatives and friends have succumbed, but none seriously. The deaths I have mourned through virtual funerals have been caused by conventional illnesses, their impact intensified by the prohibition of association with the dying and the bereaved. Whilst there has been loss in the very limited physical contact I have been able to make with my extended family during the pandemic, including the two youngest grandchildren to whom this book is dedicated, there has been no deep suffering or lasting damage. I have lived to write, and through writing, living in lockdown has been made safer and more bearable.

Daniel Defoe and later Albert Camus in their different ways wrote accounts of plagues in order to prevent history repeating itself. This social history has a more modest ambition. It is part of the process by which the pandemic has enabled us to understand ourselves better, in our vulnerabilities but also in our strengths and resources. Such knowledge has to be both clarified and recorded if it is to have value for the future. As the chapters argue in a range of contexts, the mass of the British population reacted to Covid-19 with a speed and an effectiveness that put to shame the largely ill-prepared, indecisive, and ill-judged performance of their political masters. The account is a short-run history of twenty-four months but one which requires for its narrative and conclusions a perspective of British society over the previous centuries.

For myself, retired from university teaching and administration, the daily routine of walking from the house to my office to read and write all day was largely uninterrupted by lockdown. Visits to archives were suspended, but the internet has become a cornucopia of sources, particularly where the focus of inquiry is the most recent past. Thanks normally given to librarians and libraries are due this time to the Open University's digital collection, to the digital versions of *The Times*, the *Financial Times*, the *Guardian*, the *New York Times*, and other newspapers and journals, to researchers across the humanities, social sciences, and sciences who have undertaken and published online a remarkable range of reports and inquiries in a very short space of time. In the case of more formal sources, many books have been dispatched along country lanes by distant booksellers. I am grateful to Mass Observation, and in particular Jessica Scantlebury, for allowing me early electronic access to Covid-19 diaries, and for organizing a series of seminars on their use. Finally, I must acknowledge the efforts of British Telecom, which connected my village, recorded in the Domesday Book, to fibre broadband just as it was severed from every other physical means of communication.

When Covid-19 began, I was engaged in a more conventional history project. I was, however, invited to join an international blog, *Covid2020diary*, by my friend and former vice chancellor Brenda Gourley, and her Australian colleague Anne Chappel. Writing around 150 daily commentaries in the company of a diverse range of talented contributors awakened in me the ambition of constructing a full-length history. I am particularly grateful to Brenda and Anne for setting *The Fatal Breath* in motion, and for being there at the end to review the final text. The enterprise has benefited from what became the online meetings and output of the Wellcome-funded Pathologies of Solitude project led by Barbara Taylor at Queen Mary University. Thanks also for their advice to my wise and useful brother Rob Vincent, who, *inter alia*, led the effort to make Test and Trace work in Yorkshire and Humberside, and my caring and useful niece Becci Crook, a newly qualified hospital doctor who laboured at risk to herself with Covid-19 patients in intensive care. For improving the manuscript, I thank Ros Crone, Caroline Millington, John Naughton, and Polity's rigorous referees. Charlotte Vincent, as much an expert in living through Covid-19 as I am, has, as always, sustained the labour of writing this book in every way possible.

Shrawardine, February 2023

The Infection generally came into the Houses of the Citizens, by the Means of their Servants, who, they were obliged to send up and down the Streets for Necessaries, that is to say, for Food, or Physick, to Bakehouses, Brew-houses, Shops, &c. and who going necessarily thro' the Streets into Shops, Markets, and the like, it was impossible, but they should one way or other, meet with distempered people, who conveyed the fatal Breath into them, and they brought it Home to the Families, to which they belonged.

Daniel Defoe, *A Journal of the Plague Year* (1722)

Writing the Pandemic

The Wall

Along the south embankment of the Thames at Westminster is a high stone wall. In front of it runs a pavement overlooking the river, crowded with pedestrians. For a stretch of five hundred yards the wall is now covered in more than two hundred thousand red hearts.

A plaque announces that this is the 'National Covid Memorial Wall'. It was established by Covid-19 Bereaved Families for Justice, supported by the political campaign group Led By Donkeys, in the week following the first anniversary of the imposition of a national lockdown. The hearts represent the victims of Covid-19. Each has been drawn by a volunteer using a simple template, giving the sense of a host of distinct individuals.

As with other national memorials, the wall serves several interlocking functions. Its sheer scale reflects the extent of suffering in the pandemic. Every heart is a life cut short, a level of excess deaths not seen in peacetime since the 1918–20 Spanish Flu epidemic. Together they bear witness to the volume of bereavement. The conventional calculation amongst care professionals of seriously affected relatives or friends is around five for any fatality, although a recent American study suggests the ratio may be as high as nine to one.[1] The wall is an extended public sculpture, freely accessible in a central location in the nation's capital city. Those directly affected by the pandemic and those wishing to bear witness to the scale of the suffering can bring to the monument their thoughts and emotions. There is plenty of room along the riverside: no limitation on entry, no pressure to move along.

The wall is interactive. The blank red hearts can be inscribed by anyone wishing to honour the departed and personalize their sense of loss. There is insufficient space for extended narratives. Instead, there are abbreviated messages to the departed, the briefest summaries of the pain felt by the living: 'Seamus Craig All Love Forever', 'RIP Nurse Estrella Catalan',

'Forever in our hearts Tasmir Kaur 1956'. Some of the inscriptions are in other languages, including Arabic. Most, but not all, reflect the impact of the pandemic on older cohorts: 'Tony Taylor 1951–2020', 'Anne Evans 1943–2020', '1950–2021 In Memory of Michael John Allen "Mick" XX'. It is just possible to indicate the grief of close families: 'In Loving Memory of our Mother 1948–2020 In Our Hearts Forever. We Miss You So Much XXX', '21 12 45 – 9 02 21 Nan Chrissy. We All Miss You So Much. Love All of Us', 'My Wife Chrissy. Always on My Mind'. There is meaning in the sheer limitation of language. In many cases, the texts recorded a death that occurred in intensive care units closed to family members, followed by a severely restricted funeral service. Dying of Covid-19 was a compressed experience for all concerned.

The multiple red images reflect a common trope of public memorials in Britain. The centenary commemoration of the First World War seven years earlier featured a display of 888,246 scarlet poppies on the grass slopes surrounding the Tower of London. With its home-made hearts, the Covid Memorial is a more effective response to the scale of individual deaths than the mass-produced ceramic flowers.

The wall was immediately recognized as a national event. It was endorsed by the Mayor of London, Sadiq Khan. The Leader of the Opposition, Keir Starmer, made a public visit. The Archbishop of Canterbury, Justin Welby, walked along from the neighbouring Lambeth Palace and was photographed chatting to the volunteers painting the hearts. The memorial became the most powerful visual representation of Covid-19 in Britain, used as a standard backdrop for television and newspaper reports throughout the remainder of the pandemic.

The location was perfectly chosen. Behind the wall is St Thomas's Hospital, where Boris Johnson was treated a fortnight after the lockdown was declared. That event, the looming realization that Covid-19 might cost the life of the prime minister, did more than anything else to entrench the reality of the accelerating pandemic.[2] The intense public attention paid to the sequence of minor symptoms suddenly worsening, leading to a hospital admission and then an intensive care unit and the prospect of treatment on a ventilator with a slim chance of survival, brought home the choreography of the disease. Directly across the Thames is the Palace of Westminster. Once the wall was painted, Members of Parliament could at any moment look out across the water and see the long red line, a constant reminder of their task and the consequence of failing in it.

In its conception, however, the wall was anything but a consensual event. It was a crowd-funded by-product of a campaign being waged by a group of angry relatives of early victims. Covid-19 Bereaved Families for Justice believed that many deaths had been caused by government mismanagement in the crucial first weeks of the crisis. They launched a petition for a public inquiry, claiming that,

> as more and more information comes to light, it has become clear that the UK hasn't ended up with one of the highest death tolls in the world by coincidence. Gaps in the country's pandemic preparedness, delays to locking down, inadequate supplies of PPE [personal protective equipment] and the policy of discharging into care homes among other issues have all been identified as having contributed to the level of the death toll.[3]

Boris Johnson resisted for a year, arguing that his administration should not be distracted from the battle against the pandemic. He faced a dilemma once the wall became a success, not wanting either to endorse the campaign or to disrespect the lives that were mourned and celebrated. His solution was to pay a visit to the wall on a dark evening accompanied only by a single security officer. He was spotted by a passing MP and much mocked in the next day's newspapers.

The government finally agreed to the demand for a full-scale inquiry a few weeks after the wall was finished. The team of twelve QCs led by Lady Hallett began work in July 2022, with a report not expected for at least another year. Covid-19 Bereaved Families for Justice only gained permission for their installation on the basis that it would be temporary. Were it to become permanent, the hearts would need to be properly protected with lacquer. It was intended to be a means of publicizing the alleged scale of public maladministration and consequent loss of life. At the press conference on the first anniversary of the lockdown, Johnson promised a 'fitting and permanent' memorial that would be constructed 'at the right moment'.[4] In July 2022, the 'UK Commission on Covid Commemoration' was established, with a brief to 'build a consensus around the measures which will be put in place to tell the story of this period in our history and remembering into the future those we lost'.[5] Whose monument prevails, which narrative comes to represent the national memory, will depend on the unfinished debate about the course of the pandemic.

The Fatal Breath

The title for this book, and its epigraph, are taken from Daniel Defoe's *A Journal of the Plague Year*, published fifty-seven years after the events it described. The account of the outbreak of bubonic plague in London in 1665 embedded carefully assembled factual information in the format of a fictional diary. The first-person witness was invented as a means of giving urgency and authenticity to the narrative. Defoe, who was about five years old at the time of the outbreak, grew up in a city full of memories of the event, and collected documentary material on the progress of the disease through the parishes of the capital.[6] He was no more certain than any contemporary medical authority about the aetiology of the infection. As a doctor wrote in a treatise published in the same year as the *Journal*, '[T]he Cause of the Plague is most mysterious, and not yet hitherto plainly discovered'.[7] Amongst the prevailing theories, argued the doctor, it was unlikely that 'ours was caused by the like Production of Worms or Insects, as some have rather fancied than demonstrated'.[8] It was not until 1894 that the responsible bacterium, *Yersinia pestis*, was isolated, and a further four years before the mode of transmission, fleas carried by black rats, was identified.[9]

Defoe followed the conventional diagnosis of preceding outbreaks that the plague was spread by contagion, in some way involving contact between humans. If there was no medical proof of this mechanism, there was ample experiential evidence stretching back at least as far as the sixth-century Plague of Justinian that preventing association between the healthy and the infected was the most effective means of controlling an epidemic. Exactly what passed between individuals was not clear. It was at once invisible and pervasive. In his parallel treatise, *Due Preparations for the Plague*, on the need for public preparations against a return of the plague published just before the *Journal*, Defoe summarized the capacious process and the ideal counter-measure.

Nothing is more certain than that the contagion strengthens, and the infectious particles in the air, if any such there are, increase in quantity, as the

4

greater number of sick bodies are kept together. The effluvia emitted from the bodies infected are more rank and more contagious, and are carried farther in the air the more bodies are infected, and are therefore more apt to be received from house to house; and were it possible for all the people in the populous cities and towns in England to separate on such an occasion as this, and spread themselves over the whole kingdom in smaller numbers, and at proper distances from one another 'tis evident even to demonstration, that the plague would have but very little power, and the effects of it be very little felt.[10]

The infectious particles could survive in the folds of clothing or on hard surfaces.[11] Defoe's *Due Preparations* contained a vivid account of the steps taken by a wealthy London grocer to avoid contamination by his extensive correspondence:

His letters were brought by the postman, or letter-carrier, to his porter, when he caused the porter to smoke them with brimstone and with gunpowder, then open them, and to sprinkle them with vinegar; then he had them drawn up by the pulley, then smoked again with strong perfumes, and, taking them with a pair of hair gloves, the hair outermost, he read them with a large reading-glass which read at a great distance, and, as soon as they were read, burned them in the fire; and at last, the distemper raging more and more, he forbid his friends writing to him at all.[12]

That the grocer survived and the porter eventually died of the plague merely proved the point. The particles might somehow be inherent in miasma arising from cess pits, bad food, rotting refuse, or corpses. Moreover, it had been accepted at least since the fourteenth-century Black Death that they were passed through the air from mouth to mouth.[13] Recent medical research has established that in addition to the intermediary role of rats and fleas, it is possible for the pneumonic plague, a lethal version of the bacteria, to infect the lungs and be transferred directly through coughing or sneezing from one respiratory system to another.[14] Defoe was at least partly right in his lamentation of the effect of so natural an action as breathing.

The ill-defined but insistent emphasis on contagion made the treatment of the Covid-19 pandemic seem very conventional. By the beginning of the seventeenth century, the long battle against the bubonic plague had established structures of control and surveillance that were far ahead of any other area of public intervention in non-criminal private behaviour. In Britain, a series of initiatives were consolidated into an Act of Parliament in 1604, which, amongst much else, specified that anyone infected with the plague and found in the company of others could be hanged for a felony.[15] When the disease returned half a century later, the authorities drew upon their reserve powers to specify restrictions on social activities which, given subsequent developments in popular recreations, were much the same as those imposed in the lockdowns of 2020 and 2021:

> THAT all Plays, Bear-Baitings, Games, singing of Ballads, Buckler-play, or such like Causes of Assemblies of People, be utterly prohibited, and the Parties offending severely punished by every Alderman in his Ward. THAT all publick Feasting, and particularly by the Companies of this City, and Dinners at Taverns, Alehouses, and other Places of common Entertainment be forborn till further Order and Allowance. . . . THAT disorderly Tipling in Taverns, Alehouses, Coffee-houses, and Cellars be severely looked unto, as the common Sin of this Time, and the greatest occasion of dispersing the Plague.[16]

The response to the Spanish Flu epidemic was hampered by the failure correctly to identify the microbial cause, and as a result the authorities fell back on established techniques of social distancing. As well as traditional venues like public houses and churches, prohibitions were now applied to transport systems and schooling.[17]

Covid-19 was the first global pandemic where the pathogen was fully understood almost from the outset. After an initial attempt to conceal the outbreak in Wuhan, the virus was identified and its genetic sequence was posted on the internet on 11 January 2020. However, for all the progress in medical science, there remained room for error. Global public health policy in 2020 was compromised by a misleading emphasis on fomite transmission.[18] Working within the framework of earlier research into infectious diseases, the World Health Organization (WHO) and other official bodies at first assumed that the principal mode of spreading Covid-19 was through droplets expelled from the mouth or nostrils and falling onto surfaces where they infected those who touched them and then their faces. 'The best thing people can do to prevent the spread of coronavirus is wash your hands,' advised the prime minister on 28 February 2020.[19]

It was not until later in 2020, following a range of studies, including those on the course of outbreaks on cruise ships, that greater emphasis began to be placed on aerosol infection: microdroplets suspended in the air and breathed in by those occupying the same space.[20] A year and a half after the virus was identified, the issue was still being debated in the columns of *The Lancet*. An article in May 2021 concluded that

> it is a scientific error to use lack of direct evidence of SARS-CoV-2 in some air samples to cast doubt on airborne transmission while overlooking the quality and strength of the overall evidence base. There is consistent, strong evidence that SARS-CoV-2 spreads by airborne transmission. Although other routes can contribute, we believe that the airborne route is likely to be dominant. The public health community should act accordingly and without further delay.[21]

The misconstrued emphasis on surfaces connected the early response to Covid-19 with the obsessive grocer smoking his mail in mid-seventeenth-century London. Not only correspondence but also the mounting flow of packages and parcels containing online orders were carefully wiped down or left untouched for a few days until it was assumed that they no longer carried a threat. The public was advised that whilst paper or card covers ceased to present a risk of viral transmission after twenty-four hours, seventy-two hours would be necessary to decontaminate plastic-backed books.[22] Door handles, shop counters, and bars in public houses were cleaned after every customer. Hard currency was shunned. There was a substantial diversion of effort and resources as cloths, sprays, and disinfectants were purchased and the drama of surface sterilization was conducted. The upside was a general improvement in public and personal hygiene and a corresponding fall in associated infectious diseases. But lives were lost as a consequence. The importance of masks to impede the expulsion or ingestion of aerosols was not fully and immediately recognized, nor was the need to ventilate indoor spaces adequately.[23] A clear distinction was slow to be drawn between crowded interiors, where microdroplets could hang in the air and infect everyone in the room, and outdoor encounters, where the danger was far less, irrespective of the physical distance between one individual and another.

The long debate over the causes of pandemics led finally to Defoe's 'fatal Breath', in the epigraph. The normal and necessary act of taking in and expelling air ceased to be one amongst many routes of transmission and came to be seen as the principal mechanism for spreading the disease. Further, the main location of infection moved from the streets to the interior of buildings. These might include public spaces such as restaurants and bars, and crowded public transport, but the critical, inescapable setting was the home. The only walled environments consistently more dangerous than the domestic arena were hospital wards and the institutions in which the frail and elderly lived out the remainder of their lives.

The public health controls adopted in pandemics since records began ensured that central to the experience were the most intimate personal relationships. Whether the front door was nailed shut with a watchman stationed outside to prevent escape, as in the case of suspected households in Defoe's London, or whether in Covid-19 societies adults and children were sent home from work and school to spend all hours of the day and night in close proximity, each family member was both the crucial support and principal threat to the life and wellbeing of every other. As Defoe emphasized, the presence of asymptomatic illness, a reality with both the bubonic plague and Covid-19, served only to heighten the drama. He observed in the *Journal* that the combined circumstances struck at the very heart of love and grief:

> It was very sad to reflect, how such a Person . . . had been a walking Destroyer, perhaps for a Week or Fortnight before that; how he had ruin'd those, that he would have hazarded his Life to save, and had been breathing Death upon them, even perhaps in his tender Kissing and Embracings of his own Children.[24]

The Pandemic as History

The attempt on the Thames Embankment to appropriate the historical meaning of the Covid-19 pandemic reflected a wider turmoil of debate in societies overtaken by the global event. As early as mid-March 2020, the Pulitzer Prize-winning writer Thomas Friedman identified a 'new historical divide': 'There is the world B.C. – Before Corona – and the world A. C. – After Corona.'[25] Writing in an updated account of pandemics from the

Spanish Flu onwards, just three months after the outbreak began, Mark Honigsbaum observed what had already become an industry of competing accounts.[26] Full-length histories began to appear well before the end of Covid-19 was in sight, and renewed attention was paid to past plagues stretching back to biblical times, and to more recent pandemics, including the hitherto largely neglected Spanish Flu and the sequence of viral outbreaks earlier in this century which presaged the coronavirus.[27]

The British response to the crisis was subject to sustained interrogation in the print and electronic media almost as soon as the first lockdown was declared. The *Sunday Times* Insight team published a powerful, widely read, exposé of the first thirty-eight days of the government record on 19 April 2020, which then became a four-hundred-page book, *Failures of State*.[28] Highly critical assessments of errors in the early months were written by the editor of the leading medical journal, *The Lancet*, and by the director of the largest medical research charity, the Wellcome Trust.[29] By 2022, full-length studies were appearing, drawing lessons from the event that could be applied to the widely expected next pandemic.[30] Parliamentary Select Committees and official agencies working at arm's length from government conducted a series of critical examinations of the sequence of decision-making from the first announcement of a new infection at the end of 2019. The failings in preparedness were meticulously examined by the National Audit Office in May 2021.[31] Whenever it is published, the official inquiry that began work in the summer of 2022 will add to what by then will be a mountain of articles, reports, and books, whether or not it alters the verdicts that they contain.

Covid-19 turned everyone into historians. The urgent need to write about a new epoch was not confined to professional commentators and analysts. The last occasion on which British society endured widespread controls in response to a national emergency was the Second World War. Ordinary men and women became recorders of passing time. Mass Observation, founded in 1937, was employed by a government for the first time anxious about the most private beliefs and behaviours of the general public. Narrative accounts were commissioned either as free-form diaries or as responses to particular topics. The organization gained renewed momentum in the 1980s, and began once more to collect material from witnesses of social change.[32] In 2010, it revived the project of commissioning accounts of a single day in the year, 12 May. The tenth anniversary of this exercise occurred, as it happened, on the last day of the first 2020 lockdown.[33] Whereas in previous years only a few hundred people responded to the annual invitation, the organization was inundated by more than five thousand contributions.[34]

All the writers were conscious that their experiences, however mundane, reflected an era of change which could only fully be captured in the daily lives of men and women who were now largely confined to their homes. 'I want this diary to matter to future historians of our times,' stated one of the contributors. 'I feel I speak as a mother and a world citizen.'[35] Writing diaries was a means of anchoring experience in the flux of change and shaping the perspective of posterity. 'I shall miss writing this diary somehow,' wrote another diarist. 'It's been something to "hold" onto in these strange and unusual times. I've really enjoyed recording events on a day-to-day basis and hope it will be useful for people when they come to research the coronavirus pandemic.'[36]

The observers traditionally tended to be older, more middle class, and more likely to be women than the population as a whole. A diarist reflected on her relative privilege:

> I've been giving more thought to the lock down. I don't have a crying baby, children that need educating at home, or an abusive husband. I'm not waiting for my 80% salary payment or my benefit to arrive (neither adequate if I were struggling before). I have a regular income, a garden, space, attentive sons, friends and neighbours who care for my welfare and no difficulty in shopping. As far as an easy life is concerned, I must be in the top few percentages.[37]

However, the new writers now embraced an age-range from a five-year-old (see chapter 6) to those at the other end of their lives. Contrasting perspectives were provided by other collections focusing on specific categories of experience. The valuable *Covid Realities*, a research project based at the Universities of York and Birmingham, working in partnership with the Child Poverty Action Group, collected accounts of day-to-day life by parents and carers living on low incomes, and organized social activities to support them. The material records the strategies and emotions of those struggling with over-pressed domestic budgets. There was the hope that amidst the suffering, the diary collections might constitute a new basis for attacking deprivation. A contributor explained:

Covid Realities has meant a lot over the pandemic. Our voices have been heard where we've felt previously ignored. We will have hopefully made a valuable contribution to effect changes for the future of our children, to not feel so alone in what are and were challenging times. It is important we are heard. We are not alone and we must speak up about the unfairness in society.[38]

A host of organizations recognized the need to give voice to those living through the pandemic. Newspapers and magazines, ranging from the *Financial Times* to the *Daily Mirror* and *Marie Claire*, invited accounts from their readers.[39] Enterprising radio producers commissioned material, particularly the BBC *PM* programme, which broadcast a series of recordings under the heading of *Covid Chronicles*, later published in book form as *Letters from Lockdown*.[40] Social research bodies and networks including the Young Foundation, the Joseph Rowntree Foundation, and *The Conversation* set out to establish resources of Covid-19 reminiscence with a particular concern for marginal voices.[41] Towns and cities from Aberdeen to Plymouth, recognizing that their communities had been profoundly changed by the pandemic, invited citizens to send in personal narratives.[42]

The long-established tradition of written autobiographies by ordinary men and women was extended by firms offering ghost-writing services.[43] Out on the web, bloggers turned their attention to the altered times. One of the most thoughtful and best-informed of these, John Naughton of Cambridge University and the *Observer*, subsequently published an online volume of his writings as *100 Not Out: A Lockdown Diary, March–June 2020*.[44] The author of this study contributed around eighty thousand words in blogs in 2020 and early 2021 as part of an international project, *Covid2020diary*.[45]

One motivation of these collections was archival. There was a sense that future historians would need evidence beyond the documentary records of public bodies. An accurate account would be of necessity polyphonic, embracing as many different voices as possible. It was important to shape competing accounts of the pandemic. The 'NHS at 72' campaign collected over two hundred 'NHS Voices of Covid-19' designed not just to record experiences on the frontline but also to re-centre the debate about public funding of such services. A junior doctor wrote:

The narrative that's been created about NHS staff being heroes kind of just creates a narrative where it's okay for NHS staff to die. In hero films, it's okay for the hero to die as part of the greater good. I don't think that's fair. It's not a narrative I want to be part of. I think the NHS should be properly funded, properly stocked with protective gear, and just because we work in health care does not mean it's ok to die because of this.[46]

The diary entries enfolded the present with the past and the future. The writers everywhere contrasted the sudden alteration in their circumstances with ways of living they had previously taken for granted. At the same time, they contemplated what a restored normal would look like. They were at once longing for the return of familiar pleasures but aware of the need for a better world. Central to that transformation had to be a collective understanding of circumstances that the crisis had exposed and to which the diarists gave witness.

The accounts of Covid-19 were framed as an historical plot, with a beginning, a time-limited duration, and an assumed ending, however much that had to be extended. Epidemics – in their global form pandemics – are by their nature transient events in contrast to endemic diseases such as malaria or tuberculosis. In an influential article written in the midst of the AIDS crisis, the historian Charles Rosenberg wrote that there is a

> defining component of epidemics that needs emphasis, and this is their episodic quality. A true epidemic is an event, not a trend. . . . Thus, as a social phenomenon, an epidemic has a dramaturgic form. Epidemics start at a moment in time, proceed on a stage limited in space and duration, following a plot line of increasing and revelatory tension, move to a crisis of individual and collective character, then drift toward closure.[47]

The bubonic plagues broke out, devastated societies for a year or two, and then, at least for a while, disappeared. The Spanish Flu in this sense mirrored the Great War that preceded it. However complex the causes and however prolonged the consequences, there was a point at which the first infections occurred, and another when the disease lost its potency and became a low-level endemic illness. The corona outbreaks at the beginning of the twenty-first century, SARS from 2002 to 2003, MERS in

2012, together with the lethal eruption of West African Ebola between 2013 and 2016, each had their own arcs of diagnosis, death, and retreat. Covid-19 was thus unlike the two forces implicated in the experience of the pandemic: structural inequality and climate change, whose origins must be traced back at least to the industrial revolution, if not to the emergence of civilization itself. Equally there is no end in sight for either misfortune, despite increasingly urgent attempts to put dates on the reduction of global warming.

The arguments about the decision-making of national governments and international agencies in late 2019 and early 2020 were essentially about dates of origin. Either action was taken as soon as the virus was discovered, or, as critics claimed in Britain, the starting gun was fired at least a fortnight late, which cost many thousands of lives. As soon as lockdown was imposed, a narrative of unlocking was promulgated, as was the case with further lockdowns in November 2020 and January 2021. Each intervention immediately stimulated an exit strategy.[48] Instead of 'plan', the metaphor of a 'roadmap' was constantly used, implying a destination which could be envisaged, navigated, and reached by a given time.[49] Those contributing to the Mass Observation 12 May 2020 project frequently assumed, wrongly as it transpired, that the worst was already over, and they could spend their time claiming compensation for cancelled holidays and re-booking them for the following year. Infection reached a new peak in January and February 2021, but alongside the new controls, the government laid out a timetable of relaxation during the spring and early summer with the expectation that they would not need to be reimposed. The further peak of the Omicron variants in the early spring of 2022 was accompanied by a formal declaration by the government that society was free of regulation, and central testing was no longer required.

The notion of an ending was founded on medical, political, and social realities. The first of these is the most obvious, but, in the Covid-19 pandemic, far from secure. Unlike the Spanish Flu, when record-keeping around the world was so poor that a century later there remain variations of more than fifty million in the estimation of mortality, a close score has been kept of deaths, infections, and hospitalization globally by a unit at Johns Hopkins University in the United States, informed by national agencies of varying degrees of competence.[50] In Britain, as this account is written, the Omicron variants continue to evolve. There are well-founded doubts about whether the ending will be as decisive as was the case with the last major global pandemic a century ago.[51] In bubonic plagues, the disease did not disappear everywhere at once but in stages around the world. During months and years, it was carried from port to port by cargo ships, or from country to country by invading armies or travelling merchants.[52] In an era of mass movement of people, societies celebrating victory may well be thrust back into the inferno by those where the virus is still rampant and changing its identity. Setting aside the uncharted effects of 'long Covid' in people recovering from the disease, and the prolonged damage caused to health systems dealing with a backlog of conventional illnesses, it is evident that the dance between infection and immunity is not yet over. The conflict still continues between the body's defences, reinforced by vaccination, and the virus developing further mutations.[53] Nevertheless, there will come a point, at least in countries with adequate medical services, when the curtain falls on this drama, and we wait for the next zoonotic pandemic.

It is critical to the political process that such a moment can be formally declared. Since early 2020, governments have seized powers over every-day life without precedent in peacetime. To be told who may enter your house and whether and why you may leave it, where you may travel and for what purpose, what economic activity you may and may not engage in, whom you may touch and whom not, would have seemed inconceivable in any democracy at the end of 2019. It was no surprise that Johnson's government fatally hesitated when faced with this prospect. Reacting to the reimposition of controls in the autumn of 2020, Lord Sumption, the recently retired Supreme Court judge, Reith Lecturer in the year that Covid-19 was identified, and distinguished historian of the Hundred Years War, denounced the entire political response to the pandemic, which he described as 'the most significant interference with personal freedom in the history of our country'.[54]

The most influential definition of the freedom of the citizen in the modern world was set out by John Stuart Mill in *On Liberty* in 1859: 'The only purpose for which power can be rightfully exercised over any member of a civilized community, against his will, is to prevent *harm to others*.'[55] The notion of 'harm to others' has since been much debated, but in the midst of Covid-19, it had an incontrovertible meaning: the transmission of an infectious disease that will cause the serious illness or death of large numbers of people. Although they lacked the language of political rights, that was why the fifteenth-century Venetian government put incoming travellers into quarantine, why the mid-seventeenth-century Mayor of London locked plague victims in their own houses. In the twenty-first century, such actions are not an attack on personal freedom, rather a necessary restriction on the harm caused by its unlicensed practice.

It is important to retain a sense of proportion in such an exceptional time. Lord Sumption claimed that the regime of controls meant that 'in a crisis the police were entitled to do whatever they thought fit, without being unduly concerned about their legal powers. That is my definition of a police state.'[56] A passing acquaintance with modern dictatorships would caution against such a parallel. Despite inconsistencies and confusion in the application of 118,978 fixed penalty notices over two years, the British police and courts have played a comparatively small role in the crisis (not least with regard to the incurious policeman stationed at the door of Number 10 whilst illegal parties took place inside). The regulations were not as tough as those across the Channel, where written permits were required to leave home. In Britain, observance has largely been a matter of consent. The acceptance of such controls depends on the information that can be communicated about the threat of the pandemic, on the trust that is invested in the competence of decision-makers, on the sense that everyone is being treated fairly, and on the understanding that the controls will be revoked as soon as the danger has passed.

After the Second World War, the last time when there was a widespread suspension of civil liberties in the interests of defeating a yet greater danger, most of the restrictions were lifted in 1945, although food rationing, accompanied by identity cards, remained in place for a further nine years. Conversely, a more recent threat to public safety, the 9/11 attacks, resulted in permanent extensions of the security state, some in plain sight, some not made public until the Snowden revelations in 2013. The language of a 'war on terror' imposed the concept of a time-fixed contest on a threat whose conclusion was nowhere defined. A pandemic, on the other hand, offers the prospect of an evidence-based termination. It was on the assurance that all restrictions would at that point be lifted that there was comparatively little protest at their imposition.

The final expectation of an ending was inherent in the social experience of the pandemic. The engagement with passing time varied widely. For those faced with a sudden, overwhelming collapse in their ability to breathe, every minute of every hour became critical. So too for their close family, desperately trying to maintain contact with an intensive care unit they were forbidden to visit. Conversely, retired and relatively fit households were thrust into an almost time-free existence. Then again, homeworking families with school-age children faced a day divided into unforgiving units as web-based lessons were overseen and online work meetings were conducted. For society at large, bus and train timetables, which controlled movements between home and office or school, ceased to exist for all but essential workers and their children. Television, radio, and cinema, whose schedules had in the twentieth century done so much to pattern the consumption of leisure, were supplanted by streamed films and archived programmes. Such changes in the temporal landscape were by turns terrifying and tedious, relaxing and laborious. They were all, nonetheless, assumed to be temporary. Everyone made plans for the post-pandemic future, if only in their minds. The disruption of time was never expected to be timeless, however long the lockdown days and weeks might appear. It was on this basis that the restrictions were for the most part endured without private collapse or public rebellion.

The question, then, is how best to capture the intensity and complexity of what Charles Rosenberg insisted was an event, not a trend. The short answer is that it requires and is receiving the attention of every kind of commentator and every intellectual discipline. This account has been written partly on the basis of digital cuttings from newspapers which day by day engaged with the drama, reporting a proliferating body of research conducted by government agencies, universities, think tanks, and interest groups. It was not just the genome sequencers and vaccine developers who responded to the crisis with unprecedented speed. Everywhere the arthritic processes of writing grant applications, gaining the approval of employing institutions and funding bodies, recruiting staff and where necessary survey panels, conducting analysis, writing up and publishing peer-reviewed articles and occasionally books were dramatically accelerated.

In Britain, the largest quantitative study, mounted at University College London (UCL) with support from the Nuffield Foundation, went from conception to product in a matter of weeks. The first set of results from a sample of fifty thousand respondents was published sixteen days after the declaration of a pandemic by the WHO and just four days after Johnson's belated announcement of a lockdown.[57] The survey also collected over thirty thousand written testimonials. Initially it covered various categories of stress and responses to the new regulations; a month later it was reporting on broader issues such as life satisfaction and loneliness.[58] At the same time, the Office for National Statistics (ONS) led by Ian Diamond, the single most important government organization in the UK during the pandemic, outside those dealing directly with the medical threat, adapted its well-established Opinions and Lifestyle Survey to cover a widening range of topics, publishing regular, authoritative reports throughout the pandemic. Tim Spector's Zoe Health Study mass-reporting app was launched on 24 March 2020, to track Covid-19 symptoms and was publishing data on the spread of the infection a month later. A host of disciplines across the humanities and the social and physical sciences turned their attention to what appeared to be a radical break with the past. It was calculated that 4 per cent of the world's published research in 2020 was devoted to some aspect of the pandemic.[59] The most effective, such as the social psychologist Stephen Reicher and his team at the University of St Andrews, bridged the gap between academic research and popular understanding throughout the crisis.

It may be that, in the long run, the novel is the most productive form. In terms of past epidemics, the best introductions to the experience of mass infection are both fictional. Defoe's *Journal* was, as noted, told by an invented witness,[60] and Albert Camus's *The Plague*, first published in 1947, and taking its epigraph from Defoe, described an imaginary outbreak of the bubonic plague in the Algerian city of Oran.[61] The novel form, which Defoe helped to bring into being, was particularly suited to the bounded plot that a pandemic creates.[62] Both books begin with a discussion of sources, with proper respect paid to the officials who compiled them. The only acknowledged hero in *The Plague* is the unassuming bureaucrat Joseph Grand, patiently maintaining the statistical record of the outbreak in Oran, whilst attempting to complete the first sentence of his own novel.[63] Both accounts explore the tension between the evidential record and the imaginative challenge of describing the intensity of human suffering.

At one point, Defoe's witness encounters burials in a mass grave and finds himself unable fully to describe the horror. 'This may serve a little to describe the dreadful Condition of that Day,' he writes, 'tho' it is impossible to say any Thing that is able to give a true Idea of it to those who did not see it, other than this; that it was indeed *very, very, very* dreadful, and such as no Tongue can express.'[64] The stories gave free rein to their authors' creative powers and come closer to moving the reader than even the angriest of the non-fiction accounts. In the time of Covid-19, novelists have begun to enter the fray, including Orhan Pamuk, who, following Camus, has created a fictional outbreak of the bubonic plague on the eastern Mediterranean island of 'Mingheria', as an allegory of the decline of the Ottoman empire at the beginning of the twentieth century.[65]

At this juncture, there is a particular role for novels with footnotes, which comprise the output of social historians. There are a number of reasons why their discipline has a contribution to make to understanding the crisis through which we have lived. In the first instance, the pandemic forced attention on the boundaries between personal choice and collective responsibility. In Britain, as in other developed countries, the leading causes of death in the years before Covid-19 were non-communicable. Dementia, heart disease, strokes, and cancer had complex and painful implications for those caring for the sufferers and coping with bereavement, but they were not in themselves caused by interactions with other people. Once the pandemic began, individuals adopted strategies that seemed most likely to protect their personal health, and at the same time recognized that how they behaved would directly impact on the well-being of those with whom they shared their lives. More broadly, it was immediately apparent that the time-honoured devices of quarantine and isolation, now renamed lockdown, required the subordination of private interest to a collective conception of public good.

Nothing was easy. There were a range of devices to enable withdrawal from the oppressive presence of those with whom lives were shared, and to resist severe loneliness when relationships proved no longer possible to sustain. The announcement of a national lockdown on 23 March 2020, and its subsequent reimposition later in the autumn and again early in 2021, challenged every calculation about what was possible, desirable, and ethically justifiable in the conduct of the deepest social relations. The notion of a private space within which intimate emotions might flourish was compromised by the enforced confinement and the constant presence of others. Whilst sanity might depend on the ability to escape the confines of the home, the consequent exposure to the infected breath of outsiders could threaten the health of every other occupant, particularly if they were elderly or suffering from an underlying condition. The capacity to adjust to imperfections in marital or parental relations was undermined by the obstacles to finding support or relief outside the home. Child or partner abuse was not invented by the lockdown, but the means of resistance or escape were often critically limited.

At the same time, opportunities were presented for strengthening or revaluing relationships. There was a sense of shared sacrifice for the good of the social unit, as each member restricted their activities for the benefit of others, however much they might chafe at the regulations and look forward to their removal. Interactions between partners, and between parents and children, which had for generations been attenuated by the enforced absence from the home for education or employment, could now be enhanced by the extended time in each other's company. Commuting in the company of strangers or in lonely cars was replaced by domestic time together at the beginning and end of working days. If mothers, unsurprisingly, found they acquired more responsibilities than they lost, there was a direct gain in the involvement of homeworking fathers in the learning and entertainment of their children. Those in later life, whose physical contact with children and grandchildren was now reduced to video conferences, discovered new areas of mutual support and dependency, not least in the IT services provided by younger generations. Gardens, a source of both shared and individual pleasure, had never been better looked after or used, particularly during the long, sunny weeks of the first lockdown.

Social history is founded on an engagement with time. Coping with the 'fatal Breath' involved inheritance and improvisation. Too much of the commentary on an event that contains great tragedy and widespread disruption to established routines assumes that those affected were encountering challenges for the first time or were being forced to develop entirely novel responses for dealing with them.[66] This was perhaps true of the government, which had allowed its emergency systems to atrophy and was forced to invent policy and procedures on a day-by-day basis. For those they were seeking to protect, however, the experience was suffused in history. Whilst most families found themselves, in Shakespeare's words, 'cabin'd, cribb'd, confined', by the lockdowns, they had access to ways of managing sociability and solitude that had emerged during the modern era. As Adam Tooze notes, for the population at large, 'the resources for adapting [to the pandemic] were already on hand and were deployed'.[67] Individuals and social units had developed over generations strategies and resources for coping with unexpected threats to their ways of living. These were deployed with remarkable speed before the first lockdown, and continually adapted throughout the remainder of the crisis.

The capacity to draw upon established practices was assisted by the limited scale of the pandemic. However much strain was placed on social structures, by and large they remained in place, at least in more developed countries. The major outbreaks of bubonic plague in the past had devastated entire societies. The sixth-century Plague of Justinian killed at least twenty-five million inhabitants of a much smaller world, destroying entire cities;[68] the mid-fourteenth-century Black Death cut the European population by around a third; Defoe's plague cost the lives of about a fifth of London's residents. Adjusting for subsequent population growth, the upper estimate of the toll of the 1918–20 Spanish Flu is the equivalent of about three hundred and fifty million deaths today.[69] By contrast, according to the Johns Hopkins dashboard, Covid-19 had killed six and a half million globally by September 2022.[70] The subsequent revision of this figure to almost fifteen million by the WHO, based on an interrogation of poor record-keeping in many of the most affected countries, still left the event a pale reflection of earlier tragedies.[71]

Apart from sheer scale, the age-specific mortality is critical in distinguishing the current pandemic from its predecessor a century ago. The Spanish Flu took the lives of not just the vulnerable young and frail old, but also adults in their prime. The 'W'-shaped mortality curve had a middle peak of those aged sixteen to forty, especially men, who accounted for over half the total influenza deaths.[72] This meant that family units were everywhere threatened. Homes lost their breadwinners only just back from the war; children were deprived of one or both parents; the elderly were left alone without the younger generation to support them. The subsequent loss of life in the Second World War, which in Britain killed about a third as many civilians as Covid-19, similarly struck across the age groups.[73] AIDS, which globally had killed forty million people by 2021, principally infected those in the prime of their lives.[74]

The British experience of mortality in the Covid-19 pandemic amounted to a small acceleration of trends since the beginning of the twentieth century. The doubling of life expectancy had been achieved less by people living longer and more by a continuing reduction of losses amongst younger cohorts and a corresponding concentration of mortality amongst the elderly. In 2019, of six hundred thousand deaths, 84.3 per cent were aged sixty-five and over. At the height of the first wave in the middle of April 2020, 87.8 per cent of Covid-19 deaths in England and Wales were in this age group.[75] Two years later, the corresponding figure was 90.3 per cent.[76] Conversely, the locked-down young were often less at risk than in a normal year, deprived of exposure to alcohol, violence, and road accidents. The Covid-19 deaths of the elderly were frequently explicable but never inevitable. Their lives had still been cut short, a cause of great suffering amongst the victims and their relatives. The basic population landscape, however, remained largely untouched.

The non-negotiable reality was the accumulation of years. In recent times, it had become commonplace for those enjoying the extension of active decades to convince themselves and those around them that whatever their birth certificate might say, their minds or their bodies were twenty or thirty years younger. Now the biological age ruled. Seventy really meant seventy, eighty was the new eighty. A sixty-year-old who caught Covid-19 in 2020 was a hundred times more likely to die than an infected twenty-year-old, and an eighty-year-old had a thousand times the chance of not surviving.[77] At the furthest ends of the age range, the over-nineties had thirty-five thousand times the risk of dying as school-age children with Covid-19.[78] A key variable was the presence of 'underlying conditions' or 'comorbidities', which were present on nine out of ten death certificates in the first Covid-19 wave. These were in turn a manifestation of past time. Earlier medical misfortunes and unhealthy lifestyles increased the likelihood of hospitalization and death. The official category of 'clinically extremely vulnerable' who were to be shielded from all contact with those outside their household embraced over two million people at the beginning of the pandemic.

Defoe's *Journal* is full of accounts of parents, children, and servants succumbing inside their quarantine houses. The journal of the tanner

Miquel Parets describing the outbreak of the same plague in Barcelona in 1651 had to encompass the deeply mourned deaths of his wife and three of his four children.[79] Although coronavirus infections ran through households, instances of whole families perishing were rare. The deaths in Wales of David Lewis's wife and two grown-up sons within five days of each other in November 2020 attracted much media attention, but the event seems to have been caused by an unfortunate conjunction of prior medical conditions rather than the lethal nature of the virus itself.[80] Another triple family death was attributed to a joint refusal to be vaccinated.[81] Elderly couples passed away close to each other, the second sometimes because of the first. A ninety-year-old Covid-19 sufferer just took off his oxygen mask when told of the death of his wife of sixty-three years, dying later the same day.[82] For the most part, however, demographic structures survived. Long-established patterns of behaviour and aspiration were placed under immense stress but remained recognizable.

Social history, together with its sister discipline economic history, further forces attention on the issue of agency. A problem with the multiplying surveys of states of mind in the pandemic is that they tend to fracture the subjects into constellations of attitudes, whether 'anxious', 'depressed', or 'lonely', whereas the question in all cases is the strength of their devices for coping with the complex challenges of living. The capacity to adapt strategies and behaviours to meet the exigencies of infection and lockdown was profoundly shaped by the inherited resources of everyone faced with threat of the 'fatal Breath', as it had been, in different ways in earlier plague outbreaks.[83]

Different metaphors have been deployed to describe the impact of Covid-19 on societies, including 'mirror', 'lens', and 'magnifying glass'.[84] It was not so much that the pandemic created major new structures of wealth and poverty over a few short months, although there were in financial terms distinct winners and losers; rather, as in the case of previous epidemics, it made visible the existing distribution of income and privilege and demonstrated the consequences. The long history of inequality gathered itself together and displayed its extent and effect. Whether in fundamental matters of infection and death or in the more quotidian tasks of maintaining a sustainable life amidst a host of constraints, possession of material goods and access to essential services determined a critical range of outcomes. Inherited diets and medical histories, long-term availability of health facilities, established security of employment and requirements to labour in frontline services, accumulated savings and debts, the extent and quality of domestic interiors and necessary possessions including digital equipment, access to controlled exterior space: all varied by age, gender, race, and class.

Inequality was also a matter of states of mind. Few entered the crisis in a condition of orderly calm. 'I wonder what percentage of people,' pondered a diarist in May 2020, 'had their lives in some kind of steady state when lock-down went into operation. I suspect a whole lot fewer than we think.'[85] The spectrum of disorders ranged from those making transitions from one set of domestic arrangements to another to those daily struggling to avoid the complete collapse of their family economies. In some cases, desired changes were put on hold, including ending unsatisfactory relationships and starting new ones; for others, pending disasters could no longer be held at bay. In every case, the question was the nature of the trajectory being followed and whether it was impeded or enhanced by the virus and the official response to it. For this reason, the disrupted education of developing minds was of particular significance. Adults and children already suffering from a mental illness were especially vulnerable. In every measurable category, those with a prior diagnosis found it more difficult to make the adjustments and compromises that the pandemic demanded. In turn, necessary assistance was cut off as informal support networks were disrupted and access to professional treatment became more difficult.

By its long practice, social history is accustomed to engaging with the minutiae of existence and with the range of evidence, including personal testimony, that yields information on such matters. A global pandemic raises the largest possible questions of life and death and the very future of the planet. Any account must deal with the behaviour of international agencies, including in particular the WHO, and with the record of national governments, as will be the task of the forthcoming public inquiries. But as we seek to understand how societies managed the threats, we are required to consider a plethora of experiences and resources. The chapters in this study engage, *inter alia*, with anxiety and bereavement; walking and gardening; dogs and other pets; informal giving and support; shopping and saving; licit and newly illicit sex; watching television and logging into Zoom meetings; reading books and taking part in virtual book clubs; self-improvement and online quizzes; cooking new recipes and baking sourdough bread; escaping and seeking the company of others: each of them distinct practices with their own histories, but all of them fitting together over time to comprise the response to lockdown, infection, and death.

Finally, social history everywhere raises questions of knowledge. It addresses the issue of what people know about each other and how this matters in times of crisis. Examination of the *ars moriendi* of modern society draws critical attention to how the dying communicated with those they were leaving behind. Observation of lockdown regulations and acceptance of subsequent interventions, including mass vaccination, were dependent on the information that was transmitted and, more importantly, on how it was received. The experience of nature in lockdown comprised its own curriculum of discovery. Informal networks of support were fundamentally dependent on the capacity to comprehend need and identify the most efficient means of meeting it. Learning itself, seeking and mastering new skills and information, became an important way of getting through the long weeks and months of lockdown. It is evident from past studies and from the examination of localities in the Covid-19 crisis that such knowledge is unevenly distributed, often with damaging consequences. If *The Fatal Breath* has a practical function, it may be in educating politicians and administrators about the societies they find themselves governing when disaster occurs.

Illness, Death, Bereavement

'So this is hapimji@g In fuve mumutre they piu nr yo sleeo fky tn gayd'

In November 2020, Tim Hayward was a fifty-seven-year-old food journalist, writing for the *Financial Times* and living in Cambridge. For four days he suffered from a mild respiratory infection, as did his wife and daughter:

> Then, on November 15, things suddenly got very weird, very quickly. I woke feeling unusually short of breath. I'd bought, on the recommendation of a medical friend, a little gadget that measures SAT, the concentration of oxygen in the blood. My score was not out of the ordinary – above 94 – but something felt wrong nonetheless. Just after lunch, I called 111. I felt 'out of it' and had an overpowering feeling that life would be a lot better if I could just take one decent full breath.

An ambulance was called, and Hayward was admitted to Addenbrooke's Hospital:

> By 4pm, I was in a comfortable bed, waiting for the results of my first Covid test and 'responding well' to oxygen therapy and Dexamethasone. But I wasn't destined to get off that lightly – at 9 o'clock that night, they called Al [his wife Alison], to tell her I was being put on a ventilator. Most people need to be knocked out to have a tube put down their throat but somehow, I'm told, I remained conscious, though I have no recollection of this at all.

He had some sense of what was to follow:

> [L]ike every other news junkie and doom scroller in the country, I know what this means. People who go into intensive care, who get anaesthetised and

held on life support, don't tend to have what the news euphemises as 'good outcomes'. I'm hit with awful clarity that this is probably the most significant moment in my whole life. 'It will just feel like going to sleep,' says the medic. True…but I have no idea whether I'll wake up. I have no religion. In fact, I remember thinking: 'Well, if I don't wake up, I won't know anything about it.'

Hayward's wife was not able to accompany him to the hospital:

Then they offered me my phone. I couldn't raise Al on voice or text so, almost automatically, I thumbed on to Twitter . . . 'So this is hapimji@g In fuve mumutre they piu nr yo sleeo fky tn gayd'. Later a nurse tells me I'd become 'a legend on the unit' – as I went under, they had to prise the phone from my fingers.

Later conversations with medical staff enabled Hayward to piece together his treatment:

Nourishment comes through a thin tube up your nose and goes out a catheter at the other end. To drain the constant build-up of toxic crap and to relieve the pressure of the other organs on your damaged lungs, you will probably be 'proned' on 18-hour cycles – moved to a facedown position. It takes up to nine people to do it safely, keeping all the plumbing and wiring in place. It's hard to imagine a more invasive assault on the body than paralysing it and taking over all its functions. My friend Binks is a specialist intensive care nurse who's had way too much experience of it for her young years. As she puts it: 'People don't realise how intense intensive care is.'

On the ninth day, the staff began reducing his sedation:

I don't immediately recover my own breathing and it's another day before I come round. Someone yells: 'Do you know where you are?' And I try to answer, 'Scotland.' I don't know who or where I am. I'm still delusional. The ICU [intensive care unit] nurse hooks up a FaceTime call with home in which, apparently, I croak, 'Laptop, laptop!' through vocal cords wrecked by the tubes. They tell Al not to worry and that it's not really me, but she's terrified by my insane urgency. The next day, they arrange a call with my mother. She says I was so incoherent she was convinced I'd had a stroke.

As Hayward started to recover, he became aware of the damage his physical and mental systems had suffered:

> While I was unconscious, [a nurse] explains, I 'sustained some neurological damage' – this is apparently not uncommon. My left foot is a bit numb, tests show my right arm to be mildly affected, but I have no movement at all in my right ankle and foot. No voluntary control, just very uncomfortable 'pins and needles'. I have a 'drop foot' that will require a brace to aid walking, a Zimmer frame while I learn to use it and, eventually, a walking stick. Later, I'm put into a CT scanner where they discover I have a pulmonary embolism, a blood clot in my lung. For 30 days, I didn't use most of my muscles and spent only minutes out of bed. I lost just over 14kg in weight, around two stone. I'd like to say it was all fat but, sadly, a lot of it is muscle. My legs look like two bits of grey wool, my stomach is pleasingly flat, but so is my chest. I get exhausted after about 10 minutes of anything. My voice has lost its resonance and I'm cold all the time – no muscles working to generate heat, no fat to insulate.

The aftermath was both personal and social. He was experiencing a common outcome of intubation on a ventilator, whatever the illness. At the same time, he was acutely aware of the costs of his illness for those around him:

> All the symptoms of actual Covid-19 are gone and I'm left with the injuries and impairments sustained in the process of saving my life – but, honestly, I'm just so bloody glad to be alive that it hardly matters. I do struggle with survivor's guilt. If I'd gone to sleep in ICU and not woken up, I'd have known nothing of it. My family, friends, the people the pandemic has taught us to call 'loved ones', had to confront the possibility of bereavement, unsure for days whether I was going to live or die in isolation, unable to say goodbye. Like the doctors and nurses in the hospital, I can't speak for them, but I'm left with the feeling that they all had a worse ride than I did.[1]

Tim Hayward's unusually full account illuminates the three interwoven forces affecting an encounter with Covid-19. There was the pathology of the disease itself, particularly its capacity to descend in a matter of hours from a light infection to a ventilator in an ICU where survival in the early months was no better than fifty-fifty. There was the state of the NHS, underfunded and, as the virus spread, under-provided with ventilators and PPE and under-staffed as frontline workers themselves became ill. And there was the *ars moriendi* of early twenty-first-century Britain, the structure of shared beliefs and practices that surrounded and supported the process of dying and bereavement.

The Phone

As far as Tim Hayward's wife was concerned, her husband's close encounter with Covid-19 took place on the other end of a phone. In the years before the pandemic, a debate had been growing about where to die and in what company. Since the Second World War, death had increasingly become institutionalized. Where once life ended as it had begun, in familiar surroundings amidst close family, now it was outsourced to professionals in specialized buildings.[2] At the beginning of the twenty-first century, a half of deaths in Britain took place in a hospital, with the remainder occurring in what statisticians termed the 'usual place of residence', which included care homes.[3] By then, however, voices were being raised against both the location of dying and the treatment of those who were nearing the end of their lives.

The essence of the critique was communication. A good death, it was argued, required an extensive engagement with the fears and feelings of those who knew that they were approaching the end of their lives. In her influential *On Death and Dying* of 1969, Elisabeth Kübler-Ross began with the observation that 'dying nowadays is more gruesome in many ways, namely, more lonely, mechanical and dehumanized'.[4] As the treatment of serious illness became medically more complex, the humanity of the patient was diminished. Doctors were trained only in how to keep their patients alive for as long as possible, using every procedure at their disposal.[5] 'The problem with medicine,' wrote the palliative doctor Rachel Clarke as the Covid-19 pandemic arrived, 'is its potential for dragging out and debasing the experience of dying. There is even a new name for this relentless over-treatment: "desperation oncology".'[6] There was an inherent tendency to apply yet another invasive therapy until the patient's body could no longer respond. 'A defining question of modern medicine,' concluded Clarke, 'has therefore become not how do I keep this person alive, eking out more scraps of life, but *should* I? . . . When, in short, is enough enough?'[7]

The answer was to be found in talking. Sudden deaths still occur. Each year in the UK, more than thirty thousand heart attacks occur outside a hospital, of which nine in ten are immediately fatal.[8] There were 1,752 fatal road accidents in Britain in 2019.[9] But for most of those who die, the diagnosis of a terminal disease will occur weeks, months, or even years earlier. The issue for the palliative care movement is the quality of the conversations that take place in that interval. 'If a patient has had enough time,' wrote Kübler-Ross, '. . . and has been given some help in working through the previously described stages, he will reach a stage during which he is neither depressed nor angry about his "fate".'[10] Her insight that there are always five sequential states of mind – denial, anger, bargaining, depression, and acceptance – is now seen as schematic and reductive. Nonetheless, the underlying assumption of her analysis has remained fundamental to the palliative care movement, which she did much to launch.[11] There was an overriding need to listen to patients both to help them work through their feelings about their looming mortality and to plan the most appropriate sequence of treatment.[12] Julia Samuel explained in *Grief Works* that:

> The time I spent at the hospice has taught me we should all try to talk, plan and prepare for death long before we are actually faced with the end of our life. It helps us to dig deep inside and to discover why we are scared to death of death; our fear can be diffused if we sit quietly and work out what we believe about life and death, and find a way to talk to the people closest to us – particularly those who are going to survive us – about our wishes, our thoughts, our fears.[13]

This process would take time. It is partly because most people in a secular, scientific age have little experience of thinking about the event of death, which they now rarely encounter in their daily lives. And it is partly because their outlook is likely to change as their illness progresses, if in more complex and less predictable ways than Kübler-Ross proposed.

The arrival of a global pandemic had a dual effect on the experience of dying in Britain. It increased, for the wrong reasons, the numbers dying outside hospitals and heightened the debate about the quality of care the terminally ill received inside medical institutions. Since the turn of the century, propelled by the palliative care movement, the long-term decline in deaths taking place in the 'usual place of residence' had been halted. Between 2004 and 2019, the proportion of people dying somewhere other than hospitals increased from 35 per cent to 47 per cent. The first phase of Covid-19 accelerated the change. Provisional data for 2020 showed a further sharp growth. In England, 108,242 deaths were registered in private homes in the first nine months of 2020, 25,472 more than the preceding five-year average.[14] At the heart of this change was a health service in panic at the prospect of a sudden influx of Covid-19 patients requiring beds, staff, ventilators, and PPE, which it was immediately apparent were all in critical short supply.

In the outbreaks of bubonic plague, the crisis point was when a community ran out of gravediggers. 'The pestilence began in the other regions of England,' wrote a chronicle of 1349, 'and lasted for a whole year, with the result that the living were hardly able to bury the dead.'[15] Such a circumstance was both a terrible practical problem and a measure of the wholesale collapse of Christian ritual and the civilization that depended on it. In modern societies, the equivalent moment was the overwhelming of the health services, with the result that those seriously ill from the virus were turned away from hospitals or left to die in corridors, and every treatment of the normally sick and dying was compromised or halted. In the early days of the Covid-19 pandemic, television screens were full of images of such events taking place in Northern Italy, the location of the first mass outbreak in Europe. As the numbers requiring intensive care rose through March and early April in Britain, health officials and government ministers were all too aware of how close the system was to complete breakdown. Nothing would do more damage to their reputation for competent management than queues of ambulances outside hospitals and exhausted doctors admitting that they no longer had the facilities to treat the dying.[16]

There were two solutions. The first, given wide publicity, was to acquire necessary equipment as fast as possible, institute an effective testing system, and increase capacity by building seven 'Nightingale hospitals' at a cost of £350 million. The new constructions remained largely unused because, as the King's Fund concluded, 'in an emergency you can build ventilators, you can adapt buildings and you can manufacture personal protective equipment – but unfortunately, there is no magic NHS staffing tree to shake'.[17] The second solution, hidden from view until the consequences became too egregious to ignore, was to control the numbers allowed to occupy hospital beds.

At the heart of any hospital is the 'take', when decisions are made as to whether a patient is admitted and to what form of treatment.[18] It is the means by which the best use is made of resources, and patients receive the most appropriate treatment in the shortest space of time. As soon as the lockdown was declared, work began at a national level on devising a Covid-19 triage tool, which would give doctors guidance on who should be selected for critical care. Adapting an existing National Institute for Clinical Excellence clinical frailty score, a number would be derived from three factors: age, frailty, and underlying conditions. Those over eighty or suffering from serious comorbidities would be at the bottom of the list or excluded altogether.[19] They would either not be admitted to an ICU, or ambulances would refuse to collect them from their place of residence. The tool never became an official national policy, but versions of it appear to have been quietly adopted by individual NHS trusts across the country.[20] Those facing the greatest pressure on bed spaces began to place increasing emphasis on age independently of other factors. Tim Hayward was lucky that he fell ill just before the second wave gained momentum, that he was comparatively young, and that he had no underlying conditions.

There had always been a flow of patients between the institutions caring for the elderly. The medical facilities in the more than fifteen thousand care homes were rarely more than basic; conversely, hospitals had an interest in emptying beds as soon as treatment was completed. Now the transfer became one-way. Between 17 March and 16 April 2020, twenty-five thousand patients were discharged to care homes, mostly without tests to determine whether they were infected with Covid-19.[21] They were received by staff who themselves were untested and for months were almost completely lacking in appropriate protective equipment.

The recent growth in the care home system, which by the time the pandemic commenced accommodated over four hundred thousand residents, was based on a compromise between the personal support that the elderly might receive from their families and social networks and the institutional expertise of staff trained in the emotional and physical needs of people no longer able to look after themselves. In one sense, a care home is a form of stasis, the last stopping place in the journey of life. But in another, the whole enterprise functions on movement. Family members are encouraged to visit, residents are expected to mix with each other in communal facilities outside their private rooms, and those whose health deteriorates can be transferred to specialist medical facilities.

The desperate attempt by pandemic-threatened hospitals to protect their services destroyed the whole balance. Care home managers immediately excluded all visitors except to those on the point of death, locked residents in their rooms in a token attempt to prevent infection, and were compelled to retain in the building those who fell ill for any reason. They desperately searched for PPE, which throughout the first surge of Covid-19 was prioritized for hospitals.[22] Mobility was now confined to zero-hours contract staff, calling on home after home in the course of their working days, untested and unprotected.

In the first year of the pandemic, the number of deaths in care homes was 19.5 per cent higher than the five-year average. Of these, 42,341, almost a quarter of all fatalities, involved Covid-19, although, given difficulties with testing in the early months, the figure may have been still higher.[23] These men and women died in familiar surroundings but often without specialist medical equipment and staff. They were denied the company of even a single relative until the final hours. At the Home Farm Care Home on Skye, where a quarter of the forty residents died of Covid-19, the manager operated a strict system of visits. On the last day in the life of Colin Harris, a daughter living nearby was allowed in to see her father, but when her mother arrived, she was refused permission to swap places: 'This is how Mandie watched her husband of 25 years die: squinting through a window on a sunny day. "We couldn't see clearly," says Mandie. "The sun was reflecting off the window." By the time the nurse came back to Colin's room, he was dead.'[24] Similar circumstances surrounded deaths in care homes from other causes.[25] Those who survived faced months of isolation from other occupants and from their families. The suffering was particularly acute amongst residents with dementia, who could not understand why they had been sentenced to a form of solitary confinement and struggled to recognize relatives when once more they were permitted to meet them.[26]

Only in rare instances were care home residents likely to continue their lives elsewhere. The institutions could be viewed as a form of managed dying. There was, nonetheless, nothing inevitable about the surge of Covid-19 fatalities behind the locked doors. The mounting vulnerability to incapacitating illnesses amongst the elderly demonstrates only the resilience of the human body and spirit. On average, an eighty-year-old has five serious medical conditions. Yet there is only an 8 per cent chance of their death taking place within the next twelve months. Patients may survive for years with a diagnosis of a terminal illness. Whether they are spending their days looking after themselves, with or without visiting carers, or in specialized settings ranging from care homes to hospices and palliative hospital wards, people continue to live lives which have value to themselves and to their family and friends. As he grew old, Colin Harris at Home Farm on Skye suffered from depression, Parkinson's disease, dementia, lung cancer, a stroke, hepatitis C, and a chest infection.[27] Yet he was still going at the beginning of 2020, a source of warmth and affection for his nearby family. In spite of his multiple comorbidities, his death in early May from Covid-19 was premature and, given the mismanagement of both his care home and the wider health service, unnecessary.

The number of excess fatalities in care homes in the first six months of the pandemic was almost exactly matched by the increase in private residences. There were 25,220 more deaths than in a normal year.[28] Whereas the care home residents were simply trapped, the increase of those who died in non-institutional settings was a more complex event. Efficiently run hospitals sought to manage the flow of patients by issuing potential cases with oxygen monitors, regularly checking the scores and admitting those who fell beneath 92 per cent. In other cases, the unpublicized triage system meant that ambulances did not arrive when summoned, or, after a cursory examination, left empty. Much depended on the capacity of suddenly alarmed family members to work an opaque system. Michael Rosen, the author and former Children's Laureate, recorded his encounter with Covid-19 in verse. He had been in bed with flu-like symptoms for thirteen days in late March 2020, and was beginning to have trouble with his breathing:

Get tested, says my friend John.

The GP has closed.
A recorded message at the surgery
says not to come in
and not to go to A and E.
If you think you might have Covid-19,
call 111, it says.

I call 111.

I get through to the Ambulance Service
and talk to a man
who asks me some questions.
No, I'm not coughing, I say.
No, I don't feel worse today
than I felt yesterday.

He tells me to keep taking the paracetamol and ibuprofen.

I do.

Rosen starts to feel worse:

I say to Emma [his wife]
It feels like I can't get enough air.
There isn't enough air.
'I can't catch up,' I say.
There are moments I feel hotter
than I've ever felt before
and moments when I am colder
than ever before.[29]

He rings the ambulance service again and receives the same advice. More proprietary painkillers.[30] Speed was critical in these moments. There were accounts of renewed attempts to get into hospital being resisted until it was too late. A bereaved son wrote:

My dad called for an ambulance a week before his passing, asking for help, and although the paramedics came, they did not take him to hospital as he should have been. The paramedics thought it was a chest infection. His symptoms worsened over the next week and the paramedics were called again. This time my dad was taken straight to the ICU and was put on a ventilator. I received a call from a nurse two days later to tell me my dad had died. I would like to ask Boris Johnson why paramedics were instructed to tell people that if they showed signs of the virus, to stay home?[31]

Rosen is, by the thinnest of margins, a luckier man. His wife asks a neighbour, who happens to be a GP, to pay a visit. She tests for his absorption of oxygen and takes it upon herself to negotiate with the local A and E department. By this chance connection, Rosen is saved from dying at home. As it is, he spends forty-seven days in intensive care, hovering on the edge of death.

A separate cohort lost their lives because they were not sent for tests when first reporting symptoms of other serious illnesses, or their tests were delayed because of pressures on the system caused by the pandemic. GPs were unable to arrange hospital beds for the seriously ill where previously they had been able to operate a well-understood system. An unknown number simply decided that there was no point in trying to access a health service which daily media reports told them was on the edge of meltdown or were discouraged from doing so by the non-emergency III call centres. A mother caring for an agoraphobic son described how she rang for assistance when he started gasping for air: '[H]e was told he did not need paramedics,' she said. 'He stayed at home for the next few days unable to move until he started drifting in and out of consciousness and an ambulance was called again. This time he ended up in intensive care. A few days later he died.'[32]

Some decided, as was the case in the nineteenth century, that they stood a greater chance of being infected and dying in hospitals than if they stayed at home.[33] Initially there was a sharp fall in the numbers taking themselves to A and E departments, whose business in the two decades prior to the pandemic had seen an annual average increase of 2 to 5 per cent, placing them continually on the edge of crisis. In April 2020, there was a dramatic 57 per cent drop in demand in England.[34] Scotland saw a 40.7 per cent decline in attendance at A and E departments in the first six months of 2020 and a 25.8 per cent drop in emergency hospital admissions.[35] Over the first Covid-19 year as a whole in England, attendance in emergency departments fell from twenty-five to seventeen million.[36] Some of the absence was because there were twenty fewer fatalities a week on the roads during the first year of lockdown and a corresponding reduction in injuries.[37] There were fewer industrial accidents with much of the economy closed down. Once the pubs had been shut, there was less alcohol-fuelled violence. In other cases, people just seem to have attended to their own injuries. Two years later the situation was reversed. A and E departments and the ambulance service were on the brink of collapse, caused by a surge of supressed demand, long-term staff shortages compounded by Covid-19 infections, and a lack of beds in both hospitals and care homes.

It is difficult to draw the line between self-help and self-harm in the engagement with the health service, between those who recovered or died in the familiar surroundings of their own homes and those who fatally did not access professional help when evidently they were in need of it. A Marie Curie review suggested that the pandemic 'had indirectly enabled a long-term aspiration of increasing the proportion of people who die at home'.[38] The common factor across all the non-hospital mortalities during the Covid-19 pandemic was the absence of properly informed choice. The advocates of palliative care in private homes or hospices were not in principle opposed to high-tech medicine in specialized institutions, merely to the inability of those facing death to give voice as to how and where they were treated. Care home residents sent from hospitals whilst infected or trapped in their buildings without appropriate testing regimes or protective equipment were passive victims with only their relatives occasionally able to make angry but ineffective protests.

Those who fell ill in their own homes were unaware of the triage systems being adopted by hospitals in order to deliver the government's claim that the NHS was coping with Covid-19. The poor came to the pandemic carrying comorbidities caused by years of inadequate local facilities.[39] Between a half and two-thirds of the higher mortality amongst members of minority ethnic groups was caused by forms of deprivation, including place of residence, population density, and household income.[40] In a time of crisis, they had no ability to manipulate a stretched and opaque system to their advantage and suffered greater fatalities as a consequence.

Michael Rosen's neighbourly GP willing and able to intervene on his behalf was a rare moment of good fortune. The more common experience was fear and resignation, turning back to families and communities for such support that they could render.

By effectively reducing demand for beds, hospitals saw a net increase of only seven thousand deaths in the first six months of the pandemic. 'But where, we keep thinking, is everyone else?' wrote Rachel Clarke, voluntarily transferred to an ICU. 'The people with heart attacks, strokes, kidney stones, bleeding stomachs? Coronavirus hasn't merely overwhelmed the department, it has somehow displaced from the NHS the thousand and one additional reasons to be rushed on a trolley through the locked-down dark, sirens screaming, blue lights flashing, your stricken brain or heart or guts demanding our most urgent attention.'[41] Instead, wards were converted into an ICU, which received those whose immune system had stopped attacking the coronavirus but was instead attempting to destroy the patient's lungs and other vital organs.

Covid-19 distorted the work of hospitals but did not itself invent the basic work of an ICU. Sedating and intubating a patient whose essential systems were failing was an established and highly skilled procedure.[42] It was that part of the treatment process where the last chance of preserving a life was to render the individual almost lifeless. 'Normally,' wrote Rachel Clarke, 'in an ICU, it is the patient who becomes dehumanised. Punctured and crisscrossed by a cat's cradle of wires and tubes, alive thanks only to the bedside machinery that hums and chugs and sucks and blows, a Frankenstein version of a body.'[43]

As with prisons, so with hospital wards, the managers have always exercised a right to determine not only who leaves but also who visits. The consequences of resisting cross-infection were intensified by the pathology of Covid-19, in particular the speed of the final descent into critical illness that we saw in the cases of Tim Hayward and Michael Rosen. A diarist writing for the Mass Observation 12 May 2020 exercise lamented her family's situation:

Day to day life is becoming increasingly difficult. My grandad passed away a few days ago. He went into hospital and had to stay for 2 nights. He tested negative for coronavirus. On his third day in hospital, he somehow caught it and passed away that day. Nobody could visit him or speak to him for the days he was there. When we got the call that he doesn't have long left to live, my mum was given permission to go up to the covid ward and give him our goodbyes. She was too late by a matter of minutes. My grandfather left the world without his family by his side.[44]

The absence of contact was compounded by the shortage of time. The experience of the rapid transition from a light fever to a potential death-bed exacerbated the inbuilt inequalities of power at all levels of health treatment.[45] What Rachel Clarke described as 'disaster gatekeeping – this unprecedented severing of distraught family members from each other',[46] gave medical staff more responsibilities than they could easily exercise and deprived patients and their families of what little involvement they had in the process. 'When he died,' recalled a daughter of a factory key worker, 'he had been in hospital, lying alone in a coma, for 42 days. We were ushered in to say our final goodbyes before hospital staff turned down the flow of oxygen and he died in front of us. Later, they wrapped him in a hazardous waste bag. He was placed in his coffin wearing it.'[47]

The surges in the pandemic caused established patient–nurse ratios to be diluted from one to one to as many as five or six to one. With constant adaptations and workarounds, it proved possible to deliver the basic med-ical support. Much more difficult was the maintenance of human con-tact with those undergoing life-saving treatment. The essence of effective nursing was responding to the needs and circumstances of knowable indi-viduals. In many cases, the transition from an ambulance to an ICU to a ventilator was so swift that it was impossible for any kind of familiarity to be established. The process had always depended on conversations with the patient if that were possible, and with relatives in their vigils at the bedside. The anaesthetist Jim Down observed the difficulties on his ward:

> They were also finding it harder to connect emotionally with the people in their care. There were no relatives by the bedside to humanize the patients, who were often lying face down for the whole shift. Some nurses telephoned the families and asked for personal information to help them build a relation-ship, but others found that too upsetting.[48]

The through-put of patients and the concealment of their faces by the oxygen masks attaching them to ventilators meant that many who were in their last days were known to those looking after them only as numbers, not even as names.

In turn, the doctors charged with taking the final decision about whether to continue with intrusive treatment found it difficult to conduct the face-to-face conversations with close relatives that normally occurred. Under the influence of the palliative movement, there has been a growth in recent years of care planning, where wishes about how to be treated in the event of a potentially fatal illness are set down for the benefit of medical staff, close relatives, and the person making the decision.[49] Atul Gawande reports that 'people who had substantive discussions with their doctor about their end-of-life preferences were far more likely to die at peace and in control of their situation and to spare their family anguish'.[50] Such discussions could be given legal force in the UK as an 'advance directive'. As Covid-19 took hold, only 4 per cent of the population had completed such a document.[51] In most cases, doctors were still dependent on last-minute debates with relatives about what the patient might have wanted, or what the family desired on their behalf. Although the larger proportion of victims were elderly, conversations had to take place with men and women whose lives were suddenly ending in their middle years. In an unexpected crisis, there were few prepared answers. Many of those drafted into intensive care wards had little training in such tasks. A hospice doctor reported that 'suddenly everyone wants a piece of me. Doctors less used to working with people at the end of life are asking for help in having difficult conversations about ceilings of care with patients who before Covid-19 we wouldn't have expected to die.'[52] The more sudden the crisis, the more urgent the need to talk; the greater the risk of catching the virus, the less the chance of doing so.

The PPE, when it arrived on the wards, compounded the problem. Female staff struggled to wear gowns, face shields, and respirators designed for Caucasian men.[53] If they fitted properly, the hot and sweaty face masks impeded the human voice. It was difficult to pick up clues about meaning and emotion from facial movements. Medical teams struggled to understand each other. 'Behind our masks,' wrote Rachel Clarke, 'we strain to hear each other speak and are forced to second guess our colleagues' expressions. Being protected entails being dehumanised.'[54] A protocol emerged in hospitals that a single relative would be let into a ward possibly in the short period before intubation, which might well be the last opportunity to talk, and then again if it became certain that the patient was dying. But to ensure that visitors did not spread infection in the ward or themselves become infected at the bedside, they would also be awkwardly dressed in full protective clothing. If they were conscious, the dying patients saw only these alien figures struggling to make contact.[55] John Naughton's mother-in-law, suffering from dementia in a care home, was transferred to hospital: '[O]ne of the things I can't get out of my mind is the thought of how frightening it must have been for her to come from a small, friendly care home to a Covid-19 ward full of staff who – in full PPE kit – look a bit like invaders from Mars.'[56] In turn the relative's final sight was often of a body which itself seemed barely human. A doctor witnessed a last visit to a dying son:

> At some point during the process Adam's mother arrived in the hospital. The nurses helped her into full PPE, brought her into the bay, and she walked tentatively over to the bed space to look down at her son. She saw his exposed torso, the breathing tube coming out of his mouth, the lines carrying his blood to and from the filter, the drug ampoules, the crumpled wet sheets, the crash trolley with drawers open and equipment spilling out, the fluids, the catheter, the syringes and torn packaging discarded around the bed, the machines and monitors and the eight of us surrounding him in our PPE. We paused for a second, then carried on, and she watched. Eventually she backed away to a seat by the door and listened to our efforts. Half an hour later, when I assume she couldn't bear it any more, she left.[57]

Nonetheless, in spite of every practical obstacle, the effort was made to communicate. In the often brief interval between leaving home in an ambulance and being prepared for intubation, patients tried desperately to keep in touch with the family they had left behind. Tim Hayward texted his wife until he lost consciousness. A consultant anaesthetist tried to respond to the despair of a woman who knew how much danger she was in:

> 'I'm not ready,' the patient implores me through her CPAP [continuous positive airway pressure] hood. She's breathing at more than triple her normal rate and I've been asked to intubate her as she's deteriorating, despite three days in intensive care. She is 42 years old. There's terror in her eyes. A tear runs down

her cheek. She's looking at the patient opposite who is in an induced coma, intubated and ventilated, and isn't doing well. The noise of 30-litres-a-minute of oxygen in her CPAP hood makes communication almost impossible. She repeats, 'I'm not ready', and raises trembling hands. But her oxygen saturation is only at 84%, when it should be close to 100%, and she's becoming exhausted and agitated. She tries to rip off her hood. 'I need to phone my family,' she gasps. I nod and say OK, almost shouting to be heard over the noise of the alarms.[58]

As treatment progressed, it was not so much the patient who was alone, surrounded by the teams of up to eight or nine doctors and nurses required to monitor symptoms and regularly turn the unconscious body, as the relatives daily seeking news. 'His wife is at home on her own and she can't be with him or see him,' wrote a Mass Observation diarist of a friend. 'If he dies she will have to go through all of that on her own. Her own elderly mum died last year and she took that really badly. I don't think she will cope with this. It must be horrendous for her, waiting for a phone call or word that he has died.'[59] In the interim, lockdown regulations made it next to impossible for those who were self-isolating to gain comfort from other friends and non-resident family members. Never was hugging more needed and less possible.

Nothing fully replaced the chair by the bedside, but every alternative was explored while life remained. In the bleakest of circumstances, relatives simply tried to be as close to where they knew the struggle was taking place. Rachel Clarke, transferred from her hospice to an ICU in Oxford, noticed something odd happening outside the hospital building:

A handful of parked cars began to appear each day, all of them angled so as to face the hospital. Their occupants sit impassively, sometimes for hours, staring at the threshold they are forbidden from crossing. The watchers hold vigil, strained and desperate, unable to resist being as near as possible to the person they love – a husband, a daughter, a sister, a father – now banished out of reach on a ward or in the ICU, often critically ill with Covid. They ache and ache for human contact – for holding, hugging, embracing, clinging on to – but the car park is as close as they can get. And so they sit in their vehicles, pulsing with longing, and suffer the absence of tactility.[60]

Any action which might reduce the isolation of the living from the dying was explored. There were non-verbal modes of establishing connections. The wife of a man in his last days in a care home arranged for her perfume to the placed under her husband's chin to evoke a final memory.[61] Another put together a playlist of favourite music which a nurse turned into a YouTube resource. It was necessary to abandon the assumption that communication was necessarily a two-way event. A guide to 'deathbed etiquette' for cases of Covid-19 advised that people should 'just keep talking, even if their loved one is asleep or doesn't seem to be strong enough to listen to them, actually having the sound of their voice in the background is really helpful'.[62] 'I would hold phones to patients' ears,' recalled a nurse, 'and tell families that they might be able to hear, so please talk away to them.'[63] Equipment was clamped to a bed and family members chatted about their lockdown lives to a deeply unconscious body.[64] The junior doctor Roopa Farooki did what she could for a dying patient:

> She doesn't ask for someone to come in with their phone or iPad, so she can chat to her relatives and say goodbye, although you do it anyway. She's just drowsy, non-rousable, and sleeping until the end. She barely acknowledges her son on the phone, on the screen. You put your hand on her arm, and hope that she will think it's her son's hand, when she hears his voice on the line, behind her shuttered eyes and shutting down consciousness.[65]

In the absence of a response, there was still some comfort in thinking about the news that would be of interest to the relative, and in speaking to the person as once they were free to do. Sleeping behind their oxygen masks, frequently experiencing violent hallucinations, it is not clear what a patient could ever hear, although Michael Rosen's recovery of consciousness was attributed by his doctor to the music that his wife had arranged to be played to him.[66]

An ICU doctor in BBC Radio 4's *Letters from Lockdown* captured the critical role of virtual communication. She traced the multiple uses of her phone, wrapped and sealed in a cellophane bag, during the course of a working day.[67] It was the final means of connecting a patient to her family.

> In the absence of an NHS mobile or tablet on the ward, my phone has been placed next to an old lady's ear, on her pillow as she drifts into unconscious-

ness, breathing with shallow, irregular gasps, with hopes and promises from her daughter, hoping that her mum will be able to hear her final words of love, even though she can't be there to say them. Its speakerphone plays the voice of her ten-year-old granddaughter tearfully telling her that she wants her to come home to read to her again one day soon.

Words were accompanied by pictures:

Its camera has facetimed the lovely man in Room 10 with his elderly wife and grown-up children, gathered in their living room, faces filling the small pocket-sized screen, grandchildren on more screens within screens who cannot be there with their parents because of the lockdown. Thanking him for being such a wonderful dad and grandad, telling him that they love him, and to sleep, now.

Or by sounds:

Its speakers have played favourite songs; Elvis albums and jazz compilations, songs that families have suggested will provide comfort in those last hours of life.

It enabled the overworked doctor to exercise virtual care:

Often abandoned without me, remaining in patients' rooms, an offering of humanity as I am called to assess a new or deteriorating patient.

More prosaically, the phone was also a vital working tool, at the centre of the hastily improvised systems that kept the Covid-19 ward operating. The staffing rota was now run by a WhatsApp group instead of the mechanical bleep system. By means of texts and images, the multiple tasks of caring for the dying could be managed:

On my phone are weekly pictures of property bags of the dead, piled up in the store room waiting for collection by the porters, my own death figures captured weekly in a macabre picture. Each bag representing a person I cared for, my handwriting in their notes documenting my attempts to save them, and eventually, to keep them comfortable when alive, to be followed by my handwriting on certificates after their death.

It had one final service to perform:

> The phone's torch light has proved useful for confirming deaths in the absence
> of pen torches on the ward. Pupils fixed and dilated.

At the end of the working day, it accompanied the doctor home:

> The final role my phone has played during the coronavirus pandemic has been
> when I am lying in bed at night, unable to sleep or waking from vivid dreams.
> My phone distracts me, although as I trail mindlessly through social media,
> I try my best to avoid any news – I don't want to be consumed by any bigger
> picture, for fear of being overwhelmed. Content and able to cope with my
> micro-level involvement with this pandemic, with my phone beside me that
> has allowed me both to stay connected and to disconnect. It's been my lifeline
> and without it, I think we would have all been lost.

The overworked phone in its plastic bag represented the efforts that were
made until the very last to resist the isolating effects of machinery and
lockdown. It was not always effective. A study found that 'participants
described mixed experiences of communicating with their sick relatives
through video calls on phones or iPads. While some valued the contact
this gave them, others described frustrated attempts caused by poor internet connection, problems with equipment and being unable to hear the
conversations properly.'[68] But every use represented a collective struggle against a lonely death. Over time, the pressures in wards worsened
and eased and then returned to the edge of breakdown. As he recovered in mid-November 2020, Tim Hayward was told by the nurses at
Addenbrooke's that once more the patient–staff ratios were coming under
pressure.[69] The development after the first wave of Covid-19 of additional
drug therapies provided more alternatives to an immediate intubation,
but this remained the destiny of those whose capacity to absorb oxygen
had collapsed. Throughout the crisis, stressed doctors and nurses did
what they could to link the sick with the survivors. Wherever possible,
information technology was deployed to resist the depersonalizing effects
of medical technology.

The theatre of dying during the pandemic both dramatized and qualified the arguments about treatment in hospitals. The patients and their

relatives had minimal control over the course of events and suffered from the attenuation of every form of interpersonal communication during the final days. The staff in turn found their exhaustion compounded by the brief but harrowing interactions with excluded family members. In some ways, it was worse for the many doctors and nurses drafted in from other specialisms where they had scant training in caring for the terminally ill or previous experience of working with them.[70] A diary was placed by Michael Rosen's bedside while he was unconscious, in which nurses could leave messages.[71] Many of them began with the phrase 'I normally work in . . .', on several occasions wards with children where Rosen's books were much-loved texts. At the same time, few could argue about the necessity of ICUs and their procedures when a society was beset by a fatal mass infection. Nor could they fail to be impressed by the persistence and ingenuity with which every player in the drama sought to maintain human contact as death approached.

Letting Go

There is an inverse ratio at work in the process of dying and bereavement. The faster a life is ended, the longer it takes for relatives and close friends to come to terms with their loss. Over time they merge back into the fabric of the living to be replaced by another cohort dealing with their grief. The way the victims died deepened the sense of dislocation and loss and increased the likelihood of what is now termed 'prolonged grief disorder', leading to 'high levels of loneliness, social isolation and emotional support needs'.[72] 'In the face of such difficulties,' concluded an early study of the Covid-19 bereaved, 'one might speculate that letting go, finding a place for the deceased in ongoing life, relinquishing the old ties/bonds and moving on may not be tasks that can yet be dealt with.'[73]

Research into the first wave of deaths established the particular isolation of the Covid-19 bereaved.[74] Almost a quarter felt that they had no involvement at all in the last struggle of their relative. Over a third failed to receive any support from healthcare professionals, and nearly half had not been contacted by the hospital or care provider after the death occurred. There was a contrast with those dying from conventional diseases. Seventy per cent reported 'limited contact' with individuals dying of Covid-19 compared with 43 per cent of cancer deaths. Eighty-five per cent were 'unable to say goodbye as they would have wished', whereas 61 per cent of cancer relatives were able to do so. Using an 'Adult Attitude Grief Scale', the research found that a relative dying in hospital was more than twice as likely to generate psychological suffering as when the event took place at home.

Overall, three-quarters of the Covid-19 bereaved were discovered to be encountering 'social isolation or loneliness' compared to just under two-thirds of those experiencing a loss through cancer. The score for relatives of the non-pandemic victims is a reminder of the inherent pain of bereavement, which studies since 1945 have found to be the most desolate form of being alone.[75] At its most intense and unresolved, grief could turn into what Freud described as pathological melancholia, where all attempts to form new relationships failed.[76] A network of official and voluntary agencies had grown up to respond to the widespread need for therapy.[77] Cruse Bereavement Care, which was founded in 1959, recognized how the sheer speed of a Covid-19 death intensified the emotions inherent in any loss:

> If someone dies of coronavirus or complications resulting from the virus, a number of things may be particularly hard for family and friends to deal with. Infection controls may mean that family members do not have an opportunity to spend time with someone who is dying, or to say goodbye in person. Depending on the person, the illness may have progressed and become serious very quickly, which can lead to feelings of shock. If they were not able to be present for the death and cannot view the body, it may be difficult to accept the reality of a bereavement. At times of considerable trauma, people tend to look for certainty. However at the moment, that certainty is not there. This can amplify any feelings of angst and distress. Bereaved people may be exposed to stories in the media which highlight the traumatic nature of death in these circumstances. Or they may have witnessed distressing scenes directly. People may become disturbed by mental images, which in a severe form can become Post-Traumatic-Stress Disorder (PTSD). If the health services become stretched, friends or family may also have concerns about the care the person received before they died. This in turn can lead to feelings of anger and guilt.[78]

The prospect of managing the multiple dislocation of bereavement was further undermined by the general lack of planning for the event.

The urging of the palliative care movement has in recent years caused an increase in the informal and formal dialogue between those nearing the end and their close family. Given that so many of the Covid-19 victims had serious comorbidities and were full of years, it is possible that some had already given consideration to the final illness. But the onset of Covid-19 was so unpredictable, and the journey to a ventilator and the mortuary so swift, that there was little or no time for the patient or the family to make either practical or emotional preparations. It was as if Britain suffered two hundred thousand fatal road accidents or the loss of life of more than two thousand Grenfell Towers. No one involved had sufficient time to prepare for the shock.

The lockdown regulations, which varied slightly from nation to nation, severely reduced attendance at funerals. John Naughton described the farewell to a much-loved mother-in-law:

> The aftermath is also traumatic for families, but in a different way. Normal funerals are currently out of the question. An undertaker collects the body of the deceased and essentially books a slot with a crematorium or a graveyard. So it was with Elsie. Her slot was last Thursday morning, at 8am. There would be a very brief ceremony organised by the funeral director, but – we were told – there would be a live video feed for family members. So, from our homes across the UK and Ireland, we all logged on at the appointed hour – only to have the video feed suddenly drop out. And when it returned, the service – such as it was – was over. The funeral director was as baffled and as frustrated as we were. It had gone as planned, he said. Some Beethoven on the way in and a popular song on the way out. But we saw or heard none of that. And so we're left with a curious feeling of empty incompleteness. We were denied that awful psychobabble word – 'closure'. We were – as Thomas Lynch puts it – unmoored. May that lovely woman, my children's beloved grandmother, rest in peace. And may the government which left our care homes exposed to the virus one day be held to account for its failure to take the virus seriously when there was still time to prepare properly for it.[79]

There was a rapid growth in businesses such as Obitus, which describes itself as 'a leading UK provider of bereavement technology services'.[80] There had been a modest demand in previous years, but now they became a widely used enhancement of small or non-existent congregations.

Even when the technology functioned, the engagement with the event was bleak. Viewers opened screens with the aid of a login and a password, and five minutes before the ceremony was due to begin, an empty funeral chapel appeared. There was a fixed camera at the rear, transmitting an unchanging view of the backs of a handful of mourners. The sound quality was indifferent, the visual effects often non-existent. After half an hour, the congregation left separately, unable to attend a wake larger than six people, and the online mourners turned off their screens. As with so much of the internet provision in the crisis, it was better than nothing. Harriet Sherwood described the minimal permitted event, which echoed the regulations in Defoe's plague-ridden London: '[N]o Neighbours nor Friends be suffered to accompany the Corps to Church. . . . And further, all publick Assemblies or other Burials are to be forborn during the Continuance of this Visitation.'[81] In Sherwood's modern version:

> On a cold, bright day a couple of weeks ago, a hearse drew up at a crematorium in Leicestershire for the funeral of an elderly woman. . . . Six pallbearers hoisted the coffin, decorated with spring flowers, on to their shoulders and carried it to the catafalque as Vaughan Williams' The Lark Ascending played. During a short ceremony, Sally-Ann Best, a civil celebrant, introduced music chosen by the family and read two poems. Between her, at the front of the crematorium chapel, and the funeral director standing respectfully at the back, there were rows of chairs. Every single one was empty. It was a funeral with no mourners – and not for a lack of relatives and friends. The woman's family, most of whom lived 100 miles away, were unable to attend because of coronavirus restrictions.[82]

Bereavement was a common enough experience for everyone to know what they were missing. John Naughton contrasted the fractured online funeral with its predecessor in his family:

> How different this was, I thought, from the time some years ago when her husband, my father in law, was dying in a hospice. Then we were all around, dropping in and out to sit with him, and my daughter and I were with him when he died. And then afterwards we had a big funeral, which was the usual mixture of shared joy at being together and shared sadness at his passing.[83]

A similar contrast was drawn by a professional funeral celebrant who was one of the contributors to Mass Observation's 12 May diary exercise. In pre-Covid-19 times, she found pleasure in her work. Now the rituals of the contemporary *ars moriendi* no longer functioned, to the cost of everyone involved:

> Most people think funerals are always miserable – but they aren't; they can be uplifting and joyous as people come together in solidarity to celebrate a person they loved. But in these strange times there is an additional shadow of sadness cast over everything . . . no hugs or shaking of hands, every one sat apart, no touching the coffin or carrying in. Funerals have a hollowness like I have never experienced before.[84]

The Covid-19 restrictions affected all deaths. It was estimated that during the pandemic, three-quarters of the bereaved could not arrange the funeral they desired.[85] The Church of England reported that by January 2021, seven out of ten people had been unable to attend the funeral of someone they knew.[86] The major obstacle was the restriction on attendance, which reduced the average funeral congregation from fifty to ten, leaving millions of mourners unable to take a direct part in the process of mourning. Faced with such unsatisfactory proceedings, an increasing number of relatives chose to by-pass any kind of service. SunLife's *Cost of Dying 2021* report found that during the pandemic the proportion of 'direct cremations' – low-cost, unattended events where the coffin was delivered to the crematorium and the ashes were later sent to a nominated relative – nearly doubled from 14 to 25 per cent. Almost as many were now seeking this wholly impersonal route as were choosing a traditional burial.[87]

Some use was made of virtual communication, starting with an increasing tendency to employ Facebook rather than newspapers to convey information about a loss.[88] Established bereavement counselling organizations expanded their service, with over a million people accessing Marie Curie's online information and an increase of a quarter in calls to its national support line.[89] Informal online forums were organized by groups of friends and relatives and specialized networks were established, such as COVIDSpeakEasy, 'a space for the bereaved to share their experiences, doubts and grief'.[90]

The technology was some compensation, but the Zoom calls and chat rooms could not establish an ordered pathway through mourning. Emotion kept twisting back on itself. There was a constant revisiting of the last days and hours. A daughter wrote of losing her father:

> People die suddenly all the time: they have heart attacks and car accidents; they suffer terrible violence. But what marks Covid out is the way it has kept people apart from its victims while they are still alive. For those left behind, much of the pain comes from wondering what they must have been feeling in those lost hours, days, even weeks.[91]

Private anguish was daily reinforced by the continuing debate about the mismanagement of the pandemic. Covid-19 Bereaved Families for Justice ran a large chat room which combined support for individual sufferers with a collective protest against the government.[92] Coming to terms with a personal loss was hampered by the widespread bitterness at the apparent errors within the health service and care homes and at the quality of the national and international decision-making. 'Today, I woke up with moments of anger,' wrote a Mass Observation diarist. 'Anger because I could not be there for him, because he caught coronavirus in hospital, because this outbreak was ever allowed to reach a global scale.'[93] Early in 2022, there was further outrage when those who had rigorously observed quarantine, up to and including avoiding physical contact with the dying and bereaved, discovered that the staff in Number 10 had widely disregarded the regulations they had imposed.

The scale of the pandemic and its refusal to fade away after the first outbreak in the spring of 2020 disrupted and diluted the personal narrative of mourning. The counsellor Julia Samuel observed that collective grief can be 'incredibly overwhelming, confusing, and you're treated like one [person] . . . [when] you're really a lot of very different, grieving, hurting people'.[94] There were few means of retreating from the larger tragedy. '[M]y dad died on 13 March,' wrote a bereaved son, 'and from that point coronavirus has been on the news every minute of every hour of every day. It was like someone sticking a knife into the wound all the time, there was no escaping from it.'[95] A death through cancer or a coronary might have national implications, and there were always debates to be had about the quality of the medical care. But it was easier in such circumstances to envisage an individual process of coming to terms with a bereavement over a period of time. Covid-19 constantly displaced the victims from their unique misfortune. 'Those whose lives have been shattered,' explained the Cruse counselling service, 'have difficulty occupying the centre of their own dramas when all around them are competing narratives of loss.'[96]

In earlier pandemics, the rituals of religion provided a framework within which mourning could take place. They supplied an explanation of suffering, a template for mourning, and a community for the bereaved. Those disorientated by loss were relieved of the tasks of designing and managing the events following death. The doctrines and the institutional practices provided a protected pathway through personal grief. The rituals assisted the management of time in the weeks and months after a loss. When Covid-19 arrived, Britain had become a society of many faiths and none at all. The crisis highlighted the similarities and differences of belief systems which were all challenged by the sudden increase in infectious deaths and the unprecedented interference of the modern state in the ways in which religions conducted their most sacred affairs.

During the outbreaks of bubonic plague, organized religion struggled to prevent its basic funereal and mourning practices from being completely overwhelmed and at the same time sought to impose its account of what was happening and what should be done to prevent a recurrence. Fast days were instituted in Britain during nine plague pandemics from 1563 to 1721. The theological rationale was derived from the concept of special providences and divine judgements. Natural disasters were seen as God's punishment for the sins of a community and required petitionary prayers and promises of repentance if they were to be averted. During the nineteenth century, the growing salience of medical explanations of infectious diseases marginalized this response. A decisive moment came in 1853, when Lord Palmerston, the Home Secretary, publicly rejected proposals for a fast day against an outbreak of cholera, arguing that the solution lay in better sanitation and public health.[97] There was in addition the difficulty that the growing nonconformist congregations were often reluctant to take part, and the Quakers refused altogether. More generally, it was increasingly apparent that the bulk of the population no longer paid any attention to them, seizing instead the welcome opportunity for a holiday. 'Now, what is the spectacle presented on the morning of one of these days?' asked *The Times* in an editorial on 2 November 1853. 'The shops, it is true, are shut, and the middle class on their way to their devotions; but from every court and alley, from every yard and stable, pour forth men and women, boys and girls, all eager to make the day what it is to three-fourths of the population – a day of pleasure.'

Fasting in response to a pandemic has not disappeared completely. Early in the Covid-19 crisis, the World Evangelical Alliance designated 29 March 2020 as a Global Day of Prayer and Fasting. 'The theme of the initiative,' it explained, 'is "Lord help!"' Its purpose was to 'listen to what God is saying, to intercede for those affected and to pray for the pandemic to pass quickly. The theme "Lord Help" is inspired by Psalm 107 where the people of Israel cried out to the Lord in their trouble and He delivered them from their distress.'[98] The impact of the event in Britain on either the national diet or the course of the virus was difficult to detect. Instead, the Archbishop of Canterbury responded to the closing of his churches by conducting Easter communion from his kitchen table in Lambeth Palace.

As a national institution, the Church of England found itself largely marginalized in the crisis. It could no longer present a theological explanation of the pandemic and had little contribution to make to the public discourse or programmes of action. Its leaders spoke of the need to reflect on the frailty of human endeavour and the vulnerability of the natural world, but proposed few answers. Instead there was a welcome for the opportunity for spiritual exploration. 'People are asking big questions about Covid,' said the Bishop of Ripon, '– why now, why us, what does this mean for my life?'[99] The church organized a 'National Day of Reflection' on the first anniversary of the lockdown. Unlike earlier pandemics, organized religion had a minimal role to play in the public health and welfare services and only a marginal presence in institutional care for the elderly. The vigorous national debate about Covid-19 policy and tactics was essentially secular. 'At a time when what is still nominally a Christian country craved spiritual guidance and reassurance, the Church of England went missing in action,' wrote a *Times* columnist.[100]

With some minor exceptions, the congregations and their leaders rapidly modified their rituals and practices in the interests of protecting public health. Almost all the faiths were immediately threatened by lockdown regulations. This was partly an accident of timing. The 23 March announcement was made on the eve of major religious festivals: Passover from 8 to 16 April 2020, Good Friday and Easter on 10 and 12 April, Vaisakhi on 13 April, Ramadan from 23 April to 23 May, Eid al-Fitr on 23 and 24 May. The general absence of serious tension between religious communities and the state was a tribute both to political management and to the flexibility of the spiritual leaders overseeing their rituals. The decision was taken to make no significant exceptions for any faith, but fundamental conflicts, such as insisting on cremations or dispensing with individual burials, were avoided. It remained a sensitive area, however. There were widespread protests in the Muslim community when Matt Hancock announced in a late evening tweet new prohibitions on meetings between households in northern England just as the larger of the two annual festivals, Eid al-Adha, was about to commence on 30 July. He compounded the offence by alleging without evidence that the decision was necessary because of widespread disregard of social distancing rules.[101]

The national church in England fully observed the letter and spirit of lockdown. The Archbishop of Canterbury closed all the churches immediately, forbidding even individual prayer in the buildings, a decision that was later regretted. 'What I would really like,' explained a clergyman '– and would have liked throughout the time – would have been churches (perhaps not all of them) kept open at set times for personal prayer and quiet. But surprisingly there seems to have been little expressed wish for this – though I suspect that such open churches would have been used by many people as well as church members.'[102] The role of clergy was diminished as they were unable to visit the sick who were now shielded, or the dying whether at home or in hospitals. A week after the first lockdown was imposed, 'Stephen', a clergyman, lamented his lost role:

> When I closed and locked the doors of the church I knelt down in a pew and cried. People come here to pray, to give thanks, to share their fears and their joys. But now the House of God is locked up and there are to be no services there, and I wonder if God's mercy has also been closed to us. As the priest of this parish I feel as though I have abandoned my people in their time of need.[103]

Another vicar reported her reaction to her first locked-down crematorium service:

Twenty-four years a priest but no experience like it before. .... Something inside me rages against this situation, rages that I must timidly hide away exercising my ministry by phone, by Zoom, behind barriers. ... I want to be where I am most fully alive, where I am most useful, with others – but I cannot be. Even disregarding my own safety, I cannot take the chance that I might bring illness to others.[104]

Funerals were compressed in time and by attendance, or, in the case of those choosing 'direct cremations', avoided altogether. Nonetheless, workarounds were attempted. It proved possible to conduct the last rites through computer screens to patients in hospitals. A survey found that Anglican clergy were preparing an adapted funeral liturgy, in both a short and remote form, to be used where there were constraints on attendance or the bereaved could only attend online.[105] Nine out of ten parishes created or expanded digital networks to support the bereaved and more generally to maintain the life of their congregations.[106] The locked-out vicar 'Stephen' took vestments, a chalice, and bread and wine back to his vicarage, and from there broadcast Morning Prayer to his flock.[107] New skills were deployed. '10am we stopped and went to virtual church,' wrote a diarist on the last Sunday before lockdown. 'IB [our vicar], helped by GR, live streamed a short 20 minutes of prayers, collects, a sermon and of course, notices. He was amazing, never seen him so confident where normally he is hesitant and "um's" a lot. A good clear message of hope and love, perfect love casting out fear.'[108]

There were, however, dissenting voices. Six hundred clergy wrote to the Archbishop of Canterbury protesting at his ready acceptance of lockdown.[109] A handful of evangelical congregations courted confrontation with the police by insisting on large-scale services. 'I never thought I'd say this in Britain,' said the chief executive of Christian Concern, which was organizing illegal congregations, 'but churches are going underground. These are not isolated cases – and the longer it goes on, more churches will join the movement.'[110] In the event, however, few did. By and large, the national church (in England and Wales) proved itself adaptable to the systems imposed by the state.

The challenge was greater for the four million British Muslims, whose infection rates were three and a half times the national average.[111] They observed more elaborate and urgent funeral rites than the Christian tradition: *ghusl*, the washing of the body immediately after death; *kafan*, the shrouding of the body in cloth; and *salat al-janazah*, a congregational prayer for the deceased, usually attended by large numbers of mourners. The body was to be buried, not cremated, as soon as possible, usually within twenty-four hours.[112] The response to Covid-19 disrupted every part of the process. It was not clear, especially in the early weeks of the pandemic, whether it was safe to touch a body. Many of those who would perform such tasks were elderly and vulnerable, and after 23 March, there was no question of them working in close contact with each other. Speed was a problem, particularly for those who had died in hospitals. However, the first of the five ultimate objectives of Islamic law is *hifz al-nafs*, the protection of life. In exceptional circumstances such as war or pestilence, any ritual could be altered or overridden if it seriously threatened the wellbeing of the practitioners. Modifications were rapidly accepted by Islamic leaders, working in conjunction with Public Health England. The washing could be conducted by fewer people using full protective equipment, which avoiding touching bare skin. If necessary, the process could be undertaken simply by spraying the body. The cloth wrapping could again become almost exiguous, providing the gesture was made. If demanded by the health authorities, coffins could be used and it was possible for the funeral ceremony to take place without a body. As with other faiths, extensive use was made of online services both to train practitioners in their new tasks and to conduct ceremonies in the absence of closed mosques. Staff in hospitals, some of whom were themselves Muslims, were trained how to adapt to the modified practices.[113]

Sikh rites were also flexible. Washing the body was again necessary but could be modified. Cremation was essential, although once more it was possible to work around the requirement that it be undertaken on the day of death. Congregations could attend the final service online. Orthodox and non-orthodox Jewish communities generally accepted modifications to their practices, including restrictions on attendance at funerals. The major exception was the long-established ultra-orthodox Hasidic congregation in London's Stamford Hill. Unlike its counterparts in New York and Israel, where the sect came to blows with the police, the protest was more a matter of evasion than public resistance. Regulations about gatherings in synagogues, wedding ceremonies, and schools were routinely ignored, with a consequent infection rate nine times the national average.[114]

The 2021 census revealed that in England and Wales the proportion of the population describing themselves as Christian was for the first time less than a half, dropping from 59.3 per cent in 2011 to 46.2 per cent.[115] Anglican church attendance had fallen by 40 per cent in the preceding three decades.[116] At the 2021 Church Synod, the Archbishop of Canterbury reported that an investment of £240 million between 2017 and 2019 to arrest the decline had 'not so far' shown any results.[117] On the eve of the crisis, just 12 per cent of the population were identified as belonging to the Church of England and its sister churches in Scotland and Wales and under 2 per cent regularly attended church services.[118] The age profile of churchgoers was, like that of the pandemic victims, overwhelmingly weighted towards the elderly. A third of those over seventy regarded themselves as Anglicans compared with only 1 per cent of those aged between eighteen and twenty-four.[119]

Almost all the congregations launched online services, with the Archbishop of York claiming a 'digital coming of age' during the first year of the crisis.[120] Unsurprisingly, the older worshippers were more concerned than the young about the closure of churches and were more uncomfortable logging in to take part in an event or download reading material. Nonconformist congregations, whose numbers had also been falling, found it less discomforting to take part in events outside sacred buildings and were less affected by the difficulties in performing the Eucharist.[121] The clergy sought to maintain their duties of pastoral care but were impeded by the shielded status of so many of the bereaved. Attempts to engage in broader community services, such as the provision of foodbanks, were constrained because much of the traditional volunteer base was now confined to their homes. They were also undermined by the long-term decline in the finances of the churches, accelerated during the lockdown by the loss of income from collections and property letting.[122] When the churches began to re-open at Easter 2022, there was no reversal in the long-term decline in attendance. The Quakers survived best of all, with few fixed costs, no salaries to pay, and a form of silent worship that could readily take place online. 'Isn't Zoom wonderful?' exclaimed a member of the University of the Third Age (u3a). 'I attend Quaker Meeting for Worship in Newcastle on Sunday morning, 41 of us, all on Zoom. And in the afternoon I attend my American penfriend's Meeting for Worship in Pennsylvania. 38 of us, and they are so similar to the Newcastle Friends.'[123]

Within minority ethnic communities, there was a greater prospect of faith organizations helping the bereaved through their grief. Religious leaders had more presence and authority amongst their congregations than was now the case in the Anglican church, where clergy were increasingly likely to have entered the ministry as a late-life second career and to be responsible for a network of parishes.[124] There was a tighter bond in Islam between private households and local religious structures and beliefs. The pragmatic approach of adapting burial rites to lockdown regulations ensured that those who had lost family members to Covid-19 were not cut off from traditional practices. A survey conducted at the end of the first year of the crisis found that 61 per cent of Muslims 'encountered an increased closeness to their faith throughout the pandemic'.[125] There was more opportunity for prayer and study during the lockdown, and an increased dependency on mosque-based charitable endeavours.

Across all faiths, the role of ritual was to give bereaved individuals a structure of comfort and action at a time of disorientation and despair. In the pandemic, it enabled social networks to come together to memorialize the departed and share their sense of loss. Except for those choosing 'direct cremations', the end of a life, whether from Covid-19 or all the other causes of death in the period, was marked by a formal ceremony of some kind. There is little evidence, however, that in the first quarter of the twenty-first century, religious practices were sufficiently entrenched or effective to compensate for the widespread dislocation of the process of mourning. Despite some excitement amongst commentators about the increased numbers of hits on online services and prayer sites, there was no apparent reversal of the long-term decline in spiritual belief. Instead, there was concern amongst observers of Christian denominations that they would suffer the same fate as department stores, with an expanded customer base likely to continue their involvement after the pandemic in the comfort of their own homes rather than taking part in face-to-face worship.[126]

At best, the crisis caused a temporary pause in the relentless growth of 'nones', those professing no belief of any kind.[127] However, it was reported that 'the trend for streaming services on YouTube or Zoom began during the pandemic and is here to stay for those in care homes, the housebound and even those who wish to do something else with their Sunday mornings and watch the service on catch-up later that day'.[128] The Catholic Church in England and Wales was less permissive. 'Most people have resumed the wide range of normal activities,' it observed at the beginning of May 2022, 'no longer restricted by the previous Covid measures. We therefore believe that the reasons which have prevented Catholics from attending Mass on Sundays and Holy Days of Obligation no longer apply.' The rules that were suspended at the beginning of the pandemic should now be reinstated. Except for those who were ill or caring for the sick, explained the Bishops, '"virtual viewing" of Mass online does not fulfil the Sunday Obligation'.[129]

In a secularizing society, religion served primarily to enhance rather than displace the role of the family. In March 2021, the Royal Society of Arts commissioned a survey into the needs of Black, Asian, and Minority Ethnic (BAME)[130] communities. Seventy-seven per cent identified 'friends and family' and only 29 per cent 'religious/faith groups', the least important of ten agencies listed in the questionnaire.[131] A parallel study of British society by the Christian think tank Theos asked in the midst of the pandemic, 'what things matter most when trying to live a fulfilling life?' 'Being with family' led the list of fourteen factors at 61 per cent, 'growing your spirituality, religion or faith' was second from bottom at 10 per cent.[132] In every community, the partial or complete exclusion of relatives from bedsides, funerals, and wakes caused acute suffering to which ritual practices or personal spiritual support could never fully respond. *This Too Shall Pass*, a study by the Collective Psychology Project, found that the curtailment of the existing rituals of death 'turned our mourning periods into something much more drawn out, complicated, detached, unresolved'.[133] Each bereavement set in motion a long Covid of the mind that was likely to persist far beyond the nominal end of the pandemic.

States of Mind

Knitting Teddy Bears

Amongst the diarists who recorded their activities at the outset of the pandemic was an eighty-five-year-old widow in Brighton. Unlike most of those experiencing the crisis, she had vivid memories of the Second World War. In her life, she had been married twice, raised three children, and earned a living as a probation officer. She had recovered from a serious stroke at seventy-nine but now suffered from fatigue and poor balance.

She began writing on Tuesday, 14 April 2020, around the time when new patterns of life in the lockdown were becoming established. As with everyone, her response reflected the impact of changed circumstances on inherited experiences and capacities. There were two major constraints on her emotions. She faced a daily struggle with her increasing infirmities which frustrated her gardening after three falls into the flower beds and required frequent rests during her walks to the nearby park. She had already confronted her own mortality: 'I'm also, at the age of 85,' she wrote, 'with many of my close friends gone, fairly reconciled to the idea of dying. I've made sure my wishes not to be resuscitated in any circumstances are well documented.'[1] In the background was the bereavement she had suffered seven years earlier when her second husband died of dementia. 'Had a restless night, no particular reason,' she wrote on 18 April. 'Slightly depressed. I suppose life is a bit more tedious than usual, and I don't think any widow ever really gets used to living alone nor do I think the grief ever goes. It just comes and hits you sometimes.'[2] She neither dramatized nor belittled her grief. It was the price to be paid for a deep relationship and there was compensation in the social network she had since constructed. 'I think all widows are lonely much of the time,' she reflected, 'if they had good marriages, but this is the next best thing.'[3]

Despite constant complaints about her weariness, the diarist's response to lockdown was anything but passive. She took exercise every day, outdoors when she could, indoors in twelve-minute sessions with Mr Motivator on YouTube. It was not just children whose face-to-face education moved to virtual lessons. Her u3a course on maths was transferred from the instructor's house to Zoom. She was part of a WhatsApp network in her street and cooperated with friends and neighbours in managing online grocery deliveries and preparing cooked meals for each other. There were frequent phone conversations with friends and relatives, many of whom in the lockdown were anxious to strengthen relationships that had decayed over time. Technical advice on the digital media was provided by her sons, and by an evening course on computing (to the bemusement of a fourteen-year-old neighbour who could not understand why anyone had deliberately to learn such skills). In the hours alone at home, she maintained a long-standing struggle with the *Guardian* crossword, sometimes enlisting the help of other enthusiasts when faced with a difficult clue.

In evenings, the diarist got out her wool. 'Currently,' she wrote, 'I'm knitting teddy bears at the request of the local Methodist church. In normal times I have quite a lot to do with them, despite my being an atheist. They do a lot of good work and are very friendly and community minded.'[4] The restricted role the Christian churches played in the lives of their congregations at a time of death and bereavement was discussed in the previous chapter. Here was a function which flourished for believers and non-believers alike. Having long since lost her childhood faith, the diarist enjoyed the company she found in her local church and, as the pandemic took hold, appreciated the efforts its members made on behalf of the vulnerable and shielded:

Emerged from the shower having washed my hair when the phone rang. Long conversation with a very pleasant woman who helps with the Wednesday old people's lunch I normally go to at the Methodist church. . . . She is ringing everyone who attends in turn to make sure they are ok. It's so warming to know there are so many people who care about one's welfare.[5]

Embedded in her neighbourhood on the south coast, the diarist was acutely aware of the national picture. 'So much of my time is spent each day reading the paper,' she confessed, 'but I am unable to give it up – mesmerised by the news all the time. I cannot believe how incompetent the government has been.'[6] She had clear views about how the pandemic was being managed, and about the particularity of her own position. With a comfortable house, sufficient income, a range of interests despite growing worries about her memory, and three supportive children, she knew that she was better placed than many in the fraught spring weeks of 2020. What made her a representative figure in the lockdown was the constant negotiation between the strategies for living she brought to the crisis and the challenges she now faced. Her state of mind was informed by a long life with and without others, and by the fresh set of restrictions and opportunities created by the pandemic. She neither escaped nor was overwhelmed by her circumstances as a bereaved elderly woman in uncertain health. It was not that she moved up and down a quantitative scale of less to more lonely, but rather that in complex ways the relation between her sociable and her isolated life changed its form.

Peaks and Plateaus

Covid-19, as with pandemics going back to the bubonic plagues, was from first to last a numerical event. Defoe structured his *Journal* around the weekly Bills of Mortality which allowed him to trace the progress of the disease through the parishes of London. The data generated by national and international agencies from early 2020 onwards framed both scientific and popular understanding of the scale and progress of the drama. Daily news reports displayed figures and graphs of current infections and deaths, which informed the modelling by epidemiologists and the sequence of political decision-making. As soon as it was accepted that the principal response to the outbreak would be quarantine, the search began for equivalent measures of mental wellbeing. In addition to the exposure to illness and bereavement, it was envisaged that controls on the social interactions of an entire population would have effects on its psychological health. The cost of Covid-19 would embrace not just morbidity and mortality but also states of mind. A complete understanding of the event could best be achieved by setting one set of graphs alongside the other.

There was an attraction in adding quantitative measures to the narrative accounts of emotion and suffering and aligning them with the medical statistics. However, the two sets of tables displayed a striking visual contrast. The graphs of infection, hospitalization, and death were essentially vertical. Over the course of the pandemic, the waves of Covid-19 represented an alpine range, with steep peaks and declivities over short periods of time. It is not for nothing that an authoritative account of the medical politics of the first year is entitled simply *Spike*.[7] The graphs of feeling and emotion, on the other hand, represent the rolling English countryside. There were some sharp rises at the outset, but thereafter the fluctuations were less dramatic, with a small upturn in spirits during the summer of 2020, when it appeared as if the pandemic might be ending, and a downturn in the winter of 2020/1, when lockdown returned and vaccines had yet to have an impact. The fullest survey of research into states of mind during the first two years of the pandemic, based on ninety published papers, concludes that 'studies looking at mental health trajectories for individuals suggest most of the population retained stable and good levels of mental health during the pandemic'.[8]

The ONS charted an increase in 'depression' from 10 to 19 per cent between July 2019 and March 2020, but thereafter discovered little change during the drama of further waves of infection and accompanying lockdowns. The condition reached a peak of 21 per cent between January and March 2021, falling back to 17 per cent in the summer of 2021.[9] The ONS weekly estimates of 'happiness' began at 7.2 (where zero is not at all and 10 is completely happy), reached a low point of 6.4 at the beginning of 2021, and were back at 7.1 in the last week of March 2022 as all government controls on behaviour were lifted; those for 'anxiety' (where 10 is 'completely anxious') were a little more volatile, starting at 5.2, improving to 3.6 in the summer of 2020, and ending at 4.0 after two years; the catch-all 'life satisfaction' mirrored happiness, hovering around 7 throughout the pandemic with a dip to 6.4 early in 2021.[10]

The UCL study, based on a different and not wholly representative sample and asking its own questions, looked much the same across the period.[11] 'Happiness' began at 5.8, rose a little in the summer of 2020, fell back in the following winter, before reaching a high of 6.5 towards the second anniversary of lockdown. 'Life satisfaction' had a similar profile, beginning at 5.5 and ending at 6.7. 'Depression' fell from 7 to 5 and 'anxiety' from 6 to 4 as the first wave ended, rose at the beginning of 2021, and concluded at much the same point as at the lifting of the initial lockdown. Loneliness, a basic measure of the quality of social interaction during the pandemic, appeared almost impervious to change. In the ONS surveys, those reporting in official measures to be 'often/always lonely' rose by just over two points from a base of 5 per cent at the beginning of the pandemic before falling back to 6 per cent.[12] Using the three-item UCLA-3 Loneliness Scale, the UCL survey recorded less movement, with a score of 5 on 23 March 2020, a peak of just over the baseline in the gloomy 2020/1 winter, returning to a little under 5 after two years of Covid-19.[13] The only category that looked remotely like the health graphs was 'food security', where initial high stress levels about access to supplies in the lockdown fell precipitously between the end of March and the beginning of May 2020 as the supermarkets established control over their stocks and home delivery systems, and remained almost negligible for the remainder of the crisis.

The observed changes had significance for those involved. A movement of 1 per cent in the adult British population represented over half a million sufferers of what might be serious psychological difficulty. Nonetheless, the initial question that needs to be addressed is the absence of major peaks and troughs.[14] Part of the answer is that there were fundamental differences in the process of quantification. To begin with, it is an issue of how change is measured over time. A pathogen generates exponential growth if left unchecked, whether the Black Death, the Spanish Flu, or the coronavirus. In the middle of March 2020, the Covid-19 epidemic was redoubling about every five days in Britain. For this reason, a week's delay in imposing lockdown may have cost twenty thousand lives.[15] There is no such engine driving quantified emotions. Alteration, when it occurs, tends to be relative and gradual.

The tables and graphs represent different engagements with the past. The indices of Covid-19 infection, hospital admissions, and deaths started from a zero base; the emotional indices, by contrast, measured change in an existing condition. In 2019, no one in Britain was suffering from Covid-19, whereas there were cohorts of the anxious, the depressed, the unhappy, and the lonely, with in most cases established practices of calculating them. The baseline was higher than for the new disease, the prospects of radical movement correspondingly lower.

There was a separate question of calculating figures when attached to emotions. To take one example, there was a long-standing practice of estimating 'loneliness'.[16] The UCLA Loneliness Scale was developed in 1978 and widely deployed in research on both sides of the Atlantic. It required respondents to assign themselves to four boxes: 'often', 'sometimes', 'rarely', 'never'. There was a constant tendency in the commentary on loneliness to conflate the top three categories. The most widely read recent study on social interaction and its absence is by Vivek Murthy, the nearest equivalent in America to England's Chief Medical Officer.[17] He begins his 2020 *Together: Loneliness, Health and What Happens When We Find Connection* by stating that '22 per cent of all adults in the US say they often or always feel lonely or socially isolated'.[18] The parallel figure given for the UK is 23 per cent. On closer examination, however, the paper by Bianca DiJulio et al. upon which this claim is made, a careful 2018 study of nationally representative samples of the USA, UK, and Japan, divides the lonely into those who found it a 'major problem', a 'minor problem', and who responded that although they were lonely, 'it isn't really a problem'. In the UK, just 5 per cent, and in the USA 4 per cent, belonged to the first category, where serious suffering might be taking place. The UK sample recorded 11 per cent for respondents for whom it was a minor and 7 per cent a negligible matter.[19]

It was widely assumed that the pandemic could only worsen the problem. An early study of Covid-19 and loneliness began by claiming, again on the basis of collapsed UCLA categories, that 'for quite some time, Western societies have been facing an epidemic of loneliness in which almost half of the population of the report regularly feeling lonely', and then went on to assert that in the USA, the 'COVID Response Tracking Survey 2020 finds twice the rate of loneliness as two years ago', which left the socially well-adjusted to be counted on the fingers of one hand.[20] More cautious analysis concluded that, overall, little quantitative change had taken place. The ONS employed a version of the highest category which was likely to generate serious emotional suffering. Its baseline figure of 5 per cent at the beginning of the pandemic was in line with what is known about the extent of the condition in Britain since the Second World War and with the findings of the DiJulio et al. 2018 study.[21] The relative absence of change thereafter seems to have been a consequence of increased isolation in some cases being balanced by greater, sometimes enforced, social interaction in others.[22] A review of Covid-19 literature concluded that, 'contrary to expectations, there were no significant mean-level changes in loneliness'.[23] A range of international studies indicated that 'within the context of this pandemic, it is remarkable that loneliness, on average, may be less reactive to the effects of social isolation and other sources of stress'.[24]

The expectation of dramatic change in emotional wellbeing was also a reflection of the prevailing politics of mental health. In the years before Covid-19, critics of neoliberalism had been making increasingly vocal claims that the pursuit of individual material gain was fragmenting social relations and generating emotional hardship. 'Without at first noticing,' wrote Robert Putnam in his influential *Bowling Alone*, 'we have been pulled apart from one another and from our communities over the last third of the century.'[25] The Conservative Party was uneasy about the apparent levels of community breakdown in the aftermath of the 2008/9 slump and the imposition of austerity. Following a report published by the Jo Cox Commission on Loneliness,[26] Theresa May launched an official strategy to combat loneliness in England in October 2018, entitled *A Connected Society*, and appointed the world's first 'loneliness minister'.[27] Three reviews of the strategy have so far been conducted by the Department for Digital, Culture, Media, and Sport (DCMS), and Scotland and Wales have published their own action programmes. Boris Johnson's administration did not allow itself to be distracted by the pandemic. The February 2022 DCMS report claimed that 'we have worked across government and across society more widely to drive forward action to tackle loneliness and support a connected recovery from COVID-19'.[28]

The debate about particular pathologies was heightened throughout the pandemic by the competition for resources within the broader system. Service providers and associated charities and pressure groups had been protesting throughout the previous decade about the underfunding of mental health and related social services, including care homes. The outbreak of what was assumed would be a time-limited event intensified the debate about the long-term level and distribution of public resources. It was clear that the initial effect of the crisis would be to concentrate effort and expenditure on hospital-based physiological medicine. The issue was whether this could or should be reversed once the public sector returned to a new normality. Thus, for instance, the leading campaign organization Mind claimed that lockdown had been 'devastating' for mental health.[29] The Royal College of Psychiatrists repeatedly referred to a 'tsunami' of unmet needs caused by the diversion of funding and the interruption of face-to-face treatments.[30] It is unclear how precisely this metaphor had been thought through. At its most literal, Covid-19 represented the earthquake or underwater volcanic eruption that caused an obliterating wave of mental ill-health; figuratively, it stood merely for a large and destructive event.

There was nothing new in the use of medical categories to weaponize demands for political or social change. In the midst of the AIDS crisis, Charles Rosenberg reflected on a long-standing practice: 'These clichéd usages are disembodied but at the same time tied to specific rhetorical and policy goals. The intent is clear enough: to clothe certain undesirable yet blandly tolerated social phenomena in the emotional urgency associated with a "real" epidemic.'[31] Loneliness campaigners on both sides of the Atlantic drew frequent parallels with a medical emergency. In Britain, they continued to deploy their preferred metaphor despite the global encounter with a real infectious disease. The leader of the Liberal Democrats, Ed Davey, suggested in Parliament that lockdown had 'created a silent epidemic of loneliness', and the All-Party Parliamentary Group on Loneliness issued a report demanding action to tackle a 'loneliness emergency' that the pandemic had exacerbated by denying people contact with family and friends.[32]

Tables indicating that during the largest disruption to living and working in living memory, amidst two hundred thousand deaths and more than twenty million infections, change in basic emotional states occurred within relatively narrow boundaries, drawing attention as much to the resilience as to the vulnerability of the population at large. There are perhaps three general truths that emerge from the graphs of emotion. The first is that the multiple individual cases of suffering caused by illness, death and bereavement, and the widespread controls on social intercourse did not cause a wholesale collapse in the coping strategies that were in place at the outbreak of the pandemic. Individual trauma, such as a serious physical assault, was more likely to have a sudden impact on mental wellbeing than a collective misfortune where experiences and remedies were shared. As discussed in chapter 1, the basic demographic structures of British society were not overthrown during the pandemic, and for reasons that will be explored in the remainder of the study, neither was the emotional resilience of the population as a whole.

The second truth is that the adaptations that were made to the new landscape of stress and suffering changed much less dramatically than the sequence of illness and intervention which filled the headlines over the two years from March 2020. The imposition of controls on movement and the steep rises in infection and mortality in the spring of 2020 caused immediate but not catastrophic declines in mental wellbeing. The second and third waves of Covid-19 partially reversed a subsequent recovery, before the figures once more began to approach pre-pandemic levels. For the most part, people seem to have come to terms with the radical challenge of the pandemic almost before lockdown was announced, and thereafter were slow to register changes in their emotional wellbeing, whatever was being announced at the daily press conferences.[33] Neither the boosterism of the prime minister and his colleagues, nor the fierce attacks on pandemic policy from mid-April 2020 onwards, had much effect on how citizens felt about themselves, although there were measurable impacts on the view of the political process itself. The UCL team found a sharp and lasting downturn in trust in the English government following the exposure of Dominic Cummings' flight to Durham and the televised statement in the garden of Number 10 on 25 May.[34]

The third truth is that mental suffering, where it occurred, was not consistent across the population, as will be discussed in the remainder of this chapter. Variation was caused by a range of factors, including gender, age, poverty, ethnic identity, and prior ill-health. For all that their men were often at home all day and available to contribute to child-rearing and other duties, women were most exposed to the stress of re-organizing domestic routines and managing overcrowded households. The young felt acutely the disruption to the wider social networks which had enabled them to cope with their own changing needs and identities. Those with low and uncertain incomes found it more difficult to cope with the strains of managing budgets. Male members of some ethnic communities, particularly those of Pakistani or Bangladeshi origin, displayed higher levels of distress than the population as a whole, although further research is required to establish how far the differentials were directly caused by Covid-19. The loss of agency in coping with threats to psychological wellbeing caused by a history of mental ill-health at any age was widely visible. The reverse implication of these qualifications is that

67

those who were outside the vulnerable groups had a less troubled journey through the pandemic than the averages suggest.

Getting By

Had the Brighton widow diarist been asked by a pollster whether she was happy or anxious, it is difficult to know how she would have answered. Her days were filled with finding a new balance between long-standing threats and familiar responses. Another diarist contributing to Mass Observation's 12 May 2020 survey described the activities and devices she was embracing as she came to terms with the crisis:

> Since lockdown, my days have mostly comprised working (from home) – not a huge change from pre covid19 – getting together with and looking after the grandchildren, yoga, walking, cooking, cleaning, reading, watching TV, listening dancing and singing to rediscovered records. And connecting with friends and family . . . in some cases this has meant reconnecting to the past as well as strengthening existing connections.[35]

There was plenty to occupy the passing days, but at the outset it was difficult to strike a new emotional order:

> I have experienced the emotional rollercoaster that has affected almost everyone I know, with some serious bouts of stress and anxiety – counteracted by alcohol and chocolate, and some spontaneous weeping – now all firmly back under control, as I am now more immersed and better adjusted to the new 'normal' imposed by the restrictions on movement and physical proximity to people and things.[36]

Everyone had their own short-term remedies. The overall consumption of alcohol in the pandemic was broadly static, with those drinking more balanced by those making efforts to cut back. A fall of sales in licensed premises was offset by alcohol bought for domestic consumption, particularly wine and spirits.[37] There were no closing hours at home and there was no shortage of stocks on supermarket shelves, which were cheaper than drinks purchased in pubs or restaurants. Research commissioned by Alcohol Change in June 2020 found that 13 per cent of current or former drinkers were consuming more units of alcohol, 12 per cent less, and 60 per cent were unchanged.[38] The consequence was a growth in those drinking at a higher risk to their health from six to nearly eight million between February 2020 and October 2021.[39] Alcohol-specific mortality, which had increased by 400 per cent in the half-century before Covid-19, rose by almost a fifth between 2019 and 2020.[40] Public Health England reported that 'from June 2020 onwards there were significant and sustained increases in the rate of unplanned admissions for alcoholic liver disease'.[41] Modelling suggested that this was likely to continue after Covid-19, causing, in the most pessimistic scenario, twenty-five thousand extra deaths over the next two decades.[42] More chocolates were also eaten in response to the crisis, raising concerns about Britain emerging from the crisis with a still more overweight population.[43]

There seems to have been an overall fall in acute anxiety once it was apparent that the government had a strategy of containment, however belatedly it was arrived at. In its place was the task of managing uncertainty about every aspect of personal interaction. Low-level fear was the sea in which everyone was swimming. There was no handbook for living through a pandemic. The modelling of Covid-19 consisted of calculating the least unlikely or unwelcome of a lengthening list of outcomes. Every government regulation from the 23 March lockdown onwards was both provisional and life-transforming. Each had multiple consequences for every household. Nothing could now be planned with any confidence. 'I think the anxiety comes from the unknown,' wrote a diarist. 'Will I be able to attend my nieces first birthday? When will I see my nan again? When can I see my friends again? Will I be able to travel? So many questions, and so many of them selfish ones, yet it is what dictates my mind.'[44] Moments of acceptance of the new conditions were overtaken by a renewed sense of impotence. 'Today I feel alright,' recorded a witness, 'but yesterday I felt quite miserable. Some days are good and some days I feel frustrated and weighed down by the quarantine and the state of the world. It's not possible to forget the situation for any moment in the day, which gets exhausting, psychologically and emotionally.'[45]

During the uncertain weeks of mid-March, the government's hesitation at the enormity of the changes it was being urged to implement is not difficult to understand. The choice it faced was avoiding an overwhelming catastrophe by disrupting every aspect of daily existence. A contributor to the u3a collective diary explained the difficulty she faced:

> I cannot get my head round this new way of life, which has changed beyond that of anything, anyone has ever known. Shortages of things such as milk, bread, toilet roll, hand wash etc, with the shops having empty shelves. Numbers of UK confirmed cases, and deaths increasing by vast numbers. I am scared of it all and very on edge and stressed with the uncertainty of every-thing.[46]

There were multiple challenges each with their register of success and failure. The separate difficulties and responses will be examined at differ-ent points in the following narrative, but it is necessary at the outset to stress the inherent complexity of lockdown life. A thirty-three-year-old furloughed baker in a coffee-shop wrote of the intense difficulties caused by looking after her children aged twelve, ten, and six: 'I am living in an almost constant state of anxiety not helped by trying to teach the children one of which is autistic.'[47] Her anxieties ranged across the short-term problems of a child's schooling, to her own peace of mind, to the larger issue of the consequences of relaxing the first lockdown: 'Here are 3 things I'm worried about today. 1) my youngest being allowed back to school (she wont be until I can be sure shes as safe as she was before). 2) my anxiety getting worse than it already is. 3) to many people thinking it's ok to go out and forcing a second peak.'[48]

Those struggling to manage domestic budgets found that poverty, stress, and exhaustion were mutually reinforcing conditions. 'I don't think many people really understand,' explained 'Victoria B.', 'how debilitating stress can be, especially when stress is combined with lack of funds. Someone who's stressed but has money has options to cope with their stress. Most don't.'[49] There was little relief in the constant task of planning and adjust-ing the family exchequer. 'Thinking ahead constantly calculating money and bills, is mentally exhausting', wrote 'Alex R.'.[50] Nor were the drivers of this kind of tiredness suddenly relaxed as lockdown was suspended. Many were inheriting financial difficulties incurred before lockdown; others were thrust into borrowing by the sudden closure of much of the economy. Incurring and repaying debt had a long-term cycle that was only partially related to the short-term drama of imprisonment and freedom staged by the government. 'Today things began to open up more,' noted 'Fiona T.', 'but rather than feeling joy I am mentally exhausted. I have just paid monthly bills and don't have much left to go back out and enjoy the easing of lockdown.'[51]

Every potential victim of Covid-19 was faced with a double level of choice. They had to decide whether to observe the controls, insofar as they understood what they were, then to calculate how to implement them with least damage to their wellbeing and established way of living. As Pauline Boss observed, anxiety in the pandemic was not a pathology, but rather a rational response:

[W]ith so many unanswered questions about the virus and vaccines, jobs and schools, wearing masks or not, and adapting to being quarantined, we need to be aware that our anxiety was likely a normal response to an abnormal situation. It was born out of the ambiguity that surrounded our losses – the not knowing, the lack of factual information, the confusion and doubt about what was happening, if and when it would be over, and what do to stay safe. To live more calmly now, we not only increase our tolerance for ambiguity but view the culprit as outside of ourselves.[52]

In this sense, it was misleading to present the sequence of lockdown and relaxation as a transition between losing and then regaining freedom. The most that happened was that over time, people became more accustomed to lockdown life, and with the introduction of vaccines, gradually more optimistic about their capacity to manage it.[53] Throughout the pandemic it was a question of dealing with uncertainties. Those deemed extremely clinically vulnerable at the beginning of the pandemic were unsure how to respond to the modified regulations. They were told that from 6 July they were no longer required to keep apart from the non-vulnerable with whom they lived, and that they could associate with up to six others providing they maintained social distancing.[54] By then the danger of Covid-19 to those with pre-existing medical conditions had been so thoroughly communicated that it was far from easy to re-write a personal risk-register. So much depended on the behaviour of others released from restrictions that for many it seemed safer to continue a regime of strict isolation, irrespective of the subsequent decline in hospitalization. When, from January 2021 onwards, vaccinations became available to the elderly and clinically compromised, the choice was easier, but doubts about the declining immunity conferred by each injection curtailed any sudden escape from the apprehensions with which they had long been accustomed. 'Hoping everybody is going to stay safe and sensible now more restrictions are being eased across the country,' wrote 'Eric J.' in May 2021. 'With the new variant spreading and not fully understood I myself am getting extremely anxious about leaving home again and mixing with other people.'[55]

Underlying all the emotional responses was the possibility of infection and illness. 'Some days,' wrote a student with a vulnerable father, 'it felt like we were waiting while the virus lurked outside the door.'[56] 'Everyone is terrified,' wrote another diarist, 'that they will be the one who gets a severe case, that they will be the one who develops pneumonia, that they will be the one who dies.'[57] Another witness described the perpetual low-level anxiety:

> Lockdown has a habit of getting the mind into repetitive 'what if' narratives. What if we catch the virus? What if I get ill, who cares for my kids then? What if they get ill, will I be able to care for them? What if the virus never leaves, what if lockdown lasts years, what if they never find a vaccine, what if what if what if. It's exhausting. And can easily lead one's mind down a dark rabbit hole of dispair and fear.[58]

There was the common experience of a chance close encounter in the street or an enclosed space with a coughing non-mask wearer that caused unsettling self-diagnoses for days afterwards. Test and Trace, when it could be made to work, could be seen as an essential means of controlling the disease. Alternatively, it was an anxiety-promoting mechanism as contacts waited at home examining their bodies and trying to recall exactly how close they had been to a victim's breath. Whilst tables were continually produced of positive tests for Covid-19, there was no count of those privately studying symptoms which might or might not turn out to be the beginning of a journey to a ventilator in an ICU. Efforts were made to specify the difference between signs of a cold or flu and the commencement of Covid-19, but in a stressed mind and body these were not always easy to discern.

After a year and a half of the pandemic, the NHS designated symptoms were:

a high temperature – this means you feel hot to touch on your chest or back (you do not need to measure your temperature), a new, continuous cough – this means coughing a lot for more than an hour, or 3 or more coughing episodes in 24 hours (if you usually have a cough, it may be worse than usual), a loss or change to your sense of smell or taste – this means you've noticed you cannot smell or taste anything, or things smell or taste different to normal.[59]

In the spring of 2022, the list was extended in response to the Omicron variant, adding shortness of breath, feeling tired or exhausted, an aching body, a headache, a sore throat, a blocked or runny nose, loss of appetite, diarrhoea, feeling sick, or being sick. This was an invitation to hypochondria. It needed an especially robust mind to be certain that such conditions were real rather than imagined, and specific to Covid-19 rather than some other common or seasonal malaise. A diarist recorded a sequence of concern that was shared by millions over the course of the pandemic: 'I was slightly worried by the fact I'd developed a dry cough, but I think that was due to running. My imagination of course went into overdrive and I looked up coronavirus symptoms. I'd taken my temperature and that was normal.'[60] For those who did test positive there was a period of around three weeks charting a recovery or contemplating a swift descent into a life-threatening condition, and as time passed, a further concern about an indefinite period of long Covid.

By the time the second wave of deaths peaked in January 2021, most people knew someone who had died.[61] Yet more common were relatives or friends who had suffered from Covid-19 and had wholly or partially recovered. Those escaping infection projected forward the course of the disease in themselves and others and contemplated a fatal outcome, whether or not this was avoided. Then there were family members or acquaintances who had died from an unrelated disease during the pandemic because of failures of diagnosis and treatment amidst the diversion of resources within the health service.

A life foreshortened was on everyone's mind: with varying degrees of intensity, it accompanied the progress of each day. It turned attention back to what had been achieved over the years and interrogated what was planned and undertaken or unfinished during the crisis. Until they occurred to the individual or someone close to them, the pre-pandemic fatal illnesses were largely unvisited. Specific forms of cancer, heart disease, or dementia were only studied when they invaded a family. Everyone, however, was soon familiar with how Covid-19 became terminal. A diarist reported on the bleaker moments of living in the face of mortality:

> Death stalks the world. I've been having some dark thoughts myself – What if this virus claims me and all the things I've wanted to do but never got round to doing would die with me? All those books, all those desires would lie unwritten and unfulfilled. My life would end and I would've failed to put my papers in order. What if it claims me or one or our family? What if we can't breathe? What if we get taken away, put on a ventilator, alone and put in a coma, because our lungs are sodden with fluids and can't take in oxygen? What if we die alone? Just another number in the daily statistics – what a waste.[62]

In reality, increased personal hygiene and diminished mixing with others meant that there was a general reduction in common or seasonal ailments. Nonetheless, should an infection occur, it was doubly difficult to measure its threat. The worst was immediately assumed, alternative pathways to diagnosis and remedy were neglected. For all the medical advances since the seventeenth century, Defoe described a dilemma that was widely experienced during the reign of Covid-19:

> It was a very ill Time to be sick in, for if any one complain'd, it was immediately said he had the Plague; and tho' I had indeed no Symptoms of that Distemper, yet being very ill, both in my Head and in my Stomach, I was not without Apprehension, that I really was infected.[63]

The evidence suggests that faced with an over-stressed and infection-ridden medical service, those worried about their symptoms erred on the side of caution. The NHS calculated that over ten million people who might otherwise have come forward for treatment during the pandemic did not do so.[64]

The higher level of vaccine hesitancy amongst the young, which will be considered in chapter 7, may have reflected a relative immunity to such bleak meditations. But as infection rates rose amongst millennials, and it became evident that long Covid was a threat to cohorts who might not perish from the disease, they, too, mostly queued up with their elders at the clinics when they were permitted and encouraged to do so. The persisting high levels of compliance with government regulations from the first lockdown onwards, in spite of the steep changes in infection rates and the often confused and confusing sequence of policy-making, reflected a deference not so much to the state as to the disease. The UCL studies consistently showed much lower scores in answers to the question 'how much confidence they had in the government to handle the Covid pandemic' than to inquiries about willingness to observe the controls that were being imposed by the administrations.[65] Whilst trust in English politicians, measured on a scale of 1 (not at all) to 7 (lots) sank to just over three in the bleak autumn of 2020, compliance with the majority of regulations never fell below 90 per cent.[66]

There were differences in personal discipline between the age cohorts, but these were usually minor. In April 2021, the ONS turned its attention to the question and discovered that whilst 96 per cent of the adult population said they were following the guidelines on the basic safety measure of wearing face masks, the figure only fell to 93 per cent amongst eighteen- to twenty-four-year-olds.[67] There was a larger difference in maintaining social distancing in groups but almost three-quarters of the young claimed to be doing so. In the UCL sample, the younger cohort, those aged eighteen to twenty-nine, were just ten points lower than the older, those aged sixty and over, with regard to compliance with a majority of the rules.[68] As government regulation faded into advice in March 2022, there was a wider gap between the generations. Older adults were twice as likely as the young to be wearing face masks; only 3 per cent of those under thirty were practising social distancing compared to a fifth of those over sixty.[69] As we will see below, men and women in their twenties were particularly vulnerable to a range of emotional pressures, including depression and loneliness, and even when they were confident about their own prospects, they remained part of multi-generational networks. Whilst Covid-19 was unlikely to kill them, they were aware that if they became infected, they could cause the death of older close relatives. 'I know I am healthy to fight it if I get it,' said a respondent to the ONS inquiry, 'although I know my parents will struggle if they were to catch it.'[70]

Pathologies

How far and by what means fear was kept at bay will be discussed in later chapters. Alcohol and chocolate were only the first lines of defence. Where individuals and social groups retained a measure of control over their circumstances, a wide range of cultural and material assets could be drawn upon in the struggle to get through the long weeks and months. Those, however, who inherited or developed specific forms of mental ill-health found it much more difficult to cope with the pressures created by Covid-19.

As soon as the gravity of the pandemic was realized, existing campaigns against emotional suffering gained a new energy. Inability to develop or maintain sustaining personal relationships was one of the first forms of difficulty to attract the attention of investigators. Loneliness was best understood as a form of failed solitude.[71] Seeking escape from the company of others had become an increasingly diverse and valued practice in the modern era. It evolved into a pathology when individuals lacked the capacity to connect or reconnect with their social life. Agency was the key resource. When withdrawal from society was a matter of choice and its duration was under control, it was possible to enjoy an enriched and diverse life. Hardship occurred when individuals lost the ability to move at will between registers of sociability. Preventing those who lived alone from relieving their isolation by going shopping, exchanging visits with others, or engaging in gatherings such as public houses, cinemas, or coffee shops threatened to tip the balance away from managed solitude to enforced loneliness. Equally, there were those who lived or worked with people in such stressed circumstances that it was impossible to escape a sense of emotional isolation.

Although the overall findings of the major surveys were much less volatile than had been feared, the increased interest in the topic caused more attention to be paid to the drivers of loneliness. From the outset, the UCL study asked about the impact on the condition of a range of variables, including age, income, type of household and community, presence of children, gender, and ethnicity. The young were lonelier than the old, and those living alone more than those sharing accommodation, but the most significant determinant was mental health. Bodily wellbeing was almost irrelevant. In the July 2021 data release, the loneliness scores for those with and without prior diagnoses of physical ill-health were almost identical. By contrast, a prior diagnosis of mental ill-health split the table. Those without such a condition registered 4.5 on the revised UCLA scale, those deemed to be suffering were almost 40 per cent higher at 6.3.[72] A similar pattern was revealed by the series of studies conducted by the ONS on the experience of those with 'disabilities'.[73] The research measured the impact of a range of physical impairments such as hearing, vision, and mobility, but mental ill-health was much the largest differentiator. At the height of the second wave of infections and deaths, the figure for mental ill-health amongst the 'often/always' lonely was 32 per cent and for those with what were termed 'social or behavioural' impairments still higher at 37 per cent.[74] Conversely, the returns indicated that those who were fully fit during the pandemic, mentally and physically, were barely exposed to the severest form of loneliness. In the earliest survey, a few days after lockdown was imposed, only 1.6 per cent of those without any kind of disability were in the 'often/always' lonely category, a figure rising to just one in twenty-five a year later, one-eighth of the level of those with a mental disability.[75]

It was a two-way journey. The predicted threat of loneliness in the pandemic fell most heavily on those who were already experiencing difficulties with managing their emotions. They found it harder to adapt their strategies for engaging with or disengaging from the company of others. More research is required on the experience of LGBTQ+ people in the pandemic.[76] There are indications, however, that difficulties were caused by the closure of venues where they could freely associate with company who would recognize and develop their gender identities.[77] Particular problems were faced by those now confined to unsupportive households. Online networks supplied only a limited means of dealing with their isolation.

Prior choices about the boundaries of domestic units were now set in stone. If someone's primary battle was with their own state of mind, adjusting to suddenly imposed rules about social interaction was a daunting task. 'I would describe my life at the moment as lonely and uncertain,' wrote 'Eric J.'.

I am a single father with a daughter living with me since my ex partner left about 5 years ago, I am unable to work due to mental health issues and live on benefits which is a struggle for anyone, but I have no close family or friends so since lockdown started last March I have had virtually no contact with the world outside my own home.[78]

It required a secure sense of self to react to the frequently revised restrictions on who were permitted to meet and under what circumstances. For those with no prior disabilities, acute loneliness barely registered amidst all the threats to everyday life. But for those who entered the pandemic after years of struggling with their mental health, lockdown could be a step too far. There was, as a consequence, a reverse flow of pressure. In the ONS survey taken during the second wave, 59 per cent of those with no disabilities claimed to be stressed or anxious, a figure rising to 84 per cent for those with mental health diagnoses or social or behavioural problems. In the more acute category of 'high anxiety', the returns for those with prior mental ill-health were more than double the level of those free of disabilities.

Amidst all the problems, some of those long accustomed to anxiety and isolation found an unexpected comfort in the sight of a population full of apprehension and unwilling to leave their homes to find company. They no longer worried that their fears were imaginary or their rejection of company irrational.[79] At the most extreme, Irwin James, who had served twenty years of a life sentence, saw an affinity between those inside and outside the prison walls: 'it has given people a flavour', he observed, 'of what it's like to have your choices limited.'[80] The practised solitaries found themselves ahead of the game. 'I suppose living on my own', wrote a diarist, 'and having had years of experience of spending time alone and being able to seek out outlets that help to build a social life has helped no end in the last few weeks. I see neighbours who may have been recently separated from their partners through death or their admission to care or hospital suffering such anguish.'[81] Covid-19 re-ordered the skills for living, foregrounding hitherto unregarded techniques for survival.

The category of mental disability covered a wide range of conditions. The largest group at risk were those suffering from some form of memory loss. At the beginning of the pandemic, about eight hundred and fifty thousand people in the UK were living with a diagnosis of dementia.[82] Women were more at risk than men. During 2020, more died of dementia than of Covid-19.[83] The collapse in the control of infection in care homes during the first wave placed dementia at the head of the table of lethal pre-existing conditions. Between March and June 2020, 27.5 per cent of all fatalities that mentioned Covid-19 on the death certificate in England and Wales were of people with dementia, around double their normal level of mortality.[84] Those who survived faced a severely restricted level of support. By the end of the first wave of the pandemic, almost all care homes were forbidding visitors at any time, and the provision of face-to-face assistance in the community had been severely restricted.

The essence of effective support for those with dementia was the maintenance of social contact, whether they were still living in the community after diagnosis or were now receiving regular visitors in care homes. The chief executive of the Alzheimer's Society wrote that the organization was witnessing the 'devastating impact of social isolation for people with dementia. Without family and friends able to visit, people's symptoms have worsened much more quickly and connections to their loved ones, sadly even those who play a vital caring role, have been lost.'[85] Continuing association with close relatives enabled those with weakening memories to retain a sense of their identity, constantly reminding them of who they were and why they mattered to others. By connecting to those with whom they had long been familiar, men and women in the early stages of the disease were offered the best chance of enjoying a time-infused existence. Men and women still living independently were provided with critical practical services such as shopping, cooking meals, and household maintenance. In care homes, visitors constituted a continuing link with their previous lives, supplemented paid-for services, and liaised with the staff about appropriate forms of care.

The imposition of lockdown posed an immediate threat to dementia sufferers still trying to run their own households. 'My mental health and state of mind has taken a hit because of coronavirus,' reported an early onset sufferer, 'and I know I'm not alone. I have been much more depressed and anxious. You can never underestimate the power of social contact and being around loved ones, particularly for people living with dementia.'[86] Long-established systems of support were fractured by the controls on movement between households. The relative of a sufferer in her late eighties witnessed her rapid decline: 'Dementia has deteriorated considerably in lockdown. We have not been able to visit her in her flat to help with reminders about eating, sort out cupboards and help with meal prep. She has lost weight.'[87] As with other forms of mental illness, the key issue was the continuing capacity to exercise agency in the face of externally imposed threats and controls.

'Living with a diagnosis of dementia,' lamented a sufferer, 'means that you wish to retain as much independence and control of your life as you possibly can. That independence and control has been lost due to my lockdown. I am also fiercely proud and dislike having to ask people to do things that ordinarily I would do myself. This control has been totally lost.'[88]

Once independent living had been abandoned, there was a new theatre of decline. Over time, visits to dementia sufferers in care homes constituted a slow deterioration in familiarity. The struggle to remember identities became harder, the history of relationships faded until the very concepts of parent and child, brother and sister, lost their meaning. If frequent contact could be maintained, there was less sense of step changes over what may be years of a worsening condition. As soon as the scale of the threat of infection and death was grasped by the care home managers, almost all physical contact with relatives was halted, to be gradually re-introduced on a distanced and tested basis later in the pandemic. The residents forgot their visitors, and the visitors saw the alteration as a series of downward steps. Research suggests that in many cases the sense of accelerated worsening in both cognitive capacities and physical wellbeing was real.[89] Dementia sufferers lacked the capacity to adapt to their sudden disconnection from what was left of their known world. A u3a diarist recorded the mutually painful encounter with her afflicted sister when the care home softened total lockdown with 'window visits' arranged by appointment well in advance:

I hate to relate how traumatic this first visit was. A familiar, very kind, but masked carer had prepared my sister, sitting with her by the window ready for my visit. My sister hates the masks and tries to tear them off. I've rarely seen her look so dejected. At first, though I lowered my scarf, she appeared not to know me (this is new), then when she seemed to recognise me she became very angry, trying to close the window, thrusting back at me the sweets I gave her. Perhaps she was angry at my perceived neglect of her. She can't understand what's going on nor express herself coherently. I could not comfort her. She was getting more and more upset at me and I left in a hurry. I don't know which of us was more distressed. Who knows what has been going through the minds of these 'abandoned' people, many of them, like my sister, unable to understand or communicate. [90]

Wherever possible, hospital wards catering for the mentally ill emptied their beds, if only to reduce the risk of infection with the coronavirus.[91] At the same time, those in acute need found it more difficult to access face-to-face support. Their first resort was to pharmaceuticals. In the three months to September 2020, more than six million people in England were prescribed anti-depressants, the highest figure on record.[92] There were falls in access to NHS psychological support services. Between March and August 2020, referrals for talking therapies were almost a quarter of a million lower than in the corresponding period in 2019. At the beginning of 2021, the chair of the British Psychological Society's division of clinical psychology, Esther Cohen-Tovée, raised serious concerns about the changing pattern of treatment: 'I'm shocked and extremely concerned about the massive extent of the reduction in referrals for psychological help during a time of huge anxiety, stress and distress for the whole population. This is even more concerning when there has been a huge increase in the prescription of antidepressants.'[93]

As in many other areas of the health services, change was a matter of accelerating pre-pandemic trends. In the autumn of 2019, 73 per cent of children and young people and 76 per cent of adults had accessed mental health services in face-to-face settings. Nineteen and 20 per cent, respectively, conducted a consultation by telephone and less than 1 per cent by some form of video link. A year later, demand for help had risen, and the channels of care had been transformed.[94] The proportion engaging in a live conversation halved in both cases. Forty per cent of children and young people and 47 percent of adults now discussed their problems by phone. Twelve and 6 per cent, respectively, used a version of telemedicine with small increases in email communication.[95] More broadly, in 2021, a quarter of the population were found to be 'managing their mental health' by digital devices.[96]

The shift away from face-to-face discussion was not always resisted. There were those who preferred to stay in their homes and fit an appointment around other domestic activities. Less need to travel meant a reduced risk of infection. Some with troubled minds preferred not to be exposed to the physical presence of an unfamiliar adult. But over a third found telephones or digital systems difficult to use, and almost a quarter reported that their problems were worsened by remote consultation.[97] It was an intensification of obstacles facing everyone using the internet in the pandemic which are discussed in chapter 7. The telephone was a familiar technology, but studies conducted in 2019 found that over a fifth of the population lacked the digital skills for everyday life, a figure rising to 35 per cent for those with a disability.[98] Conversely, professionals were not always fully equipped for remote working, nor enthusiastic about the task of assessing people they could not see. 'Our days right now are the opposite of how we normally work,' wrote a social worker. 'The enforced distance and lack of face-to-face conversations mean we can't build that rapport. We can't read body language, or offer a tissue when things get painful to talk about.'[99] As elsewhere in the field of mental health, it was a matter of informed and managed choice. The acceleration away from face-to-face care was too rapid to be appropriate for substantial numbers whose state of mind was under severe pressure from the disruptions in their basic interpersonal experiences during the crisis.

Amidst the multiple forms of mental suffering in the pandemic, the abuse of children and women caused immediate alarm. Lockdown was recognized as a particular threat to groups in society whose circumstances were already the subject of intense concern. As soon as the formal restriction was announced, observers began referring to a 'perfect storm' faced by vulnerable women and children.[100] The danger was generated by a combination of three factors: the exposure in enclosed households to maltreatment by partners or family carers; the stresses within domestic units caused by overcrowding and poverty; and the isolation of those in need of professional protection and support.

Deprivation did not by itself cause child abuse. But when combined with forms of mental ill-health, or exacerbated by substance abuse, it could lead to what is referred to in the literature as 'negative coping strategies'.[101] Lockdown increased the incidence of child poverty, which had been growing during the previous decade of austerity and magnified its consequences.[102] Inadequate accommodation became still more overcrowded as the entire family spent every day in each other's company. The inability to spend money on electronic devices became critical as schooling and entertainment became digital. There was a separate risk of children spending too much unsupervised time online and being exposed to harmful material.

The impact of lockdown on children was a dangerous form of invisibility. The epochal child protection legislation of 1889 and 1908 had made possible protection from abuse by removing from parents an absolute right to deny outsiders knowledge of how their children were being raised. Over the succeeding century, an elaborate structure of direct and indirect intervention had been established, ranging from specialized welfare officers to the now universal encounters with schoolteachers. The National Society for the Prevention of Cruelty to Children (NSPCC) summarized the threat posed by lockdown:

> The conditions created by COVID-19 have increased the likelihood that both stressors and vulnerability will increase, at a time when the protective services we normally rely on have been weakened, and families have reduced social support and connections to rely on. . . . Lockdown has meant that families are having fewer interactions with the services and social institutions designed to help them and are receiving only a fraction of the support and scrutiny that would normally work together to protect their children from maltreatment. At the same time, friends, relatives, neighbours and the community are also prevented from offering as much social support to families and checking on children's welfare; while some of the systems and services that function behind the scenes to support families or detect criminal activity have also been compromised.[103]

Reports to the NSPCC of the physical abuse of children rose by just over a half during the first phase of the pandemic.[104] The systems of intervention and care, which were at breaking point before Covid-19, depended on multiple channels of detection and referral. These were disrupted or halted altogether by the sharp reduction in face-to-face encounters. GPs no longer saw children in their surgeries, welfare clinics and community health services less often encountered families, and above all, schooling went online. In Ofsted's 2019–20 Annual Report, Amanda Spielman, the Chief Inspector, drew attention to the consequences:

> A big concern for us during the period when schools were closed to most children was the lack of visibility of vulnerable children. Schools are crucial to

children's safety and welfare, and not just while they are on school premises. In normal times, around 20% of notifications to local authorities about children come from schools and early years settings. Teachers know their children and often recognise when something is not right. . . . The low numbers of children in school during the first national lockdown therefore directly affected the ability of local safeguarding partners to identify neglect and harm. Combined with disruption to community health services, which are the universal service for very small children, it became more difficult to identify children's and families' need for early help and protection. Instead, local authorities are more likely now to be responding to a legacy of abuse and neglect.[105]

At the point at which families broke down altogether, there was a further crisis in the adoption services. Barnardo's reported that in the early months of the crisis, children identified as needing foster care rose by 44 per cent, whereas people inquiring about becoming a foster carer fell by 47 percent.[106]

In the case of abused women, the issue of agency was more complex. A range of voluntary organizations had grown up in the previous decade with which victims could make contact for advice or practical assistance such as the provision of temporary refuges. The danger posed by the pandemic was so obvious and so critical that both reports of abuse to police in London and recorded criminal offences of violence against women began to rise a fortnight before Johnson finally announced a national lockdown.[107] A diarist reported how the complex arrangements with her separated husband collapsed, leaving her in physical and financial peril:

> Due to lockdown and school closures and I am now coparenting and home schooling with me ex husband who is also my abuser. He has taken the opportunity to make a child maintenance claim against me too. I am a single parent with 2 jobs whilst he is a part of a couple and does not work. Feel like the system is constantly working against me.[108]

All the players could see what was coming. The support groups rapidly increased their efforts to enable online reporting and to supply advice, assisted by an emergency public grant of £2 million just nineteen days after lockdown was promulgated. At the beginning of May 2020, a further £76 million was made available for work in this area, of which

£25 million was specifically to support domestic abuse services, including £10 million to fund safe accommodation. In the midst of the second wave of infections, the Ministry of Justice allocated another £10.1 million on 18 November for rape and domestic abuse support.[109]

With more money and effort invested in responding to the plight of women trapped in their homes with abusers, it is difficult to be certain how far the rise in the use of helplines and chat rooms was a consequence of changed behaviour on the part of perpetrators, better recording by the police, or the increased ability of their victims to seek assistance by means of virtual communication.[110] Between April and June 2020, there was a 65 per cent growth in calls to the National Domestic Abuse Hotline compared with the same three months in 2019.[111] An investigation by the BBC's *Panorama* programme and Women's Aid in the summer of 2020 found that two-thirds of women in abusive relationships said they had suffered more violence since the pandemic began and three-quarters were finding it more difficult to escape their abusers.[112] Refuge, which claimed to be the largest organization working in this area, reported a 61 per cent growth since the beginning of 2020 in the average number of calls and contacts logged on its database between April 2020 and February 2021.[113]

A detailed study of the work of the Metropolitan Police discovered that lockdown was having a complex effect on the vulnerability of women.[114] Up to mid-June 2020, there was an 8.1 per cent growth in criminal offences by current partners since the beginning of lockdown, and a further 17.1 per cent growth in offences by other family members. These rises were, however, partly offset by a 11.4 per cent fall in offences committed by former partners, who were less able to move about and harass women with whom they were no longer living. There was a net increase, but scarcely the overwhelming flood of abuse that had been predicted. Further, the requirement for neighbours to spend all their days at home altered the source of complaints. Tracking the origin of calls to the Metropolitan Police revealed that almost all the increase came not from the victims themselves but from third parties, particularly in crowded neighbourhoods with high levels of deprivation. As used to be the case in the slums of London, a price of poverty was the loss of privacy.[115] Then as now, the first line of defence for abused women was other women hearing and seeing what the men were doing.

As with many other inequalities of power and resource in Britain during the pandemic, it may be that the principal consequence of lockdown was not so much to cause abuse as to heighten public consciousness about its long-standing extent and harm. In the year ending March 2021, there were 845,734 domestic abuse-related crimes in England and Wales, an annual increase of 6 per cent.[116] Covid-19 broke out as the long campaign against domestic violence was beginning to generate Parliamentary action. Unlike other forms of injustice, remedial action was taken before the virus had run its course. In addition to the series of emergency subsidies to charities in the field, a major law was passed in April 2021. The Domestic Abuse Act created a statutory definition of domestic abuse, established the office of Domestic Abuse Commissioner,[117] improved court proceedings, introduced a domestic abuse protection notice and order, and placed a duty on local authorities to give support to victims of domestic abuse and their children in refuges and safe accommodation. The legislation had been under discussion for several years; it took the widespread sense of crisis for it finally to reach the statute book. Implementation of the new powers was, however, obstructed by the practical obstacles created by successive lockdowns. At the end of the year, campaigners were unconvinced that women were any safer than they were at the beginning of the pandemic.[118]

The most extreme indicator of a society under stress is the rate of suicide. The period between a death and the registration of a suicide, compounded by the widespread delays in the court system that were exacerbated by Covid-19, means that at the time of writing there are only reliable figures until the end of 2021. These indicate that suicides during the first period of the pandemic were 9.2 per cent lower than in 2019.[119] The fall was confined to men, particularly those in their thirties, and largely to the first month of the full lockdown. Thereafter, the monthly figures were broadly comparable to previous years.[120] These findings are in line with what is known of other countries.[121] It will be several years before the scale and causes of fluctuations in the rates are fully understood. One possible explanation of the early fall in suicides was an unanticipated consequence of the cessation of road and rail travel at the beginning of the pandemic. The ONS reported that methods of suicide were generally constant, except for 'jumping or lying in front of a moving object', which saw 'a statistically significant decrease in April to

December 2020 (3.1%) compared with the same period in 2015 (5.0%)'.[122] As with domestic abuse, it is unclear whether the overall figures reflected the level of stress or the effectiveness of mechanisms for responding to what was expected to be an increase in the number of people in crisis. The Samaritans recorded a rise of 12 per cent in calls or emails in the first year. It appears, however, that the principal cause of anxiety reflected the major source of pathologies in the pandemic. Analysing their traffic, the Samaritans found that 'the mental health of people with pre-existing mental health conditions appears to have been affected most'.[123]

PTSD

One of the known consequences of domestic abuse was post-traumatic stress disorder (PTSD).[124] Younger women without employment and struggling to raise children with low levels of social support were particularly vulnerable. As with so many forms of anxiety in the pandemic, the impact of new difficulties was magnified by existing conditions and the fragility of strategies for coping with them. This most severe reaction to what the NHS defines as 'very stressful, frightening or distressing events'[125] was identified amongst survivors of earlier virus epidemics such as Ebola.[126] Its origin lay in both the exposure to trauma and the associated breakdown of mechanisms for reporting and treatment.

Of all the psychological damage caused by the pandemic, perhaps the most immediate was that experienced by those directly engaged with sickness and death. Within eight weeks of the first outbreak, a survey reported a range of problems amongst frontline NHS staff. A poll conducted on behalf of the Institute for Public Policy Research found that half of healthcare workers said their mental health had deteriorated since the Covid-19 crisis began.[127] A year later, the Samaritans reported that 'healthcare workers have experienced a significant and direct impact on their life and work as a result of the pandemic. Our research finds that stress and burnout, fears of infecting family members and anxiety about attending work have all been common features of Samaritans contacts.'[128] The NHS and its employees were already under stress, and the ill-planned, poorly equipped response to an unprecedented crisis rapidly exacerbated the difficulties. In August 2021, sixty thousand NHS workers were estimated to be suffering from PTSD.[129] Anxiety had multiple sources.

There was the technical challenge of keeping patients alive. Untried treatments had to be devised for an unknown disease which required a rapid re-organization of the work of hospitals and the responsibilities of their staff. There was the emotional challenge of dealing with dying patients and having to substitute for close relatives excluded from the bedsides. There was the direct fear of infection as doctors and nurses engaged with the sick without appropriate protective equipment and colleagues began to die.

Above all, there was the pervasive apprehension that staff would take the disease home. Whilst the civilian population exposed to forms of anxiety could, like the widow in Brighton, find comfort and distraction in established social networks, for the frontline staff, families frequently compounded the difficulties. Health workers quarantined themselves in separate bedrooms after work and ate their meals separately. Some ICU doctors moved out of their homes altogether to avoid infecting their children. Rachel Clarke reported a painful conversation with her nine-year-old daughter demanding to know why her mother, who had volunteered to work in an ICU, was putting her children at risk of infection or bereavement. 'Why do *you* have to be the one who sees all the coronavirus patients in the hospital?' she asked. 'Why can't it be someone else who doesn't have children so if they die, it isn't as bad?'[130] The pressures accumulated in staff who were working punishing hours. 'Over time, the anxiety became unbearable,' reported a nurse. 'I wasn't sleeping, worried about infecting my family and terrified about the prospect of passing the virus to the people in my care. Eventually my GP signed me off work owing to stress.'[131]

The experience on the Covid-19 wards rendered them different from any other medical practice in living memory. The essential issue was connectivity not with machines but with other people. The staff were technically challenged and physically exhausted and at the same time fearful of their patients. Unlike the standard fare of cancer, heart attacks, and strokes, Covid-19 was a direct threat to doctors and nurses forced to work in prolonged contact with those on ventilators. The oxygen was very noisy, and it was necessary to get close to the breath of a patient to hold a conversation. Doctors and nurses, particularly in the early weeks when, in spite of their protests, they had little or no protective clothing, sought to save patients who might, and sometimes did, kill them. The

Royal College of Physicians reported early in May 2020 that almost half of all its members were 'concerned or very concerned for their health', a figure that rose to just over three-quarters amongst BAME staff.[132] 'I was stressed and I was fearful,' wrote the ICU doctor Jim Down. 'I am not claiming that Covid didn't frighten me. Like almost everyone I was waiting to get it, expecting at any moment to develop a fever and a cough, and take to my bed.'[133] Roopa Farooki described her feelings equipped with just a regular surgical mask and gown on a Covid-19 ward during the first month:

> You'll walk straight into the virus. You'll soak it up in your hair like a sponge. You're going to get it, too. It's inevitable. You're surprised you haven't got it already. You've been more exposed than anyone you know. Face to face and hand on hand with patients who have gone on to test positive. You take that knowledge home, every night.[134]

She was fearful for her own health and that of her four children, and in turn her husband was of her: 'Your children's father is scared of you. When you come in the door, he keeps well away. He wipes the handles that you touched with ungloved hands.'[135] After a month of examining herself for symptoms, she indeed caught Covid-19.

By May 2021, more than seventy-seven thousand hospital staff in England had caught Covid-19 and nearly a quarter a million had taken sick leave related to the virus.[136] The present writer's niece, a newly qualified doctor, lasted just one unprotected week on an early Covid-19 ward before she noticed that she could no longer taste the chocolates donated by well-wishers. She was young and fit and soon recovered, but was forced to isolate, together with a flatmate, taking two freshly trained doctors away from the frontline at just the time they were most needed. When she returned to work, she still lacked appropriate protective equipment.

Almost immediately it was evident that BAME staff were particularly vulnerable. In the first month of the pandemic, they constituted 63 per cent of all deaths.[137] The cumulative figure for all fatalities from Covid-19 in health and social care had reached one and a half thousand by June 2021.[138] In turn, the medical staff had a constant responsibility to ensure that through their interactions with patients sick from other causes, or with relatives called in during a medical crisis, or with their own family to which they returned at the end of a shift, they did not themselves become agents of the 'fatal Breath'. Care workers stood still less of a chance of adequate protection as they earned a barely adequate living. 'I do feel anxious,' wrote one such care worker, a diarist for the Joseph Rowntree Foundation:

> When I left last year everything was normal. Now, I'm going to have to return to my kids each night worrying about whether I'm bringing home the virus. In one sense it will be a sort of normality but I'm scared because I will have to put myself out there. But there is no choice. My family can't afford for me not to work.[139]

Unlike domestic violence, where an established system of reporting and responding to abuse was expanded immediately the pandemic began, the NHS was slow to engage with the stress of its staff. A study conducted in June and July 2020 found that around 45 per cent of a sample of doctors, nurses, and others working in ICUs were self-reporting 'symptoms of probable PTSD, severe depression or a severe anxiety disorder'.[140] Outside the ventilator wards, healthcare professionals watched person after person dying alone. Staff were suffering from PTSD at double the rate displayed by military veterans with recent combat experience.[141] A further 8 per cent were drinking too much, although it was not clear whether this was a contribution or a response to symptoms. Eventually, almost a year after the outbreak, there was an official recognition of the scale of the problem. In February 2021, the NHS announced that it was setting up forty 'mental health hubs' in England, which would supply advice and where appropriate refer staff to psychologists and mental health nurses.[142] PTSD is by its nature a condition which can have short-term causes and long-term consequences. As with all the forms of stress and illness caused or exacerbated by Covid-19, its outcome may not be fully apparent for years to come.

4

Connections

Clapping

One of the components of life in a community is the familiar background of sound. The most dramatic impact of the first lockdown was registered aurally. Whilst most of the population took time to develop new ways of associating with others, there was a sudden change in the level of everyday noise. For a few weeks in late March and early April 2020, traffic stopped almost entirely. The noise it had generated over centuries of horse-drawn and motorized transport was replaced not by a complete silence but by sounds which for the most part had long been drowned out. Quiet conversation became possible in the street. Town-dwellers found that they could hear particular birds in specific locations. The government's edict neither created nor shaped the spring chorus of 2020, but made it audible to many urban residents for the first time in their lives. All that was left was the wailing of ambulances transporting Covid-19 victims to hospitals.

It was appropriate, therefore, that the first collective response to the pandemic was to make noise in the street. 'Clap for Our Carers' took place at eight o'clock every Thursday evening for ten weeks from 26 March 2020.[1] Although focussed on the British National Health Service, it was inspired by a European initiative. Its originator, Annemarie Plas, was a Dutch national living in London. She derived the idea from similar spontaneous events in Italy, France, Spain, and her native Netherlands. The objective was to create a volume of sound that could be heard across a neighbourhood. Clapping was merely the headline action. Residents came out of their front doors with whatever instruments came to hand. A u3a witness wrote that:

The highlight of the week (so termed by one of the neighbours) is when we all get together (socially distancing of course) and clap for the NHS on Thursday nights. Except we don't just clap – we make as much noise as possible! With hooters, a bongo drum, pan lids; metal watering can being battered with a big stick, frying pan and wooden spoon, plus honking a car horn. Afterwards we all socially distance in the middle of the road and have a brief chat, before disappearing behind our front doors for another week.[2]

Behaviours that normally occurred in the specialized surroundings of football matches or bonfire nights were now enthusiastically embraced by normally reticent householders. 'I went out into the back garden for the 8pm clap for the NHS,' wrote a Mass Observation diarist. 'It was so lovely to hear all the whoops and cheers coming from all around the park. Some people were even letting off fireworks! I really hope all the staff in the hospital could hear as it was so moving.'[3]

The immediate and lasting effect was on the neighbours themselves. In given streets, there were always distributed networks of friends and familiar faces, particularly of parents with young children. But with so many absent from their homes during working hours and recuperating in private in the evenings and at weekends, there was rarely even visual knowledge of most of the residents in many localities. Most shopping took place in the anonymous spaces of supermarkets. Now strangers from a few doors away revealed themselves, publicly embracing a shared sentiment that brought people together at the heart of the pandemic. 'Last night at eight,' wrote a diarist, 'we joined in with those standing on their door steps and looking out of their windows, clapping for the NHS and other valued workers. We saw neighbours we'd never seen before but we will, I am sure, introduce ourselves properly when all this is over.'[4] There was a sense of discovery about who lived only a few yards away. 'Made sure that we were out on our doorstep at 8pm to clap all the NHS,' wrote another diarist. 'There were so many people out on Amersham Road, George said he'd wondered where they'd all come from! I banged two saucepan lids together and it was wonderful to hear the clapping and noise echoing up and down the road.'[5] The connections were fleeting and mostly non-verbal. There were nodded greetings, occasional conversations, and then everyone went back inside.

In London in early spring, the sun set around the time the clapping began. There was little incentive to stay on the streets in the dark, even though it was unseasonably warm. Nonetheless, 'Clap for Our Carers' engendered a consciousness of community which in pre-Covid-19 times had at best been unspoken. 'Yesterday evening at 8 pm was wonderful,' recorded a u3a witness. 'I live in a little street but quite a few of us stood at our windows or doorways and clapped and shouted to support the NHS and those amazing people who are risking their lives for us. It also made me feel part of a community. I hope we can do something like that regularly.'[6]

The clapping and associated gestures such as displaying painted rainbows in front windows were a source of encouragement for the NHS workers. There were accounts of stressed staff reduced to tears by the noisy performances in the streets where they lived.[7] One of the long-term losses as a result of the post-war welfare state was the connections between the former ramshackle structure of hospitals and the communities they served, despite the subsequent work of groups of 'friends' and other fundraisers. The gain of a national system came at the expense of local involvement. On Thursday evenings, the noise may not have penetrated the sealed spaces of ICUs or the double-glazed windows of care homes, but for once the staff felt a real sense of appreciation from their home territory.

As the event became a media phenomenon, however, questions began to be asked about the conflict between thanking and acting. Senior members of the government were quick to associate themselves with the weekly ritual. After the third Thursday, the health secretary, Matt Hancock, posted a video on Twitter of himself apparently clapping to the whole of London from the roof of his Department, together with the message: 'A huge THANK YOU to our incredible NHS & social care staff. We can never thank you enough for all that you are doing for the nation.'[8] On the seventh Thursday, the prime minister arranged to be filmed clapping outside Number 10 Downing Street alongside the chancellor of the exchequer, Rishi Sunak, at Number 11 (possibly the first time in history that the occupants had appeared on the street just as neighbours). A week later, he was back on the doorstep with his fiancée, Carrie Symonds. As both Johnson and Hancock had recently been treated for Covid-19, they had cause to give personal thanks to medical staff. But what frontline workers urgently required was not applause but ventilators and adequate PPE. Performing thanks in front of the cameras increasingly appeared a calculated distraction. 'You feel angry watching the politicians, though,' wrote the junior doctor Roopa Farooki, working in an ICU in the first month. 'Credit-grabbing feel-good photo opportunists. Led by the prime minister. Smug mop-headed bastard.'[9]

Community spontaneity was being appropriated by politicians anxious to divert attention from their failings. The shelf-life of the gesture expired as the consequences of inadequate planning and provision became impossible to ignore. After the end of May, the peace of Thursday evenings was no longer disrupted. Attempts to revive the practice in honour of the seventy-second birthday of the NHS on 5 July 2020, and in the form of a broader 'Clap for Heroes' in January 2021, were met with diminished enthusiasm. There was mounting bitterness about the gulf between the rhetoric of thanks and the reality of practical support for those risking their lives on the frontline.

A large-scale study late in 2021 cited a senior doctor: 'I feel, at times, that I am considered totally expendable and that if I die or become ill not only will it have been preventable with political will, I will simply be an inconvenient statistic. I'm not a COVID hero, I'm COVID cannon fodder.'[10] In turn, medical staff were now finding themselves criticized by ministers and right-wing newspapers and abused by anti-vaxxers.[11] The *BMJ* reported a sharp rise in 2021 of violent incidents in GP surgeries.[12] Efforts to respond to lockdown turned to local initiatives. A centralized attempt to mobilize the desire to help by establishing a national register of NHS volunteers was over-subscribed and under-utilized. In the longer term, the government confined itself to issuing guidance to those who wanted to do something. 'Anyone can volunteer during the coronavirus pandemic,' advised the Department for Digital, Culture, Media, and Sport.[13] How they did so, however, was largely a matter of their own initiative and capacity.

Helping

'Clap for Our Carers' created a legacy of community participation. 'The lockdown is when I actually first met my neighbours,' a diarist reported. 'A lot of the time, I didn't really speak to them. It was a case of when we went outside for the NHS clap, it created that link and then we carried on speaking with them.'[14] Amidst the conversations, more concrete forms of activity grew rapidly. Within seven days of the start of lockdown, three hundred thousand people had offered their services to help those affected by Covid-19.[15] A survey conducted by King's College London in partnership with Ipsos Mori between 1 and 3 April found that six in ten of the population had already volunteered to help others and 47 per cent had received help from others.[16] A month after the first lockdown was imposed, the ONS asked its sample how often in the past seven days they had checked on neighbours who might need help. Sixty-three per cent reported that they had done so between one and seven or more times. Conversely, a significant proportion of those at risk knew that they could count on some kind of neighbourly support. Almost two-thirds agreed with the proposition, 'If I need help, other local community members would support me during the Coronavirus (COVID-19) outbreak.'[17] A parallel survey found that those in their seventies and eighties were most confident in receiving support, and those in their sixties most likely to enquire about the wellbeing of others.[18] In succeeding months, the numbers grew.

The initial burst of activity was sustained as the pandemic waxed and waned. A national survey carried out in December 2020 found that 12.4 million adults, about a quarter of the adult population, had so far volunteered during the pandemic. Many of these had previously taken part in some form of unpaid activity, but 4.6 million had become involved for the first time.[19] According to a *Times*/YouGov poll taken at the end of the year, 40 per cent of respondents believed that Covid-19 had enhanced 'the sense of community'; a figure rising to just under half amongst those over the age of sixty-five.[20] The UCL study asked participants in July 2020 and September 2021 how they felt about their neighbourhood. In the first summer, a little over a quarter felt that levels of communal support had increased since the pandemic started. In the second autumn, that figure had risen to over a third, although the number who thought it had deteriorated had increased from 5 to 15 per cent.[21] More generally, the UCL study found that in July 2020, 'nearly a third (28%) of respondents said that there was an improvement in how willing people were to help their neighbours and this rose to 35% in September 2021'.[22]

There was a permeable boundary between measurable participation in charitable structures and informal, unrecorded assistance to immediate family and nearby friends and residents. The baseline was keeping in touch with those known to be vulnerable and acting effectively and reliably where need was discovered. There was a wide range of small-scale activities that could make a fundamental difference to the lives of those who were now unable to leave their homes. A couple in Neath explained how their weekly shopping routine had lately been extended: 'We may need to take food/medication to an old aunt who lives not far away. I've also been picking up prescriptions for a neighbour.'[23] 'There has been a good sense of community,' wrote a u3a member, 'with wonderful stories of people helping each other and looking out for others. I'll always be grateful to my neighbours who have shopped and got my prescriptions.'[24] 'We have a shopping list for us,' explained another diarist, 'plus one for my wife's 84-year-old aunt who is essentially in isolation at her home. She lives a couple of miles from us and we simply drop the bags onto her doorstep.'[25] What once may have been a personal endeavour now became a wider service, employing where necessary the increasingly available online services.

In this world, there were no clear lines between the needs of relatives and others living nearby. 'My neighbour put a list of shopping she needed through my door,' wrote a diarist, 'my mother in law phoned me with her list and my mum rang with her list. I then went onto the Sainsburys online website placed the order. I shop for 4 people every week including myself.'[26] In her spare time, she found new value in her favourite pastime: 'I have been raising money for the local Parkinson's Support Group by selling plants on my drive, to date since lock down I have raised £535. I put out a small stall. I then spent time in my green house.'[27]

A consequence of Covid-19 was to make goodwill apparent. Few if any of these activities were called into being by the pandemic. Prescriptions had long been collected, shopping undertaken, household repairs made, gardens tidied, by the able-bodied on the part of the less-abled. As the leader of the King's College survey put it, '[W]e have got this reservoir of helpful behaviour between neighbours and communities which is there, but just not very visible. Definitely, the levels we are seeing now are higher than in "normal" times, but we have an underlying propensity [to help each other]. The crisis has just given us a way to express that.'[28] The sheer speed with which these multiple forms of assistance were mobilized was evidence of the depth of existing practices. A week before the announcement of lockdown, a Mass Observation diarist reported that, 'I've just had a printed card through my door from the local volunteer bureau giving me a number to ring if I need help. So kind and an amazingly quick response.'[29] Another diarist in a village north of York reported on 20 March that

> Burke's 'Little Platoons' have sprung into action. AL, in his capacity as parish councillor, delivered a message from the newly formed 'Terrington CV Support Group', comprising of around a hundred residents, offering practical, non-medical help to those in need. These stalwarts would pick up and deliver groceries, prescriptions, walk dogs, put out bins or chat on the phone if people feel isolated.[30]

The edict of 23 March caused social scientists to undertake surveys which found a culture that had always been there, if on a smaller, less urgent scale. A few weeks earlier, a national lockdown seemed to the government an inconceivable intrusion of state power. When it was forced to act, the private response to the demands it created needed only modifications or extensions of familiar channels of personal assistance. 'The virus gave us permission to be kind again,' said the manager of a community centre in Hartlepool. 'We should celebrate the way communities have responded. Millions did a good thing.'[31]

The critical change was not so much the accumulation of acts as knowledge of their availability. A basic consequence of lockdown was that neighbours got to find out about each other, on Thursday evenings but also in casual conversation. The proportion who recognized similar values with their neighbours rose from 9 to 32 per cent between July 2020 and September 2021.[32] It was a partial return to times when social life was led out of doors. 'The chat over the back-garden fence had ended,' wrote a Liverpudlian who had grown up on a council estate. 'The outside world has been shut out. Piercing a neighbour's bubble by communicating over the fence is against all the rules: their privacy is sacrosanct. Except that now it isn't. There's suddenly a lot to talk about. The sunny days of lockdown are like back-to-back childhood Sundays again.'[33]

Need did not always arise immediately. At the outset, individuals had different stocks of goods. The demands of their housing or gardens varied by the season. Medical prescriptions altered over time. People's health might permit a self-sufficient life at one point and reduce them to dependency at another. As lockdowns were imposed, relaxed, and reimposed, their freedom to manage their existence independently of others changed in ways that were easy neither to anticipate nor to manage. Trust in the possibility of assistance was of paramount importance. A diarist recorded how much it meant to her simply to know that support could be called upon: 'When I went down to make breakfast, I noticed an envelope pushed through the front door into the porch. It was a card from neighbours across the road offering help if I needed it and giving me their mobile number. People are so very kind.'[34] For this reason, one of the earliest actions of the proliferating neighbourhood support groups was to compile a register of those likely to require assistance in the future. At a national level, there was the listing of those deemed clinically extremely vulnerable to Covid-19, which began with data held in GP surgeries. It was assembled centrally and then made electronically available to supermarkets and local authorities to enable them to pay attention to the wants and wellbeing of over two million people who were now confined to their homes.[35]

The most reliable forms of support were extensions of organizations that were already in existence when Covid-19 broke out. They had the administrative and technical systems, the necessary equipment and buildings, the experienced volunteers and coordinators. These could readily and reliably be expanded to meet new demands. They knew their localities, and how to raise donations and source goods to meet legitimate needs. Religious organizations had a long record of involvement in food banks, often in coordination with the Trussell Trust. It was estimated that nine in ten Anglican churches were engaged in this work during the pandemic.[36] Involvement in such basic assistance had always been a feature of the work of mosques.[37] The Sikh community, meanwhile, adapted its tradition of the *langar* or shared meal to provide an emergency food service for its own members and NHS staff.[38]

Over the previous decade, networks had grown up to facilitate the exchange of services (Nextdoor) and unwanted food (Olio) and household goods (Freecycle) in local neighbourhoods. These were immediately able to respond to the new scale of demand as lockdown began. The founder of Freecycle reported that his operation 'went from maybe 60,000 posts a day to 120,000 posts a day overnight'.[39] Olio, an app which enabled people to share edible food waste, also saw its users double from two to four million. In this respect, as in many others, the voluntary sector was much better prepared for the crisis than the serially challenged agencies of the state. A diarist described how her locality's efforts coalesced around an existing organization:

> Our village Community Council has stepped up to the mark without hesitation. We have dedicated, hard-working people who have organised a volunteer group (which we are part of), a food larder for free food for those who are in need (all the result of donations) and a link to all the information and advice available. That doesn't even scratch the surface of the kindness and neighbourliness all around us from local businesses, tradesmen, delivery services and all the usual essential services that we take for granted. It's heartwarming and humbling to see such values. It's not all about money.[40]

Across the whole period of lockdown, there was an outpouring of goodwill and organizational effort and skill. There were, however, countervailing pressures which were difficult fully to overcome.[41] Much of the sense of community in the pre-pandemic era had depended on face-to-face association and the freedom of volunteers to leave their homes to support those in need. As libraries, educational centres, village halls, coffee shops, bars, and shops closed their doors, there was a sharp reduction in opportunities to meet with others and gain access to a range of formal and informal assistance. A diarist reported a succession of closures in a long-established programme of voluntary endeavour:

> On an ordinary Tuesday I'd be driving 25 minutes through Exeter's rush-hour to work in a small charity, where 3 days week I coordinate a project for unpaid male carers. I also do freelance work – largely community engagement and project evaluation, but also as a simulated patient at local university medical schools. None of those things are happening now – no face-to-face teaching in universities, no community events or other public gatherings.[42]

The smaller the community, the more visible the sense of loss. Groups which had been in existence for many years, sometimes as branches of national bodies, were instantly suspended. In the corner of Shropshire where this book was written, there was a sharp curtailment in long-established gatherings that combined socializing with forms of support, particularly of older residents. The monthly *Parish News* for May

2021 (price 30p, delivered throughout the crisis in hard copy) contained the following entries: 'Mytton Book Club. The club is on hold until further notice'; 'Montford Bridge Lunch Club. This is Still on Hold'; 'Fitz Knitting and Sewing Group. Meetings have been cancelled for the time being'; 'Fitz Flower Group. Will Resume when the Hall is reopened and even then only if the organiser feels it is safe to do so'; 'The Friendship Group for over 55s. The programme will resume a soon as possible'. It is too early to know whether all these small but valued bodies will reappear, but by the autumn of 2022, the Fitz Friendship and Flower Groups were once more meeting in the village hall.

A further threat of loss was created by the medical response to the first wave of Covid-19. For men and women deemed 'clinically extremely vulnerable', the issue was as much risk as incapacity; many were otherwise fit enough to lead a normal everyday life. Those who were of retirement age had frequently been volunteers in some respect. Now they were thrust into dependency, reliant on the goodwill of others for their daily needs. The advice was relaxed at the beginning of August 2020, although warnings remained in place for those with particular medical conditions, who were prioritized in the subsequent vaccine programme. An unintended consequence was a loss to their own sense of self-worth and to the contribution they could make to the needs of others. The Trussell Trust reported that it was difficult to meet growing demand because 'a large proportion of their volunteer base were asked to shield'.[43] A seventy-seven-year-old retired woman wrote of her frustration at her house arrest: 'I can go out once a day for a constitutional but not shopping or any other more social or communal activity. I find this enormously restricting as generally I would be carrying out some sort of voluntary activity as part of my weekly norm and now I do none.'[44]

The loss of those protected from Covid-19 was partly countered by the creation of a cohort of economically inactive men and women under the furlough scheme. Those still nominally on the payroll occupied their spare time serving as delivery drivers, packers of food parcels, and other locally organized helpers. Their numbers explained the large over-subscription to the appeal to help out the NHS, which attracted nearly three-quarters of a million offers of assistance by the end of March 2020.[45] Many found a sense of purpose and public recognition that they had never before enjoyed in their daily lives. A woman in Blackpool, herself on Universal

Credit and making use of a food bank to support her family, reported her pleasure in also being able to help others in need: 'I went to Stanley Park Sports Club today to help pack food into bags for free school meals and family packs. We all stood 2-metres apart and wore gloves and masks. I really enjoyed it, knowing that I was helping the community.'[46] There were press reports of cheery encounters on doorsteps, sometimes involving celebrities exploiting their public profile. At the beginning of the pandemic, the comedian Johnny Vegas, backed up by an online message of encouragement from his friend the Hollywood actor Russell Crowe, was widely photographed delivering food parcels in his native St Helens on behalf of a charity run by a former rugby league star.[47]

An additional resouce was the expanded use of online facilities. Amidst the cancellations reported by the rural parish news, one branch of the Women's Institute was able to turn to digital communication. It was reported that the Bicton and Oxon branch would 'meet via Zoom on Wednesday 5th May at 7 30 pm when Penny Thompson will give an anecdotal talk Hatching, Matching and Dispatching'. There was now sufficient expertise in networking apps to overcome difficulties of physical association and shortages of volunteers. WhatsApp, in particular, was easy to adapt from family exchanges to community building. By its nature, it lent itself to instantly formed, small-scale collective activity. Villages, streets, ad hoc groups of neighbours, friends, and relatives were able to collate information about local requirements and coordinate efforts to meet them. A diarist described her work, which constituted the basic building block of engaging with the difficulties caused by lockdown:

> I have been one of the volunteers from our road since lockdown began, the need being much greater now that people can't visit to collect food themselves. The woman on our road who organised and set up our street WhatsApp group volunteers there every week and had begun working there more regularly since she couldn't do her 'normal' job during lockdown. There are about 4 or 5 of us (with cars) in our road's group who do deliveries throughout Southwark during the week and I spent just over 2 hours doing deliveries to 5 different households today.[48]

More ambitious endeavours crossed the line into professional uses of the web. There were rules to be observed about the deployment and storage of personal information, and skills to be learned about how to counsel and support vulnerable adults and children. Experienced volunteers or those with knowledge gained in their employment found themselves working behind the frontline to ensure that there was an orderly and legal use of digital systems. 'In the afternoon,' recorded a diarist,

> I did some online training on data protection for the parish council I sit on, not fascinating but necessary. I have done something similar for work. I filled in a volunteering form to support people by telephone through church. I registered for some online safeguarding training I will need to do for that. I rang an isolated gentleman who I am supporting through another scheme.[49]

For all the conscious outpouring of goodwill from before the first lockdown, however, Britain remained a society under acute stress. There was a problem of networking throughout the pandemic, for which volunteers setting up physical or online systems could offer only a partial solution. Those delivering services were constantly aware of demand outstripping the capacity to respond. The food charity the Trussell Trust, a barometer of basic physical deprivation in the pandemic, reported that its business had grown by a third in the first year.[50] The Independent Food Aid Network saw a still higher growth in its work.[51] This was partly a consequence of failings in the state welfare system and long-term issues of low pay, which will be examined in the following chapter. But it was also caused by the erosion of interpersonal aid. When it came to not being able to feed dependants, there had always been a range of family and neighbourhood resources that could be called upon. The less those locked down in their homes engaged with the experiences of others, the less easy they found making even small gestures of help, the more likely it was that the requirement for food parcels would grow. The Trussell Trust explained the problem:

> Before the pandemic, the vast majority of people referred to food banks had either exhausted the support that was available from family and friends, or had resource-poor social networks who weren't in a position to help. Others were unable to access more formal support such as advice services, or debt

management agencies. The pandemic has caused huge disruption to people's social circles and informal support networks, as well as civil society organisations, making it harder to receive this kind of support.[52]

It was not just an issue of eating or not eating. Every approach to a food bank represented a series of fractured channels of assistance. In this regard, as with systems of mental health discussed in the previous chapter, it was critical that those in trouble could find their way through pathways of advice and referral that were everywhere disrupted by lockdown. Equally, it was essential that the donating bodies were as sensitive to local dietary practices and individual need as family and neighbours might have been. 'We received a wonderful food parcel this week,' reported a recipient, 'Put together by a local church group (but funded by the government) it was the best, most considerately thought through parcel we've ever had. They called and asked about dietary requirements first. It contained no useless "treat" food, but loads of fresh fruit and veg, and even really good quality meat (1kg beef mince and 24 sausages)!'[53]

The pandemic exposed systems of dependency that were already under enormous stress. Demand for Trussell Trust food parcels had grown by just under a fifth in each of the two years before Covid-19.[54] The organization analysed its users, and found that on the eve of the pandemic, of those referred to food banks, '95% met the definition of being destitute, three-quarters were severely food insecure, and one in five were homeless'.[55] Seven in ten food-bank households had someone with ill-health or disability, four times the national average. Immediately after the first lockdown, referrals spiked by 85 per cent. The health crisis intensified the pressure on already-overstretched channels of aid between those in a given week or month who were just above the absolute poverty line and those who were falling below it.

However much it said about the goodwill inherent in British society, a world divided between volunteers and recipients reflected an increasingly fraught existence amongst the least prosperous and a persistent exposure to shame as recourse was made to assistance. 'I've also had to rely a few times on food parcels from charities,' wrote a *Covid Realities* diarist, 'that was soul destroying and life saving all at the same time.'[56] 'I never say no to free food,' wrote another.

how can I these days. But the shame I feel. Not cos anyone is making me feel ashamed, my neighbours are all very gracious and they act like it's no big deal to them at all. And I'm not the only person who gets this kindness in our little community, and, though rare, when I can I share also. So I shouldn't feel shame. Yet I do. I wish I had the ability to just switch off years of trauma and get into work, I wish I wasn't reliant on others for aid. I wish I was more the type of mother we're told we're meant to be, able to magically juggle household and children and career. But I'm not. I'm on the dole, I get food aid, my kids are on free school meals, they wear mostly hand me downs from strangers and donations, and I shouldn't feel ashamed and yet I deeply do. I'm grateful to have the help. I wish we didn't need.[57]

Snitching

A further reflection of a stressed society was the rise in what became known as 'snitching'. The National Police Chiefs' Council reported at the end of April 2020 that forces had received 194,000 calls about people alleged to have broken lockdown regulations.[58] Sara Glen, a deputy chief constable with responsibility for tackling coronavirus, said: 'We have members of the public who are coming in on the phones and [via the internet] to report where they've got concerns either at gatherings of people that they can see from their locations, or if they think people aren't adhering to the regulations and that's actually putting them at risk.'[59]

Neighbours were informing on neighbours, expecting that fines or other punitive action would follow. The Chairman of the West Yorkshire Police Federation complained not only that his force was having to deal with a growth in domestic abuse reports, stimulated by the efforts of support groups to ensure that victims were not rendered defenceless in their homes, but also that there had been a rise in calls from people reporting others for potential flouting of regulations.[60] Further south, it was noted that the 'avalanche of complaints about twice-a-day jogs or overly frequent trips to the supermarket has been such that the Thames Valley Police Commissioner Anthony Stansfield felt obliged to go on the BBC and urge citizens to stop tattling on one another'.[61] Elsewhere in Europe, more draconian regulations were matched by more active tale-telling. The mayor of Rome set up a website for people denouncing those who breached the quarantine regulations. In Spain, 'snitchers' were said to be not only reporting infractions but also taking direct action against rule-breakers.

The police responded by directing complainants not only to the existing non-urgent 101 telephone number but also to specially created online reporting systems. By the second week of April, over half of the police forces in England and Wales had launched dedicated web pages to collate information.[62] The Metropolitan Police, for instance, posted a form which invited Londoners to 'Tell us about a possible breach of coronavirus (Covid-19) measures.' There was a short-lived proposal to create a cohort of 'Covid marshals' in every town and city, which would 'engage, explain and encourage best practice and national COVID-19 secure guidance'.[63] In the early autumn, there was a renewed burst of activity when the government introduced the 'Rule of Six', which was intended to restrict social interaction short of imposing a new lockdown. From 14 September, it was illegal in England for households to meet with people from other households in groups of more than six, either indoors or outdoors, except for 'secure venues such as places of worship, restaurants and hospitality venues', where 'groups of up to 6 must not mix or form larger groups. This rule will not apply to individual households or support bubbles of more than 6 who will still be able to gather together.'[64] A week later, a further set of restrictions was announced covering the wearing of face masks, opening hours of businesses selling food and drink, and attendance at weddings and funerals.[65] The regulations were difficult to comprehend and varied between the four nations. In England, they were accompanied by a structure of fines culminating in £10,000 for repeat offenders.[66] At the same time, the government announced 'an initial £60 million to support additional enforcement activity by local authorities and the police'.[67]

The regulations generated more hostility than the initial lockdown, both from those who believed they were evading a necessary second full lockdown, and from those who considered them an unacceptable extension of the surveillance state. Local authorities were unenthusiastic about recruiting and managing the underfunded army of 'Covid marshals'. The police, coping with a rise in the crime rate that initially had fallen, were reluctant to assume extra responsibilities.[68] The head of the National Police Chiefs' Council explained that the police would respond to the new regulations on the basis of the 'four Es approach': engage, explain, encourage, and enforce, with minimal emphasis on the final action.[69] The minister responsible for maintaining law and order was more robust. Priti Patel made headlines when she was asked how she would respond if she saw two families of four bumping into each other and stopping for a chat. 'I'm rarely at home,' she replied, 'but if I saw something that I thought was inappropriate then, quite frankly, I would call the police.'[70] The prime minister both supported and distanced himself from the regime he had called into being. Anxious not to soil his libertarian credentials, he advised that discussion with transgressive neighbours was a preferable first step.[71] In the language of his schooling, he said he had 'never much been in favour of sneak culture'.[72]

At the centre of the criticism was the locus of action. It was assumed that the Rule of Six regime was less an imposition on society than a co-option of its more responsible members in a disciplinary project. The journalist John Humphrys drew attention to 'an outcry against this attempt to turn us all into Covid vigilantes on the grounds that it would turn us into a nation of snitchers'.[73] In the words of the excitable Lord Sumption, the scheme required the creation of 'a Stasi-style surveillance state with a poisonous network of informers'.[74] The allusion to the East German state was instructive. The Stasi raised reporting by neighbours to a bureaucratic art-form. Before the fall of East Germany in 1989, it was estimated that as many as a third of the population were acting as informers. The totalitarian regimes of twentieth-century Europe had maintained their power through an army of civilian spies.[75] Seven thousand Gestapo officers exercised control over a population of sixty-six million by acting as a clearing house for written complaints about illegal activities or opinions. Stalin's apparatchiks were in receipt of a torrent of correspondence about comrades betraying the Soviet project.

Beyond the growing opposition on the right wing of the Conservative Party to the continuation of any controls over social behaviour, there were two objections to the home secretary's willingness to report everyday activity to the police. The first was the ownership of the outcome of the pandemic. From the outset, the government had insisted that survival depended more on the behaviour of individual citizens and social networks than on the decisions and actions of the state. 'It's not dobbing on neighbours,' insisted Priti Patel, 'it's all about taking personal responsibility.'[76] Rather than focussing on political failings such as the late imposition of the first lockdown and the evasion of the second, or on shortcomings in the provision of PPE and an effective Test and Trace system, or on structural problems of inequality and underfunded public services, attention was turned to the basic values and self-discipline of the population.[77] Despite additional funding, improved reporting lines, and systems of fines, there was a limit to what could be expected of the police and the courts. The key was the natural tendency of neighbours to watch each other, and to take what action was necessary to enforce agreed and necessary standards of conduct. Controlling the spread of infection, in this discourse, was essentially a matter of self-discipline and reinforced by collective surveillance.

The second objection was that the distraction from political misconduct threatened the erosion of mutual confidence within the communities that were celebrated through 'Clap for Our Carers' and other gestures.[78] The leading motive for observing the regulations was the evident risk not to the individual but to the local community, particularly its more vulnerable members.[79] The sense of mutual obligation was weakened if the political rhetoric of widespread individual disobedience gained traction. Further, if it was thought that neighbours were constantly alert to every casual meeting, to any small excursion to relieve the imprisonment of the home, to each occasion when a mask was not worn properly or at all, it was impossible to maintain any kind of relaxed social intercourse. The structure of mutual assistance depended on those able to help generating information about those who needed it. Inquiry, observation, and action were critical to the support of others, but now these same actions were destructive of collective security and respect.

The complex regulations associated with the Rule of Six weaponized almost every aspect of the daily round. It was easy to take complaints to the police, and to cause embarrassment and financial harm to those who found themselves in the courts. 'Curtain-twitching,' wrote John Humphrys, 'grassing, ratting, snitching – call it what you like – is the mark of a society that isn't working not one that is. The thing that matters most in any society is trust and once that's undermined it's hard to grow again.'[80] There was a danger of stigmatizing deviant groups, and, as the crisis progressed, the young altogether as they sought outdoor entertainment and proved more hesitant about vaccination.

The debate about snitching required a sense of historical proportion. There were no grounds for describing the practice as either non-British, or specifically a product of the Covid-19 crisis. In the Great Depression, the nearest comparable combination of acute community stress and enhanced state interference in everyday life, there had been extensive reporting of misbehaviour to the authorities.[81] The Means Test placed a monetary penalty on a wide range of activities. Matters that had always formed the substance of street gossip, such as who had a hidden source of income, who had acquired a new possession, who was sharing whose table or bed, were now relevant to the work of the inspectors policing the benefit system. They acted less as detectives and more as processors of a flow of tales of alleged misconduct. As George Orwell observed in *The Road to Wigan Pier* in 1937, 'there is much spying and tale-bearing'.[82] At the heart of the practice was the absence of power in a threatening world. Unable to control their material circumstances, the unemployed asserted their sense of fairness amidst collective suffering and appropriated the authority of the state to settle otherwise unresolvable disputes with neighbours.[83]

The Covid-19 lockdown and subsequent iterations of the rules controlling personal conduct created similar circumstances.[84] An entire society was told it had responsibility but no security. Until the arrival of vaccines in early 2021, every action was defensive, with no guarantee of effect. Avoidance of the 'fatal Breath' required both self-discipline and collective good conduct. Each day was a matter of calculating the best means of reducing the risk of infecting or being infected by others. Thoughtless behaviour by others constituted a threat to life which the medical system was palpably incapable of dealing with. Ringing the telephone lines or completing online forms were means of diminishing perceived dangers and, as in the 1930s, asserting a collective interest in good behaviour. At a time when it was impossible for neighbours to escape each other's company, they were also a device, as in the past, of appropriating external authority to settle local disputes. There was evidence that the requirement for families to stay at home, particularly in poorer areas, was already trying the patience of neighbours who were now spending much of the day in each other's company. In the first lockdown, the number of complaints about noise rose by almost a half in Greater London, despite the reduction of road traffic.[85]

The line between mischief and justified grievance was hard to draw. In the midst of the Rule of Six crisis, a police spokesman told *The Times* that 'many members of the public were reporting even small transgressions and sometimes reporting because of a grudge against neighbours'.[86] A toxic combination of political malice and personal misjudgement was responsible for the highest-profile case of snitching in the second phase of the crisis. Dominic Cummings' time of trial following his flight to Durham began when his father-in-law's neighbour spotted him in the town and informed the police. Scotland's Chief Medical Officer was forced to resign after being exposed for twice visiting her second home. The epidemiologist Professor Neil Ferguson, whose work was instrumental in persuading the prime minister to impose the initial lockdown, was reported to the *Daily Telegraph* for breaking the rules of household isolation by receiving at least two visits from a married woman who was still living elsewhere.[87] The *Telegraph*, no friend of state-imposed regulation, delighted in his discomfort. In turn, the health secretary, Matt Hancock, welcomed his resignation from the Scientific Advisory Group for Emergencies (SAGE), despite Ferguson's previous contribution. 'The social distancing rules are there for everyone,' he said piously. 'And they're incredibly important, and they're deadly serious, and the reason is because they're the means by which we've managed to get control of this virus.'[88] He would not stand in the way of a police prosecution. Just over a year later, his career was in turn destroyed by accidental electronic surveillance of similar misbehaviour in his private life. Whilst he had not 'broken the law', he later wrote, 'the recommendation remained that everyone should follow the one-metre-plus rule, and we clearly had not.[89] Eventually, the prime minister himself was undone when he failed to quell the flow of stories from inside Downing Street about illegal parties.

The trusting society envisaged by critics of snitching was not to be found either during the pandemic or in the past. The encouragement of reporting to the authorities reflected a judgement by the government that such behaviour would occur as it had previously. However, it took place on the margins, not at the centre of the collective response to the pandemic. The volume of complaints reflected only a small minority of an entire society embraced by lockdown. The initial perception that there was something in the British character that would resist a draconian closure of social life was quickly shown to be wrong. Observance of the rules was almost universal at the outset, and the UCL study found that 'majority compliance' was still over 90 per cent when the police 101 line was being flooded with calls in September 2020; a year later it had only fallen to the upper eighties.[90] Most people were observing the rules and thought others were doing so. What changed was popular understanding of the regulations, which was almost universal during the first, very simple lockdown, and fell to below a half in England once the absolute prohibition on leaving home was replaced by a more complex set of rules governing social interaction. A mere 14 per cent of English respondents claimed a total comprehension. The figures were higher in Scotland and Wales, possibly because of better government communications.[91]

Misreading the scale of snitching had consequences. At the outset, most people took precautions in the interests not of themselves but of their community, particularly its vulnerable members. The stress by ministers on the scale of rule-breaking weakened mutual trust. 'The question matters,' wrote the social psychologist Stephen Reicher, 'because it has implications for how people act. If someone senses that everyone else is breaking Covid-19 restrictions, this will undermine their own determination to stick by the rules.'[92] Better to celebrate the remarkable level of community discipline and focus attention on the scale of the difficulties political mismanagement had caused. In any case, it was a ministerial fantasy to suppose that exhortations to report on neighbours would have any influence on such behaviour. The decisions about whether to talk about a difficulty, or, on comparatively rare occasions, register a formal complaint, were made for complex reasons, private to the individuals involved and the social networks in which they lived. In the midst of the Rule of Six drama, the columnist Zoe Williams robustly defended the impermeability of citizens to external persuasion:

> [T]he very idea that a government could have an impact on neighbourly behaviour runs counter to any understanding of human beings. We have known this since the Stasi. Someone who will call the police on a neighbour will do so anyway, whether it is their brother-in-law or their direst foe, whether they have been asked to or not – all they need is the hotline. And someone who would not go to the authorities over another person's law-breaking, even

while the hot tubs are overflowing and the hydroponic lamps are beaming straight into their conservatory, will never do it. And nothing Johnson, Patel or anyone else says will make the slightest difference.[93]

Tracing

In the absence of a vaccine or some other pharmaceutical intervention, there is only one way of controlling the outbreak of an infectious disease: those who are infected must be isolated, together with those who have been in contact with them. It is difficult to conceive of any other task facing an early twenty-first-century government that is exactly the same as that undertaken by the vestigial public administrations of the medieval and early modern period. It was the reality in Defoe's London. The 'ORDERS concerning infected Houses, and Persons sick of the Plague' decreed that: 'IF any Person shall have visited any Man, known to be infected of the Plague, or entred willingly into any known infected House, being not allowed: The House wherein he inhabiteth, shall be shut up for certain Days by the Examiners Direction.'[94] Defoe discussed the ideal length of quarantine and decided that the traditional forty days was too long, settling instead on fifteen or sixteen days, almost the same as the fortnight decreed by the collective scientific wisdom in 2020.[95]

Following outbreaks of trans-national diseases earlier in the century, every state with a functioning bureaucracy had made plans for mass quarantine in the event of a recurrence. On 2 March 2020, nine days before the WHO formally declared a new pandemic, Boris Johnson declared in a Downing Street press conference that 'this country is very, very well prepared. . . . [W]e've got fantastic testing systems, amazing surveillance of the spread of the disease.'[96] This statement, together with subsequent claims by Matt Hancock, the health secretary, that Britain possessed or was developing 'world-beating' systems of testing and tracing, were reminiscent of Mary McCarthy's summary of the accuracy of Lillian Hellman's writings: '[E]very word she writes is a lie, including "and" and "the".'[97] Six months after lockdown was announced, SAGE, faced with unmistakable signs of a second wave of Covid-19, compiled a summary of how the various 'non-pharmaceutical interventions' had fared. Its verdict on the Test and Trace programme was damning:

An effective test, trace and isolate (TTI) system is important to reduce the incidence of infections in the community. Estimates of the effectiveness of this system on R [the number of people that one infected person will pass on a virus to, on average] are difficult to ascertain. The relatively low levels of engagement with the system (comparing ONS incidence estimates with NHS Test and Trace numbers) coupled with testing delays and likely poor rates of adherence with self-isolation suggests that this system is having a marginal impact on transmission at the moment. Unless the system grows at the same rate as the epidemic, and support is given to people to enable them to adhere to self-isolation, it is likely that the impact of Test, Trace and Isolate will further decline in the future.[98]

There were a range of performance indicators associated with the Test and Trace system, but the fundamental measure was its impact on the spread of the coronavirus. In the view of the government's own scientific advisers, the procedures for discovering and isolating those who had been in contact with the disease had been, and remained, almost useless.

At the onset of the pandemic, it was rapidly discovered that successive governments had let disaster planning atrophy, allowing stockpiles to run down and operational systems to decay. In 2016, Exercise Alice had examined preparedness for a possible MERS-like coronavirus epidemic and Exercise Cygnus tested readiness for an outbreak of a fictional 'swan flu'. Exercise Alice, which was the closest to the Covid-19 outbreak, recommended better provision of PPE, the imposition of quarantine, and community sampling.[99] It was kept secret during the pandemic on the grounds that publication could 'lead to loss of public confidence in the government's and the NHS' Covid-19 response . . . based on misinterpretation of the report', but publication was eventually forced in August 2021, under the Freedom of Information Act.[100] 'The UK's preparedness and response,' discovered Exercise Cygnus, 'in terms of its plans, policies and capability, is currently not sufficient to cope with the extreme demands of a severe pandemic that will have a nationwide impact across all sectors.'[101] Late in 2021, the National Audit Office conducted a full review of preparedness for the coronavirus. 'Although the government had plans for an influenza pandemic,' it concluded, 'it did not have detailed plans for many non-health consequences and some health consequences of a pandemic like COVID-19.'[102] It was otherwise in those countries where the SARS outbreaks were recent memories.

These failings were compounded by the culture of public administration inherited by the Conservatives. At least as far back as the Fulton Inquiry of 1968, doubts had been growing about the capacity of the civil service to meet the technical challenges of the modern world. The subsequent rise of the new public management stressed the need to import the skills of the commercial sector into Whitehall, or export whole areas of policy formation and delivery. Under Margaret Thatcher, expenditure on outside consultants rose from £6 million to £246 million.[103] Employing outside staff meant that the civil service establishment was kept down and there was less risk of subsequent crises causing an unplanned and unwanted growth of the state. The Third Way subsequently embraced by New Labour saw no necessary contradiction in employing private companies to deliver a range of public services, including parts of the prison system. At the same time, the long-standing disregard for the capability of local government was compounded by the Lansley health reforms to the English NHS of 2012, which had dismantled regional health authorities and concentrated responsibility in the centralized Public Health England. The new role of community-based Director of Public Health, which had emerged from the re-organization, was insufficiently connected to the funding streams and policy making of the NHS.

Faced with an unanticipated crisis early in 2020, and an unwelcome discovery of their lack of preparedness, ministers instinctively turned to consultancies and outsourcing companies. These were eager to promise both speed and efficiency in the delivery of critical systems such as testing and tracing Covid-19 infections. 'We excel in the business of human potential,' claimed Boston Consulting, one of the principal beneficiaries, 'and believe in its power to shape strategic, organizational, economic and societal change.' The US firm that managed the new contact system claimed that 'at Sitel Group, we know the employee experience *is* the customer experience – and we are committed to transforming the contact center industry. Our 90,000 people around the globe are redefining the way brands connect with their customers – 3.5 million times each day.'[104] The NHS signed over 600 contracts with private providers, in its haste frequently by-passing established practices for tendering and transparency. Around fifty firms were placed in a 'fast lane' for awarding contracts on the basis of opaque contacts with government or its supporters.[105] Despite widespread criticism of the charges levied by the firms, the Public Accounts Committee found that as late as February 2021, the NHS Test and Trace programme was still employing around 2,500 consultants at an average daily rate of £1,100 and a peak of £6,624. It was told by the Department of Health and Social Care that such rates were 'very competitive'.[106]

The initial attempt to create a comprehensive Test and Trace system was overwhelmed by numbers before it could begin to operate properly. On 10 March, the government abandoned community testing, confining its surveillance to those who had already been hospitalized by Covid-19.[107] At the beginning of May, with the first wave of infection receding, it began to plan NHS Test and Trace (NHSTT) at a budgeted full-year cost of £22 billion.[108] Twenty-one thousand contact tracers were hastily recruited on a basic salary of £10 an hour, some from call centres operated by the currently moribund travel industry.[109] They were given a mandatory training during a single eight-hour shift, mostly relating to child and adult safeguarding and data protection, and handed a script prepared by 'experts from Public Health England' from which they were advised not to deviate.[110]

The launch of the contact tracing programme on 28 May was a shambles, with political haste and managerial incompetence compounded by a failure in the Synergy script software and the continuing postponement of a customized NHS tracing app, which was finally abandoned a few weeks later. Stories filled the press of the new recruits sitting on the end of silent phone lines. *The Times* reported that 'thousands of tracers were left with long, empty shifts with no calls to make. One reported going 20 shifts without speaking to a single coronavirus patient, spending the time upholstering furniture and watching Netflix.'[111] 'I have a friend,' wrote a diarist,

> who volunteered to be a 'tracker' when the Government first launched the scheme. She didn't receive a single notification of someone she should contact to ask them to self isolate. She had no communications from the person she was told was her 'Track & Trace Team Leader'. She left the programme after a short time because she was utterly bored with having nothing to do.[112]

It was otherwise in the devolved nations, which combined improved national reporting systems with reliance on long-established structures of monitoring and managing outbreaks of infectious diseases. Scotland followed much the same chronology as England, abandoning contact tracing for every case on 12 March and introducing a new system on 28 May.[113] This enhanced the central digital systems of collating information, but relied on the fourteen regional health boards to undertake the task of locating, monitoring, and assisting those who needed to isolate.[114] 'Scotland's approach to tracing,' explained the Edinburgh administration, 'uses established, tried and tested contact tracing techniques, delivered by health protection professionals in local teams, with support arrangements at national level.'[115] 'Our approach,' said the Welsh government, 'will bring together and build on the existing contact tracing expertise of our local health boards and particularly our local authorities to deliver this strategy on the ground.'[116] In Northern Ireland, the new system built upon the resources of 'the Health Protection Team in the Public Health Agency', which had 'specialist experience in delivering contact tracing'.[117] There were no large-scale contracts with consultants, no newly hired, centrally managed contact tracers.

The launch of NHSTT encountered more than mere teething problems. There was a fundamental flaw in the centralized, call-centre approach to tracking and quarantining. It assumed an English population comprised of forty-four million disconnected adults, each one of whom could be sufficiently known to a distant stranger asking questions from a prepared script. The requirement for national oversight and funding of the tracking process was confused with the task of understanding personal circumstances and communicating effectively with often highly stressed men and women. A midwife, faced with the requirement to self-isolate, was not impressed by her distant interlocutor: 'It also annoyed me that the track and trace personnel were reading from a script asking about mental health as it came across as fake and phony concern.'[118]

Immediately the NHSTT began work, voices were raised criticizing the scheme. As the Public Accounts Committee drily noted in March 2021, 'a range of stakeholders have queried why local authorities and NHS primary care bodies were not more directly involved in testing and tracing activities at the outset, given their existing networks, experience and expertise'.[119] The reliance of government on outside contractors and centralized callers was challenged not just in principle but with reference to systems and structures that had long been in place. 'Local authorities, public health teams are trained to do contact tracing', observed Sir Chris Ham, former chief executive of the King's Fund, 'and even more important they know their communities. And it's been very clear . . . in recent weeks and months, unless you are part of a community where you're doing the contact tracing, then your ability to reach contacts and then support to isolate is very, very limited.'[120]

The key figures were the 135 Directors of Public Health who were employed across 153 local authorities in England.[121] They had statutory responsibility for tracking infectious illnesses and ensuring that appropriate action was taken. Whilst outbreaks of food poisoning, influenza, tuberculosis, or sexually transmitted diseases might not make national let alone international headlines, they mattered to the communities involved. The secretary of state had to approve the appointment of the Directors to ensure coordination between the centre and the periphery, but their principal focus was on local needs. They advised elected members and officers on the improvement, protection, and delivery of public health.[122] The essence of their role was connectivity. They were involved in decisions about the allocation and use of resources, worked with directors of children's and adult social services, engaged with the voluntary sector, and networked with care homes and health professionals in GP surgeries and hospitals. They had both a long-term role in improving the wellbeing of a local population and a short-term duty in emergency planning and response.

The Directors of Public Health knew immediately that the centralized structure of contact tracing was not working. In early August 2020, for instance, a group of seven leaders of upper-tier Yorkshire local authorities wrote to Matt Hancock, the health secretary, and Dido Harding, Chair of the Test and Trace programme, pointing out that in one of their areas 'on average 30% of cases and 60% of contacts known to the national system are lost to follow up'.[123] At a time of widespread cold-calling for improper purposes, there was a basic problem of answering a phone call from an 0300 number rather than a recognizable local code.[124] There was a yet more fundamental issue of London-based, poorly paid, and inadequately trained tracers trying to talk to people from widely differing ethnic backgrounds. The Yorkshire council leaders wrote:

We know that some of the challenges we face include language barriers, access to some household members, behaviours of some young people who are not themselves at high risk, and, above all, gaining and retaining trust. Through our strong links to our communities and networks of community leaders and voluntary organisations and other communications channels we can deliver arrangements that are sensitive to local culture, ethnicity and faiths.[125]

The Director of Public Health in Sandwell in the Black Country characterized the tracking system as 'designed for affluent areas where you've got most people speaking English. It's just not working well in areas where there is a lot of diversity.'[126]

Above all, the local leaders knew that the central task of tracking infection was not just a binary issue of finding or failing to find people. A functioning system ensured that tests were widespread, and that those taking them were willing and able to act on the results for the full quarantine period. Nationally and internationally, trust in the community was a more powerful driver of conformity than trust in the state.[127] As the social psychologist Stephen Reicher repeatedly argued, there was no point in telling people they were infectious unless they were able to take time off work or make alternative arrangements for looking after children or elderly relatives.[128] An effective process, properly interpreted, also permitted reverse tracing, discovering the conditions that were causing peaks of Covid-19. In northern English communities, as in many other parts of Britain, economic factors were critical in determining not only the exposure to disease but also the capacity to take appropriate action to control its spread. The Yorkshire council leaders explained:

Evidence indicates that people on low incomes are disproportionately affected and research with families in West Yorkshire suggests that high proportions are struggling financially and experiencing anxiety about job security. . . . There is a significant risk that low wage employees may feel that they cannot support their families through self-isolation, especially if they are not entitled to an appropriate level of sick pay due to their contractual conditions. Failure to comply with self-isolation guidance as a result of economic insecurity will of course present an increased risk of the spread of infection, particularly among our poorest communities and BAME populations, thereby increasing the inequalities associated with the impact of COVID-19 on these groups.[129]

The seven Yorkshire councils offered the government the following service: 'communicating the level of risk; clarifying the practical implications of current regulations; encouraging safe behaviours; encouraging the take-up of testing; reporting the outcome from tests; pursuing contacts; providing advice; providing support including for enterprises and individuals whose livelihoods are affected by the need to self-isolate'.[130] Three days later, after mounting pressure from the localities and growing evidence of the failure of the 'world-beating' system to meet the essential target of contacting and quarantining 80 per cent of victims within forty-eight hours of a positive test, the government gave way.[131] For both ideological and contractual reasons, it could not dismantle its centralized system altogether. Instead, it conceded that after twenty-four hours, the NHSTT staff would pass to localities the names of those they had failed to contact, and allow the Directors of Public Health and other staff to locate and support them.[132] Although the local authorities had the structures in place, the operational burden, coming after a decade of budget cuts, required additional national support. On top of the £300 million which had been allocated to local authorities in June to fund work on Covid-19 generally,[133] a per capita sum of £8 was awarded for enhanced contact tracing. Dido Harding now claimed that her approach had always been 'local by default'.[134] Those who had to go out to work struggled with instructions to isolate on the basis of sick pay of £95.85 a week, one of the lowest levels in the OECD.[135] After further lobbying, a 'Test and Trace Support Payment' of £500 could be claimed in England by those who demonstrated that financial pressures were preventing them observing quarantine requirements. This only amounted to £35 a day during a fortnight's quarantine, and two-thirds of applicants were rejected.[136]

Knowing

In October 2020, Public Health England published an account by the Director of Public Health in Calderdale, one of the seven Yorkshire councils that had lobbied Matt Hancock and Dido Harding in August. She described how the new partnership was being made to work. Eighty-three per cent of the names passed on by NHSTT in September had been contacted and completed by local tracers, 4 cent had already finished their isolation period, and just 9 per cent could not be reached, together with one person who had died. The success was based on the deployment of staff who were familiar with their community and were willing to use all possible means to reach it. 'Our team of local contact tracers,' she explained, 'use text messages, telephone and home visits to contact the COVID case to identify people they may have infected and to offer support with self-isolation.'[137] Her staff found that leaving their offices and knocking on doors was worth the effort:

> We have also started to visit cases where the information given by the individual on the phone was not detailed enough to allow us to carry out the contact tracing we need. This is working particularly well in Calderdale. We have some people who have provided more detailed information when speaking face to face and have been much more receptive once they're aware of the support available to them.[138]

It was a two-way flow. Those who needed to be isolated were located, and the council was able to build up a more detailed picture of the sources of infection in the area and the steps needed to contain it. In turn, those who had come into contact with Covid-19 were given advice and encouragement about how to manage quarantine in the context of their family economy and other cultural demands.

At the heart of the process was the construction and mobilization of local information. In the Covid-19 crisis, a critical factor was knowledge of the suffering of others and the capacity to take action to alleviate it. The 23 March lockdown and subsequent iterations drew tighter boundaries around the spatial dimensions of neighbourhoods, placing increased emphasis on who could be met and talked to within walking distance of home. It also enhanced the role of local structures of support, whether in the form of elected councils and their officers or the institutions of civil society such as voluntary organizations or churches. At every level, from the most informal assistance rendered by relatives and neighbours to the management of Test and Trace once it had been at least partially devolved in England, the critical factor was knowing what the need was and how to meet it.

The children of ageing parents made runs to pharmacies and shops, increasing their use of social media to keep abreast of changing circumstances. Volunteers with cars undertook journeys along familiar roads transporting the sick to appointments and distributing parcels. WhatsApp groups in particular streets collected data on who was vulnerable and who might be able to assist them. Food charities extended established distribution networks and sources of supplies. Individual churches, mosques, synagogues, and temples increased their support of the charitable sector. The national register of the clinically vulnerable collated data from GP surgeries and returned it to local supermarkets as they prioritized deliveries to those trapped in their homes. Council employees, overseen by Directors of Public Health and their counterparts in the devolved nations, located the infected and sought to manage their quarantine.

The knowledge was mobilized with remarkable speed once the scale of the health crisis was recognized because in most cases it was already latent. Formal and informal systems of support had long histories, their importance growing in the decade before Covid-19 as inequality and deprivation were increased by austerity. In the quarantine process, the leaders of the devolved administrations recognized immediately that they should deploy and enhance established structures for controlling infections. Only in England, with by far the largest population and national budget, was the decision taken to by-pass existing local mechanisms for finding and supporting Covid-19 victims and their contacts. Whilst the initial policy was modified after it was seen to be failing to reach the minimum 80 per cent target, a year later the main outsourcing agency, Sitel, was still advertising short-term £10-an-hour posts for centrally employed telephone contact tracers.[139] The knowledge required to combat Covid-19 was context-based. Those requiring assistance had to be understood in terms of the material, social, and cultural circumstances of their lives in particular places. The vastly expensive NHSTT programme demonstrated how little could be known if the subject was conceived of as a discrete individual divorced from his or her neighbourhood.

Those who could help felt better about themselves, and about the places where they lived. British society as a whole saw more of its generous self during the months of crisis. At the same time, local knowledge could be mobilized in less positive responses to the tensions in neighbourhoods riven by Covid-19. Snitching was a way of redressing the absence of power and protecting those who felt threatened by others, often with good reason. The drama of giving and receiving bound social networks together, but also exposed deep-rooted need and the dislocation of many existing ways of meeting it. The following chapter will examine in more detail the strategies for survival amidst the disruption and anxiety created by the pandemic.

Getting and Spending

The Marmot Reviews

Every previous epidemic, going back to the sixth-century Plague of Justinian and the fourteenth-century Black Death, exposed and amplified existing inequalities. As the wealthy fled an outbreak, abandoning the poor to die or starve, the scale and consequence of material injustice became impossible to ignore. The effects were amplified by the prevailing theological explanations of the plague, which foregrounded the iniquity of riches and self-indulgence. In some regards, the debates about the role of poverty during Covid-19, and related issues of regional, racial, and gender discrimination, were a pale echo of earlier epidemics. There were departures to second homes in the country, but the rich (as distinct from the super-rich) on the whole did not leave town or travel abroad. The Archbishop of Canterbury refrained from blaming the whole event on excessive wealth and conspicuous consumption. Whilst, as will be seen, the poor did become poorer and the comfortably-off still more comfortable, the furlough scheme and the uplifting of Universal Credit prevented widespread destitution for as long as the initiatives lasted. The dominant role played by the NHS in the treatment of victims and the distribution of vaccines placed boundaries on how far privilege shaped direct encounters with the virus.

Nonetheless, the patterns of getting and spending and of access to essential services during Covid-19 attracted attention from the outset. In the midst of the first major economic crisis of the twenty-first century, the epidemiologist Michael Marmot had been commissioned by the secretary of state for health to conduct an independent review 'to propose the most effective evidence-based strategies for reducing health inequalities in England'. His report was published in February 2010, three months before the long period of Labour rule came to an end. It found that there was a significant 'social gradient in health' which was a consequence of a wide range of social inequalities.[1] Numerous reforms were proposed covering early years and education, the tax and benefit system, the labour market, the NHS, and the role of local government and communities in the enhancement of public health.

A decade later, in *Health Equity in England*, Marmot returned to his report to find out what had happened to its recommendations. His conclusions were deeply pessimistic:

> Austerity has taken its toll in all the domains set out in the Marmot Review. From rising child poverty and the closure of children's centres, to declines in education funding, an increase in precarious work and zero hours contracts, to a housing affordability crisis and a rise in homelessness, to people with insufficient money to lead a healthy life and resorting to foodbanks in large numbers, to ignored communities with poor conditions and little reason for hope. And these outcomes, on the whole, are even worse for minority ethnic population groups and people with disabilities.[2]

After 2012, the core metric of life expectancy had for the first time in a century ceased to improve. The years of ill-health towards the end of life had increased, as had broader health inequalities.[3] A combination of low wage growth, in-work poverty, declining social mobility, and, above all, cuts in public expenditure from 42 per cent to 35 per cent of GDP had entrenched or worsened the scale of deprivation a decade earlier. A parallel report by the Joseph Rowntree Foundation found that 'even before the COVID-19 outbreak destitution was rapidly growing in scale and intensity'.[4] The Institute for Fiscal Studies (IFS) found that relative child poverty was at its highest level since 2007 on the eve of the pandemic, largely as a consequence of benefit cuts after 2010.[5] Overall, concluded the Resolution Foundation, household income in Britain fell by 2 per cent between 2007 and 2018, the third worst performance in Europe after Greece and Cyprus.[6]

Health Equity in England was presented as an indictment of the Conservative programme of austerity. It was published on 25 February 2020, just a fortnight beyond the tenth anniversary of the 2010 review. In the event, the timing had a quite different resonance. That week, the WHO was still debating whether to declare Covid-19 a global pandemic, SAGE was becoming increasingly concerned about the levels of infection in China and Italy, and Downing Street was making one last effort to pretend that nothing was happening.[7] A month later, the government declared the worst infectious disease crisis for a century, shut down much of the economy, and confined most of the population to their homes. The review of the last decade unintentionally became the baseline for assessing the impact of the disruption that was now set in train.

At the end of the year, Marmot took up the challenge. *Build Back Fairer: The Covid-19 Marmot Review. The Pandemic, Socioeconomic and Health Inequalities in England* assessed the pattern of illness and death since February. The core finding was the absence of significant change. The first year of Covid-19 was like the decade of austerity, only more so. 'COVID-19,' the review concluded, 'has exposed and amplified the inequalities we observed in our 10 Years On report and the economic harm caused by containment measures – lockdowns, tier systems, social isolation measures – will further damage health and widen health inequalities.'[8] By now, some seventy thousand people in England and Wales had died specifically of the disease.[9] The victims looked very much like those of other diseases: 'Inequalities in COVID-19 mortality rates follow a similar social gradient to that seen for all causes of death and the causes of inequalities in COVID-19 are similar to the causes of inequalities in health more generally.'[10] The most that happened was that the differentials amidst the top five deciles of prosperity were a little smaller under Covid-19 than was the case more generally, whereas the variations amidst the bottom five were slightly more pronounced. In spite of a novel infection and unprecedented government intervention, the outcome seemed all too familiar. England, and by extension the UK, had entered the crisis displaying entrenched trajectories of inequality which determined much of what then happened. 'The unequal conditions into which COVID-19 arrived,' concluded the report, 'contributed to the high and unequal death toll from COVID-19 in England.'[11]

Marmot returned to the subject once more in the summer of 2021, examining the impact of Covid-19 in Greater Manchester. The North West as a whole had experienced the largest decline in life expectancy in England during the pandemic, falling by 1.6 years for men compared to 1.3 nationally, and 1.2 years for women compared to 0.9. Rates of Covid-19 mortality in the city region were 25 per cent higher than England as a whole, and Greater Manchester displayed the highest socioeconomic inequalities in the country. The report found that 'the COVID-19 mortality ratio in the most deprived decile was 2.3 times greater than in the least deprived decile between March 2020 and January 2021.'[12] As in the earlier national study, the causes were embedded in the growing inequalities in children's early years, engagement and attainment in the education system, increasing poverty, rising unemployment, and deteriorating mental health for all age groups.

The conclusions of the linked reviews forced attention on the recent past as well as the specific conditions of the crisis months of the pandemic. The structural forces that had accentuated inequality since 2010 were deeply embedded in both public policy and the broader economy. In one sense, the findings were a tribute to government interventions during lockdown, which had ensured that, for better or worse, the basic lineaments of poverty and privilege were still recognizable, in spite of the vast disruptions in ways of living and working. In another, the profound elements of continuity demonstrated yet more clearly why inequality mattered. Suffering had been intensified during the pandemic; injustice was measured by avoidable mortality.

Getting

'Furlough' was originally a military term dating back to the seventeenth century, describing the procedure by which a commanding officer permitted soldiers to take leave of absence from the army. By the later twentieth century, it had been extended to both the early release of prisoners and the temporary layoff of civilian workers. During the pandemic, it was the most effective response of the government to the profound dislocation of the economy. Following discussions with employers and trade unions, the chancellor of the exchequer announced a job retention scheme (JRS), which became popularly known as the furlough, on 20 March 2020. Termination dates were set and superseded as the pandemic continued before it was finally closed on 30 September 2021. In the initial formulation, 80 per cent of wages up to a ceiling of £2,500 per month were to be paid by the government.[13] Workers would stay at home but remain in employment, with their employers expected to make up the remaining 20 per cent.

Unlike the large expenditure on Test and Trace, the JRS was not out-sourced but administered with considerable efficiency by Her Majesty's Revenue and Customs, which opened it to claimants ten days ahead of schedule on 20 April 2020. A separate scheme embracing those working for themselves, the Self-Employment Income Support Scheme (SEISS), was launched on 13 May, and went through four subsequent versions. It encountered more administrative problems due to uncertainties about eligibility and definition of profits. At the outset, the JRS attracted nine million applicants. The numbers fell to two million as Covid-19 retreated and lockdown was eased during the summer, before rising again to 4.5 million in January 2021. There were just over a million claimants when the scheme was closed at the end of September 2021. Altogether, some 11.6 million employees were furloughed at some point during the pandemic.[14]

The JRS was expensive, costing some £70 billion over its lifetime. It was also effective. During 2020, the UK recorded its worst economic performance for more than three hundred years, when a largely agricul-tural economy was suffering from the Little Ice Age. The contraction was greater than the Great Depression, or during the 1918–20 Spanish Flu.[15] There were many economists, including the authoritative Office for Budget Responsibility, forecasting that unemployment would rise towards levels not seen since the first Thatcher administration, when almost 12 per cent were out of work.[16] In the event, it increased from 3.8 per cent in 2019 to 5.2 per cent during the second Covid-19 wave between October and December 2020, before declining to 4.6 per cent in the summer of 2021, and to just 3.5 per cent in the June–August quar-ter of 2022, the lowest rate since 1974. Job losses during the pandemic were at about the same level as in 2016 and 2017, and considerably lower than the aftermath of the bankers' crash, which saw a peak of 8.5 per cent in the autumn of 2011.[17] As had been hoped, the furlough discour-aged employers from severing contact with their workers, and when the scheme was concluded, most firms were able to take staff back on to their full-time payroll. Whilst some enterprises had gone out of business in the meantime, workers in their fifties and sixties had left the job market altogether, causing record levels of job vacancies.

Outside the medical arena, nothing did more to contain the sense of crisis during the pandemic. Whilst there were major disruptions in how and where work was conducted, there remained a fundamental sense of continuity. To retain a contract of employment, to have the certainty of at least a basic income week after week, instilled an impression of order and security amongst the workforce. Although it was envisaged as lasting only a few months, the JRS was kept going for long enough to see a significant revival of economic activity. For the better paid, such as the numerous airline pilots who were furloughed while their industry almost completely ceased to operate, the maximum sum payable represented a serious loss of income, but it was around twice the minimum wage and prevented recourse to the deeply disliked bureaucracy of Universal Credit, where benefits had been raised by £20 a week.[18] As the government struggled to retain the trust of a beleaguered population in the face of catastrophic misjudgements in the imposition of lockdown and well-publicized failures in the administration of quarantine and personal protection, the furlough scheme represented the capacity of the state to take unprecedented but well-managed risks with the public finances in the interests of the working population.

In 2020, household income was broadly similar to 2019, despite GDP falling by almost 10 per cent.[19] Nonetheless, the dynamics of the pre-Covid-19 economy remained clearly visible. The characteristics of lockdown interacted with long-standing inequalities. The occupations most affected by the closures, particularly arts and leisure, non-food and non-pharmaceutical retail, and passenger transport, contained large numbers already on or below the minimum wage and were more often staffed by the young, by women, and by workers from minority ethnic groups.[20] The IFS found that 'workers under the age of 25 are twice as likely to work in a shut-down sector as those aged 25 and over, whilst employees in the bottom 10% of the weekly earnings distribution are seven times more likely than those in the top 10% to do so'.[21] In the first lockdown, women shortened their hours of work twice as frequently as men in order to take care of children sent home from school.[22]

Those with the least power in the labour market were more at risk of being furloughed, or working shorter days, or losing their job altogether. The self-employed suffered from continuing difficulties with their version of the furlough scheme.[23] Workers in the rapidly expanding gig economy had no contracts that could be subsidized and suffered the largest fall in hours worked. Ethnic minorities, in particular Bangladeshi and Pakistani communities, were concentrated in occupations such as taxi-driving and food and beverage sales. The Covid-19 crisis in some cases confirmed occupational vulnerabilities and in others exacerbated them. The young in particular, accustomed to moving at will between relatively unskilled and poorly paid occupations, found their choices suddenly curtailed.[24] They were two and a half times more likely than other employees to have been making a living in a shut-down sector.[25] Between the spring and autumn of 2020, youth unemployment rose faster than at any time in the previous decade.[26]

A further engine of inequality was the location of employment for those who avoided furlough or losing their jobs altogether. The initial injunction was to work from home except in designated key occupations. Whilst there were some high-status jobs which required physical attendance, most obviously doctors in the overcrowded hospitals, for the most part there was a sharp class divide between those sitting before computers in hastily converted spare bedrooms and those forced either to pursue their occupations out of doors or to travel to their labour. Defoe was struck by the sheer bravery of those who ventured out into the plague-ridden streets of seventeenth-century London in order to feed their families:

> It must be confest, that tho' the Plague was chiefly among the Poor; yet were the Poor the most Venturous and Fearless of it, and went about their Employment, with a Sort of brutal Courage; I must call it so, for it was founded neither on Religion or Prudence; scarse did they use any Caution, but run into any Business, which they could get Employment in, tho' it was the most hazardous; such was that of tending the Sick, watching Houses shut up, carrying infected Persons to the Pest-House; and which was still worse, carrying the Dead away to their Graves.[27]

In the towns and cities of the early twenty-first century, there were more sophisticated funeral procedures, but 'brutal courage' properly describes the staff who in the early months of the pandemic continued to attend to the needs of care home residents, knowing that Covid-19 was running out of control in their place of work and that their PPE was inadequate or non-existent. They were fully aware that they were risking their lives, and that they were in danger of bringing home not only a paltry minimum wage but also a virus that could infect their own families. At the end of 2020, it was reported that healthcare workers had been seven times more likely to get severe Covid than other workers.[28]

The risks taken by those who continued to leave home to earn their living called into question the conventional understanding of 'key workers'.[29] Those endangering their lives for others in hospital wards obviously belonged to this category and were awarded priority in the provision of PPE as it belatedly became available. They were readily embraced by the Thursday-evening clapping. But voices began to be raised about the significance and sacrifice of hitherto disregarded and mostly unlisted occupations which were vital to the continuation of some semblance of normal life. 'I'm not complaining,' wrote a Joseph Rowntree diarist, 'but it does make me think about who the government is really recognising as key workers. Supermarket staff are getting no recognition at all. They are not allowed to go to the front of queues because the emphasis is on the NHS and that's right but there just isn't much understanding for the less talked about jobs.'[30] Bus, taxi and delivery drivers, construction workers, personal carers, cleaners and security staff, grocery shelf-stackers and till-operators, food processors, all of whom had traditionally enjoyed low status and corresponding levels of pay, could now be seen to be performing crucial roles amidst the constant threat of dislocation and breakdown. As John Naughton wrote, '[W]e are discovering that the people who are suddenly described as "critical workers" – the people who actually keep this society functioning – are almost without exception poorly paid and insecurely employed.'[31]

The fundamental expression of inequality in the Covid-19 society was the association of deprivation with death. Across developed countries, there was a correlation between the degree of inequality and the levels of excess mortality during the pandemic. In Britain, inhabitants of the poorest 10 per cent of areas were 2.6 times more likely to die from Covid-19 than the richest 10 per cent. The largest differential was amongst those of working age, where men and women in the least prosperous areas experienced a death rate of almost four times that of the wealthiest.[32] This suggests that the causal factors embraced not just the absence of money, but also the way in which it was consumed and earned. The residences of poor families were more crowded and were less likely to have properly heated spaces into which home-schooling children and homeworking parents could escape, or large attached gardens.[33] The 'brutal courage' that drove workers out to earn a living had a direct impact on their health. 'When looking at broad groups of occupations,' reported the ONS, 'men who worked in elementary occupations [routine manual tasks requiring no educational qualifications] or caring, leisure and other service occupations had the highest rates of death involving Covid-19.'[34] There were some striking anomalies – guarding the property of others was about as lethal as working in care homes – but for the most part it was not difficult for either statisticians or those making the choice whether to go out to work in the morning to comprehend the threat to their wellbeing and those of their partners and dependants to whom they returned at the end of their shifts.

From the beginning of the first wave of Covid-19, attention was drawn to the mortality of BAME men and women. Whereas, prior to the pandemic, the death rate in the white community was generally higher, now the situation was reversed. Covid-19 deaths for Black African men were 3.7 times greater than for the white population, and 2.6 times for women. For people of Bangladeshi ethnic backgrounds, the figures were 3.0 and 1.9, for those from Black Caribbean backgrounds, 2.7 and 1.8, for those from Pakistani backgrounds, 2.2 and 2.0.[35] During the second wave, those from Bangladeshi backgrounds rose to the top of the table, returning mortality rates 5.0 and 4.1 times higher than their white counterparts. In the Omicron wave, the differentials were lower but displayed the same hierarchy.[36]

Research into the causes of these differentials is still continuing. Prior medical conditions played a part, with a greater susceptibility in some groups to diabetes, cardiovascular disease, hypertension, and obesity. At the end of 2021, the Medical Research Council identified the LZTFL1 gene, carried by 60 per cent of people of South Asian origin, which could make them more susceptible to dying of Covid-19.[37] The principal drivers, however, were those causing inequalities across the population as a whole, compounded by racial discrimination. 'Our statistical modelling,' said the ONS, 'shows that a large proportion of the difference in the risk of Covid-19 mortality between ethnic groups can be explained by demographic, geographical and socio-economic factors, such as where you live or the occupation you're in.'[38] The working and home lives of BAME households were more stressed and less safe than those of the broader population. BAME families were between two and three times as likely as white families to be in what the Social Metrics Commission described as 'persistent poverty'.[39] For a range of material and cultural reasons, they were more likely to have endured lockdown in overcrowded accommodation. Outdoors, nearly 40 per cent of BAME children had no garden compared to around 25 per cent of all children from low-income homes.[40] BAME income earners were more commonly key workers and employed in riskier jobs in the health service. The British Medical Association reported that in the middle of 2021, a fifth of all NHS staff were from BAME communities but they constituted three-fifths of deaths amongst healthcare workers, partly because a disproportionate number had been filling patient-facing roles with inadequate PPE.[41]

The connection between how people earned their living and how they died is illustrated by the everyday task of driving buses, where the age-standardized death rate in the early months of the pandemic was three and a half times the national average.[42] The fate of those carrying people to and from work attracted much attention. They were doubly victims of the occupational requirement to leave home: vital to the transport needs of generally impecunious commuters and themselves spending their working days amidst the public. A newspaper story featured Nadir Nur, who drove a bus in Hackney, east London, and died on 2 April 2020, leaving a wife and five children, including a ten-month-old daughter. The report concluded: 'His wife, Bishra, described her husband as a "hero on the frontline helping healthcare workers to hospitals". She said he was a "loving, kind, caring helpful person whom everybody loved" and said bus drivers needed further protection to prevent any more deaths among transport staff during the pandemic.'[43]

Under pressure from the unions, the supervisory body Transport for London commissioned Michael Marmot's Institute for Health Equity to conduct an independent study. The conclusions were a familiar combination of the structural and the contingent.[44] Bus drivers tended to be older than the working population as a whole, to have a larger intake from the BAME community, particularly Black members, and to live in areas of relatively high deprivation. They had also long been known to suffer from health problems associated with their sedentary but stressful life on the traffic-filled roads of London, including hypertension, coronary disease, and diabetes. When Covid-19 broke out, they were victims of the slow and uncertain provision of PPE throughout the economy. The Mayor of London, Sadiq Khan, explained on 8 April:

> On a number of occasions we've sought advice from not just Public Health England, not just the Department for Transport, not just the Department for Health, but also the World Health Organization. What they've told us is that personal protective equipment should only be used in care settings. There is a shortage of PPE anyway for the NHS and social care staff. As recently as yesterday we chased the government on this. Their advice is quite clear – that transport workers should not be wearing PPE.[45]

The early emphasis on fomite transmission meant that the bus companies invested effort in cleaning the buses but were slower to block the screens through which passengers talked to the drivers and to alter the procedures for getting on and off. The daughter of another victim, a sixty-seven-year-old immigrant from Zimbabwe, protested that all he had been given to protect himself from infection was a pair of gloves, which he had never used.[46] As with many other occupations, the independent review concluded that the lives of at least some bus drivers would have been saved had lockdown been imposed earlier. When the infection rules were relaxed after the second wave, the drivers, in common with many others in face-to-face contact with customers, were exposed to further stress and occasional violence as they strove to maintain recommended practices about wearing face masks and maintaining social distance.

Set against the life-threatening pressures of going out to work in the pandemic, the circumstances of those forced to work at home seemed essentially benign. Not only were they more protected from Covid-19, their absence from crowded trains and offices meant that they were less likely to fall victim to the menu of seasonal illnesses. As the educational sector shut down, children no longer brought home the viruses that flourished in nurseries and classrooms. There had always been a substantial cohort prevented by long-standing health conditions from travelling to a job. Prior to 2020, the disability employment rate was 53.7 per cent compared to 82 per cent for the able-bodied workforce.[47] Now employers were more willing to make arrangements for those who had always found it difficult to leave home. Whilst the enforced exclusion from the office was a novel experience, setting up a desk in a room in the house was not a wholly unfamiliar task; with increasing use of digital communication, the number of homeworkers had been rising before the pandemic.

It is no surprise that when the first lockdown ended, most managers and professionals ignored the government's injunctions and chose to stay at home. Those who did so encountered growing debates about the strains of virtual conferencing, and the dangers of allowing employers to gain a digital foothold inside the homes and leisure time of their staff. They also found themselves working more unpaid hours than those who had gone out to work. There was a tendency for employees to treat at least part of the time previously spent commuting as falling within the daily regime of labour. On average, those working at desks in bedrooms or on kitchen tables contributed an unsupervised six hours a week of unpaid overtime, compared with 3.6 hours for those toiling under direct supervision.[48] The more serious problems were faced by those trying to compress work and often schooling into ill-equipped and overcrowded domestic spaces. The structures of inequality that determined who had to go out to earn a living also shaped the experience of staying at home.

Never was Virginia Woolf's injunction to possess a room of your own more critical. The ultimate luxury was one or more dedicated studies, sound-proofed and connected to the internet. Failing that, the requirement was for accommodation that could be converted for other purposes when either or both parents sat down to earn their living. Where the domestic space was already overcrowded and ill equipped, the new regime of employment was a further cause of mental and physical stress. If there was no work to be done, confinement to a cramped domestic arena because of furlough or unemployment placed strains on the whole household. A single, unemployed father with two children, living on the Broadwater Farm Estate in London, recorded his dominant concern through lockdown: 'Even if our flat had one extra bedroom, I or my children could isolate and we could talk to one another over the phone but it's not that easy for us. Overcrowding is on my mind every minute and it keeps me awake at night.'[49]

For every household, but particularly where it was impossible to maintain physical distance, there was fear of cross-infection. Doctors reported using different bathrooms and sleeping in separate bedrooms when they came home from hospital shifts, but this was not an option for less well-paid key workers or for the poor more generally. On the Broadwater Farm Estate, it was an endless worry : 'I've woken up feeling very tired this morning because I kept checking on the children last night. I'm terrified of them becoming unwell and not being able to isolate them properly in this flat. Their bedroom only measures 3.5 by 2.5m and they have to sleep side-by-side.'[50]

Spending

As there always had been, there was a basic paradox in the management of domestic budgets in the pandemic. The poorer the family, the more expensive their way of life.[51] Over a fifth of households experienced an increase in spending during the first lockdown, mostly amongst the least prosperous sectors of society. Those with dependent children were 40 per cent more likely to do so. The Resolution Foundation found that 'over one-third of families with children in the lowest income quintile reported increased costs in spring 2020, closely followed by a significant share in the second household quintile'.[52] The initial lockdown foregrounded online communication. Homeworking was dependent on at least the intermittent use of digital devices, and even more so home schooling. More prosperous homes were already equipped for these challenges, whereas those at the bottom of the income scale found themselves faced with new financial demands. It was no longer sufficient to possess just a digital phone, or a single battered laptop that could be shared between family members for their separate purposes. Broadband connections that had once been just about adequate failed to cope with streamed videos and online conferences. Around 10 per cent of primary school students and 15 per cent of secondary school students had no access to a computer, laptop, or tablet during the first lockdown and 5 per cent of children lacked any kind of internet access.[53]

'Old tech not up to the job,' reported a *Covid Realities* diarist, 'or not enough tech to go round the family.'[54] Another described the constant struggle for access in the home: 'Also, both our children have a phone but we don't have a computer which is tricky for some projects. Our WiFi isn't brilliant either.'[55] The consequence was either a degradation of essential services or a deviation from established tactics for managing a tight budget. Another *Covid Realities* diarist, low-paid parent 'Alex R.', explained the choices that the change in his children's schooling imposed on the family:

> More tough decisions to make! At the start of the pandemic I signed up to broadband so my daughter could complete her school work and interact with her friends, with a Talk-Talk package advertised as having no price increase during the 18 month contract. I have now received an email saying there will be a £2.50 increase per month from July and in April it will increase again by the rate of CPI + 3.7%. The money I receive has not increased in several years so I am facing a real struggle to find the extra money, this will mean even less food in the cupboard and a really tough time during the winter as I have now got to a point I will not be able to afford the cost of heating our home even for a short period of time each day.[56]

The simple fact of all the rooms in a home now having to be heated and lit throughout the day imposed additional costs. Whatever might be said against office work, at least the services were free. So were the school classrooms in the state system. 'More spent on gas and electricity as at home more,' observed 'Alex R.'.[57] 'It's been a long week again money is tight even though we are going nowhere the cost of fuel, food and bills with the kids home is a lot,' wrote 'Lexie G.'.[58] Families had intricate strategies for managing tight budgets that were now under increased strain. Another diarist explained how dependent her household economy had been on the unquantified assistance of her children's grandmother, whom they were now forbidden to visit:

> We spend so much more on electricity, food, gas as we are at home most of the time. We used to have lunch or dinner at my mums after i got the children from school. Mum always picked up little thing for us when she does her shopping like washing powder or sweets or toys. Now we no longer can visit.[59]

As chapter 4 discussed, integral to the financial survival of hard-pressed families was the web of informal assistance provided by relations and neighbours who were now placed out of bounds. It was a tightly managed voyage, threatened with capsize by unanticipated squalls, which during a global health crisis were all too likely to occur. 'My grandad died,' wrote 'Gracie H.' 'It's been awful. He was like my dad. I cry all the time. We are spreading the cost of the funeral Between us. Flowers alone are £40 each between me and my 6 cousins. They have no idea that I had to take out a loan. I had no choice.'[60]

Life on the margins was constantly endangered by minor increases in expenditure that were barely noticeable in more prosperous households. The micro shopping strategies which had been essential for managing inadequate incomes were placed under new pressure. It was a life of endless calculation and decision-making. A *Covid Realities* diarist reviewed her choices:

> My food shop has gone up, previously I was likely to spend probably on average of £100/wk. this week's bill was £150 although that did include some £8 shorts for my son. All of a sudden, he has shot up. I'm not sure if that is down to the continual munching he does. There seems to be a lot less offers in the shops now. Morrisons tended to do the 2 for £3 on fruit and these don't seem to be so easy to come by. Tesco's don't seem to have the same sort of offers as before, such as the offers of the week on veg and fruit. I do tend not to go to the same shops so much as I used to due to the offer situation and have recently shopped more in Asda of late.[61]

There was relief when after the first few weeks of lockdown, the major supermarkets re-filled their shelves and adapted home delivery systems to meet the needs of the large shielding population and others who felt unable to go out of doors to stock their larders. But the two discount chains, Lidl and Aldi, declined to provide this service, although the latter began delivering a limited number of items to those living within a six-mile radius of participating stores through a partnership with Deliveroo towards the end of 2020.

At the other end of the market, Waitrose and Ocado/Marks & Spencer expanded their business to meet rapidly increasing demand from their customers.[62] Remote shopping was a crucial service during lockdown, but it imposed costs. As a disabled woman explained,

> [T]he Covid reality is that shopping online at one of the bigger supermarkets is not economical at all. You have to spend over £40, which is the minimum basket charge – even at Iceland it's £35 but at least you get free delivery, and then they charge you a fee for pick, pack and deliver of at least £3, depending

on the time of day you chose. Even if you are able to click and collect it still costs £1.50 for pick, pack and deliver.[63]

The financially secure had little trouble finding provisions. A seventy-six-year-old wife of a clinically vulnerable husband made an arrangement with a local supplier: 'Must concentrate on my shopping lists for L.,' she noted, 'and our home delivery from the local Farm Shop. Still not used to not being able to browse in the supermarket and see what's new on the shelves.'[64] Farm shops, which during the previous decade had become a commonplace resource in the hinterland of prosperous communities, combined good quality with high prices. For those shopping closer to home, the alternative to the cheaper supermarkets was the corner shop or the outlet attached to a local garage. Convenience came at a cost. 'We get the basics at the petrol station,' explained a *Covid Realities* diarist, 'but certain things we can only get at Tesco or Iceland. At the petrol station the prices are a lot higher.'[65] Household budgets long balanced by minute calculations about the price of necessities were suddenly overstretched by the daily shopping.

In the early days of lockdown, the government responded to the needs of the clinically extremely vulnerable who were unable to arrange home deliveries. They were invited to complete an electronic form which generated the arrival on their doorstep of a free weekly food box. This contained a menu of provisions little changed since the Second World War: potatoes, apples, UHT milk, tins of chopped pork or corned beef, Heinz tomato soup and baked beans, tea and Maxwell House instant coffee, sliced white bread.[66] The only concession to seventy-five years of dietary evolution was the inclusion of two jars of Bolognese sauce and a packet of pasta. Individuals with 'any allergies or religious/cultural dietary requirements' were advised to contact their local authorities for further assistance.[67] The government also established the £3.45 million Food Charities Grant Fund, which made available awards of up to £100,000 to frontline food aid charities that were 'unable to meet an increased demand for food from vulnerable individuals or supporting charities'.[68] The Fund was closed on 13 July 2020 'due to a high volume of applications'.

The acceleration in the demand for food bank parcels during the pandemic was discussed in the previous chapter. The Food Standards Agency (FSA) calculated that up to May 2021, between 8 and 10 per cent of the population was wholly or partly dependent on this service.[69] Applications for support were generated by intersecting circumstances: 27 per cent of families in June 2020 reported 'a delay or problem with benefits payments'; 29 per cent in August, and 33 per cent in November and December reported that 'someone in the household was self-isolating or shielding from Covid-19'; and in September, the most common reason cited was 'we had difficulties travelling to get food our-selves'. In October 2020, the precipitating factor was simply that 'we did not have enough money to buy food'.[70] When they were unable to get a good delivery, the poor cut back on eating. The FSA survey found that 'at its highest in November and December, 19 per cent of participants reported skipping meals or cutting the size of meals because they did not have enough money to buy food'.[71] Those who were tightening their belts tended to be young, from larger households, or with at least one child. The better off, on the other hand, enjoyed improved diets during lockdown, as more meals were taken at home, prepared from healthy ingredients. More pleasure was taken in the basic tasks of cooking, such as making bread.

For hard-pressed households, asking for food parcels was an unwelcome but necessary means of survival. Even if only supplementary items were available, they were warmly welcomed. 'There is a food bank at my children's school,' recorded a stressed mother, 'and this afternoon I took some bread, oatcakes and fresh fruit. This is a huge help to us and we are very grateful.'[72] 'When the pandemic started things became unmanageable,' recorded a single parent.

> It was my daughter that spoke to a worker at a young carers group that she attends and they put us in touch with a food bank. To start with I found it very hard to accept the fact that I needed this help, but it was a life line that I feel I could not have managed without. For the first time since my partner left we were able to eat fresh healthy food which has made a huge difference to both of us.[73]

Food insecurity, which became a more common experience during the pandemic, was not just a matter of latent or actual hunger. Above all, it was a condition of perpetual uncertainty and anxiety, with intermittent moments of relief. A mother explained her tactics:

I don't want to go downstairs today, have to try and make something edible from ingredients kiddies dislike. Yesterday we ate like Kings, the local youth group dropped off tuna, sweetcorn, and cheese and wraps, it wasn't a lot but we made warm tuna wraps from [them]. I also defrosted our last meat (which I try to ration) and made cheese burgers to enjoy with the last of the bread.

There were good days and bad days, but no escape from the constant drama of eating that affected everyone in the household. Her account concluded:

I just wish I could give them more meat. Dinner tonight will likely be pasta, they hate pasta. They won't complain and I know they'll try eating it bless em. I also know they'll hate it. I can't believe that all we can think about lately is food. It's surprising how much food can affect the emotions within the house. From tense to excited to relieved.[74]

Savings and Debt

There was a long tradition in global pandemics of the rich escaping the misfortunes of the poor. Defoe began his *Journal of the Plague Year* with an account of the exodus from London: '[T]he richer sort of People, especially the Nobility and Gentry, from the West-part of the City throng'd out of Town, with their Families and Servants in an unusual Manner.'[75] When the twenty-first-century plague broke out, there were fears that history would repeat itself, with reports of large-scale departures by the richer sort of people for the three-quarters of a million second homes in England and the twenty-five thousand second homes in each of Scotland and Wales.[76] As a measure of increasing inequality during the era of austerity, the number of English householders who felt sufficiently prosperous to acquire and maintain an additional property solely for their own use had risen by a third in the decade following 2008–9. In addition to those travelling to fixed addresses, the lesser sort were accused of filling caravan sites and parking camper vans along remote country roadsides.

The desire to escape the cities for the sake of mental and physical health was deep in the national psyche and was causing debate before the first lockdown was announced. The *East Anglia Daily Times* reported on 19 March that 'residents in Suffolk's seaside towns of Southwold and Aldeburgh say they have become increasingly busy in the last few days, with those from London who own second homes in the area taking advantage of the opportunity to escape the capital and the potential of a lockdown'.[77] A Welsh diarist witnessed 'second home owners leaving London and coming down here where they are not registered with the GPs and the local hospitals are not geared up to cope with larger numbers'.[78] Similar pressures were identified in the West Country, and the national parks, particularly the Lake District. Although the flight to second homes was observed in many European countries and the USA, in the event it failed to become a major phenomenon in the UK.[79] This was partly because there was not as stark a contrast between urban danger and rural safety as there was assumed to be in mid-seventeenth-century England. Over time, the Covid-19 infection rates varied across towns and cities and less densely populated areas, but at no point was there an overriding need for the wealthy to save the lives of themselves and their families by fleeing to the countryside. Moreover, they could not escape their age or their medical condition, which were the prime indicators of risk in the peak months of mortality.

Further, the UK was a different kind of polity than Defoe's world. There were national governments seeking to exercise control over all their citizens. The rural authorities demanded that action be taken to prevent their services, particularly underfunded GP surgeries and hospitals, being overwhelmed by incomers who might themselves be carrying the virus. The Department of Health and Social Care was alert to the danger that the already malfunctioning quarantine system would collapse altogether if people were allowed to move freely about the country if they could afford to do so. The announcement of the three lockdowns in March and November 2020 and January 2021 were accompanied by regulations forbidding travel for any but essential purposes. The only concession, made at the end of March 2021, was the 'Stanley Johnson loophole', for owners of second homes needing to visit them for urgent repair or renovation for rent or sale. North of the border, the government, fearful of a flight to remote islands to escape Covid-19, moved quickly to protect their populations. Transport Scotland announced that 'from Sunday 22 March 2020, until further notice, ferries will be for those who live on our islands, who have an essential need to travel to or from the mainland and for essential supplies or business. Nothing else.'[80] On Easter Sunday, 146 people used the Hebridean ferries, compared to one hundred and twenty thousand the previous year.[81] At the beginning of November 2020, the Welsh government closed the border from Chepstow to Chester to prevent English residents escaping newly imposed restrictions. The first minister, Mark Drakeford, was asked whether this was the hardest border that had ever existed between the two countries. 'That may well be the case,' he replied, 'for several centuries at least.'[82]

In the longer term, Covid-19 intensified what was already a growing demand by city dwellers to find property in villages and smaller towns to escape, if not the virus, then more general health-threatening environmental conditions. The discovery that homeworking was a feasible means of reconciling the demands of work and families accelerated the search for quieter surroundings. During the course of the pandemic, there was no certainty about how far office regimes would be re-imposed, but there was a general expectation that the future would remove at least some of the frequency, pain, and cost of long-distance commuting. The largest online property website reported that in the first six months of 2020, there had been a 126 per cent increase in enquiries from people living in cities considering properties in village locations, and a 68 per cent increase for small towns. During 2021, 91,750 Londoners bought homes outside the capital, an increase of 59 per cent over the previous year.[83] The identified motives for such upheavals were a desire for a bigger garden and access to parks or countryside, larger affordable accommodation, and, in the coming era of electric cars, a drive or garage where a charging point could be fitted.[84] These dreams were not created by Covid-19; they merely appeared more pressing.

For the seriously rich, there remained ways of evading the mundane restrictions of lockdown. There was a marked increase at the top end of the property market, with purchasers looking to a create a protected universe of comfort, complete with butlers, cooks, housekeepers, and gardeners. A leading estate agent reported selling twenty-one estates valued at over £15 million in 2020, compared to one in 2019.[85] Alternatively, there were means of escaping the plague-ridden island altogether. The government gave sufficient notice of the first lockdown to cause a sharp rise in bookings for private jets earlier in March 2020.[86] The jet broker Air Partner reported being overwhelmed with enquiries. During the remainder of the year, the industry was hit by the global cancellation of business conferences and the closure of many holiday resorts. But whereas the commercial sector almost ceased to operate, the private jets business only declined by 43 per cent and it began to recover rapidly in early 2021.[87] The attraction, heavily marketed by the companies, was travel in a controlled environment, avoiding the risk of infection in crowded airports and multi-seated cabins full of low-paying strangers.[88] Those who had once been content with the luxury of first-class seats now began to contemplate for the first time hiring an entire jet. Journeys for leisure by any means were illegal under lockdowns, but it was always possible to claim a necessary business need.

The benefits of private international travel were further increased by the introduction of Covid-19 vaccines at the end of 2020. The decision in the UK to restrict the treatment to the NHS was a powerful engine of equality in the midst of the pandemic. The rich could not buy immunity – unless, that is, they could fly to a country with weaker controls over its pharmaceutical industry, such as the United Arab Emirates (UAE) or India. Media interest was aroused in January 2021 by the marketing programme of Knightsbridge Circle, a private concierge service that charged a basic £25,000 a year for 'a carefully curated membership' which 'ensures that clients receive unparalleled access to the very best of everything that life has to offer'.[89] This now included jumping the vaccination queue. The founder of Knightsbridge Circle, Stuart McNeill, explained to the *Daily Telegraph* the recent addition to his service: 'It's like we're the pioneers of this new luxury travel vaccine programme. You go for a few weeks to a villa in the sunshine, get your jabs and your certificate and you're ready to go. Lots of our clients have business meetings in the UAE.'[90] Preserving health was not cheap. It was reported that a month-long 'vaccination holiday' in Dubai, including first-class flights, accommodation, and two doses of the vaccine, started at £40,000.[91]

The Knightsbridge Circle still knew the difference between right and wrong, claiming that it had not arranged for the vaccination of anybody under the age of sixty-five. 'We still have a moral responsibility to make sure that people that really need it get it,' said its founder, 'and that's what we are focusing on.'[92] Commentary on the service was less positive, and further press enquiries were not answered, leaving it difficult to estimate just how many had made use of this manifestation of the well-established industry of health tourism. Amidst the manifold inequalities of exposure to Covid-19, there remained a basic hostility to preferential treatment. Whilst there were significant variations in the quality of community medicine, once infection happened, the ambulance would fail to call on a stricken household irrespective of its wealth, and the medical staff would lack PPE no matter whom they were treating. It was accepted that the queue for vaccines should be controlled by information from medical records, not by bargaining or bribery. However, whilst the basic treatment for the coronavirus remained free at the point of demand, a thriving industry of wellness clinics grew up to deal with the increasing numbers of long Covid sufferers. A stay in a private facility in the Austrian alps might assist recovery, but it remained out of reach for the healthcare workers, teachers, and care home staff who were the most numerous sufferers from the condition.[93]

The use of private jets to evade lockdown restrictions was further condemned on environmental grounds. The carbon footprint per passenger of this form of travel was estimated to be up to fourteen times higher than taking a commercial flight and at least fifty times worse than taking a train. The average private jet owner was calculated to have assets of £1.3 billion.[94] Unlike earlier recessions, serious wealth increased during the Covid-19 crisis. Oxfam calculated that 'since 2020, the richest 1% have captured almost two-thirds of all new wealth – nearly twice as much money as the bottom 99% of the world's population'.[95] The 2021 *Sunday Times* 'Rich List' recorded the largest annual increase in the number of UK billionaires since the register began a third of a century ago.[96] Forbes calculated that the first nine months of the crisis created a £400 billion windfall for the world's richest ten men.[97] In 2021, the number of the 'ultra-rich' in the UK (with assets of more than £24 million) increased by 11.3 per cent, just above the global average.[98] Credit Suisse estimated that 5.2 million people entered the ranks of the dollar millionaires around the world during the peak of the pandemic and the number worth at least $50 million grew by a quarter. 'The contrast between what has happened to household wealth and what is happening in the wider economy can never have been more stark,' concluded the bank.[99]

There was a surge in the purchase of Rolls-Royces, which the chief executive attributed to an enhanced sense of mortality amongst the rich: 'Many people witnessed people in their community dying from Covid-19 and that made them think life can be short and you'd better live now rather than postpone until a later date.'[100] Demand for super-yachts increased by a quarter in the first year of the pandemic, again allegedly driven by a sudden awareness of the transience of existence. 'This year will smash all records for super-yacht sales,' claimed the editor-in-chief of *Boat International* at the end of 2021. 'After lockdown, people are thinking, "I might as well buy one so I always have access." They're thinking, "Life is short. Let's buy a boat."'[101] There was the added advantage that the seriously rich came to believe they could run their businesses without ever again having to set foot on dry land. 'A lot of people say they appreciate the safety of being on a yacht during the pandemic,' explained a leading broker. 'But it's also because whereas in previous eras the people with enough money were too busy in the office to justify the purchase, these days they can work from anywhere.'[102]

The gains partly derived from the particular dynamics of the Covid-19 economy. Technology stocks initially prospered, led by shares in Zoom, which in the first nine months of 2020 increased their value by 750 per cent, before falling to a mere fourfold increase as its competitors began to push back. The price of Apple, Netflix, and Amazon shares doubled as demand grew for their services. Conversely, the prospect of the pandemic coming to an end in the spring of 2022 sowed uncertainty across the sector, as growth forecasts began to be revised. In April, Netflix announced that it had lost subscribers for the first time in ten years. By July, its shares had fallen by 67 per cent.[103] In Britain, there were bankruptcies across the fixed-site retail sector, but the specialist online grocery firm Ocado saw its value grow by a half. More generally, the long-term growth in wealth was the product of the availability of cheap credit. During the decade since the 2008–9 crisis, those seeking to make money had never found it easier to borrow it. In the face of the disruption caused by the need to protect public health as Covid-19 spread, central banks maintained their strategy, injecting $9 trillion into economies to protect them from the effects of lockdown and the disruption of global trade.[104] After short-term falls, stock market and property values rose once more.

The consequence was a growth in inequality in Britain, as elsewhere. The average family had gained £7,800 in wealth per adult by the middle of 2021, but the richest 10 per cent had prospered by £50,000 and the poorest 30 per cent by just £86.[105] This was partly due to the increase in the value of the investments and property of those who already possessed them and partly due to the contrast in patterns of expenditure. The sight of billionaires making more billions amidst and in some cases directly as a consequence of so much suffering aroused fierce moral condemnation, but the changing balance of savings and debt across the population had a more pervasive impact on the wellbeing of households. In a national crisis, there is a general instinct for domestic budgets to be tightened, if only as a cautionary measure. The looming prospect of the worst health emergency since the bubonic plague was cause enough to husband resources.

This tendency was compounded by the nature of lockdown. Those with a stable or increasing income found less to spend their money on. They began to save by default as much as a deliberate strategy. Transport costs, whether the maintenance or replacement of cars or weekly expenditure on fuel or bus and train tickets, almost ceased during the three periods when all but essential workers were confined to their homes. They only partially recovered when restrictions were lifted because employees proved resistant to official injunctions to start travelling to their offices once more. Overseas vacations, except for the super-rich, were cancelled or redirected to a booming staycation market. After decades of growth, there were 58.7 million holidays abroad in 2019.[106] What had become an accustomed luxury disappeared almost completely during 2020 and 2021, plunging the industry into crisis but removing a significant item from the annual domestic budget. Expenditure on clothing was cut back as there was no need to appear presentable in an office or dress up for a night out. Little or nothing was spent on cinemas, theatres, restaurants, and bars.

Many households appear to have adapted with speed and discipline to the unwelcome Covid-19 regime. Initially, it was assumed that life would return to normal in a few months, and consumers whose outgoings were suddenly falling seized with alacrity the chance of attending to their finances in the meantime. 'Checking banking and other admin,' wrote a diarist on 6 April. 'Paid off credit card – our spending during lockdown has plummeted.'[107] It was reported by the Bank of England that £7.4 billion of private credit was repaid during April 2020, the largest net repayment since data began to be collected in 1993. By the end of the year, a record £16.6 billion had been repaid in contrast to a growth in personal borrowing of £13.2 billion in 2019.[108] The household savings ratio, which had fluctuated between 5 and 10 per cent since the last financial crisis, suddenly increased from 7.2 in the first quarter of 2020 to 23.9 in the second quarter, the highest level since records began in 1963.[109] It declined to 14.0 as lockdown was eased, before rising again during the further lockdowns, reaching 18.3 in the first quarter of 2021 before falling back to pre-pandemic levels at the end of the year.[110] Savings varied with the cycle of opportunities to leave the house and spend money. In the year to February 2020, flows into 'deposit-like accounts' were an average of £4.7 billion a month. They tripled in March 2020, whilst the government was still debating what to do about Covid-19, and reached a peak of £27.4 billion in May, before falling back to £12 billion as the economy was partially re-opened in the third quarter. The second and third lockdowns caused deposits to rise once more, reaching £18.5 billion in January 2021 and then slowly returning to the original level by the end of the year.[111]

Those who could afford to do so adjusted their household finances to the changing cycle of opportunity and constraint, creating a reserve of savings which the managers of the national economy hoped would kickstart a recovery once the pandemic ended. It was otherwise for those with little or no choice about how they spent their money. In the financial year ending 2020, the poorest tenth of the population spent 43 per cent of their outgoings on food, drinks, clothing, housing, fuel, and power compared to 24 per cent by the richest tenth.[112] Low-income families were adept at time-consuming tactics for making small sums go further. The difficulty in lockdown was that the rules kept changing. The places where bargains were known to be available were unreachable or poorly stocked. Prices in the corner-shop alternatives were high enough to make the difference between just coping and going into debt. Households on tight budgets in lockdown faced a continuing challenge reconciling increasing needs with diminishing opportunities to shop efficiently. As one stressed parent reported:

> Our only saving has been £2.50 a week we spent on playgroup, and on petrol as we drive out to places less. On a whole we have seen our spending increase. Our electricity and gas bills have gone up for a start, as we're at home more. We have spent a lot more on food, especially during the first lockdown when there were shortages and we had to buy expensive brands. My children snack

more when they're at home too, my fruit spending has gone up considerably. We've also found that we've made outgoings with regard to entertaining the children that we wouldn't have pre-Covid – Disney+, crafts, and books (especially when all the libraries and charity shops were shut). We rely on charity shops a fair bit so when they were closed we spent more. I would have bought my daughter's school uniform from the supermarket but couldn't because it sold so fast and had to buy it at a higher price online. The Covid restrictions have also meant that my daughter's school have changed uniform requirements at the last minute – requesting two days to wear joggers and trainers – which has meant an increased spend on uniform.[113]

The greatest pressure was felt not by those on long-term benefits, who to an extent had adjusted their lives to what was available. They gained from the emergency uplift in April 2020 of £20 in Universal Credit, until it was withdrawn on 6 October 2021, in the middle of the annual Tory Party Conference. While it lasted, the increase kept up to eight hundred and forty thousand people out of poverty, including two hundred and ninety thousand children.[114] Since March 2020, the number in receipt of Universal Credit had doubled from three to six million. Making the uplift permanent would have cost around £6 billion a year.[115] Its removal was the single most gratuitous act of harm against the poor during the pandemic. 'The removal of the £20 uplift,' wrote a *Covid Realities* diarist, 'will mean I will have to choose between heating my home and myself and my husband eating. The removal of £20 may not seem a lot to people in government who see it as pocket change but to us as a family it really does mean choosing between heating and eating.'[116]

The uplift was replaced by a £500 million Household Support Fund, to be administered by local authorities who could use it to make 'small grants to meet daily needs such as food, clothing, and utilities', a scheme which made the nineteenth-century Poor Law seem a model of generous, predictable assistance.[117] Three weeks later, following widespread protests by the poverty lobby and MPs, a third of the cut was reinstated in the autumn budget. The taper rate was adjusted to enable those in jobs to keep a larger proportion of every pound they earned above their worker allowance. The concession was of no benefit to unemployed claimants. The major disruption to the management of marginal budgets during the pandemic was experienced by those who were plunged into short-term working or lost their work altogether.[118] 'What big changes have you gone through in the past year?' a diarist was asked.

> My upheavals have been my husband lost his job due to COVID which was horrific, stressful and beyond heartbreaking. That left us needing to apply for benefit help which left us with no money for weeks which obviously resulted in debt (debt is something I don't normally do, I was raised if you can't afford something you save until you can) so the impact on all of our mental health has been major.[119]

As the overall savings ratio increased, so also did the level of personal debt amongst the poor. The Financial Conduct Authority (FCA) reported in February 2021 that three in eight adults had seen their economic situation decline because of Covid-19, and for 15 per cent their situation was a lot worse. In this context as in many others, the consequences of the pandemic were magnified by long-term failings. In February 2020, almost two-fifths of families already lacked what the FCA defined as financial resilience, resources amounting to three months of expenses which could act as a buffer against unanticipated misfortunes, including the loss of the main source of household income. Between March and October 2020, the number of economically vulnerable adults increased by over a third.[120] A third of the three million new Universal Credit recipients had no savings of any kind at the beginning of the crisis.[121] The most at risk were the young, the self-employed, those earning less than £15,000 a year, and BAME adults.

Where possible, expenditure was forgone, but every month there were recurrent demands that either were paid or began to generate debt. With a second lockdown on the horizon in October 2020, Citizens Advice, the largest organization supplying guidance to the financially stressed, calculated that six million adults had fallen behind on household bills during the pandemic.[122] The biggest category reflected the changing nature of necessities in lockdown: 3.4 million adults now owed money on their mobile phone or broadband accounts. The remainder of debts reflected more traditional costs: three million unpaid water bills, 2.8 million unpaid energy bills, and 1.2 million behind with their rent.[123] Despite subsidies of £38 million allocated by the government to the debt advice services, the overall figure of unpaid bills had reached 7.3 million by the spring of

2021.[124] Some bills, particularly council tax, where the consequence of non-payment could be prison, were almost impossible to avoid. The only alternatives were payday loans or credit cards. A joint study by the Joseph Rowntree Foundation and Save the Children found that at the end of the first lockdown, six in ten families on Universal Credit and Child Tax Credits had been forced to borrow money.[125]

Households incurred debt as a device for managing their budgets at varying levels of prosperity and with differing levels of urgency. Across society, nearly nine million adults were borrowing more money than usual at the end of 2020. In total, the number of debtors rose from 10.8 per cent of the population in June to 17.4 per cent in December.[126] The poorer the family, the less choice in taking this action. The Resolution Foundation reported in November 2020 that just over half of adults in families in the lowest income quintile had borrowed more since the first lockdown to cover basic costs.[127] The contrast in financial strategies was most striking in the field of home ownership. The government was so exercised about the prospect of large-scale mortgage defaults as the economy contracted that it introduced a three-month mortgage repayment holiday, later raised to six months and extended to July 2021. Almost 1.9 million borrowers, one in six of the total, took advantage of the scheme.

At the other end of the market, the rise in the price of houses, driven by a stamp duty holiday, generated a greater sense of prosperity. The consequence was that in July 2021, there was a net repayment of mortgage debt for only the second month in the previous decade, the other occasion being the general clearing of debt that occurred in the first full month of lockdown.[128] Those who were comfortable with their payments could look forward to a future of rising assets as the value of property continued to grow. Those who spent every month of the pandemic avoiding creditors and searching for loans would emerge from the crisis still further behind the rest of the economy.

Nature

'We can go on one walk a day'

One of the youngest Mass Observation diarists was a five-year-old from West Sussex. His entry for 12 May 2020 read, in its entirety, 'We stay at home. We can go on one walk a day.'[1] The two short sentences perfectly summarized the government's quarantine strategy. There were exemptions to the requirement to remain indoors, covering shopping for basic necessities, medical needs, and travelling to work, which did not concern the schoolboy. The only general escape from domestic imprisonment was 'one form of exercise a day, for example a run, walk, or cycle – alone or with members of your household'.[2] The regulation seemed to preclude mixing the type of recreation; there were to be no mini-triathlons. It set no specific time limit, although it was generally assumed that an hour a day was all that was permitted.

The young diarist did not seem unduly cast down by his circumstances. The brief text was accompanied by a colourful illustration of a smiling boy standing above green and below blue squiggly lines representing respectively the grass and the sky, with, on one side, a yellow sun sending out six rays and, on the other, what was possibly a palm tree from which a coconut was falling. How society more generally responded to the regulated encounter with nature is the subject of this chapter.

There was little novelty in the prescribed activities. Walking in nearby streets, lanes, parks, or countryside had for centuries been the basic recreation available to every level of society. It was so commonplace that it has for the most part escaped the attention of historians, except where it became the focus of literary commentary or organized endeavour.[3] Cycling for pleasure pre-dated the motor car. Jogging against the clock can be traced back to the craze for competitive walking in the later eighteenth and early nineteenth centuries.[4] Gardening had a long and rich history ranging from country-house parks to competitive flower growing by groups of artisans in the midst of the industrial revolution.[5] Not surprisingly, the wealthy had larger gardens than the least prosperous, but few homes were without any kind of attached green space.[6] Despite all the urban sprawl and high-rise flats of the modern era, seven out of eight households had access to their own gardens as Covid-19 spread, and amongst those aged sixty-five and over, who most needed shielding during the spring of 2020, the figure rose to 92 per cent.[7]

The first lockdown began to be relaxed on 13 May, when other recreational purposes were added to the list of activities outside the home, and it became possible to meet a person who was not a member of the household. The two subsequent lockdowns were broadly similar, with increasing emphasis on the benefits of socializing out of doors as the danger of aerosol transmission in closed spaces became more apparent. Even during the periods of relaxed regulation, there was a general acceptance that taking exercise outside the home was both a required and a privileged activity. What changed during the pandemic was not only the volume of walking, gardening, and related encounters with nature, but also the meanings that were invested in such activities. There was an increased sense of the polarity between inside and outside the home. Where once occasional pedestrian expeditions or cycle rides or bouts of weeding and lawn mowing had been woven into the household regime, now they stood in conscious contrast to the physical construct of the home, which represented the fundamental defence against the pandemic. The permitted escapes made lockdowns bearable and at the same time emphasized their necessity.

In this binary universe, time took on a new significance. Engaging with nature was not just a way of using up spare moments. It became a means of giving structure to increasingly formless domestic and work routines. As there was only one opportunity to get outside in any given day, the expeditions were planned and undertaken with a new discipline. Out of doors, there was a fresh awareness of sight and sound, particularly during the first lockdown, when, for a few precious weeks, the noise of traffic almost disappeared, and air pollution fell. It was not so much that flowers were brighter or birds were louder, but rather there was an incentive to engage the senses with what could be seen and heard. 'I live opposite a park,' wrote a retired civil servant, 'so took some of my daily constitutionals walking around the lake and through the woods, absorbing the glorious sound of birdsong, and watching the progress of newly born ducklings, goslings and cygnets. I had never spent so much time over there in all the 38 years that I have lived here.'[8] In turn, conscious learning was required as half-remembered plant names and half-familiar birdsong were no longer sufficient.[9] The changing seasons offered an alternative narrative to the drama of infection and death, supplying both a memory of past endeavours and an investment in alternative futures. They were a resource for the preservation of mental health, a defence against the perpetual anxiety that accompanied the pandemic. They provided at least the illusion of control in a world ruled by an unmanageable disease. And as the final section of this chapter will discuss, the regulated encounter with local nature directed attention to global environmental change, both as an issue in its own right and as a cause of past, current, and future pandemics.

Exercise

The permitted daily excursions were a throw-back to a much earlier association between exercise and the locality. From the later eighteenth century onwards, there was a growing inclination to take a journey in order to walk. Firstly by horse or coach, and then by trains and buses, those with money and time on their hands travelled to areas unspoiled by the smoke and noise of the industrializing towns and cities. In 1835, William Wordsworth, whose poetry had done much to kindle this enthusiasm, was persuaded to write a guidebook to his native Lake District for a market created by 'travellers' who had begun 'to wander over the island in search of sequestered spots distinguished as they might accidentally have learned, for the sublimity or forms of Nature there to be seen'.[10] As the railway network was extended, ramblers formed themselves into associations to purchase excursion tickets that would permit a day's exploration of local beauty spots. More adventurous and better-funded travellers crossed the Channel and headed for distant mountains and coasts.

The first lockdown returned walking to its original form and purpose. Driving for pleasure was prohibited; trains and planes ceased operation. Instead, the daily release from the home extended only as far as the pedestrian's time and energy would permit. Writing in late February 2021, a regular hiker described the curtailment of his activities: 'My lady friend and I have walked all over the world: Peru, New Zealand, Tasmania, the Himalayas – and we've done most of the long-distance paths in the UK. For the past six months we've only been walking from the house; we haven't put petrol in the car since the start of December.'[11] The 'one walk a day' became a means of both escape and confinement. It was integral to the process described in chapter 4 of increasing the sense of community as a physically bounded space.

Streets previously only glimpsed from inside a bus or a car became combinations of gradient and length, exposed to the sunlight at different hours or to winds on particular days. The surrounding built landscape was examined afresh, as were the fragments of the natural world that flourished in the interstices of urban spaces. 'We noticed things we'd long forgotten to see,' wrote the scholar Matthew Beaumont: 'intriguing buildings that had always been obscured by buses or the press of commuters; songbirds in trees blackened by decades of pollution; wildflowers and weeds in the grass verge beside roads that had until recently been choked with commuter traffic.'[12] Opportunity and restriction redefined the meaning of exploration. 'We have become nosy tourists in our own neighbourhoods,' observed the journalist Amy Fleming. 'We seek out less-travelled backwaters, eyeing curiously the fragments of human and animal lives that we pass, gazing on seasonal changes like besotted new parents.'[13]

Efforts to find variations in the daily expeditions led to unexpected discoveries. Long-occupied localities yielded green spaces within reach of the home that previously had not been known to exist. 'I have seen unusual things even in my small urban Southampton environment,' wrote a contributor to *Letters from Lockdown*. 'A woodpecker in a front garden by a normally busy main road. The clear sound of a blackbird serenading with no traffic noise to disturb. The flowers in the garden seem more vibrant and prolific this year.'[14] Instead of the swings to which the children had always been taken, parks and fragments of countryside were located almost on the doorstep. A diarist recorded her sense of pleasure and surprise:

[W]e decided to go for another walk and head in a direction we don't normally go. It turns out that we have another park/nature reserve just around the corner from our house and had never realised! We had both heard of it, having been in its very far end before, but had no idea it came so close to us. Despite the fact that it was drizzling, it was lovely to go out and walk along the stream. We also saw a beautiful cream barn owl swooping over the meadow which is something I had never seen before.[15]

Residents who thought they knew where they lived found that they still had much to find out. 'Gradually I've found myself exploring my area more and discovering new places,' reported a lockdown walker. 'I hadn't realised there was a nature reserve about five minutes away, and now I go pretty much every day. You sometimes take what's right in front of you for granted.'[16]

However, in the UK world of Covid-19, the rules kept changing. The tightly contained regime of the spring of 2020 gave way to a more expansive set of regulations. All that was illegal were groups of more than thirty people out of doors, and the frightening prospect of 'raves', which could attract fines of £10,000. It remained almost impossible to take holidays abroad. Instead, families got into their cars and headed for the national parks, which experienced the largest influx of new visitors in their history. Walking was no longer co-extensive with locality, nor was it governed by the basic rules of good conduct overseen by settled communities or drawn up by experienced ramblers. Walkers arrived ill prepared for the terrain and the British climate. There was a record call-out of rescue teams in the Peak District in 2020.[17] Emyr Williams, chief executive of Snowdonia National Park, referred to the 'Spain people', who in another year would have taken their summer holidays on the Costa del Sol.[18] Now they created all kinds of difficulties, lighting fires in dry areas, overwhelming sanitary facilities, parking in the wrong places, heading into wild landscapes with inappropriate clothing, and leaving litter everywhere.[19] It was a matter of purpose. If they were taking exercise for the sake of the 'scenery, culture, heritage, landscapes, exercise, great', said Williams. 'If they are coming for a party, no.'[20] By the beginning of 2022, the misbehaviour of enthusiastic refugees from the pandemic had become so serious that the government was reported to be planning to introduce Asbo-style public space protection orders for the national parks.[21]

The sense of escape varied with the evolving restrictions, but throughout there was an enhanced sense of the otherness of nature. As will be discussed in the next chapter, electronic communication, whether for homeworking and home schooling or maintaining contact with family and friends, played a larger role in everyday lives, particularly for older generations, who might previously have left such activities to the digital natives. Nature was reality unmediated by a computer screen or an iPhone. 'We felt reassured,' wrote Matthew Beaumont, 'by the sheer "thisness" of the material world beyond the virtual one we inhabited in our bedrooms and living rooms.'[22]

It was of course possible to take equipment on walks or runs. The Sony Walkman, the first successful portable device, was introduced as far back as 1979. By the time the pandemic arrived, there were a host of means for listening and talking while in motion. There were vastly improved headphones for blocking external sound and delivering music and speech with a clarity previously only found in heavy speakers. But with no traffic noise to block out, at least at the beginning, and so much to gain from an aural encounter with nature, such devices lost their attraction. 'I used to listen to podcasts or audiobooks on my runs,' reported an experienced jogger, 'but just lately, with time out of the house being so precious, I've been enjoying just taking in my surroundings without the need for extra distractions.'[23] Those who persisted in using such technology defeated a key purpose of the escape from lockdown. 'Started as usual getting out of bed at 6-ish,' wrote a 12 May diarist, 'tied my laces and went out to do the 5k "short" run, great time to catch up with the news – it's generally the Radio 4 today programme with more and more covid info, being blasted through my headphones.'[24]

For those who left their phones at home or switched them off, there was a two-stage discovery. Firstly silence. 'All traffic noise ceased,' recalled the ornithologist Steven Lovatt of the day after lockdown was announced, 'and you could hear litter scuffing down the empty streets.'[25] In conurbations in every country, there were reports of an unprecedented absence of noise and vibration. The only regular interruptions to the peace of British towns and cities were the sirens of ambulances taking Covid-19 victims to hospital. 'Yet the world's city centres are not completely silent', observed the natural historian Stephen Moss. 'Rising like a tide of hope, from gardens, parks and open spaces, is a surge of sound: the individual songs of millions of birds coming together to create a very timely and welcome chorus.'[26] It helped that in the northern hemisphere the lockdowns coincided with the spring chorus. In any year, those who wanted to listen would have noticed a sudden upsurge in birdsong. Nonetheless, as human social life almost ceased, the court-ship rituals of the birds had never seemed so loud. 'A little tentative and sputtering at first,' wrote Steven Lovatt, 'by the end of March it filled the air. Broadcast from aerials and hedge-tops, a rising choir of chirps, trills and warbles brought life to gardens and echoed off house-fronts, shut-tered shops and bland retail silos, seemingly suddenly obtrusive with no motor traffic to smother it.'[27]

The absence of engine noise, and also, in the larger cities, of aeroplanes taking off and landing, was so striking and pleasurable that it lingered longer in the memory than in fact it lasted. The enterprising Museum of London acquired at this time a series of gramophone discs of London street sounds made in 1928. They were thought to be the earliest such recordings, commissioned by the *Daily Mail* as part of a campaign against the unbearable noise of the modern city. The Museum had the idea of undertaking for the sake of comparison a parallel set of recordings in the same streets, which were made on the afternoon of 7 May 2020. The 1928 thoroughfares were indeed full of a wide range of noises, with not only motorized cars, buses, and lorries grinding through their gears, but also steam vehicles, horse-drawn carts clopping along the road, and the bells and screeching wheel-flanges of trams.[28] At the end of the first week of May 2020, the soundscape was more of a monotone, just the undiffer-entiated roar of the combustion engine. But it seemed no quieter. Given the different recording technologies, it is not possible to make a precise comparison, but on their own terms the streets of London were already returning to their previous cacophony just six weeks after the imposition of lockdown. Birdsong and passing conversations could faintly be heard in just one of the recordings, made in the relatively traffic-free space of Leicester Square. Neither of the two subsequent lockdowns attempted or achieved anything like the same cessation of traffic as in late March and April.

Common to accounts of this moment out of time was the acute con-trast between the cause and the experience of taking daily walks or cycle rides. The first lockdown was imposed too late to prevent thousands of deaths, and barely held in check the mounting numbers fighting for their lives in ICUs. But if the controls on movement were without precedent, so also was the weather. 'April was the most beautiful spring I can ever remember,' wrote a 12 May diarist, 'and with time almost all belonging to me, I have marinated in nature, in the lanes and woods next to the house and in watching my meadow grow day by day.'[29]

Unlike the wet beginning to 2019, there was every incentive to engage with the world outside the home. A week after lockdown was announced, another diarist wrote,

> I am making a more conscious effort, a more mindful purpose, to see, really see, what is around me, as I go out and about in these restricted times. Blossom trees abound, so many beautiful varieties. Magnolias are in all their majesty and splendour, in gardens and on road way verges of grass, merging pastel colours of pinks, creams and whites, the billowy blossoms cheer the heart and lift the soul.[30]

The Met Office later confirmed that March to May was the sunniest spring since records began in 1929, April the warmest April, and May the driest calendar month in England. The proximate cause was not the absence of traffic pollution, but rather a buckling of the jet stream that trapped an area of high pressure over Britain. But since the beginning of the century, all kinds of weather records had been broken as climate change took effect. Seven of the ten warmest springs on record had occurred since 2000.

The requirement to stay inside the home for much of the day threatened the creation of a new generation of couch potatoes. The UCL study found that over a quarter of the population became 'less physically active'.[31] But a combination of sunshine, quieter roads, and officially sanctioned opportunity increased the amount of purposeful pedestrian exercise. The Department for Transport calculated that compared to 2019, there was a 7 per cent increase in distance walked per person in 2020, reaching a total of two hundred and twenty miles, the highest since 2002, and a growth in cycling from fifty-four to eighty-one miles per person.[32] Serious pedestrians, who carried an app to measure their footsteps, multiplied sixfold in London and the South East during 2020.[33] There was a surge in the purchase of bicycles, the mode of longer-distance transport least exposed to the 'fatal Breath'. The volume of sales rose by a quarter in the twelve months to May 2021, and the value by 40 per cent.[34] As with any recreation, large sums could be spent on equipment, from walking and running shoes to hand-made cycles. But the essence of the daily escape was that it need cost nothing at all.

Whereas the possession and in particular the size of gardens were directly related to wealth, and also ethnicity, access to some kind of green space in towns and cities was inversely related to income. Thanks to the creators of municipal parks in the later nineteenth century, most towns and cities possessed a 'lung' in proximity to the poorer streets and estates.[35] In the midst of the pandemic, the ONS found that just over a quarter of the population of Britain lived within a five-minute walk of a public park, and almost three-quarters less than fifteen minutes away. The figures rose to 52 per cent and 95 per cent if playing fields were included, although the ONS was not certain about their availability to the public. The only qualification was that of space. The average facility catered for two thousand people, and no less than forty-six thousand had London's Clapham Common as their nearest park. More than a little care would have to be taken to avoid the breath of others in such surroundings.

Those who took exercise noticed what they saw along roadsides, in parks, and in the countryside. A survey conducted for the Royal Society for the Protection of Birds (RSPB) at the end of the first lockdown found that almost three-quarters of the respondents in England had 'sought out places where they could enjoy nature while taking their permitted daily exercise', and a similar proportion 'agreed that they had noticed more nature in their neighbourhoods since the Coronavirus outbreak in the UK than they would normally at this time of the year'.[36] The British Trust for Ornithology (BTO) responded to the growing interest by making membership of its Garden BirdWatch survey free, increasing participation by almost two-thirds.[37] There was a reciprocity in the intention of government and the motives of the walkers and cyclists. At a time when there was deep uncertainty that the public would accept the unprecedented controls on their freedom, it was hoped that the concession of a daily escape would reduce the prospect of a widespread rejection of quarantine. The permitted exercise was conceived as a means of reducing the stress of home confinement and the looming threat of infection. Helped by the weather, the locked-down population largely conformed to official expectations. There was an unexpected acceptance of the regulations, levels of serious stress rose at the beginning of the pandemic but were largely unchanged thereafter, and there were perceived gains in the regular encounters with fresh air. Seventy-seven per cent of the RSPB survey endorsed the proposition that 'visiting nature has been important for their general health and happiness', and four-fifths agreed 'that they had felt happier whilst/after spending time visiting nature'.[38]

Such responses reflected the growing advocacy of the benefits of exercise out of doors. The association of encounters with nature with enhanced spiritual wellbeing went back to classical times. It had been given a new focus by the Romantic movement, and throughout the nineteenth and twentieth centuries the urbanization of a small island had enhanced the perceived benefits of walking through the streets and natural surroundings that could be reached. As with so many of the responses to Covid-19, there was little that was completely new. The journalist Rachel Cooke drew an explicit comparison with Charles Dickens, whose fierce, fast walks through London were a means of finding physical and mental release from the static toil of writing and editing:

> Many of us are experiencing what was hitherto only theoretical: the connection between the rhythm of our footsteps and what I suppose I'm going to have to call our creativity, to my mind a word that can, and should, be extended to almost any aspect of daily life, from thinking, to cooking supper, to sorting your knicker drawer. Out on the city streets, I often think of Dickens, that great, compulsive walker: there are Boz-like figures everywhere in London now, doggedly trekking the pavements. Some stare at their feet, their minds far away, their regular circuit so familiar they could navigate it in their sleep. Others look up, seeing old things with new eyes, raising their phones prayerfully, as if to offer benediction to this peeling facade, that tinned-up pub.[39]

In the years before the pandemic, increasing efforts had been made to identify specific health benefits of outdoor activities.[40] Regular exercise was held to improve mood, self-esteem, decision-making, attention span, and mental wellbeing more generally. The burgeoning mindfulness movement embraced the practice as a means of locomotive meditation.[41] The effects were a product of both sensory experience and physical movement. 'I run 5 or 10k three or four times a week,' reported the chef Michael Roux, 'I find it really relaxing: I come back physically tired but mentally energised. Running is a great release, a stress reliever, especially during lockdown. It is more than a pastime; it is part of my wellbeing routine – it's vital for mental health.'[42] Rachel Ann Cullen, author of *Running for My Life*, was in no doubt about the benefits:

> Running makes me feel alive and free. I can press 'pause' on any anxiety I might have and spend time in nature, whatever the weather – I even run in snow. It makes me feel immensely grateful for my health and fitness and it gives me an inner resilience that I otherwise might struggle to find on difficult days. I honestly believe that running has saved my mental health throughout this pandemic – it makes sense to me when little else at the moment does.[43]

For those content to move at a slower pace, a similar contrast was drawn between the mounting complexities of surviving Covid-19 and the calming, ordering experience of the daily walk. 'I want to be outside for the first hour or two of the day: no phone, no distractions,' explained the nature writer and presenter Kate Humble.

> I'm sure we all wake up with a million things going on in our heads, all these disjointed thoughts, worries and anxieties. For me, that part of the day, when all I have to think about is one foot going in front of the other and not falling over, creates a headspace that allows all my thoughts to settle in a way that feels much more manageable.[44]

'Fresh air is medicine,' claimed one of the army of walkers.[45] As a contribution to surviving Covid-19, this was a valid but limited claim. The encounters with nature were neither a prophylactic against the disease nor a cure. Outdoor exercise provided many millions of people with what Isabel Hardman termed 'mental muscle'.[46] It helped them deal with vast disruptions to their way of life, resist multiple forms of anxiety, and deal with death and bereavement. Studies established that pedestrian encounters with nature helped to reduce the stress hormone cortisol.[47] At the most basic level, meeting others out of doors was safer than in closed spaces. Physically healthy members of the older cohorts stood a better chance of surviving the disease, although a prior history of good living was more important than practices embraced when the pandemic struck.

The real battle against infection and death took place elsewhere, however, in laboratories and hospitals. The long-established wellbeing movement made exaggerated claims for the ways in which individuals could be fully responsible for their own physical and psychological condition. There was a critical difference between promoting mental health, where exercise had multiple beneficial effects, and responding to mental illness, which could require a range of long-term treatments. As we shall see in chapter 7, the debate over vaccination generated claims that there was no need for pharmaceutical intervention provided the individual embraced an appropriate fitness regime. 'There is nothing more irresponsible,' wrote Isabel Hardman, 'than the natural health lobby, which throws away reams of peer-reviewed research and claims that you can cure severe illnesses through diet or hobbies.'[48]

As time passed, encounters with nature lost some of their original attraction. The problem with walking, jogging, and cycling, as with so many other aspects of the crisis, was that Covid-19 kept returning, and with it a renewed emphasis on the daily escapes from the house. What had appeared pleasurable pastimes in the sunshine and quiet of the first spring became an increasingly weary routine as the second and third lockdowns were imposed in the cold, dark months of autumn 2020 and the succeeding winter. The Canadian writer Monica Heisey viewed with disbelief the continuing routines of her adopted London. She was fully in favour of purposeful explorations of nature, but not

> joylessly trudging around the same bit of my neighbourhood, for the fourth day in a row, in the interests of scavenging a crumb of mental health. . . . [J]ust as I have never had a profound awakening at the Hampstead Heath ladies' pond in London, neither do I suspect I will find one tramping through a field, meditating on the uncharacteristically lax approach applied by the British to the definition of the word footpath.[49]

Leaving home at all carried with it an element of stress. Well-used thoroughfares and popular parks were full of people, some of whom were already infectious. 'I am always scared and vigilant that I may bump into another person,' wrote a 12 May diarist.[50] Such threats multiplied during 2021 as mask-wearing became more casual, to the concern of those still anxious to protect themselves and others.

In many cases, what kept the daily excursions going was not so much a state of mind as the demands of canine companions. The long-domesticated animals fared better in this pandemic than in earlier outbreaks of the plague. Daniel Defoe described the routine but drastic action that was taken in mid-seventeenth-century London: '[I]n the beginning of the Infection, an Order was published by the Lord Mayor, and by the Magistrates, according to the Advice of the Physicians; that all the Dogs and Cats should be immediately killed, and an Officer was appointed for the Execution.'[51] A similar cull was described by Camus in his fictional outbreak in Oran.[52] During Covid-19, on the other hand, dogs, who are known to catch the disease but not transmit it to humans, not only survived but also prospered, at least in the West; in its efforts to control the Omicron upsurge in the spring of 2022, the Chinese began destroying domestic pets.

The controlled, disciplined exercise of the animals had a long history. Fearful of rabies, an earlier pan-European epidemic, the state had imposed a system of licensing as early as 1796 to ensure that dog-owners behaved responsibly when accompanying their pets in outdoor spaces. When reliable records began to be kept after 1867, it was discovered that there were 1.4 million taxed animals in Britain, and it was assumed that there were as many again escorting owners who had failed to pay.[53] The licensing system was abolished in 1987 and replaced by a series of bye-laws controlling matters such as fouling the streets. Henceforward, canine numbers were counted by pet food manufacturers, whose business was growing rapidly. On the eve of the Covid-19 pandemic, it was calculated that the population of dogs had more than quadrupled in a century and a half. Daily routine walks with an animal tugging on a leash were not invented by the lockdown government.

In other European countries, an accompanying dog became a legal requirement of leaving home once a day during lockdowns, leading to well-publicized tales of exhausted animals being borrowed by or rented out to the owner's friends and neighbours for multiple walks. Although there was no such obligation in Britain, it was immediately apparent that such companionship would make it easier to undertake regular exercise. By the end of the first lockdown, the *Financial Times* reported that prices for puppies had doubled.[54] During the first year of the pandemic, the estimated number of pet dogs rose from ten million to twelve million.[55] There were fevered stories in the press about unscrupulous puppy farms and the concomitant rise of dog stealing.[56] In May 2021, amidst all the challenges facing the government, the environment minister announced the formation of a task force to investigate the thefts.[57]

The dogs provided company and an element of security for lone walkers, particularly women. Above all, they supplied discipline. 'The routine of dog walking continued to shape all our days,'[58] explained a solicitor otherwise housebound because of her clinical vulnerability. However much locked-down residents might wish to forgo another expedition along over-familiar streets in the wet and cold, they were compelled by their needful and enthusiastic pets to step outside, day after day.[59] With about one dog for every 2.3 households, the pressure on the population to engage in at least nominal pedestrian exercise was widespread and relentless. Difficulties arose, however, as the lockdowns came to an end. In the autumn of 2021, with schools restarting and increasing numbers of owners returning to work for at least part of the week, there were reports of canine stress as pets found themselves alone in empty houses. Professional dog-walkers experienced an increase in demand for their services. As in the aftermath of any Christmas, attempts were made to sell back animals bought in haste at a time of need, and the growing cost of living crisis in 2022 led to reports of dogs being abandoned and re-homing charities no longer able to cope with unwanted pets.[60]

Gardening

Gardening shares with walking the close encounters with flora and fauna in the fresh air. The fundamental difference is the requirement to change what is seen. The challenge of the countryside is not to spoil the view by viewing it. Every effort has to be made to ensure that traffic does not impact on the landscape, that footpaths are maintained and observed, and that litter is not left behind. Large numbers of people travel to see nature unaltered by travellers. As we have seen, the immediate consequence of the relaxation of lockdown in the summer of 2020 was to imperil the beauty of the national parks. The heavily used municipal facilities had from their Victorian creation employed keepers to ensure that as far as possible the grass and the flower beds were protected from users. In any domestic garden, on the other hand, change was inescapable, unless the space was paved over or covered in artificial grass. No matter how small the plot, plants had to be chosen and tended. If the owner ignored the beds, patio pots, or window boxes, nature would rapidly transform them in its own and not necessarily welcome ways. The oxymoron 'wild gardening', which was becoming increasingly popular at the time of the pandemic, itself demanded a strategy of sowing and seasonal care.

Following the epochal Tudor Waters Report of 1918, municipal housing was built to a density of eight houses per acre in rural areas and twelve in urban. Private developers informally adopted this standard, which determined the provision of gardens until late in the twentieth century, when more of the space around houses began to be devoted to parking cars. High-rise flats constructed after 1945 tended to replace slums where there had been no gardens at all. The average size of a cultivated plot in 2016 was just over two thousand square feet.[61] On the eve of the pandemic, there were probably more gardens than there were active gardeners in Britain. Not everyone liked the activity or had the energy or physical fitness to undertake such regular labour. The young had other interests; their grandparents might eventually become too old for such pursuits, although after retirement they tended to invest more effort in such pleasurable tasks than any other cohort. Nonetheless, by 2020, gardening had long been the second most time-consuming hobby in the country after watching different kinds of screens.

As a response to the national health crisis, gardening had a number of salient strengths. The most obvious was that the materials for such a practice were already in place. Commercial nurseries supplying plants and other materials had been flourishing since the eighteenth century. By the second decade of the twenty-first, the industry was calculated to be worth £5.5 billion. Most households could lay their hands on the essential tools, which, apart from mechanized mowers, strimmers, and hedge-cutters, had changed little since the Georgian era. A vast range of knowledge was embodied in books, television programmes, internet resources, and skills passed down from one generation to another.

The major practical problem in March 2020 was one of perishable supplies. Lockdown was imposed at just the moment in the northern hemisphere when gardeners were beginning to stock up for spring. Nurseries were closed, although later were amongst the first retail outlets to be re-opened, on the grounds that most of the shopping took place out of doors. Helped by the unusually fine weather, the normal seasonal surge in demand immediately accelerated as gardeners realized how much more time they would now have for planting and raising flowers and vegetables. One diarist reported that he had sown every unused packet of seeds he possessed, some purchased as far back as 2013, and was unable to find replacement packets online: 'I'd tried to get seeds on the internet – but they were all sold out.'[62] The leading seed merchant Suttons reported sales up to twenty times higher than the same day in 2019.[63] On both sides of the Atlantic, there was growth in normal levels of purchases, particularly for items that might contribute to the threatened food shortage such as lettuce, beetroot, and tomatoes.[64]

Owners of gardens who for lack of interest or opportunity had in the past paid little attention to their plots needed to embark on a rapid course of learning. As spring advanced, there was no time to lose. Established sources of information were inundated. The Royal Horticultural Society (RHS) reported that over 3.5 million had taken up gardening, and in the first hundred days after the initial lockdown was declared, it received fifteen million enquiries in contrast to its normal annual traffic of twenty million.[65] Large numbers were asking about matters as basic as how to grow potatoes. Other gardening apps and websites flourished. Allotments were in demand, old hands helping horticultural neophytes. 'We jumped at the chance,' recalled a new member. 'We were desperate for something to distract us from the escalating madness. We had no gardening experience and it's been a steep learning curve, helped along by more experienced plot holders. The allotment has been the silver lining to the big, black cloud that's been over us.'[66]

Gardening perfectly fitted the official strategy of full lockdown alleviated by healthful escapes from the house. Unlike other national cultures such as the United States, British gardens had generally been tended behind fences or hedges. They were liminal spaces, outside the home but maintaining the same rights to privacy and physical security, particularly at the rear of the property. Whilst in normal times owners had regularly missed key moments of flowering or ripening by going away for annual breaks, now the pandemic gave them the pleasure of witnessing every week of the seasonal round. Millions who had always taken holidays at set times of the year, often dictated by the school calendar, saw as never before particular flowers at their peak and harvested all the produce at the right moment.

Tending to plants and vegetables in the pandemic conformed to a long tradition of official encouragement. By the beginning of the twentieth century, the state had come to view gardening as a time-consuming distraction which could make a significant contribution to diets and the cost of living, and if pursued with sufficient effort could turn the working class away from less desirable pursuits such as drunkenness or disruptive politics. Better to spend the evenings digging potatoes or pruning roses than in the public house or a seditious meeting. Under the Smallholdings and Allotments Act of 1908, councils were required to make available plots to 'persons belonging to the labouring population'.[67] The take-up was immediate. By the First World War, there were over half a million allotments being tended by gardeners with little or no land of their own. The 'Dig for Victory' campaign of the Second World War further entrenched the national value of gardening in public consciousness, although the subsequent growth of cheap food imports undermined the long-held ambition that domestically grown fruit and vegetables could be an economic proposition.

By the time the pandemic broke out, the association of gardening with wellbeing had been strengthened by research into the effects of tending plants and lawns. A recent large-scale study by the University of Exeter found a range of benefits specifically associated with gardening as distinct from engaging with nature more generally. 'Reported use of the garden,' it concluded, 'was important in deriving benefits: compared to people who did not use the garden, respondents who both relaxed in the garden and gardened had better general health, mental wellbeing, higher levels of physical activity.'[68] Having tended their own flowers and vegetables, they were also likely to make more frequent visits to the countryside or public gardens. *The Well Gardened Mind*, a recent full-length study of the impact of the activity by the psychiatrist Sue Stuart-Smith, is concerned with gardening as a persistent practice. It is an absorbing engagement with change in a particular portion of fenced nature. 'A garden gives you a protected physical space,' she wrote on the eve of lockdown, 'which helps increase your sense of mental space and it gives you quiet, so you can hear your own thoughts. The more you immerse yourself in working with your hands, the more free you are internally to sort feelings out and work them through.'[69] The emphasis is on process rather than outcome: '[T]he way I thought about mundane tasks such as weeding, hoeing and watering changed; I came to see that it is important not so much to get them done, but to let oneself be fully involved in the doing of them.'[70]

At the very least, lockdown meant much more time looking out of the window at the changing sequence of growth and decay. Where once it was necessary during the working week to leave at dawn and often not return until dark, now the movement of light and shade from hour to hour could be enjoyed together with the constant alterations in the beds and borders. 'As a gardener and working as a volunteer outdoors,' wrote a retired administrator, 'I have always loved the changing weather, light, growing things, that we experience in the UK. But this year it has been more special to me. More than ever I am focussing on my garden as a piece of land to nurture and I am seeing it in more detail.'[71]

If most of the population went into lockdown already responsible for a patch of enclosed nature, many fewer had actually watched it from day to day across the seasons. 'As Spring has approached personally,' wrote a Mass Observation diarist, 'the change is more noticeable perhaps as I have time to look around our small garden and actually notice what is happening rather than rushing about and only giving a fleeting glance.'[72] In so short a time as the first lockdown, there was little prospect of a significant gain in cultivated space, although the allotment societies were able to attract new members. But in the sense that many householders now paused to look at what previously they had taken for granted or neglected altogether, there was a real expansion in the experience of gardening and the benefits it generated.

The spread of Covid-19 made the public calendar more urgent. Every morning brought new data on the spread of the virus, revised predictions about its course, fresh advice or instruction about how to behave. The essential attraction of gardening was that its cycle of change remained independent of the medical and political timetable. As the health situation, nationally and globally, continued to worsen, the days in the northern hemisphere became longer, lighter, and warmer. Whilst lockdown was bringing normal life to a standstill, seeds were sown, weeds reappeared, lawns once more needed to be mowed. The unusually fine weather in the spring accentuated the contrast between the natural disaster that was filling the hospitals and mortuaries and the constant rhythms of cultivated nature. 'Whenever I got to my allotment,' recalled a late beneficiary of the early twentieth-century reform, 'I was able to focus on repetitive tasks and stop worrying about the pandemics and what ifs. I found great comfort in the predictability of nature and the changing seasons. The great wheel was still turning, despite us being in a scary and strange limbo.'[73]

Everyone was to a greater or lesser extent fearful of what the next day would bring. Working the soil permitted an alternative perspective on the passage of time. 'When the future seems either very bleak, or people are too depressed to imagine one,' explained Sue Stuart-Smith, 'gardening gives you a toehold in the future.'[74] It was a combination of cyclical motion unaffected by human endeavour and the gardener's responsibility continually to anticipate and shape what happened next in their plot, however large or small. 'I need this to continue,' wrote a 12 May diarist. 'I need to watch and marvel as nature does her thing. I need to see there is a way ahead. A future. Things to look forward to. Patterns, seasons leading into each other.'[75] The worse the encounter with the pandemic, the more valuable an alternative way of conceiving the daily round. The world of the journalist and presenter Kate Garraway was turned upside down when her husband suffered an acute form of long Covid, rendering him immobile and semi-conscious. She and her children found solace in their labour outside the house:

> When you're living day to day on a knife edge, doing something that gives you a future just helps with a sense of progress, where there is actually none from the direct situation. It's been the most important space for us . . . a place to find joy, hope, go a bit crazy and feel a bit unleashed in a stifling physical and emotional time that we've all lived through. It just gives you that sense of moving forward. You can't think short term in a garden, you have to plan. You have to have hope, invest in a future.[76]

Those fortunate to be in possession of larger gardens were able not just to maintain them but also to engage in creative ventures. There was little that could be done to improve the interiors of homes. Tradesmen were at first locked down themselves, and when the economy began to get moving in the second half of 2021, there was both a shortage of labour and a rapid inflation in building materials. However, as soon as the garden centres re-opened in 2020, ambitious gardeners could commence transformative projects: redesigning and replanting borders; digging pools and watching them fill with wildlife; fulfilling long-held plans they had always been too busy to implement. One gardener reported that amidst a crisis he was incapable of shaping, he had undertaken a major alteration in his own surroundings: 'A small vegetable plot and seating area completes the garden. It has been a cathartic experience, and is doing wonders for my wellbeing.'[77]

As with any recreation, gardening provided substitute dramas which distracted from the larger misfortunes of life. However skilled and hard-working and knowledgeable about planning, planting, and cultivation, no gardener was more than partially in command of their destiny. Bad weather caused delay or destruction. The second spring of the pandemic was nothing like as benign as the first. Predators ate their way through carefully nurtured flowers and vegetables. Conversely, there were intermittent triumphs that defied expectation. Wilting plants that had been written off suddenly sprang back into life. Seeds germinated in unprecedented profusion. Fruit trees were bowed down by an unusually heavy crop. Amidst the encounters with infection, illness, and death that dominated the personal and collective experience of Covid-19, there were alternative scenarios of victory and defeat. Which narratives had the greater purchase at any moment or in a particular life depended on the scale of the gardening and the impact of the virus, but at least there was the possibility of achieving some kind of balance in the struggle to survive the crisis.

Perhaps the greatest value of a cultivated patch in the midst of a pandemic was the simple one of safety. Even within a family, there was less exposure to the 'fatal Breath' out of doors than inside a house. The respect that was given to the privacy of a domestic garden, and the care that was taken to control access to allotments, meant that the danger of infection was at a minimum no matter how many hours were spent on the pastime. There was no prospect of close encounters with strangers as there was on the daily walk. This characteristic was felt most strongly by those who were most at risk at their place of work. Returning to a crowded household at the end of a shift only increased the stress. In these circumstances, it was the intensely localized *cordon sanitaire* of a garden or allotment that was its fundamental attraction. 'I have continued to work fulltime through the pandemic as an occupational therapist,' wrote a regular gardener, 'visiting people in their own homes after they've been discharged from hospital. My allotment was one of the only places I felt safe, especially in the early days of lockdown. I was really scared I would catch the virus and bring it home to my family.'[78]

The Blip

On 17 August 1348, Bishop Ralph of Shrewsbury wrote to the archdeacons of his diocese of Bath and Wells:

> Almighty God uses thunder, lightning and other blows which issue from his throne to scourge the sons whom he wishes to redeem. Accordingly, since a catastrophic pestilence from the East has arrived in a neighbouring kingdom, it is very much to be feared that, unless we pray devoutly and incessantly, a similar pestilence will stretch its poisonous branches into this realm, and strike down and consume the inhabitants.[79]

Unfortunately, the prayers and the processions that he ordered failed to prevent the Black Death crossing over from France. A year later, the Prior of Canterbury asked the bishops in the southern province to take action:

> Terrible is God towards the sons of men, and by his command all things are subdued to the rule of his will. Those whom he loves he censures and chastises; that is, he punishes their shameful deeds in various ways during this mortal life so that they might not be condemned eternally. He often allows plagues, miserable famines, conflicts, wars and other forms of suffering to arise, and uses them to terrify and torment men and so drive out their sins.[80]

The populations of the fourteenth century were at once powerless in the face of the devastating pandemics and active agents in their own destiny. All were exposed to the wrath of a vengeful God, but through prayers, penitential processions, and reformed morals it might be possible to hasten the end of a plague and delay its recurrence.[81]

Three centuries later, the renewed visitation of the Black Death to Europe evoked a response that contained a larger role for secular explanations. In Barcelona, the tanner Miquel Parets drew frequent attention to the attempts by the city's inhabitants to placate an evidently angry God. 'There are no words,' he wrote, to describe the prayers and processions carried out in Barcelona, and the crowds of penitents and young girls with crosses who marched through the city saying their devotions. The streets were constantly full of people, many greatly devout and carrying candles and crying out 'Lord God, have mercy!' . . . But Our Lord was so angered by our sins that the more processions were carried out the more the plague spread.[82]

However, the authorities were also conscious that such public demonstrations could themselves spread infection, because, as Parets wrote, 'this disease does not favour gatherings of people'.[83] The clergy themselves took care not to get too close to those they were easing into the next world: 'Each carried a torch, for when confessing the sick the torch was held between the priest and the sick person, and they kept their distance because it is said that the plague is carried by one's breath.'[84] Looking back from the early eighteenth century, the dissenter Daniel Defoe took a more jaundiced view of the torrent of sermons that the plague brought forth in London. He left a nominal role for divine intervention but framed his account of the arrival and disappearance of the plague in terms of the actions of doctors and municipal authorities and the contrasting behaviours of rich and poor citizens.

In the early twenty-first century, the Christian churches, pushed to the side-lines by the increasingly secular response to disease, sought to reclaim the leadership of what they saw as a new moral crusade. 'I think the future we are called to build,' wrote Pope Francis in response to Covid-19, 'has to begin with an integral ecology, an ecology that takes seriously the cultural and ethical deterioration that goes hand in hand with our ecological crisis.'[85] The Archbishop of Canterbury wrote in 1375 that, 'in our modern times, alas, we are mired in monstrous sin and the lack of devotion among the people provokes the anger of the great king to whom we should devote our prayers. As a result we are assailed by plagues or epidemics.'[86] In a pale echo, the 105th incumbent asserted: 'Around the world, climate change is affecting food security, creating social vulnerability, and disrupting peace and security. There is no doubt we need to act.'[87]

Since the bubonic plagues, the practical tasks of devising and managing responses to a pandemic gradually transferred to governments and scientists. The moral drama of sin, retribution, and repentance has, however, continued in a new form. As the Professor of the History of Medicine at Oxford has written, "'[E]merging diseases", as they are often termed, have been seen as Nature's retribution for environmental degradation.'[88] Humankind has misbehaved, is being punished, and, with increasing urgency but limited optimism, is seeking effective forms of repentance and improved behaviour.

Successive outbreaks of respiratory diseases in this century have been blamed on an increasing exposure to infected wildlife. SARS (Severe Acute Respiratory Syndrome) in 2003, MERS (Middle East Respiratory Syndrome) in 2012, and now Covid-19 have crossed the species barrier, probably directly or indirectly from bats, which carry a wide range of pathogens.[89] The same is true of other zoonotic infections such as AIDS, which transferred from chimpanzees and gorillas in the early twentieth century, or Ebola in successive outbreaks from 1976 to the present day. Contemporary epidemiologists are certain that, like the Black Death in the fourteenth century, one pandemic will be followed by another in a matter of years. 'There will be a disease Y,' warned the Oxford vaccinologist Sarah Gilbert at the end of her Dimbleby Lecture in December 2021. 'This will not be the last time a virus threatens our lives and our livelihoods. And I would like to finish on a high note, but the truth is, the next one could be worse. It could be more contagious or more lethal or both.'[90] As this study is completed, there is an outbreak of monkeypox in the global north.

'Greater encroachment into the natural world means that new diseases are emerging ever more frequently,' argues the Coalition for Epidemic Preparedness.[91] Animals may be the proximate cause of this outbreak or the next, but the fundamental problem is the behaviour of people. Land has been cleared for population growth, the exploitation of raw materials, and industrial farming, and as a consequence there are lethal encounters with hitherto isolated reservoirs of viruses.[92] The risks are compounded by the growing wildlife trade, the overuse of antibiotics, and the continuing increase in international travel, tourism, and commerce. The pandemics have thus become a metonym for the ecological crisis more generally. As with global warming, the role of humankind is at once diminished and enhanced. The notion of an Anthropocene era is challenged. Humans can no longer see themselves as apart from the natural universe. Rather they are just multicellular organisms in which viruses can flourish as well as in other animals.[93] At the same time, their strategies, responses, and actions are foregrounded in the effort to restore a working balance with the planet on which they live.

The impact of Covid-19 on global warming was discernible before the UK government accepted the inevitable and imposed a full lockdown. The roads were already getting quieter, and by the beginning of April traffic was almost three-quarters below the level at the same time in 2019, the second largest fall in Europe after Germany.[94] There had also been declines in asthma attacks amongst children, and in work absences due to pollution-related illnesses.

Nature itself seemed to be released from the confines imposed by population growth and environmental destruction. There were multiple reports of wildlife flourishing in hitherto prohibited urban landscapes.[95] Goats wandered through the streets of Llangollen; ocean-going seabirds nested on the Tyne Bridge in the centre of Newcastle; porpoises, dolphins, and occasional whales were seen in the Thames; wildflowers, assisted by the warm spring, bloomed along roadsides. However, the vision conjured up by lockdown was scarcely a lament for a lost, known world. Country dwellers may have recovered the sights and sounds of a time before the wholesale mechanization of farming after the Second World War, and the more recent growth in car ownership in villages deprived of local services. But since the Middle Ages at least, the towns and cities had not been quiet; nor had their air been breathable. Traffic levels fell to 1955 levels, but that was the last year before the epochal Clean Air Act. Following the Great Smog of 1952, which killed around twelve thousand people immediately or in the subsequent weeks, the state finally began to tackle the life-shortening smoke and soot generated by factories and domestic coal-burning fires. There was no basis in living memory for the absolute peace and cleanliness of the London streets for the few short weeks in the spring of 2020.

Neither did lockdown present a secure vision of the future. As we have seen, cars soon began to return to the roads. The parallel with 1955 had already advanced to 1962 a fortnight after 23 March. By the end of the first lockdown, the streets and motorways seemed as noisy as ever and there was no further reduction of aural and atmospheric pollution, not least because of a prolonged reluctance to use crowded public transport amongst those needing to travel. More than three months after the guidance to work from home was temporarily lifted in July 2021, rail commuter travel was still only at 45 per cent of pre-Covid-19 volumes.[96]

Stalled economies began to move again, rapidly increasing pollution. In the UK, a study found that thirty-nine out of forty-nine towns and cities were suffering pre-pandemic levels of air quality by December 2020.[97] A range of urban pollution-free zones were delayed due to other priorities in the health emergency and lack of money in hard-pressed local authority budgets.[98] Despite the emergency closure of industry and travel, globally 2020 registered the highest temperature on record jointly with 2016. Whilst there were gains in the condition of some wildlife species, there were also losses. Eco-tourism, which constituted the financial basis for many conservation projects, collapsed almost completely.[99] COP26 in Glasgow, the critically important climate change conference, was postponed by twelve months.

Environmental scientists tracked the rapid recovery of the pre-pandemic dynamic of global warming. The annual *Greenhouse Gas Bulletin* of the World Meteorological Organization (WMO) at the end of November 2020 found that 'the rapid reduced activity associated with COVID lockdowns is expected to cut carbon emissions by 4–7 per cent this year'. Set against the established trajectory of growth, this was little more than a temporary fluctuation. 'We breached the global threshold of 400 parts per million in 2015,' explained the WMO Secretary General. 'And just four years later, we crossed 410 ppm. Such a rate of increase has never been seen in the history of our records. Lockdown-related fall in emissions is just a tiny blip on the long-term graph. We need a sustained flattening of the curve.'[100] If there was a lesson to be learned from the impact of the pandemic, it was how relentless were the forces leading to catastrophe. Closing down the world economy and halting most forms of travel was a strategy that in the long term was not repeatable, effective, or affordable.

The changed encounter with the natural world during the lockdowns is better seen not as blueprint for the future but as a dream that was outside time altogether. John Naughton took his daily lockdown exercise on his bicycle in the countryside around Cambridge in the early weeks of the first lockdown. 'The quietness of the roads,' he wrote, 'is almost magical.'[101] In an era when so much of the debate about global warming was couched in terms of anxiety, calculation, and prayer, the excursions into a fleeting beauty and silence, bathed in the sunshine of the 2020 spring, seemed like a vision of the world before the fall. There was, however, no way back, just a glowing sense of the possible. At a more mundane level, nature was a key resource at a time when the day-to-day survival of mind and body was of overwhelming importance. Whatever the fluctuations in global carbon levels, for the weeks and months of home imprisonment, walking out of the house, cycling along the lanes, digging the garden, were vital pleasures. In future, that season may be a way in which the memory of Covid-19 is anchored. A Mass Observation diarist recorded her experience on the last day of the first lockdown:

It's a fabulous spring. I've fallen in love with trees this year, I hadn't realised what a fantastic array of flowers they have; many are small, green and insignificant, but lots are very fragrant. I suppose you just need time to appreciate these things, which, thanks to lockdown is something I currently have.[102]

Communication

The Thursday Murder Club

If there was a book of Covid-19 in Britain, it was not Defoe's *Journal* or Camus's *The Plague*, nor Boccaccio's *Decameron* set in the fourteenth-century Black Death, although all saw an upsurge in sales in the early months of lockdown.[1] Neither was it any of the instant accounts written before the event was over. By far the most successful publication was the first novel by the quiz show host Richard Osman. *The Thursday Murder Club* was the literary sensation of 2020, selling over a million copies. In the full pandemic year of 2021, it was top of the bestseller list, with its sequel, *The Man Who Died Twice*, occupying fourth place.[2] It was also the most borrowed book from public libraries. The story centres on four elderly residents of 'Coopers Chase', a retirement village in Kent. Their leader is Elizabeth, a former member of MI6. She is assisted by a nurse, a psychiatrist, and a trade union organizer, who have all long since taken their pensions. The club meets in the 'jigsaw room' once a week to review cold cases from the records of the local police force. 'She wasn't really supposed to have the files,' the nurse explains about Elizabeth, 'but who was to know? After a certain age, you can pretty much do whatever takes your fancy. No one tells you off, except for your doctors and your children.'[3] The club becomes involved in a series of new murders which they solve with occasional assistance from two official detectives.

The novel was completed before the pandemic and when it was published could scarcely have been further from the circumstances of its setting. In the middle of 2020, sudden death was a presence inside not outside residential homes. The chances of four occupants together surviving Covid-19 were almost non-existent. Its realism lay in the sympathetic depiction of the ageing middle class. 'You can't move here until you're over sixty-five,' explains the narrator, 'and the Waitrose delivery vans clink with wine and repeat prescriptions every time they pass over the cattle grid.'[4] There is a sense of time running out: 'Many years ago, everybody here would wake early because there was a lot to do and only so many hours in the day. Now they wake early because there is a lot to do and only so many days left.'[5] If the particular threat of 2020 was missing, the novel was clear-sighted about the quotidian fears the elderly have to negotiate: 'Memory was the bogeyman that stalked Coopers Chase. Forgetfulness, absent-mindedness, muddling up names.'[6] The murders were perfunctory; the detection would not have troubled Miss Marple. But Richard Osman received a seven-figure advance for a project that seemed perfectly attuned to its moment. The gently witty narrative delivered a plot in which those who in real life were most at risk of Covid-19 emerged triumphant to fight another day in another book.

The Thursday Murder Club both drove and reflected an increase in the oldest form of communication technology. Despite the closure of bookshops for long months during lockdown, there was what the *Financial Times* described as a pandemic-induced 'reading boom'.[7] Whilst there was a 6 per cent fall in printed books in 2020, this was more than compensated for by a sharp rise in digital sales.[8] There was a renewed enthusiasm for audio books, whose market expanded by over a third in the first year of the crisis.[9] In the following year, with a less interrupted market, total book sales reached their highest level for a decade.[10] 'It's clear that many people rediscovered their love of reading last year,' said the chief executive of the Publishers Association, in April 2021, 'and that publishers were able to deliver entertaining and thought-provoking books that so many of us needed.'[11] A long-term fall in fiction was halted. By the end of 2021, sales were over a quarter higher than they had been in 2019.[12] Crime novels, science fiction, and romance all increased.[13] Conversely, the non-fiction market declined, although there was an expansion of no less than 50 per cent in the publishers' category of 'mind, body, spirit' as readers sought answers to living amidst the rising death toll.

Too much should not be concluded from the specific categories. The popularity of 'romantic fiction and sagas' owed something to the fact that such material tended to fill the display stands in supermarkets, which, unlike bookshops, were open throughout the pandemic.[14] There was substance in the claim by the Publishers Association that 'the nation turned to books for comfort, escapism and relaxation in 2020'.[15] It repeated behaviour during the Second World War, when there was a marked increase in the consumption of novel reading.[16] There were, however, plenty of readers seeking more challenging material or equipping themselves with guides to new interests and pastimes. The essence of a market that sold 212 million books in 2021 was that it could meet every taste and enthusiasm.[17] Sixth in the 2021 bestseller list was *Guinness World Records*, now in its sixty-seventh year.[18] Seventh and ninth were memoirs of familiar celebrities.[19]

The publisher Bloomsbury enjoyed a notably successful pandemic, increasing its share value by a half.[20] A growth in sales in the first year of the crisis continued during the second. The company reported a rise of almost a quarter in the twelve months ending February 2022. 'The surge in reading,' explained its chief executive, 'which seemed to be one of the only rays of light in the darkest days of the pandemic, is perhaps now being revealed as permanent, with the simple act of reading shedding light and giving joy to millions of people.'[21] Unlike ephemeral digital media, books survived over time. Bloomsbury was still deriving profits from the Harry Potter franchise, which started life in 1997. Newly purchased volumes sat on the shelves next to older acquisitions. The market expansion in 2020 and 2021 merely added to long-accumulated personal libraries. To adapt an old adage, books now furnished the rooms behind the Zoom calls. Visually and substantively, the printed word was everywhere in the pandemic, diverting, comforting, instructing, and informing.

Multi-media

Those who were confined to their homes turned to the full range of media to keep in touch with friends and family with whom they could no longer talk face to face. Successive communication revolutions have overlaid rather than replaced existing means of maintaining contact over distance. They have constituted what John Naughton describes as an 'ecosystem', with technologies as old as civilization itself co-existing and interacting with the latest digital innovations.[22] Correspondence was already a commonplace device amongst male artisans in the eighteenth century, and, following the introduction of the Penny Post in 1840, became widely used by the increasingly literate products of mass schooling.[23] In the years preceding the pandemic, the volume of addressed letters had been falling, both absolutely and in relation to the expanding parcel service. This decline continued in the first year of the crisis, but nevertheless a total of 7.8 billion items of mail were posted and received.[24] Some were merely hard copy marketing. Some were from the NHS writing regularly to the shielded and later the unvaccinated. But as in previous epochs, many were connecting the disconnected, pen between fingers. In 2021, with the period of absence between family and friends lengthening, and patience with Zoom meetings diminishing, there was for the first time in a decade an increase in correspondence amounting to 11 per cent over the previous year.[25] The National Literacy Trust found that a quarter of all children and young people had written a letter in the previous month.[26] With staff shortages increasing because of illness or quarantine, the Royal Mail found itself with more letters than it could manage early in 2022, causing a sharp decline in delivery times.[27]

After centuries of innovation in virtual communication, it was commonplace for relationships to be maintained through a variety of channels. In the year that the smartphone was introduced, the 132-year-old device of the telephone, still mainly in the form of a landline, was the second most common means of 'catching up with close friends and relatives', just behind face-to-face conversation.[28] With mobiles an almost universal possession by 2020, punching in a number was an automatic response to the Covid-19 restrictions. 'I think I've spoken to more people on the phone today than I have done for years,' wrote a diarist four days after the first lockdown was announced.[29] Such traffic formed the backdrop to the evolving crisis, scarcely worth itemizing. 'There is always a number of phone calls every day,' recalled a witness, 'instigated by me or others. I forget to mention them, though I suppose they are important in the circumstances.'[30] As the channels for maintaining social networks became ever more varied, there was comfort in the sheer simplicity of starting and ending a spoken conversation. 'Lately I've taken to making phone calls to friends,' explained the journalist Gaby Hinsliff, 'like in ye olden days, instead of firing off distracted WhatsApps while simultaneously doing three other things at once.'[31]

Old technologies were put to new use, and more recent innovations in social media were rapidly deployed in response to the pandemic. Throughout the quarantine period, the most consistent losers were grandparents, whose established routines for maintaining contact with their grandchildren were brought to a halt. Even if very small children lacked the patience for long video calls, they were adept at playing with the devices almost as soon as they could talk. A contributor to the BBC series of lockdown letters had grandchildren aged two and four:

> Today is Monday and my heart leaps with joy when you appear on my phone screen initiating the video call. I see you sitting at your kitchen table in Bristol bursting with pleasure and excitement because you have ice lollies for pudding. . . . Our video calls replace my fortnight granny visits. Our play is evolving to suit the medium. You carry me around the house and garden showing me about your favourite places. You both take turns to hold me virtually in Mummy or Daddy's phone.[32]

A century of demographic change had reduced the number of grandparents living either with other generations or in neighbouring streets. Instead, there was a tendency for the extended family to be distributed across the country and around the world. Thus, for instance, a South African now living in England maintained his network: 'We played charades with the grandchildren in Cape Town, Sheffield and York, feeling profoundly thankful for the communication made possible by IT.'[33]

It is striking how creative the communications became. Merely talking was insufficient. In the first flush of discovery of the conferencing sites, users invented all kinds of diversions. 'The digital, social media age has been a god send at this time,' wrote a diarist,

> as it has enabled people to keep in touch 'virtually'. The new Friday night out is done via 'houseparty' or zoom apps – they enable you to bring countless friends and family into your living room. The online quiz is the big thing at the moment – we have done several as a family. Ironically, being in lockdown has meant that we are probably speaking more to our family than before.[34]

In some cases, it was a matter of turning conventional contests into virtual competitions. Bridge could be played with partners in different locations.[35] Other games which had always been associated with face-to-face contact could be converted for locked-down households. A new calendar of diversions rapidly took shape. A diarist reported that by the end of the first lockdown a full weekly programme had been established:

This evening, as usual on a Tuesday, my husband and I will be playing cards online via Zoom with my mum, who is in Wiltshire and my sister who is in Southampton. We do this three times a week – either cards or scrabble/other board games, and we are really enjoying it – in fact we plan to continue doing it even after we are able to see each other again. One of the few upsides of this situation is that we are all embracing the 'video call' culture, something which I never thought I would do, let alone that my 84 year old mum would do![36]

The most inventive means of connecting with others was devising and conducting quizzes (which was also a popular diversion inside Downing Street during lockdown). At one level, every day was a struggle against the uncertainty of infection and regulation. At another, it consisted of endless tests of what was known about ever more arcane subjects.[37] There were always answers to the questions; no one died from getting them wrong. The widely popular pub quizzes were replicated online once it became impossible to meet over a drink. 'We have kept in touch with family members through Zoom and Facetime,' wrote a retired further education lecturer, 'holding a family pub quiz each Friday evening, taking it in turns to set the questions. This then becomes a catching-up session, trading what little news there is.'[38] The activity appealed to all ages. 'After dropping Grandma's shopping to her and checking in with her from afar,' wrote a teenager, 'I logged onto zoom for the weekly quiz with my best friends. Zoom, is such a great way to keep in contact with everyone each week we have a quiz the rounds usually include general knowledge, history, a round on our friendship and on the individual who created the quiz.'[39]

For those content to participate more vicariously, the radio and television schedules were full of contestants undergoing some kind of examination. Alongside his novel writing, Richard Osman was co-host of *Pointless* on BBC1 and presenter of *Richard Osman's House of Games* on BBC2. Quizzes and other mental challenges such as crosswords essentially belonged to a pen-and-ink age, however they were now embodied. The purest form of digital competition was online gaming. Ofcom reported that nearly two-thirds of adults and over nine in ten of sixteen- to twenty-four-year-olds played games on an electronic device, 'and over half of all gamers agreed that gaming helped them get through lockdown'.[40] A nine-year-old diarist explained what he had been doing with his friends: 'Fortnite is a game and in the game you have to defeat people and be the last one standing. We had a blasting time.'[41]

Well-established forms of cultural networking went online. Book clubs flourished in many pre-pandemic communities, and whilst there was a loss of sharing company and refreshments in other people's homes, the essential task of debating a text that had been read in common could be undertaken virtually. Some amongst the gatherings had a longer journey to full digital literacy than others, but, given persistence and mutual support, much could be achieved. A diarist described her communication universe:

> I also delivered a book to one of the members of our Shared Reading Group which is now meeting weekly on Zoom and the extract I have chosen for next week will be delivered as a scan rather than word document so the screen share would be unhelpful. Most of our members use two devices for reading aloud at the meeting. 8 out of 20 members can now use Zoom successfully and, after many hiccups and lots of patient generosity with time and perseverance on the part of our members, we are now in the swing of it while the other members are reading the texts at home.[42]

Zoom choirs were attempted, although fully aligning voices by digital means posed technical difficulties.[43] Cinemas and theatres were shut for long periods, but the multiple streaming that had developed during the previous decade made it possible to catch up with what was being missed.[44] Expenditure on video sites increased by a quarter during the first year, with *Frozen 2* the most popular film.[45] Again, what was a pleasure for the isolated individual or household could also become a networking activity. Ad hoc film clubs were formed, with participants linking up to discuss what they had simultaneously seen on their screens at home. 'Culture in quarantine has really flourished,' wrote a u3a member, 'with the Hay Literary Festival going digital. If I think of all the operas, ballets, theatre and music events we have all been able to access daily in our homes, the choice has been staggering. The growth of digital platforms has been fast. The range of online resources for learning is huge.'[46]

A few weeks into the crisis, a change in behaviour was noticed amongst online users. They were looking for more than diversion and emotional connection:

The internet also used to be a place where you could learn about anything – that is, until the information overload became overwhelming. Now cabin fever and boredom have led people back to the internet to learn again, crowd-sourcing the best sourdough recipe, mastering new languages, or picking up any number of other useless or handy skills.[47]

Covid-19 itself constituted a curriculum which everyone had to learn, with constant updates of information. Around the medical challenge, a host of private studies were conducted. The 2021 Lloyds Bank *UK Consumer Index* calculated that almost three in five of the online population had used the internet for some form of learning during the year.[48] Hobbies and pastimes provoked enquiry as practitioners reached the limits of their expertise or explored unfamiliar realms of activity. With more attention paid to home cooking in the absence of restaurants, recipes were collected not just from books but also from interactive sources of information. The short-form videos on the rapidly expanding TikTok site soon entered the kitchen. A year after lockdown began, at least 150 million downloads of a Finnish recipe for feta pasta had been made.[49] Domestic chefs photographed their creations and uploaded them for the applause and instruction of their friends.

There was no age limit on the curriculum that was attempted. An eighty-five-year-old woman reported studying 'Egyptian fractions' in a course on advanced mathematics: 'I got a lot of the tests wrong to my dismay. I was proficient in 1950!'[50] U3a, with its strapline 'learn, laugh, live', provided encouragement and online facilities for study. The four hundred and fifty thousand members were amongst the most likely to be confined to their homes in the pandemic. They were able to exploit their networks of voluntary endeavour to instruct themselves and others. Any topic that appealed to a local group, whether new languages, mastering musical instruments, exploring philosophy, or studying nature, was transferred from face-to-face meetings to home-made video classes.[51]

The realm of more formal study, the Open University, whose supported distance learning model was far better placed to withstand the pandemic than the rest of the higher education sector, reached out to those who wanted to commence or continue a personal course of intellectual exploration. In 2006, it had launched 'OpenLearn', in which over a thousand courses containing multi-media extracts from externally validated programmes were made available free of charge either for self-contained study or as portals to degree-level curricula.[52] At the beginning of the first lockdown, daily visitors increased overnight from forty thousand to over two hundred thousand, causing the total number of users since the site commenced to pass a hundred million.[53] Two million 'statements of participation' were issued during 2021.[54] New material was added to meet the particular needs of home-schooling students or employees on furlough, or of those who wanted better to understand Covid-19 itself. The use of the site reflected the appetite for learning in the pandemic. In the twelve months from March 2020, the number of discrete visitors to OpenLearn grew from seven and a half to seventeen million.

From shopping to networking, to playing, to learning, the internet performed a central role in the response to lockdown. The average time spent interacting with a screen in 2020 was three hours and twenty-seven minutes a day.[55] The figure described a society never far from an iPhone or a tablet, or from a laptop, whose sales were recovering after a period of decline. However, this overall usage was only marginally the consequence of the pandemic. The hours spent online had been increasingly steadily in previous years. The growth between 2020 and the pre-Covid-19 year of 2019 was just nine minutes a day, exactly half the increase of eighteen minutes between 2018 and 2019.[56] Using a slightly different measure, the ONS reported that in 2020, 92 per cent of adults in the UK were recent internet users, up only one point from 2019.[57] There was more volatility on a short-term basis. In the crisis month of April 2020, usage was four hours and two minutes, thirty-seven minutes higher than in the same month a year earlier, leading to headlines that a quarter of waking hours were being devoted to digital communication.[58]

The relative stability of usage partly reflected the scale of change since the invention of the World Wide Web. By the time the first lockdown was imposed, Britain, like most developed countries, was reaching saturation point in levels of capacity. In 2020, only 4 per cent of households lacked internet access, an improvement of three points since 2019. When the ONS began keeping such records in 2006, just over a half of households were online. Poverty still played a part in levels of connectivity, but the digital divide, which had greatly concerned observers earlier in the century, was ceasing to be as salient a factor. The major agent of differentiation was now age.[59] Between the years of sixteen and forty-five, virtually everyone was online. The corresponding figure for those aged seventy-five and over was 54 per cent.[60] However, this was almost double the level in 2013, and during the pandemic it was amongst elderly users that the major changes took place. According to the Lloyds Bank 'digital engagement index', the rate of growth of those over sixty was more than twice that of more experienced younger users.[61]

It was amongst this cohort that the gain in changing skills and behaviour was most apparent. Whilst they might still turn to their children or grandchildren for advice and support, they were less willing to delegate the whole process of online communication. An eighty-five-year-old reported that he was 'enthralled' by his discovery of the web:

> I was nervous of the internet before the pandemic. I had never used Google or surfed the web. I'd decided, because of all the stories of scams you hear, that it was safer just not to get involved in that world at all. But when my local Probus meetings moved online during the pandemic and after some encouragement from my younger friends, I began to explore and I must say, computers are marvellous![62]

A still older user described the course of learning she had nervously embarked upon in order to celebrate her ninety-third birthday: 'My daughter has introduced me to Zoom and I've a call scheduled. I'm feeling a little apprehensive because it sounds complicated. Learning how to use FaceTime and Zoom in the same week is a bit much.'[63]

The lack of overall change was also a consequence of the averaging of behaviour. Prior usage was so high that there was likely to be some displacement of activities once lockdown commenced. For all the relief from the pandemic older children found in online games, they had to make time to take part in school lessons or Zoom conversations with relatives. Those managing the family economy needed to prioritize the new essentials, such as food shopping online. Not all users had the opportunities that many of the diary writers enjoyed of spending long hours browsing the web for necessities or diversions. The poor still faced problems paying for access or purchasing adequate equipment. A key worker such as a bus driver or a care assistant who was away from home during the day made little or no use of digital devices at work, and was too weary to begin elaborate games or lengthy internet conversations once back at home.

Medical staff had constant interactions with screens as they extracted or entered information about the progress of patients or coordinated with colleagues, but sheer exhaustion prevented more lengthy usage. A recurrent event in the diary of the intensive care doctor Roopa Farooki during the first forty days of lockdown was falling asleep in the evenings with her keyboard still open in front of her.[64]

Despite the multiple variations that were made in the use of digital media, the activities were less of a disruption to established practices than at first appeared. There was extensive commentary in the press about the strains of online communication. Even experienced users of social media found that they needed to learn a new set of skills and manners.[65] They had to adjust to the variable technologies involved in a group discussion, with some of the participants equipped with better devices or internet connections than others. Patience was required for the uncertainty that the connections for a meeting had been properly established and that a new participant would be let in on time. Contributors found they had to learn a new etiquette of when to speak or remain silent, and how to intervene in a flow of conversation. They needed to decide how formally to dress and what, if anything, to wear beneath the waist (it was decreed that MPs in the first virtual Parliamentary debate should conduct themselves according to the normal dress code). Groups had to establish rules about whether speakers were on mute unless they had something to say, or whether the video of those not speaking should be turned off to prevent the signal from being overloaded.

There was a general consensus that video conferencing was more tiring than face-to-face conversation, and more limited in its outcome. It was partly a matter of concentrating for long periods on what was often a poor-quality image or sound. Outside work meetings, few conversations ever lasted for a prolonged period without pauses or breaks. There was the distracting prospect of not only the interlocutor on screen but also the speaker's frequently ill-dressed and, in the lengthening absence of hairdressers, unkempt image. However carefully arranged and conducted, less was communicated than in a casual conversation. As the *New York Times* explained,

> This is foremost because human beings are exquisitely sensitive to one another's facial expressions. Authentic expressions of emotion are an intricate array of

minute muscle contractions, particularly around the eyes and mouth, often subconsciously perceived, and essential to our understanding of one another. But those telling twitches all but disappear on pixelated video or, worse, are frozen, smoothed over or delayed to preserve bandwidth.[66]

'I knew that I never wanted to endure another social interaction on screen again,' wrote a commentator at the end of 2020. 'It was reality flattened and condensed, drained of what it should be.'[67] However, daily active users of Zoom, the most successful meeting platform, rose from 132,000 in the UK when the first lockdown was announced to almost 1.7 million at the end of November 2020.[68] Users became accustomed to a wide range of technologies and platforms. 'I communicate with my colleagues via Microsoft Teams and over the telephone,' wrote a homeworking wine merchant. 'I had French lessons on Teams. We both communicate with family via telephone, WhatsApp (calls and text) and Zoom.'[69] It was not that participants were unaware of the defects of online discussions. Rather, as had been the case with earlier forms of communication technology, they were prepared to trade the benefits against the losses.

Correspondence, the dominant mode of virtual exchange from the Middle Ages to the early 1970s, presented a greater difficulty of face-to-face emotional exchange. The recipient of a letter had to reconstruct the writer in the absence of their physical presence.[70] 'The problem with correspondence', wrote Laura Berlant, 'is that it is conversation without context, intimacy without intimation.'[71] In the centuries before the Penny Post, the vagaries of the delivery networks meant there was no certainty that the sender was still of the same mind when the letter was written or indeed remained alive and in good health. The successor technology to letter-writing, the telephone, provided a more immediate conversation and a range of meanings that could be conveyed vocally, but it was still a poor alternative to the visual clues exchanged by two people in each other's presence. Nonetheless, both forms of pre-digital communication were used billions of times a year and continued to be employed alongside social media during the pandemic.

There was in all forms of virtual communication a balance of risk. On the one hand, there was a threat that relationships would attenuate or cease altogether in the absence of physical association. On the other, there was a danger that intimacy would be undermined by the constraints of alternative channels of information. Committing opinion and feeling to a sheet of paper, albeit protected by a seal or, from the 1840s, by a gummed envelope, exposed private sentiment to public scrutiny. Other members of a household might come across a letter before it was sent or after it was received. Once the state established an effective monopoly of carrying mails after 1840, there was an immanent danger of official surveillance, despite general but ill-defined legal protection.[72] The telephone was similarly vulnerable to other domestic listeners, to switchboard operators until automatic exchanges were introduced, and later to more technical forms of interference. The development of mainframe computers for civilian use in the 1960s provoked immediate claims that privacy was dead,[73] and for more than half a century the corpse of intimate secrecy kept rising to be once more apparently killed by successive developments in digital media.

Survey evidence suggests that internet users took a pragmatic view of the balance between gains and losses during the pandemic. In the Lloyds Bank *UK Consumer Digital Index 2020*, 83 per cent of respondents assented to the proposition that 'the internet provides me with more benefits than it does disadvantages', rising by five points a year later.[74] They continued to log on although they were alive to the threat to their privacy. Two-thirds of the sample in both years agreed to the statement that 'I am concerned about using sites/tools where I have to enter my personal details'. At the beginning of lockdown, the sudden increase in digital conferencing cast light on the safety of the platforms, and Zoom moved quickly to improve its end-to-end encryption.[75] It is not clear just how many of those playing quizzes with friends and family were simultaneously concerned about surveillance of the answers they gave. Lloyds conducted a further survey of the one in twenty in their sample who were still offline and found that 51 per cent were 'worried about my privacy and security', and the same proportion were 'worried about having my identity taken'.[76] In both cases, the concerns had risen from just over a third the previous year. Amongst these refuseniks, the threat to privacy was three times more important than poor connectivity in explaining their behaviour.

'This year proved once and for all: screens are no substitute for real life,' wrote the journalist Ross Barkan at the end of 2020.[77] But few supposed they were, any more than pre-digital communication technologies were seen to be. They were a means of maintaining a bearable existence amidst a vast disruption to social intercourse. The levels of connectivity and capacity were so high at the beginning of the pandemic that they permitted an immediate and wide-ranging deployment of digital media to overcome the isolation threatened by Covid-19. If there was little overall increase in the time spent online, there was a flexible and focussed use of those tools relevant to the challenge of lockdown. Those least equipped to participate, men and women who had reached adulthood long before the arrival of the web and personal computers, made the most effort to learn new skills. As had been the case in the years before the pandemic, UK internet users managed to be both alert to the threat to privacy and for the most part willing to log on to the major platforms. In doing so, they made their lives far more resilient to disruption than the government initially feared they would be.[78] Debate continued, however, about the dark sides of the web, some of which will be examined below, and about the continuing increase in the power of the major providers.

At the same time, there were glimpses of the hopes originally entertained for the internet. John Naughton, who has chronicled the growth of the digital world since the 1990s,[79] caught sight of the prelapsarian vision as the first lockdown began:

> One of the interesting things about the current crisis is the way it has prompted people other than geeks to rediscover, in a way, what the Internet is really for. Those of us who were in on it in the early days saw it as a miraculous way of enabling human beings to connect with one another at a distance. That got lost a bit in the frenzied growth of social media. But what we're now seeing is people discovering tools like Skype and Zoom as a way of meaningfully connecting with people to whom they are close, or congenial, rather than via the manipulative, etiolated channels of social media.[80]

This led in turn to speculation about just how far the successful imposition of quarantine regulations in Britain as elsewhere was dependent on the devices and applications of social media:

> I saw a tweet the other day. 'Imagine,' it said, 'if this lockdown happened before the Internet.' And my feeling – shared by some of the people who responded to the tweet, was that it wouldn't have happened. Or, at any rate, it

would have been much more difficult for governments – at least governments in democratic societies – to sustain. The UK has neither the police nor the military resources to, say, enforce a curfew if a significant number of citizens decide that they have had enough of being shut up. So maybe the Net is the reason there seems to be such an orderly shut-down.[81]

Anti-Vax

'There are some things, surely, more hideous than death,' insisted William Cobbett in 1829, 'and more resolutely to be avoided; at any rate, more to be avoided than the mere *risk* of suffering death. And, amongst other things, I always reckoned that of a parent causing the blood, and the diseased blood too, of a beast to be put into the veins of human beings, and those beings the children of that parent.'[82] The debate over vaccination began in 1796, when Edward Jenner infected the eight-year-old son of his gardener with lymph from a cowpox blister. Cobbett's attack on the attempt to eradicate the endemic disease of smallpox, which then killed about one in three of those it infected and disfigured the faces of many survivors, was reprinted in the nineteenth century as part of the burgeoning anti-vaccination literature.[83] The controversy became more heated when a national scheme was introduced in 1840, and was made compulsory for children under three months in 1853. From 1867, parents could be fined the substantial sum of £1, more than a week's wage for an unskilled labourer, plus legal costs, every time they refused to attend a vaccination station with their child.

For two centuries, debate about the legitimacy of the medical procedure was kept alive by unresolved conflicts over the status of professional and commercial medicine, the role of the state in managing the bodies of its citizens, and the competing authority of official and private channels of communication. By the time Covid-19 was declared a pandemic, the social media platforms had established the business model of what Shoshana Zuboff had recently designated as 'surveillance capitalism'.[84] It was an automated version of an earlier communications economy in which consumers acquired information from publications which became the means of selling them products marketed by third-party vendors. Instead of advertisers subsidizing the cover price of newspapers, the information was now nominally free. In the specific area of pandemics earlier in the twenty-first century, as in the public arena more generally, there was ample evidence of how inaccurate or wholly false facts could by this means spread and influence behaviour.

It is striking that the global body responsible for fighting Covid-19, the WHO, immediately assumed that it needed to wage a parallel battle against what its Director General termed 'an infodemic'. Alongside the declaration of a 'Public Health Emergency of International Concern' on 30 January 2020, its twenty-strong 'risk communication team' set up an information platform called the WHO Information Network for Epidemics (EPI-WIN). Its leader, Sylvie Briand, recognized that she was adding another chapter in a narrative that stretched back to the outbreaks of bubonic plague. 'We know,' she told *The Lancet*, 'that every outbreak will be accompanied by a kind of tsunami of information, but also within this information you always have misinformation, rumours, etc. We know that even in the Middle Ages there was this phenomenon.' What were modern were speed and reach: '[T]he difference now with social media is that this phenomenon is amplified. It goes faster and further.'[85] As part of its communications strategy, the WHO launched an online 'Mythbusters' site, where it briskly dismissed prevailing misconceptions that vitamins or alcohol were protections, relieved readers of the apprehension that shoes spread Covid-19, and denounced hydroxychloroquine and bleach as remedies.[86]

The major media companies were already embroiled in a series of controversies about their dissemination of conspiracies and alternative facts, particularly in relation to the recent American Presidential elections, and the Brexit referendum and subsequent Parliamentary elections. As soon as the scale of the pandemic was grasped, Facebook, Google, YouTube, Twitter, and Microsoft announced on 16 March 2020 that they would be 'jointly combating fraud and misinformation about the virus [and] elevating authoritative content on our platforms'.[87] WhatsApp announced a similar ambition in early April. The stated intention was finally to exercise effective control over the content of their platforms. It was partly because it was obvious that so epochal an event would be a playground for every conspiracy theorist and vendor of instant remedies. And it was partly because Mark Zuckerberg and his colleagues seemed to believe that this time truth mattered and could be recognized. More so than politics, there were provable facts and institutional authorities to define them. Whilst the impact of misinformation on elections was endlessly debatable, in the case of Covid-19 the consequences could be measured in deaths and infections on an unprecedented scale.

Decisions announced in California were fully relevant to the communications economy in the UK. In the short term, there was little that the British government could do to discipline Facebook and its competitors, but it rapidly accepted the responsibility of seeking to control the popular narrative of the pandemic. According to Matt Hancock's diary, as early as 3 July 2020, a team was created in the Cabinet Office which led an online campaign 'based on providing an overwhelming counternarrative. Instead of focusing on responding directly to false claims, the main effort is to provide clear, objective positive material. . . . What we want to do is harness the enthusiasts, reassure the mass ranks and stop the anti-vaxxers persuading the hesitants not to have the jab.'[88] The daily news agenda was managed through televised Downing Street briefings, usually involving the prime minister or a senior cabinet member flanked by the Chief Medical and Scientific Officers or their colleagues. These sought to combine encouraging rhetoric with the judicious use of charts and medical metaphors. Two websites were developed to supply authoritative data on the progress of the pandemic. The 'Covid Dashboard' was 'the official UK government website for data and insights on coronavirus (COVID-19)'. It described itself as

> an up-to-date and authoritative summary of key information about the COVID-19 pandemic. This includes levels of infections, the impact on health in the UK and on measures taken to respond. We update it daily to present a dynamic contemporary picture. The dashboard meets a strong public need for timely updates at national and local level to ensure good understanding of the day-to-day progress of the pandemic.[89]

It was managed by the UK Health Security Agency, which adapted an existing mechanism for tracking seasonal flu. Visitors to the site were given the national data and could click through to their own area. Each day's report was carried by the television news, interposing 'sadly' before the death statistics, to demonstrate that newsreaders had feelings too.[90] The ONS compiled a weekly infection survey, calculating Covid-19 mortality on the slightly higher basis of the content of death certificates rather than the time elapsed since an initial diagnosis, combining this information with a regular 'latest insights' report covering vaccinations, wellbeing, and lifestyle through the pandemic.[91]

In addition to the two principal official sources, there were a host of surveys rapidly designed and conducted by academic researchers, polling organizations, and other interest groups, whose findings were then summarized in the press. The progress of vaccination from a distant prospect to active trials to a general roll-out received widespread coverage. As the statisticians David Spiegelhalter and Anthony Masters observed in *Covid by Numbers*, '[T]he discussion about the pandemic has been awash with data.'[92] In part, the speed and accuracy of the counting were a legacy of the tradition of official statistics in Britain which began with the creation of the General Registry Office in 1836. In part, it was a response to the widely perceived threat of an alternative discourse on social media. Unlike earlier crises, where the rebuttals to false information were frequently fragmented or too late, or frustrated by the power and inertia of the media companies, battle was joined from the moment the pandemic was recognized. The ambition was to replicate with statistics the medical response to Covid-19. 'One approach for dealing with this,' explained Spiegelhalter and Masters, 'supported by empirical evidence, is the idea of "inoculation" – pre-empting misinformation and telling people about the incorrect interpretation before they catch it in the wild.'[93]

There were in practice a number of obstacles to realizing this objective. Social psychologist Stephen Reicher and his team found that trust in scientists was more important than trust in government in determining how the population would behave.[94] Surveys in the summer of 2020 found that three in five considered scientists to be generally trustworthy, with 55 per cent having confidence in scientists advising the government on Covid-19.[95] These figures were higher than for many other groups involved in the pandemic, including politicians, and remained relatively stable. In the UK, 'confidence in healthcare professionals in the community to effectively deal with the coronavirus' rose from 71 to 79 per cent during the first twelve months of the crisis, whereas confidence in the capacity of Boris Johnson's government to meet the same challenge fell from 65 per cent at the beginning of February 2020 to 37 per cent a year later, the biggest fall amongst larger developed countries except Japan.[96] The support for scientists was on its own terms impressive, even more so if the middle band of a five-point trustworthy scale is added. Nonetheless, there was a solid minority of 13 per cent who found them untrustworthy or very untrustworthy, rising to 15 per cent in respect of those working with government. This was a large enough number to populate the anti-lockdown and anti-vaccination messaging on social media.

Scientific discourse in medicine, as elsewhere, was still vulnerable to failure. It took the leading medical journal, *The Lancet*, twelve years finally and fully to disown the most notorious attack on vaccination in the recent past. It had published an article in 1998, by Andrew Wakefield and colleagues, which suggested there was a link between the combined measles, mumps, and rubella injection (MMR) and autism in children. This relatively obscure, and, as it later transpired, partly fraudulent, piece of research mattered because it ignited a media storm, fed by the anti-vaccination community, and by parents anxious to find an explanation for their children's condition. Most of the stories were written not by specialist science reporters, but by journalists engaged in wider polemical debates.[97] The consequence was a fall in MMR vaccinations and a consequent rise in outbreaks of measles. More generally, the global scientific research community was now so large, and the pressure to publish so great, that poor-quality work was continually finding its way through the refereeing process and into journals, some of it manufactured by fake-paper factories.[98] Once published, it could be cited by those seeking to develop counter-narratives to the prevailing orthodoxy.

Although the coronavirus vaccine development programme was a triumph of disciplined, tested discovery, there was room for debate as it was rolled out at immense speed across populations. The full picture of risk could not be established solely by trials. Minor side effects occurred. Questions were raised about the length of protection generated by a particular dose, the timing of boosters, and the efficacy of vaccines against new variants. The balance of gain amongst those unlikely to be seriously affected by the earlier forms of Covid-19 was not always clear. Nonetheless, the reactions to a needle in the upper arm need to be placed in the context of earlier vaccines. In the case of smallpox, nineteenth-century public vaccinators, wholly ignorant of antiseptics, used a lancet to score a pattern of lines into the flesh in at least four places. Matter from an infant vaccinated eight days earlier was smeared into the cuts.[99] Parents had justifiable cause for concern.

Three centuries after the Enlightenment, the pursuit of knowledge through systematic rational enquiry was still open to question. Medicine was an applied example of a more general attack on the status of any form of accredited, disciplined, intellectual endeavour.[100] Devi Sridhar, Professor of Global Public Health at the University of Edinburgh, was a leading figure in the public debate about Covid-19, advising the Scottish government and making frequent appearances on national news programmes discussing the decisions taken by politicians and the consequences for the general public. She had enjoyed a distinguished academic career, including being the youngest ever American Rhodes Scholar at Oxford. This counted for nothing in attacks by 'influencers' on social media. She found herself accused of having no published scientific papers or being a plant for the Gates Foundation or for the World Economic Forum.[101] The leading scientists in the search for a vaccine became public figures, subject to every kind of social media abuse, up to and including death threats.[102] The communities editor of *New Scientist* gave a mordant summary of the life cycle of academic research: 'Study 3 years of degree. Study 3 more for PhD. Join lab, start working. Spend years studying problem. Form hypothesis, gather evidence. Test hypothesis, form conclusions. Report findings, clear peer review. Findings published, reported in press. Guy on internet: "Bullshit."'[103]

The self-sufficient judgement of vaccination critics was fuelled by the burgeoning wellness industry. The purchasers of an increasingly diverse and expensive range of supplements and remedies were the direct successors of early twentieth-century consumers who took 'a curious pleasure in experimenting with mysterious compounds'.[104] By the time of the pandemic, they had created an empire with an annual turnover calculated by McKinsey to be worth £1.5 trillion with a growth rate of between 5 and 10 per cent. 'Wellness enthusiasts,' it observed, 'are high-income consumers who actively follow brands on social media, track new-product launches, and are excited about innovations.'[105] Amongst them were to be found those who sought not merely to complement orthodox medicine but to by-pass it altogether. They regarded health as a personal choice, the consequence of disciplined living and nurtured natural immune systems. The individual was entirely responsible for their own body; no outside agency had the right to intervene in its management. The observable fact that Covid-19 mortality was conditioned by prior personal behaviour such as poor diet, smoking, and insufficient exercise demonstrated their argument. Their claim that the pandemic was invented in order that big pharma could make money from treatments subsidized and imposed by the state was seemingly borne out by Pfizer, which made nearly £27 billion in sales of its Covid-19 vaccine in 2021, doubling the company's overall profits.[106]

The wellness industry was embedded in digital communication. Its products were advertised and sold principally through social media. Overarching arguments about the philosophy of wellness and the iniquity of professional medicine were posted by entrepreneurs seeking to profit from the demand they created. The Centre for Countering Digital Hate reported in the spring of 2021 that two-thirds of all the anti-vaccine content shared or posted by Facebook between 1 February and 16 March of that year could be attributed to just twelve vendors of alternative medical products.[107] In a parallel study published in January 2021, the Bureau of Investigative Journalism found a plethora of sites on Facebook denigrating masks and vaccines and promoting 'immune-boosting' supplements.[108] It foregrounded the Health Freedom and Humanity account, which denied the existence of coronavirus and advertised bottles of spray claimed to cleanse the body and brain of the heavy metals allegedly deposited by vaccinations.[109] This was a year after the social media companies had proclaimed a policy of rejecting Covid-19 misinformation, and two months after Facebook, together with Google, had signed an agreement with the British government committing to 'the principle that no user or company should directly profit from Covid vaccine mis/disinformation. This removes an incentive for this type of content to be promoted, produced and circulated.'[110]

The major social media companies were not necessarily indifferent to the pandemic, which was running out of control in the country in which they were based, nor were they themselves opposed to vaccination and other orthodox medical interventions. However, they had created a business model and a set of algorithms that were continually working against their professed hostility to anti-Covid-19 propaganda.[111] Whilst for the most part they did not directly profit from such material, they gained from the increased flow of users to their sites and the consequent growth in revenue from other advertisers. Their software was designed to promote virality, the fastest possible flow of material to the largest audiences.[112] The WHO's 'Mythbusters' site, deliberately created to challenge false claims about immunity supplements and other products, stood little chance against the entrepreneurial promoters of monetized misinformation. Above all, the sheer scale of the sites prevented effective control of the content that they were attracting. Facebook by this time had almost three billion users. Attempts to censor information or close down accounts were repeatedly overwhelmed by new material. It was too expensive and complex a task to exercise the kind of policing which throughout the pandemic they were regularly promising to undertake.

There is evidence that the heterodox narratives reached a wide audience. At the beginning of the pandemic, Ofcom asked respondents whether they had 'come across any information/news about the coronavirus that you think has been false or misleading in the last week'.[113] Almost half the sample said they had done so in the first week, falling to one in seven in week fourteen, at least in part because once the initial excitement was over, they were consuming less news altogether. Just over a third of the respondents said they were concerned about the volume of false or misleading material they were exposed to. A particularly disruptive conspiracy theory that gained traction was the alleged threat from the 5G network that was under construction. A researcher in Bradford reported that 'we came up against some discussions where people thought 5G masts were being put up, and they're spraying out Covid every three or four days'.[114] In an international survey, this belief was shared by 9 per cent of the population in five countries.[115] Consequences followed, with at least sixty masts in Britain being set alight.[116] More generally, it was reported that 'exposure increased susceptibility to misinformation and negatively affects people's self-reported compliance with public health guidance'.[117] With 15 per cent of the international sample inverting cause and effect, believing that the coronavirus was invented so that governments could fulfil a long-held ambition to impose mandatory vaccination on their populations, there was a clear threat to the entire medical programme.

The term 'vaccine hesitancy' has been introduced to the discussion. It has value in that it embraces attitudes which range from mild caution to outright rejection. In another sense, however, it distracts attention from the key issue. Much of the analysis of conspiracy theories is concerned with states of mind, why beliefs are held, and how they are formed. In the case of vaccination, what matters is action. The coronavirus has no interest in whether an arm is being offered to a needle out of complete indifference, suppressed hostility, or boundless enthusiasm. In its initial formulation, 'hesitancy' was only measured once there was an available vaccine,[118] but in the crisis months of 2020, it was more widely applied to public attitudes to a future discovery.

The findings were a cause for concern. According to an authoritative survey by the Royal Society and the British Academy in October 2020, 'around thirty-six per cent indicated that they are uncertain or unlikely to be vaccinated against Covid'.[119] The successful deployment of a future vaccine was faced with an 'infodemic generated by: (1) distrust in science and selective use of expert authority, (2) distrust in pharmaceutical companies and government, (3) simplistic explanations, (4) use of emotion and anecdotes to impact rational decision-making; and, (5) development of information bubbles and echo chambers'.[120] Much the same account could be given of the nineteenth-century anti-smallpox campaign. A YouGov study on behalf of the Commission for Countering Digital Hate in the UK found that one in six 'probably', or 'definitely', would not get vaccinated, and that the greater the dependency on social media for news and information, the greater the likelihood of refusal.[121] Similar findings were reported in the *BMJ*. Use of social media was discovered to be 'highly predictive of the belief that vaccinations are unsafe'.[122] There was further alarm when the Household Longitudinal Survey reported, just as the first vaccinations were taking place, that 72 per cent of the Black population, 42 per cent of the Pakistani/Bangladeshi community, and 26 per cent of the non-UK/Irish White group, or Travellers, had no intention of accepting an injection.[123]

In the event, vaccine refusal in Britain was much lower than had been feared. There were two reasons for this. The first was the gap between intention and action. The online surveys were a snapshot of attitudes especially in relation to the state or to orthodox medicine They gave respondents a cost-free opportunity to express their griefs about various forms of authority. No one ever died of giving a negative answer to a pollster. Nor did they transmit an infection by refusing to commit to what at the time was a non-existent treatment with unknown effects. The results did not predict what people would do when a trialled vaccine was offered to them.[124] The second reason was that whilst conspiracy theories and huckster-driven misinformation continued to provide a negative commentary on the official battle against Covid-19, their actual impact on behaviour was less significant than long-standing inequalities, especially those of ethnicity.

As soon as the UK vaccine programme was launched, the ONS and the NHS began to report on attitudes and behaviour. At the time of the first injection, 'hesitancy' stood at 16 per cent of the population, the consequence of the year-long debate about the possible efficacy of a vaccine which had yet to be developed, tested, or approved. However, by the second half of January 2021, this had almost halved to 9 per cent, and it almost halved again to 4 per cent by the end of May.[125] In the middle of 2021, just 3 per cent of the population were recorded as refusing a vaccine that was offered to them.[126] Amongst the elderly, who were most at risk, take-up remained high throughout successive vaccine doses. By February 2022, only 2.7 per cent of those over sixty remained unvaccinated, one of the lowest levels in the world, and 91 per cent had received three doses. The principal reasons for refusal were uncertainty about long-term outcomes and short-term side effects, and a desire to just wait and see. The true representatives of the anti-vax campaigners on social media were those who reported that they simply did not think the vaccine would work or were opposed to vaccines in principle. In the ONS survey, they constituted respectively one in ten and one in eight of the small group who were fairly or very unlikely to refuse an invitation.[127]

More concerning was the continuity from hesitancy to non-take-up amongst ethnic minorities. The first report by the NHS on this issue in April 2021 covered the period from the beginning of the programme in December 2020. There was a striking gap between the most vaccinated population group, the White British at 94 per cent, and the least, the Black British Caribbean, at 62 per cent.[128] Those of Asian Indian and Pakistani heritage were between the poles at 86 and 73 per cent respectively. Despite widespread commentary and attempts to increase take-up, including a commitment by the government in January 2021 to spend £23 million countering misinformation in BAME communities,[129] the overall hierarchy of ethnic groups was little changed throughout the remainder of the year, and the gulf between the top and bottom closed only marginally. At the end of June, it stood at 95 to 66 per cent, and for the whole of 2021, it was 96 to 69 per cent of an ethnic group comprising just under six hundred thousand residents in England and Wales.[130]

Once any section of society fell behind on the first vaccination, there was a cumulative effect on the take-up of subsequent doses, which required a lapse of time before they could be administered. By the end of 2021, a third of the Black Caribbean group had received three injections, just half the level of the White British population.[131]

Across British society as a whole, poverty by itself was a less powerful cause of vaccine inequality. The NHS calculated that on the ten-stage index of multiple deprivation, those at the bottom of the table had a take-up of 90 per cent at the end of the first four months compared with 98 per cent amongst the least deprived. During the first year of vaccination as a whole, the ratio narrowed to five points.[132] The damage was caused when the experience of the labour market interacted with a long-standing alienation from the state and its agencies ranging from police, to education, to health. The chief executive of the Runnymede Trust attributed the low vaccine take-up of ethnic minorities to the 'deep-seated multigenerational reservations and fear that some people in BAME communities have about accessing the NHS'.[133] The UCL study found that 6.7 per cent of people from ethnic minorities who refused vaccines had 'experienced racial/ethnic discrimination in a medical setting since the start of the pandemic'.[134] Provision of facilities and treatment in their communities had been historically poor, as had levels of health from childbirth onwards. There was inadequate access to such services as were available, and a lack of trust in the performance of systems and personnel from GP surgeries to emergency care. A Parliamentary report found that 60 per cent of Black people did not believe that their health was protected by the NHS to the same extent as White people.[135]

There is little evidence that misinformation on social media was a decisive factor in the disparities in take-up once vaccines became available in Britain. Many ethnic communities paid little attention to any kind of official messaging in the mainstream media, and, as a consequence, younger, digitally active members had a disproportionate role in disseminating knowledge about the progress of the Covid-19 campaign. It was discovered that young Chinese residents were particularly influenced by sites operating in their own language, but there is no reason to suppose that the Black Caribbean community was exceptionally exposed to online disinformation in a way that the White British or Asian populations were not.[136] The sharp decline in vaccine hostility once the programme was rolled out demonstrated the extent to which social media theories flourished when everything was speculative. The most popular Covid-19 conspiracy in 2021 was that the coronavirus was manufactured in a laboratory in Wuhan, and either deliberately or accidentally released into the local population.[137] Given the censorship exercised by the Chinese government, it was very difficult finally to prove or disprove this thesis.[138]

The fast and authoritative approval process in Britain, and the belated discovery by the government of how to manage an efficient system in the pandemic, radically changed the rules of the debate. The more people who were vaccinated, the stronger the evidence of long-term impact and the less serious the incidence of short-term side effects. There were more problems in countries such as France, where there was a long-standing mistrust of big pharma, or the United States, where in the year before the pandemic the three least trusted of twenty-five leading organizations were 'the healthcare industry', 'the federal government', and, at the bottom, influenced by the opioid scandal, the 'pharmaceutical industry'.[139] A YouGov survey conducted in the summer of 2020 found that a third of the populations of the United States and France thought the proposition that 'rumours that side effects of vaccines being hidden' were '"definitely" or "probably" true', with just a fifth of the UK population agreeing. Out of twenty-one countries, only Denmark was lower.[140]

The debate called into question the depth of mistrust, not in orthodox channels, but in the content of digital sites. Suspension of belief worked in both directions. Just as the promoters of conspiracies and alternative medicines sought to undermine confidence in official information, so those who consumed this material out of curiosity or as an expression of other grievances had limited confidence in its integrity. 'My information about vaccines,' wrote a robust Mass Observation diarist, 'come mostly from the BBC news, occasionally from articles in The Guardian. I am not on Facebook, but I understand it has many anti-scientific, nonsensical, conspiracist rabbit holes for gullible users to fall into.'[141] 'I have no time or patience for anti-vaxxers,' wrote another, 'with their little tinfoil hats and their nutty theories about microchips and 5G and government surveillance.'[142] 'Overall,' concluded an international survey, 'we find that the majority of people in the countries we surveyed do not report finding misinformation about Covid credible, consistent with the spread of fake news in other contexts.'[143]

As it became clear that a global vaccination campaign was becoming a reality, the WHO issued guidance on its conduct: 'Community engagement,' it announced on 31 January 2021, 'should be at the centre of all COVID-19 vaccine introduction activities.'[144] At the heart of this approach was a particular mode of communication. It was essential that those who were still uncertain about the process should be able to discuss their doubts with familiar and trusted voices. Their concerns should be treated with respect. The questions they asked deserved to be heard; the answers needed to be framed in terms they could understand and discuss.[145] Whilst there was a need for a national flow of information about the vaccines and their administration, take-up was conditioned by a spatially confined network of information, particularly within those sectors of society that previously had displayed high levels of hesitancy.[146] There remained a role for digital media, with use made of neighbourhood or street-level WhatsApp groups. But the channels also included the distribution or display of print and posters, home visits by administrators, discussions in clubs or other social venues, and the staffing of vaccination centres by practitioners with appropriate language and social skills.

If the polling about vaccine intentions during 2020 had value, it was to alert authorities to the need for action at the community level once the vaccination programme became a reality. On 10 December, two days after the first vaccination in Britain, *The Lancet* set out what should now be best practice: 'In this new phase of the COVID-19 response, successful vaccine roll-out will only be achieved by ensuring effective community engagement, building local vaccine acceptability and confidence, and overcoming cultural, socio-economic, and political barriers that lead to mistrust and hinder uptake of vaccines.'[147] Particularly with regard to those with a well-founded mistrust of the health services, it was critical to 'adopt comprehensive local approaches that give communities a voice, and the necessary resources to put ideas into action'.[148] Case histories of successful initiatives were highlighted. In Liverpool, in place of the nationally administered vaccination centres, 'pop-up clinics' were established in neighbourhood centres, and medical students from BAME backgrounds, particularly Urdu- and Arabic-speakers, were recruited to help run them.[149]

Two prominent politicians from the Muslim community, Labour's Sadiq Khan, Mayor of London, and the Conservatives' Nadhim Zahawi, the vaccines minister, put aside their political differences and made a joint appeal for an effective partnership between central and local government. They announced that there was to be an expansion of the community champions scheme in order that

> communities have trusted local leaders who can help answer questions about the vaccine and work with the NHS and public health teams to support local communities. We are both working with faith leaders, grassroots organisations representing our diverse communities and charities and have listened to their ideas about how we can protect our communities from coronavirus and get vaccines to as many people as possible.[150]

According to Zahawi, vaccine hesitancy amongst Black and Asian communities halved between February and June 2021. Much depended on the strength of local organizations, and it may be that the continuing vaccination disparities within the ethnic communities were a reflection of the effectiveness of mosque-based networks and the comparative weakness of faith-based networks in Christian Black Caribbean neighbourhoods.

All the polling about Covid-19 beliefs and intentions, and all the consideration of best practice, established two truths that had become apparent at the end of the nineteenth-century struggle against smallpox. The first was that despite the noise made by the anti-vaccination campaigners in their publications and speeches, the real obstacle to take-up was inertia on the part of those taking the decisions; in the case of smallpox, the parents of the children who were to undergo the alarming medical intervention. The critical action was too often put off until some greater certainty or better opportunity. The 1896 Royal Commission debated whether to continue with a system of fines:

> Why, it is asked, should not vaccination cease to be compulsory altogether, and be left to the free choice of parents? If no penalty were attached to the failure to vaccinate, it is, we think, certain that a large number of children would remain unvaccinated from mere neglect on the part of their parents, or indisposition to incur the trouble involved, and not because they thought it better in the interest of their children. This appears to us to be a complete answer to the question.[151]

The second truth was that the best approach, as so often with Covid-19, was that adopted north of the border:

> We have no hesitation in expressing the opinion that the Scotch system is in some respects, to which we have called attention, superior to that prevailing in the other parts of the United Kingdom. Its great merit lies in this, that the defaulters are sought out at their own homes by the official vaccinator and then and there vaccinated by him, unless the parent objects or circumstances render postponement desirable.[152]

As would also be the case more than a century later, despite the revolution in communication technology, face-to-face conversation, with a known figure in familiar surroundings, was the most effective form of getting the message across.

Home

Lockdown

In its 2021–2 survey of consumer behaviour, the supermarket chain Waitrose celebrated a decisive change in British society. Demand for its products indicated that the prolonged experience of lockdown had 'transformed us into a nation of homebodies'.[1] 'The past year,' it concluded, 'has made us fall back in love with our homes.'[2] This excited verdict reflected the shift in consumer expenditure from restaurants and other public venues to the domestic arena. More money was being spent on a wider range of cooking ingredients and on a host of ancillary objects for use in the kitchen and other rooms in the house. It was a break with the past, the company hoped, that was created by and would outlast Covid-19.

After a series of missed deadlines, the pandemic officially began in Britain on 23 March 2020, with the prime minister's address to the nation: 'From this evening I must give the British people a very simple instruction – you must stay at home.'[3] Initially, the Covid-19 regulations were to be reviewed after three weeks, but the recurrent surges of infection meant that varying levels of instruction or advice to keep indoors remained operational for much of the following two years.

The controls, which the police were given powers to enforce, reversed two centuries of change in the balance of work and domesticity. During the industrial revolution, offices were increasingly separated from dwelling places, and manufacture was relocated from workshops below living accommodation to specialized factories. Making a living meant leaving and returning home at set times of the day. The term 'commuter' was coined for the users of the proliferating urban transit systems. By the beginning of the twenty-first century, it described the routines of much of the workforce. Then in the last week of March 2020, the roads fell silent, and the underground and the railway stations were deserted.

There were two categories of domestically confined workers: those on some form of furlough who were economically inactive; and those who were attempting to conduct their employment duties from their kitchen tables, the corners of their bedrooms, or hastily converted studies. In the autumn of 2020, with Covid-19 infections beginning to rise once more, 60 per cent of employees were back in offices or other external locations and 9 per cent were on furlough. Nearly 30 per cent were still working remotely, despite repeated urging by the government after the first peak of the pandemic that they should resume their old routines, if only to revive the retail and leisure industries which depended on them.[4] The chief secretary to the Treasury said he was 'keen to get people back in the office. . . . We think that's best for the economy, to get back to normal as part of our recovery.'[5] But ministers lacked the legal powers to force workers back to the office, and employers were reluctant to test their authority in the midst of the pandemic. Two years after the first lockdown, a quarter of all employees were still working from home, and a third of those aged thirty to forty-nine.[6] They resisted a return to the office partly because of continuing fears about exposure to the highly infectious Omicron version of the 'fatal Breath' on public transport and in crowded, poorly ventilated workplaces, and partly because they were in no hurry to recommence the time-consuming, body-tiring, spirit-wearing rituals of commuting.[7]

The desire of a significant minority of employees to make homeworking succeed in the long term reflected changes that were in train before the arrival of Covid-19. The erosion of the modern division between home and work began with the invention of the BlackBerry and the iPhone and the coming of a reliable, user-friendly internet. By the end of the second decade of the new century, about one in twenty of the employed and self-employed were already working fully from their domestic accommodation, and a further one in three were spending at least one day a week without the burden of the daily commute.[8] For a still larger proportion of the workforce, the arrival of digital communication meant that they had become accustomed to performing employment tasks at home in addition to a regular day in the office. A perceived benefit of the new regime was the prospect of a better work–life balance, where the conflicting demands of a family and job could be subjected to more effective personal control.[9] Aside from these operational considerations, there was an increasing awareness of the ecological benefits of reducing the circular journeys five days a week and diminishing the incidence of international plane travel for the sake of meetings that now could be conducted online.

Outside the realm of employment, the edict of 23 March imprisoned every member of the household. The social space outside the home and garden almost completely disappeared. Initially, no physical contact could be made with anyone beyond the front door. 'You should not be meeting friends,' instructed Boris Johnson. 'If your friends ask you to meet, you should say No. You should not be meeting family members who do not live in your home.'[10] Over time, a series of partial and reversible relaxations in the form of 'bubbles', tiered variations, differentiated national strategies, and shifts between regulation and advice altered the precise rules of confinement, but throughout the encounter with coronavirus there was a basic opposition between the physical boundary of the domestic unit and the world outside it. Whereas the young and healthy took such opportunities as were created to escape their homes, the 2.2 million people deemed 'clinically extremely vulnerable' were confined to their residences by instruction or advice until the special arrangements that had been made to ensure access to food supplies and other services were finally removed on 15 September 2021.[11] Even then, the shielded remained cautious about going out, particularly when the subsequent Omicron variant took hold.

In the midst of the crisis in late March 2020, it passed unnoticed that for the first time since the church courts of the seventeenth century, adultery in its classic form – engaging in sexual relations with a member of another household – had become illegal. There were elements of continuity in the Covid-19 regime. Since the Middle Ages, the front door, both in law and in custom, had constituted a basic barrier between the domestic unit and the outside world, no matter how frail its construction or whether it was adequately locked. Privacy was embodied not in the individual but in the household, which had the right to forbid access to neighbours, landlords, and agents of the state.[12] By the twentieth century, radical improvements in the construction of the housing stock were increasing the capacity of families to keep their lives to themselves. There was no longer any need to share sanitary facilities or escape from overcrowded interiors to join the life of the street. 'In England,' wrote Margery Spring Rice in 1939, 'side by side with the passionate wish to preserve the integrity of the family, there is found the determination to keep it as a whole *separate* as possible from other families and from any outside intrusion.'[13] The only major public inquiry into privacy in the era, the Younger Report of 1972, found that 'the modern middle class family . . . are probably more private in the sense of being unnoticed in all their everyday doings than any sizeable section of the population in any other time or place'.[14] By the beginning of the next century, this generalization applied to most of the population. 'The door is a crossing,' wrote Edwin Heathcote in his 2012 study of the home, 'a junction marking the divide between the realm of the public and the private, between the chaos of the unformed world outside and the sacrosanct order within, and as such it represents a profoundly symbolic moment that needs to be marked.'[15]

The government's requirement that the front door be kept shut except for a few specialized purposes was not, in this sense, a fundamental breach of accepted behaviour. The inclination of the general public immediately to accept lockdown, which surprised many observers, stemmed partly from the shared perception of the threat posed by Covid-19, and partly from the established practice of withdrawing behind the walls of the home. A host of material, marketing, and consumer practices had made household accommodation a place of unprecedented comfort and diversion. At a time of national crisis, it was the natural place of retreat. The difficulty was consent. The direction of travel in the modern era in all forms of social interaction was the substitution of collective regulation, whether legal or cultural, by private choice. Individuals might prefer to spend much of their time indoors in narrowly defined groups, but when they wished to mix with others in different ways in different places, they should be free to do so. This tension helped to explain the contrast between personal behaviour and emotions, which over the course of the pandemic remained remarkably stable, and the constant modifications to regulations and advice as the governments of the four nations sought to minimize what was perceived as an attack on basic liberties.

Despite the happy warriors of the upmarket grocer, the home was not the subject of a new love affair during Covid-19. Its strengths and values were too entrenched for so dramatic a change of sentiment, and there was too great a variation in domestic circumstances. Not everyone could participate in 'Trend Two' identified by Waitrose, 'The Return of the Dinner Party'.[16] Rather, the prolonged lockdown invited each home's occupants to reconsider the life they led behind their front doors. There were two fundamental questions, whose resolution varied according to temperament, material conditions, and exposure to the destabilizing impact of the coronavirus. The first was time. The furlough, homeworking, and home schooling, together with the enforced cancellation of the rituals, celebrations, and holidays that punctuated the annual round, removed most of the ways in which days, weeks, and months were structured and experienced. The longer lockdown lasted, the more acute the difficulty of exploiting the freedom from external calendars. There was a constant tension between the creation of fresh opportunities and the sheer weariness of life in the Covid-19 household.

The second question was personal relations. Face to face with the same people day in and day out invited at least tedium and at worst serious conflict from which it was almost impossible to escape. Conversely, there were opportunities to explore or discover new strengths in partners as the domestic unit dealt with the manifold threats of the pandemic. Parents, particularly fathers, spent increased time with their children, allowing them to learn more about who they were and how they were developing. Loneliness took on new forms as many of the outlets for socializing were removed. At the same time, solitude became a yet more prized experience in crowded houses which no one ever left.

Time

The most striking aspect of the spring of 2020 was how quickly households adjusted their behaviours in the light of the new regulations. It was not just a binary choice between acceptance and refusal. Instead, there was a swift and creative response to circumstances that were wholly unforeseeable three months earlier and had no precedent in the lives of any living adult. The managers of family economies took rapid actions, causing, as we have seen, the largest repayment of private credit since 1993 in the month following the imposition of lockdown. Where possible, the financial decks were cleared for what promised to be a prolonged and uncertain period of income and expenditure. Still more fundamentally, couples made immediate decisions about commencing or extending a family. At the Department of Health and Social Care, Nadine Dorries tweeted a week after lockdown: 'As the minister responsible for maternity services, I'm just wondering how busy we are going to be, nine months from now.'[17]

The answer was less than at the beginning of the year. Although she was a prolific author of historical romances, Dorries seemed to have little grasp of the extensive evidence of behaviour in past epidemics and natural disasters.[18] Where there was a major loss of life, conceptions were generally delayed until a stable future was re-established.[19] If there had been significant mortality amongst young families, there might then be a subsequent recovery in the birth rate in order to replace missing offspring. Covid-19 Britain initially conformed to the pattern. Births in the first quarter of 2021 were almost 4 per cent lower than they had been in the same period a year earlier, accelerating a downward trend since 2012.[20] This was a much smaller fall than the Covid-19-imposed contraction in weddings, further accelerating the number of children born outside marriage or a civil partnership. However, the absence of a collapse in employment and domestic income meant that, in the second half of 2021, the birth rate returned to the level of 2019 in Britain and other developed countries.[21] Given the momentum of the previous decade, forecasts of renewed strain in the economy, and the fact that Covid-19 deaths were concentrated amongst the elderly, it is unlikely that the long-term decline in reproduction will be reversed.

Unable to leave their homes except for the permitted daily exercise, household members hastened to change their recreational habits. As noted in the previous chapter, there was a surge in book sales. A sample survey conducted by Nielsen between 29 April and 1 May found that 41 per cent were reading more since lockdown, with the average time spent with a book increasing from 3.5 hours a week to six.[22] Only 10 per cent reported that they were so distracted or depressed by their new circumstances that they were reading less. According to the Reading Agency, eighteen- to twenty-four-year-olds, who might be supposed to be pining for their outside entertainments, had taken to books with particular enthusiasm.[23] At the same time, there was a rise in a form of recreation that had dominated homes until the arrival of social media. Ofcom calculated that at the peak of lockdown in April, the television was on for six hours and twenty-five minutes a day, a third higher than the same month a year earlier.[24] It was a matter of filling the spaces that were suddenly opening up in weekdays and weekends, and ensuring that as far as possible, the resources were present to occupy the coming months.

The sharpest change of all as lockdown became a possibility and then a reality was in shopping practices. 'People can feel it coming,' wrote Matt Hancock in his diary on 14 March. 'The streets are empty. Folk are cancelling engagements. Retailers released a joint letter asking people not to buy more than they need, as panic buying continues.'[25] There was an urgent search for items which were essential, but which also might easily become unavailable. A diarist with an unusually long temporal perspective explained her strategy:

> I feel very grateful that about three weeks ago, before all this kicked off, I could see the way things were going. Whether it's all my reading on social history on the second world war, but I said to George I thought we should get some supplies in. I'm sure he believed I was overreacting but the very next morning went down to Morrisons and brought lots of tinned goods, dried pasta, UHT milk, bottled water and lots of toilet rolls as they've been as valuable as gold and virtually unobtainable anywhere![26]

Other shoppers made bulk purchases of flour, yeast, and dried pasta.[27] Tinned food, which in most forms was increasingly obsolete, became suddenly attractive for its extended storage qualities.[28] Hand sanitizer was particularly in demand given the early emphasis on transmission by touch.[29] In the prevailing absence of a direct pharmacological treatment for Covid-19, paracetamol was purchased as a means of at least alleviating the early symptoms.[30] There were empty spaces as shops struggled to manage their supply chains in the first few weeks. The most notable shortages, particularly for bread flour and toilet rolls, were compounded by changes not in the volume but in the location of consumption. There was no overall increase, for instance, in the need for lavatory paper, but it was far from easy to repackage products prepared for large-scale delivery to hotels and offices into smaller units that could sit on supermarket shelves.[31] In the same way, bread flour, which previously had been dispatched in bulk to commercial bakers, now had to be turned into packets that could be placed in baskets and trolleys.

There were some changes in consumer behaviour that seemed more symbolic than practical. Demand for firewood suddenly increased at a

time when winter was ending rather than beginning, reflecting some ata-
vistic concern to protect the home against all eventualities. 'Kindwood',
a firm claiming to be 'the UK's first and only true sustainable firewood
brand', experienced a 320 per cent rise in sales at the beginning of lockdown.[32] There were altercations between shoppers competing for scarce
items, and arguments with supermarket staff attempting to police temporary rationing regulations. A Merseyside Tesco worker recounted her
experience:

> We've had people continuing to try and grab all of the pasta off the shelves
> despite clear signs saying 'max 2 per customer'. People who are still trying to
> buy too much are becoming aggressive at the tills when the cashiers try to
> take excessive products back. We've had to deal with the frustrations of people
> who can't find any bread, milk or toilet roll after the panic buyers have hit;
> people without any allergies not finding what they need and so hitting our
> 'Free From' section instead.[33]

There was much discussion in the press of 'panic buying', but for the
most part, shoppers were acting entirely rationally. As an early study of
the phenomenon stressed, the label was a misnomer.[34] In the midst of an
unprecedented national crisis, in Britain as elsewhere, people were rapidly laying in stores for which there was likely to be a demand over time.[35]
The shortages were caused not so much by excessive purchases as by most
people buying just a little more in the face of uncertainty.[36] With so much
that was unknown about the nature and duration of the pandemic, there
was every cause to ensure that the home was stocked with non-perishable
necessities, directly or indirectly linked to the threat to health.

The urgent behaviour of the managers of the domestic economies contrasted sharply with the litany of hesitation and delay that characterized
those who controlled the national strategy during this period. Had the
government started to hoard PPE, testing kits, and ventilators in earlier years, or, more immediately, on 24 January 2020, for instance, when
SAGE was told that there was now a serious threat to public health, or
on 11 March, when the WHO declared a global pandemic, thousands of
lives would have been saved and there would have been no need to spend
the rest of 2020 panic-buying medical necessities often at inflated prices
and of questionable quality.[37] Conversely, over-purchasing during the

disorderly process of issuing and managing contracts left the government spending more than £5 million a week in the summer of 2022 just storing around fourteen billion items of unused and increasingly unusable PPE in warehouses.[38]

The problem with the use of time began after the initial flurry of activity. Once the initial changes to life in the home had been made, and the necessary shopping undertaken, there was a dawning realization that lockdown existence was far from temporary. 'To begin with,' wrote a diarist on 12 May,

> there was plenty to do in the garden, and I busied myself with painting the shed – now ready to be used as a pseudo summer house. But as the new reality set in, I found that motivation started eluding me. Days began to merge with less being achieved. A week or so ago I read a social media post asking what we'd tell our grandchildren about our time during lock down, and it got me thinking – what would I tell them I'd been doing?[39]

Another diarist charted the decline since March in his spirit of enterprise:

> It is Wednesday, another day on the calendar ticks by. The days seem to yawn ahead, with a soft sigh. It is still the strangest thing, not going anywhere. We have stopped asking each other, 'What are we going to do today?, or, 'What have we got planned?' At the start of the 'Lockdown' time, I actually made a two page list of things to do. I am reluctant to look at it now, almost six weeks later, because it would look daunting, as if a stranger had written out a massive challenge list for me to achieve. All that has happened instead, has been a kind of apathy, covering everything, with a few bursts of activity in-between. A malaise, has crept in, even writing this journal comes into that category too.[40]

In the drama at the end of March 2020, everything was new. Rules had to be learned in fear of death or prosecution. Adjustments had to be made to every occupational or domestic routine. The basic household tasks of looking after children and feeding a family had to be reconsidered and replanned. But then one week began to follow another with little discernible change. 'After the first shock,' wrote a diarist, 'and then anxious excitement of contacting friends old and new my life has settled into a dull predictability: Getup, potter about, eat lunch go for walk, read, eat, read or watch a screen, bed.'[41] On the last day of the first complete lock-down, a Mass Observation witness summarized the leading characteristic of the life:

> The main one is boredom. Whilst social media and the press are bandying the message that we are 'doing our bit' etc, it doesn't take away the boredom of it all. Whilst we crave the respite of our homes when we are in the midst of a busy work week, when there is no variety from the four walls, when you are daily reminded that the walls are wonky, or that you need a trip to the tip (can't – they are closed) or that the living room floor desperately needs replacing but you can't afford to do so, it does eventually get tedious. . . . You start to long for bedtime, just to wake up and live Groundhog Day yet again and hopefully one day closer to freedom.[42]

Subsequent relaxations caused variations to the routines, but then Covid-19 forced a reluctant government to reimpose controls on movement. Further lockdowns lacked novelty in their impact. It is notable that whilst the initial event provoked an outpouring of diary entries as everything was without precedent and required recording and interpretation, later iterations seemed much less worthy of commentary. John Naughton's vivid online diary was concluded and collected into a single text after a hundred entries.[43] The international *Covid2020diary* slowed to a trickle and then ceased altogether in the midst of the third wave, despite the fact that the medical emergency was as acute as ever and the assault on social freedoms no less great. 'The pandemic has created a new boredom,' observed the writer Marina Warner a year into the crisis: 'not yawning lassitude, but foreboding, emptiness and a lack of expectation.'[44]

Weekdays ceased to be distinguishable one from another, weekends had less meaning for those working at home, and none at all for those on furlough or out of employment altogether. The shielded population of over two million people could look forward only to weekly online grocery deliveries. 'A sustained, long-run lockdown,' wrote the commentator Jonathan Freedland a month into the first lockdown, 'means that a vast stretch of undifferentiated time is unfurling ahead of us, stripped bare of the usual divisions and markers. We are facing a form of confinement that will not be brief. . . . Right now our lives resemble an unpunctuated sentence, shapeless and confusing.'[45] The private programme of birthdays, holidays, and social events was erased and replaced at best by an improvised sequence of online get-togethers. The calendar of public holidays was emptied of meaning. 'Suddenly I did not have to make use of my diary,' wrote a retired accountant, 'daily outings, appointments, nil. I kept "losing" days, very odd.'[46] The experience was variously described as 'a week's worth of Sundays', or 'opening a cupboard and ninety Bank Holidays tumble out'.[47]

A diarist struggled to find something new to write about, because, as she explained, 'essentially the days/weeks are like Groundhog Day and nothing seems too different from one day to the next. . . . I know we are so fortunate not to be ill or immediately suffering the effects of Covid but "treading treacle" (as it feels like at the moment) is hard work.'[48] Although the observers of the non-Christian faiths made determined efforts to maintain their festivals, there was less commitment to the now mostly secularized Christian events. Good Friday and Easter Sunday, three weeks into the first lockdown, had never seemed to have less meaning.[49] At the end of the year, Christmas was all but cancelled as the government struggled in vain to avert a further lockdown.

The principal differentials between one day and another were the updated tables of infections, hospital admissions, and deaths, and the regular televised briefings by the leaders of the devolved national administrations and their scientific advisers. At the height of the waves of Covid-19, the hours stretched out between rising and retiring for those not directly involved in the crisis. A large-scale French study conducted in the midst of the first lockdown found that 'time seemed to pass more slowly during lockdown compared to before. This feeling of a slowing down of time has little to do with living conditions during lockdown and individual psychological characteristics. The main predictor of this time experience was boredom partly mediated by the lack of activity.'[50] There was a general consequence for sleep patterns and a more specific incidence of 'brain fog', which described various forms of limited cognitive function, including memory loss and problem solving.[51]

Amidst the tedium, there was an enhanced opportunity to commune with the inner self and its development.[52] The present moment was emptied of urgency, leaving space for conversations with former identities. In a material sense, the objects that filled the home, bearing signals from earlier times, were subject to review. The diaries of the first lockdown describe bouts of spring cleaning as the days lengthened, and long-postponed projects to go through the accumulated clutter of a domestic unit.[53] It was partly a matter of assessing what still was useful in the home, and queues built up at household recycling centres once they re-opened. And it was partly an exercise in finding meaning in recollection. Online genealogy sites were interrogated to complete family trees that had been started but abandoned in busier times.[54] Standing still in order to stay alive provoked curiosity about the journeys that had been undertaken to this moment of crisis. An elderly woman enjoyed sorting through fifty years of family photographs, distributing duplicates to children and friends with whom she had shared her life.[55] With overseas holidays suspended, another made 'an inventory of all our different, eclectic possessions inherited, and collected from our travels abroad. Pleasure strangely mingled with a sort of bereavement/sadness as it had prompted lots of happy memories, but now left a void about what I would "DO" next!'[56]

That void demanded a more relaxed balance of planning and retrospection. The mind was free to revisit past actions but had to learn not to think less of the passing week because fewer objectives had been achieved. 'Honestly,' advised the writer Anne Enright,

> there's a lot to be said for tooling about all day, looking up recipes and not making them, not bothering to paint the living room and failing to write a novel. In the middle of the messy non-event called your mid-afternoon, you might get something – a thought to jot down, a piece of gossip to text to a pal. Boredom is a productive state so long as you don't let it go sour on you.[57]

A solution to this challenge was to place more emphasis on domestic rituals and routines. One of the less predictable shortages in the pandemic shopping surge was eggcups.[58] With families freed from the tyranny of commuting and the school run, it was no longer necessary to consume breakfast on the go.[59] Instead, a proper meal could be cooked and consumed. During the week, increased effort was invested in preparing food and bringing the household around a table at set times.[60] 'We are baking and cooking,' wrote a lockdown diarist, 'and it gives a sense of purpose and meals shape the day.'[61] The shop-emptying demand for bread flour in the early phase of lockdown reflected a desire to enjoy the result of the slow process of mixing, kneading, and proving. More emphasis was given to the ceremonies of eating. Waitrose reported that over a third of its survey had introduced a 'happy hour' of drinks at the end of what was not necessarily a working day, for which they were purchasing a wider range of aperitifs.[62]

For parents and much of the pre-retirement population, planning the day had been in the hands of external authority in the classroom or the workplace or the timetables of public transport. Through the use of online lessons and conferencing, external discipline gradually invaded the lockdown home, but there remained extensive areas of domestic responsibility for organizing the passing hours. Household managers took pride in their new time-management skills. It was no easy matter ensuring that study, exercise, meals, and downtime were organized in the interests of frequently mutinous children whose principal ambition was just to hang out with their friends, or, failing that, to be left alone to explore the online universe.

For those with less pressing responsibilities, there was the possibility of structuring the unforgiving hour by the revival or embrace of time-consuming hobbies. A shielded woman explained:

> Today is a good day. I've got a proper routine for myself these days. My husband and I went into self-isolation on the 17th March, with virus symptoms, and have barely left the house since. . . . The husband will be home for lunch shortly; after that I've got some art to do. I've been completing art challenges – partly to keep busy, partly to improve – with a group of friends. It's great to see what we make of each theme! I know I wouldn't have the time out of lockdown, so I am grateful for that.[63]

Amongst the winners in the lockdown economy were the retailers of do-it-yourself products and the industry servicing domestic hobbies. Despite the intermittent closure of their stores, Kingfisher, owner of B&Q and Screwfix, made record profits during the pandemic.[64] Hobbycraft, which claimed to stock twenty thousand products for two hundred and fifty activities, saw their business double during the year.[65] According to the social psychologist Daisy Fancourt, 'Creative hobbies and learning new skills can help by distracting people from their worries; it can help them come to terms with or reappraise things and get a new perspective; plus it can really boost confidence and self-esteem.'[66] They were by their nature an absorbing escape from the pressing drama of Covid-19, and, unlike much else in the lockdown home, yielded a practical return for the investment of time. 'I've been painting,' recorded a diarist, 'experimenting with new ideas, taking part in some of the challenges set by various groups, where they interest me and it has actually been a very creative time. I bought a small etching press and have been doing some printmaking for the first time in many years.'[67] The concentrated, repetitive use of the hands was a means of creating the mental space in which more extensive interior exploration could be conducted. 'It is only a small test piece,' explained a woman working on her tapestry, 'but there is something so soothingly meditative about weaving. There is no space to be anything but calm when moving the thread in and out, building a picture slowly.'[68]

Human planning, creativity, and endeavour helped to structure the pandemic day in the home. And then, as we saw in chapter 6, there were the permitted daily engagements with the temporal cycles of nature and the discipline enforced by pets. A major insurer calculated that 5.7 million new pets were bought in the first six months of lockdown.[69] It was not just a question of dogs requiring their daily walks. There were almost as many cats in lockdown homes, and their owners insisted that they, too, imposed their own timetables of care. 'We found ourselves losing track of time,' wrote John Naughton, 'and realising with a start that it was 6.30pm and we hadn't given a thought to supper. In fact it got to the point where the only creatures in the house who had any sense of time were the cats.'[70] Almost any living creature required regular attention. 'Fish-keeping is a hobby that requires a degree of involvement from easy through to very sophisticated,' explained the chief executive of Pets at Home. 'It is very rewarding. A fish tank is an incredibly peaceful thing to have in your home. . . . Fish-keeping is a practical choice but also provides a mental workout as owners must grapple with maths, physics and biology to keep their fish alive – and that's before you get into what type of fish you are going to own.'[71] In all sorts of ways, pets supported the need to structure time, although a woman in Spain was rightly fined for insisting that the national regulations allowed her to take her tortoise for a daily walk.[72]

Like every other resource in the response to Covid-19, time was a function of circumstance and prosperity. Even amongst the relatively fortunate witnesses of the pandemic who patterned their experience by keeping diaries, there were variations in the freedom to organize their days. 'One thing that really wound me up when we were in the deepest, darkest days of lockdown,' wrote a woman looking after her school-age child and a dependent mother, 'was everyone on the radio/tv/social media etc going on about how much time they had to do exercise/learn a new language/ bake frickin' sourdough bread. I've never had less time. It was just all work, schooling, housework, eat, sleep, repeat.'[73] Another diarist, 'suffering from Zoom overload, conference call chaos & desperate to keep my own small business afloat', recorded her bemusement when hailed by a friend with the greeting, 'Isn't this lockdown divine. . . . AT LAST I've got time to tackle my tapestry.'[74] Hospital staff, from nurses to consultants, spent the entire pandemic in a state of exhaustion, first from attending to Covid-19 patients and then catching up with the backlog of conventional illness. They came home only to collapse into bed. There was little or no time for interior reflection or taking up neglected pastimes. The same was true of less celebrated employees, for instance those filling supermarket shelves during long nights or spending spirit-sapping days dealing with ill-tempered customers. In one of the 'key worker diaries' collected by the Joseph Rowntree Foundation, a wife reported her husband's work routine:

> Adam got home from his night shift at Asda at 6:20am. It was his 4th night in a row and to say he's exhausted is an understatement. He told me last night was very full on, they had a huge delivery come in, which is great to know as the shelves are becoming better stocked again but tiring for the people working around the clock to keep up the pace.[75]

The consequence of poverty was measured by the availability of free time. Much of a week could be consumed assembling family meals from a combination of food charities, state benefits (when they were available), and ever more ingenious ways of making limited resources go further. A Nigerian migrant described her weeks: 'I have run out of basic things such as bread, eggs and cereals. I've been forced to use food banks and need support from charities in order to get basic things such as period products and toilet rolls.'[76] Not for this level of society the planning and preparation of elaborate meals using novel ingredients, preceded by a 'happy hour'. 'We had toast and milk for supper,' reported a key worker, 'with some salad on the side. I try to make sure the children have the most balanced diet I can give them but this is going to get harder at a time when they need the vitamins to boost their immune system the most.'[77] Although the category of key worker embraced all levels of income, the preponderance were manual workers, disproportionately from ethnic minorities. They were still subject to the routines of public transport, returning to households which were struggling to manage the changing restrictions. Where home schooling might be absorbed into the business of households already equipped with the necessary computing facilities and competencies, the closure of classrooms imposed immense strains on parents faced with the unfamiliar demands of online instruction at set times in the day. Without spacious bedrooms or large gardens in which to pursue personal activities, everyone's agenda had constantly to be negotiated with every other family member.

Then there was Covid-19 itself. The low-level anxiety that accompanied every witness of the pandemic was essentially the product of an inability to control the passage of time, never knowing when or whether the infection would reach into a home or take the life of a close relative. If the worst case happened, all grasp on the present and future was destroyed. In a matter of three weeks or so, an entire life could run out, from full fitness to a body bag, from participation in a wealth of social networks to a lonely, sparsely attended funeral.

Personal Relations

Throughout the pandemic, many household members spent more time in each other's company than they had ever imagined possible. At its most welcome, the sequence of regulated and self-policed withdrawal caused a fundamental reconsideration of the work–life balance. A Mass Observation diarist, who had been in hospital before the pandemic, celebrated his good fortune:

> Normally I am a commuter. I spend long hours travelling to London and back. I think I am enjoying the lockdown the most. Since my illness forced me to take a break from work, for the first time in many years I have been able just to be with my family at home. I imagine there are many others like me who are enjoying this forced break from commuting life.[78]

The change was particularly valued in the early years of a family. One year might seem much like another in a long-term adult relationship, but if insufficient attention was given to the formative period of young children because of the demands of commuting and long office hours, the loss could not be made up later. The father of a fifteen-month-old son celebrated what he described as his 'unexpected second paternity leave'. He had not needed to find his own diversions in lockdown, 'because instead I've been far too busy getting on with my new and all-consuming preoccupation: enjoying the wonderful gift of finally being able to hang out with my son, full time, all day and (more often than not) all through the night as well'.[79] Even when they lacked the excuse of commuting, men on average tended to spend less time on family responsibilities than women, but the gap had been reduced. The ONS reported in May 2020 that there had been a 58 per cent growth in childcare undertaken by men, increasing their contribution from 39 per cent in 2015 to 64 per cent during the first lockdown.[80]

The change in priorities was reflected in the consumer market. At the beginning of lockdown, shoppers did not confine their emergency purchases to such practical necessities as toilet paper and hand sanitizer. In the first week of domestic confinement, the sale of board games and jigsaw puzzles increased by 240 per cent.[81] John Lewis experienced more demand for these items than in its normal peak period of Christmas. During 2020, there was a growth of more than a third in the purchase of puzzles. The market leader, the German firm Ravensberger, struggled to meet global purchases of an additional twenty-eight million boxes, with particularly strong sales in the UK.[82] There was little novelty in the trade. Puzzles of every size, difficulty, and price had become widely available between the wars with the invention of dye-pressed cardboard pictures.[83] There were products designed for all age groups from toddlers to the elderly with time on their hands. The only noticeable change in the pandemic was an increased market for thousand-piece challenges. There was a similar surge in the purchase of classic board games such as Monopoly, Cluedo, and Scrabble. Hornby, manufacturers of train sets since the early decades of the twentieth century, which had experienced a chequered recent history in the face of competition from computer games, saw a renewed growth in its market.[84] LEGO, whose construction kits now embraced all levels of complexity, expanded their sales by over a fifth in the first year of the pandemic and nearly a quarter in 2021.[85]

The proliferation of domestic pastimes reflected the long period of growth in the home as a place of recreation and consumption.[86] 'Family life is both communal and individual,' explained the Parker Morris Report of 1961, which set out standards for public and private housing. 'There is the process of coming together for activities in which the family joins as a whole – meals, conversation, common pursuits, and so on; and there is the need for privacy to pursue individual activities such as reading, writing, and following particular hobbies.'[87] The reduction in family size and the increasing provision of dry, heated, sound-proofed, and illuminated rooms made it possible to conduct a wide range of activities during the course of the day, and retreat to separate bedrooms at night. The street ceased to be a location of pastimes and social interaction. The coming of television entrenched the living room as the basic location of entertainment, later distributed to other rooms as sets became portable and were succeeded by laptops and iPhones. At least in the short term, those confined to their homes had plenty of recreations to which they could turn, and no shortage of ways of supplementing them through online shopping. In March 2020, the proportion of retail sales made over the internet jumped from a fifth to almost a third, peaking at 38 per cent in the January 2021 lockdown before falling back to just over a quarter in March 2022.[88] In addition, there was the proliferating range of digital diversions which were examined in the preceding chapter.

It is impossible to draw a firm line between those pastimes that enabled individuals to retreat from each other's company, and those that generated increased levels of family sociability. Puzzles could be undertaken as personal or joint projects. There were adults as well as children extending their train sets during lockdown or turning to model making. Board games might be confined to children or fall within the category of 'kid-ult' entertainments which bound the generations together. Hobbies and pastimes, such as the tapestry weaving which a number of diarists practised, were private undertakings for show to the family once they were completed, as were do-it-yourself projects around the home.

Cooking was a case in point. Waitrose reported that 41 per cent of its sample were taking more pleasure in eating together.[89] There was a renewed interest in preparing meals, founded both on more ambitious menus and on the revival of skills long since overwhelmed by the demands of commuting and office work.[90] Thus a retired university professor celebrated the activities of both herself and her husband:

> I have also spent more time in my kitchen. I rediscovered how to use a bread maker (last used 12 years ago when my son was born). The suppliers dropped food we didn't usually use and both myself and my male partner cooked in different ways. He made soup – he hasn't done that in 20 years. I invented things and 'made do' but still felt we were eating well and it was exciting not to have everything conveniently packaged. I felt a connection with the women in war-time and I thought of my grandmother and her generation, their words and phrases and recipes started to come back into my head. I felt somehow more like a real mother, than the professional that orders things in from Waitrose and opens vegetable packets.[91]

With restaurants closed, there was also exploitation of a more recent innovation, the purchase of prepared 'meal kits' which required completion at home. Sales of the market leader, HelloFresh, more than doubled during the first period of lockdown.[92] The hours in the kitchen were both a personal satisfaction and a contribution to the wellbeing of the household. From eating together at regular times to playing games after the day's tasks were finished, there was an enhanced awareness of the interdependency of the domestic unit, no matter what the level of prosperity. A Polish social care support worker, struggling to feed her children, celebrated what could be done together amidst the crisis: 'My eldest daughter has made a wonderful roast dinner for us all and afterwards we enjoyed playing Pictionary. The pandemic is making it clear what is precious in my life, and my family means everything to me. It's for them that I work so hard and carry on.'[93]

There were unpredictable variations in personal choice and intimacy whilst the economy was closed down. With offices shut and most excursions from the home confined to daily exercise, there was less concern about personal appearance. Wardrobes were not refreshed with the same urgency. It remained possible to purchase occasional new items online, but the absence of hairdressers for months on end posed a more serious problem. A woman in her sixties, who had been dyeing her hair back to her 'schoolgirl blond' for the past fifteen years at an annual cost of some

£600, decided to give way to her years. 'The beauty of my natural grey hair begins to feel "right",' she explained, 'and freeing, as if I'm shedding a raw, unpolished persona – an authentic, more elegant me emerging from the shackles of moody youth. . . . The Covid-induced lockdown has forced me to let go of my negativity towards the visual signs of ageing and given me the courage to wear my grey with pride.'[94] An unknowable outcome of Covid-19 is whether there will be a permanent increase in the proportion of grey or white heads in the population, and a consequent loss to the hairdressing industry.

For those who decided to deal with their roots or their lengthening locks, there was no option but to trust to their own or their partner's capacity to learn and apply new skills. 'I cut my hair for the second time during lockdown,' reported a diarist on 16 June 2020. 'It's odd, even if it went okay the first time, it doesn't give you any extra confidence for the next attempt. Anyway, it looks fine, much the same as before, but I'll be glad when a professional can do it again. I find it nerve-racking.'[95] The operation required courage and forbearance in equal measure.[96] The stakes were far higher than trying out a new recipe or conducting a household repair. A relieved Covid-19 witness celebrated his achievement:

> Today was a first! I had to dye my wife's hair to overcome the grey that was starting to show through! Never done that before but needs must in the lockdown! . . . We watched a YouTube video first, to give me some idea of what I was supposed to be doing. I did my best and the results met with my wife's approval. She thought that, in the circumstances, it was first class. So PHEW! Glad I got that right.[97]

Amongst the increases in demand in the spring of 2020 were domestic hair-clippers, which soon became unobtainable. However, some households were in luck and could disinter this long-unused device from the back of a cupboard. 'George has found a pair of electric hair clippers that had never been out of the box,' reported a diarist,

> and wanted me to trim his hair, so we turned the kitchen into a barbers. I put a dust sheet down and then started. I started carefully with a grade 4. I don't think I made too bad a job of it. George was certainly impressed and said afterwards he didn't think he'd go back to the hairdressers again. High praise

indeed! . . . Then down came a tiny blue tit and gathered up bits of George's hair that were still laying around on the lawn.[98]

There is a tension in all the accounts between apprehension and relief. Successful outcomes displayed a hitherto unexplored area of service and dependency in a partnership.

There was less of a course of learning in the more profound form of intimate relations. The most thorough early report on sexual practices, conducted in July and August 2020, reached the unsurprising conclusion that the principal loss was amongst those who were not cohabiting. In general, the evidence indicated that 'most people in Britain were sexually active following the initial national lockdown'.[99] Where couples were already sharing a bed, there was only a small decline, possibly as a consequence of the difficulty of finding sufficient privacy in a suddenly crowded household.[100] But where the relationship was being conducted at a distance, or where, more particularly, it had yet to reach the stage of regular intimacy, there were greater problems. The study found that only a quarter of those not in a steady relationship at the onset of the crisis were engaging in partnered sex.[101] The small minority who practised intimate physical contact outside the household tended to be young and associated with reported risk factors such as condomless sex and higher alcohol consumption.[102] There was some anecdotal reporting on the growth of non-partnered sexual activity, although the evidence was thin, as was an adequate pre-pandemic baseline. The lockdown shopping surge included condoms.[103] Whether they were for immediate use or were a further dimension of cautionary hoarding remains unclear. There was a striking change in the level of sexually transmitted infections in England. These had been largely stable throughout the previous decade but suddenly fell by 34 per cent between 2019 and 2020, rising by only 1 per cent in 2021.[104] This was a consequence of less risk-taking, fewer sexual partners, and also under-reporting and under-diagnosis, storing up problems for the future in this area as in so many aspects of non-Covid-19 ill-health.[105]

A central problem in personal relations of every kind was not that they were impractical, but that they became frozen in the form they had assumed before lockdown. Troubled intimacies could not find the space for repair or escape. Setting aside the particular issue of domestic abuse discussed in chapter 3, it was not easy to explore alternative ways of living during the pandemic. Ending a relationship, finding new accommodation, dealing with children who might now belong to two separate households, posed all kinds of practical difficulties in a binary world of permitted and forbidden contact. Equally, the process of developing a new emotional and sexual connection, exploring its potential, taking decisions about when, whether, and where to set up home together, was endlessly complicated by the phases of control and relaxation of social intercourse. Young people seeking to come out found themselves trapped in potentially homophobic families. In any given week, according to national regulations, it was legal or illegal to meet with a potential partner. At one point, a lover could be arrested crossing from England into Wales to conduct a courtship. Internet dating was only the preliminary for face-to-face encounters, not a substitute. Social media supplemented rather than replicated physical touch and embrace.

For a settled household, alteration was constant but difficult to frame. Previously, family members had left each other's company to engage in different narratives of challenge and achievement at school or in the workplace, which they might or might not share with other family members on their return home. Under lockdown, they were in each other's presence from the beginning to the end of the day, but the repetitive round of internet meetings and walks and meals and games clouded the sense of change in personal identities. The ceremonial measurements of development, particularly birthdays, either were abolished or shrunk to token domestic events, possibly extended by an internet link-up (hence the particular outrage in January 2022 when Johnson was found to have celebrated his fifty-sixth birthday on 19 June 2020 with a party and cake in the Cabinet room in Number 10 and a further party in the garden).[106] There were in addition no weddings or other rites of passage. Less structured encounters in pubs, coffee shops, and restaurants where it was possible to catch up with the lives of other relatives and friends became fugitive events.

Holidays were cancelled, the cost reclaimed, re-booked for the following year, and then cancelled and reclaimed once more.[107] The Mass Observation diaries, completed in many cases by the comfortable middle class, revealed just how embedded overseas travel had become in the annual round. The pandemic turned events which once had been taken for granted into forbidden luxuries. Thus a contributor lamented the scale of his loss early in the pandemic:

> The other thing that has changed in the last 2 weeks has been that I have can-
> celled all of my holidays for the near future. I should be in Berlin right now.
> That clearly didn't happen. I should be in Basel next weekend visiting my best
> friend – that now isn't happening until August. The cruise I was going on in
> July to the Baltic I've moved to 2021 instead.[108]

The following year seemed no more secure, despite the new vaccine programme. 'It doesn't make me feel safer about foreign holidays,' wrote a
retired librarian, 'and I will be cancelling my holiday to Italy booked for
October. I am going to Shropshire in August on a coach holiday.'[109]

The cancellations also removed the means by which memories were
created and celebrated. There was, for this reason, a particular pleasure
in those born during the pandemic. They had a presence in time which
transcended the drama of Covid-19, however long it lasted. 'This baby,'
wrote a pregnant mother, 'has become a beam of light in the middle of
a dark storm. . . . I love this baby even more, knowing that we are going
through this together.'[110] Once they came into the world, they disrupted
and dominated domestic routines for reasons that had nothing to do with
the coronavirus. The mother of a seven-month-old revelled in her baby's
immunity from the vast disordering of everyday life:

> She sleeps and feeds and plays with her jungle gym, blissfully unaware of how
> life has been upended across the globe. . . . Life stopped in the blink of an eye.
> . . . Yet still my baby smiles at me in the way she always has. And I have begun
> to watch her habits more closely than before. . . . There may be fewer faces to
> examine on our walks, but she absorbs herself in the beauty of the flowers, the
> trees and the faded façades of painted houses.[111]

She celebrated how her small child was insulated from the calendar of
misfortune:

> As I watch my baby each day, I know we can control one thing at least: our
> response to this. . . . I watch her tolerate the empty days, not worrying about
> tomorrow or wallowing in yesterday, but just staying present in each and every

moment. . . . When this ends, those dresses in her drawer won't fit. But I will smile, knowing that while our society, our economy, our productivity, our minds, our achievements, and our dreams were forced to slow down, the growth of a little baby continued, unhindered.[112]

However, as soon as external timetables became a reality, the sense of dislocation caused by the Covid-19 confinement bore in on both parent and child, generating a range of disruptive behaviours as arrangements were constantly revised. A care worker and mother of a three-year-old recounted the growing difficulties:

> Today was a challenging one. It's been tantrum after tantrum with my son. He usually has a good routine going but that's out of the window at the moment. He doesn't understand why he can't go to nursery or why he's not seeing his friends, family, or why we can't go to the park. He's missing it all. Normal life as he knows it has just disappeared. It must be so weird for him. He's at an age where he knows something is up but is too young to understand what is happening.[113]

At least the parent could be present as small infants went through their early stages of growth, and toddlers took their first steps and pronounced their early words. Amongst the major victims of lockdown were those who were excluded from the unrepeatable events in family life. New fathers were forbidden from attending childbirth on a scale not seen for at least two generations. Grandparents were reduced to video meetings in which the youngest generation had little or no interest. Whereas some features of the domestic calendar, including holidays or even weddings, could be postponed until the Covid-19 controls were lifted, there were others, such as the growth stages of children, which were either witnessed at the time or lost forever. At the other end of the life course, funerals could be delayed for a few weeks, or the interment separated from a later memorial service, but for the most part death shrank the supportive unit, locking the grief into the remaining household.

The household was the focal point, not the boundary, of family life. It was the centre of networks which, despite the efforts that were made, could only atrophy as the initial lockdown turned into nearly two years of full or partial confinement. The home was at once impoverished and enriched by the quarantine regulations. With its members no longer absent for long periods of the day, there were opportunities for finding fresh value in each other's company and developing a new understanding of the mutual dependency which was the centre of any well-founded social network. The long-established consumer market ensured that all but the most deprived domestic units had access to a wide range of entertainments and diversions. At the same time, the sense of imprisonment grew once the early drama subsided into a sequence of release and reimposition from March 2020 to February 2022. In the long term, there were contrasting outcomes: an increasing sense of loss as the necessary developments in family life were put on hold; a growing sense of tedium as the currency of change in the home was devalued. And throughout there was a persistent apprehension as the 'fatal Breath' reached inside the front door, placing each member at risk from those closest to them. Whilst the consequences in the early waves might be lethal, the sheer infectiousness of Omicron in the winter and spring of 2021/2, made every member of the household a mutual threat. As noted in chapter 6, the only really safe setting for the occupants of a home during the pandemic was out of doors in their garden, should it exist and be of sufficient size.

Solitude

The recurrent lockdowns had a complex effect on the balance between sociability and solitude in the home. The most obvious outcome was an intensification of interactions between all members of the household, and a corresponding reduction in contacts with family, friends, and colleagues elsewhere. With the schools closed altogether in the first phase of lockdown, and around half the workforce initially either on furlough or working from makeshift offices around the house, it was difficult to avoid the company of partners and children, especially in smaller residences with little or no outdoor space. This had the effect of driving up the demand for time alone. The *UCL COVID-19 Social Study* on two occasions asked its sample what they were missing most in the pandemic. Meeting with outside friends and family was consistently the main aspiration. But almost a third of the respondents in May 2020, and over a fifth in February 2021, reported a longing for 'having time on your own'.[114]

The finding in the midst of the first lockdown was six times higher than the corresponding ONS figure for reported acute loneliness.[115]

Care has to be taken with this measure. Unlike loneliness, solitude has almost never been counted. There is no baseline to compare with the ONS or UCL surveys and there are no parallel quantitative studies. The most that can be said is that at least as many people appeared to be seeking their own company as were concerned by the absence of others. To a greater extent than loneliness, the desire for solitude was skewed by age. In the second UCL survey, 38 per cent of the young, 22 per cent of the middle-aged, but only 8 per cent of the elderly were in in search of more peace and quiet.[116] This may reflect how older members of society had come to terms with their ways of living. Some already lived by themselves and had all the peace and quiet they would ever need. Others had worked out how to live with their partners, respecting each other's boundaries, knowing when to engage and when to find time and space by themselves.

The young and middle-aged were more likely to be living with other family members, or more uncertain about the levels of sociability they required in a time of crisis. The central issue was simply the absence of privacy. The long arc of change in domestic living was partially reversed in the pandemic. For most of the working-class population at the beginning of the twentieth century, the whole of daytime family life had been conducted in the kitchen, which was usually the only warm and adequately lit room in the accommodation. Over time, household sizes had shrunk and more specialized, usable living spaces had emerged, allowing those still at home to retreat to private spaces to conduct their own activities, or just read or listen to music. Now, once again, too many activities were going on in too few rooms. 'As it happens,' wrote Stig Abell of *The Times* a month into the first lockdown, 'my own current difficulty is not isolation, but overcrowding. I reside cheek by jowl with my wife, my chosen partner in life's great quarantine, and three children who never leave.'[117] Solitude mattered on a daily basis, and it acquired a particular significance during bereavement. There was an often unmet need for the presence and comfort of others at such a time, but also for the ability to retreat and mourn a loss. 'I wanted to be alone,' wrote the daughter of a Covid-19 victim, 'which I realise is a privilege of falling into the category of frazzled parents, especially women, with young children whose problem during lockdown was not isolation, but the impossibility of carving out a goddamn moment of peace.'[118]

Finding space for yourself was a matter of negotiation with other members of the household. Through some combination of trust, goodwill, and mutual knowledge, it was understood that there was an intermittent need for withdrawal from company and from the tasks which needed performing for the wellbeing of the domestic unit as a whole. 'Lockdown has taught me how important it is for me to be on my own every once in a while,' wrote a civil servant working from home. 'I am starting to claw a bit of time back (for example coming upstairs to write this today) but I think I need more. I need quiet in my mind and that's difficult with an extrovert partner and a lively five year-old boy.'[119] Properly managed, times of absence within an intimate relationship were a reflection of its strength rather than its weakness. There were always problems of adjustment as the dynamics of the home changed, and these worsened under lockdown. Initially, the freedom from the constraints of commuting, and from working at all for those on furlough, reduced the pressure on time. There appeared to be more opportunities for pursuing individual projects, and, as we have seen, there were the permitted daily walks which could be taken alone. But whilst the hours of freedom increased, the size of the accommodation diminished as more of its members were present for more of the day. When temporary workstations were set up, the bedroom was no longer a secure place of retreat. Isolating five minutes for yourself without children banging on the door or partners demanding their own quiet moment became more difficult. For this reason, the permitted daily exercise assumed a particular value. 'That walk each day,' wrote a woman with a husband and children continually at home, 'became something I really looked forward to as not only did I get to have some fresh air but it was the one time of the day when I got to really be on my own.'[120]

The psychotherapist Josh Cohen observed that during lockdown, 'privacy, which is wrested from non-privacy under duress, feels like a matter of survival rather than thriving'.[121] More labour had to be invested in tuning out the noise of other lives, and agreeing acceptable patterns of solitary and social behaviours.[122] Particularly for those on low incomes, living through the pandemic was an all-consuming effort, leaving little or no time for the private self. In over-filled households and in the ever-present media, there were people with their own demands and narratives. A witness in the *Covid Realities* project described the suffocating presence of others amidst the constant pressure of struggling to survive on a low income:

> I'm constantly surrounded by people and I am desperate to be alone. I am fed up of the mundane realities of living in lockdown. It feels like we are living in Groundhog Day and I can't see a way out. Even when the schools return next week I will still be here working from home and living the same day over and over. I'm also fed up of seeing people on social media telling me their plans for when lockdown is over. Booking holidays and festivals. I can't afford that. When lockdown is lifted we will still have to stay at home because financially we won't be able to afford to go anywhere else. I want to be on my own for an hour or two just to think my own thoughts without anyone interrupting.[123]

Those who were living alone before the pandemic faced different challenges in maintaining their solitude. There had been a major demographic change in Britain and other European countries since the Second World War as single-person domestic units, hitherto uncommon, had grown to become almost a third of all households. It was striking that this transformation had not caused a corresponding increase in loneliness. Men and women of all ages were living by themselves for shorter or longer periods either because they liked doing so, or because it was the least worst option at a time of bereavement or relationship breakdown. Independence from parents or adult children was a long-prized condition that was made increasingly feasible by developments in the housing stock, employment, pensions, mass communication, and domestic consumption.[124]

Emotional survival in such surroundings was dependent on a range of strategies for living. In a still unequal economy, there were more opportunities for single women and young people to keep themselves. There were a greater range of recreational outlets and holidays for lone individuals, more products for those catering for just themselves, a wider menu of digital devices for entertainment or for communication with others, and the community of the workplace. Quarantine disrupted these devices for survival. Receiving visits or leaving the home to meet friends or family was either impossible or subject to varying controls. Holidays were cancelled. Trips to the shops or recreational facilities were in turn illegal or a possible threat to health. And there was a particular loss in the exclusion from the society of fellow employees. Conversations around the water cooler, interactions with others on joint projects, had once provided important forms of sociability.

The positive solitude of a quiet home threatened to become destructive loneliness if there were no alternative forms of personal intercourse. A fragile social life ceased to function once leaving the home was forbidden. 'I'm lonely,' complained 'Claire M.', 'and even though I was quite isolated before all of this I'm now completely isolated from everyone bar my partner and kids I care about.'[125] 'Loneliness and isolation getting to me,' wrote a single mother. 'Am I that bad a person that no one wants to know me? Just a sad middle aged mum of a teenage girl with autism. Not worthy of a conversation from anyone.'[126] The National Centre for Social Research found that during the pandemic those who were both living alone and working from home suffered more distress than those locked down with other people.[127] A woman whose relationship had ended at the end of the first lockdown found the resulting isolation difficult to manage as the pandemic continued: 'The flat is great – but my "office" is also my bedroom, dining room and lounge. I really have to see more than the same 4 walls. It adds to the loneliness.'[128]

The impact of the pandemic on solitude depended on the trajectory of pre-Covid-19 behaviours. Fred Cooper's study of the workers who cared for those no longer able to manage their own homes has demonstrated how the crisis could deepen both the thirst for company and the desire for withdrawal.[129] The era of austerity had increased the pressures on the underfunded personal support sector, as on the welfare system more generally.[130] Care workers were poorly supervised and increasingly overworked. Moving constantly from client to client often on zero-hours contracts, they had no opportunity to build up relationships and no recourse to a community of fellow employees. When, finally, they obtained PPE for themselves and those they were paid to look after, effective communication became still more difficult. In the early months, they suffered from the diversion of resources to the hospital sector. Later in the pandemic, the intensely infectious Omicron variant caused extensive staff shortages which further limited the opportunity for engaging with those who needed their support. The largely unsung sector of the carers, who were clapped in the early weeks, suffered the same dilemma as nurses and doctors of needing to keep their distance from other family members in case they brought Covid-19 home with them.

At the same time, care workers reported an unmet need for what the first modern theorist of solitude, Johann Zimmermann, described as 'a tendency to self-collection and freedom'.[131] There was a persisting aspiration to reflect on their calling in the midst of death and the fear of death, to find space between the incessant demands of their employment and their innermost motives and desires. The conflicting aspirations of care workers were not the invention of the pandemic. Underfunding and overwork in a gig economy had been increasing throughout the previous decade, and there is no reason to suppose that their dilemmas will be resolved in the immediate aftermath of Covid-19. The patterns of draining isolation and restorative solitude during the crisis were in all contexts the outcome of the pressures on inherited strategies for managing the boundaries of the self and social intercourse. Erecting barriers around the home, placing further pressure on those who had to deal with its breakdown, constantly challenged the often fragile balance between withdrawal and mutual support.

Aftermath

The Normal

Defoe examined the aftermath of the seventeenth-century London plague: 'I wish I cou'd say, that as the City had a new Face, so the Manners of the People had a new Appearance: . . . but . . . it must be acknowl-edg'd that the general Practice of the People was just as it was before, and very little Difference was to be seen.'[1] Following the replacement of the Johnson administration by two more Conservative governments, it is difficult to take a more optimistic view of the scale of change caused by the twenty-first-century pandemic. Defoe concluded that, 'It was not the least of our Misfortunes, that with our Infection, when it ceased, there did not cease the Spirit of Strife and Contention, Slander and Reproach, which was really the great Troubler of the Nation's Peace before.'[2] This account of the general practice of the people during the first two years of Covid-19 looks back to Defoe and the subsequent history of pandemics, and throughout foregrounds the importance of the recent and more dis-tant past in comprehending the scale of change that took place during the crisis.

Criticized for worsening the pandemic by its slow and often mis-judged reaction, Boris Johnson's government made repeated attempts to declare a decisive victory and the commencement of a new age of health and prosperity. The first 'Freedom Day' passed on 19 July 2021 with the health secretary quarantined and the prime minister and chancellor of the exchequer self-isolating because they had been working with him. The next 'Freedom Day', the following February, allegedly the earliest in Europe, was marked by the general public only with a continuing relaxa-tion in numbers wearing masks and indications that they were beginning to return to public transport and, to a limited extent, their offices.

Elsewhere, attempts were being made to plan a new future as soon as the first wave of infection began to subside. In June 2020, the New

Economics Foundation reported that '350 leaders call for us to "to build back better" as new poll shows only 6% of the British public want things to go back to how they were before the crisis'.[3] The proponents of radical change included the Director General of the CBI, the General Secretary of the TUC, former heads of the civil service and the Church of England, and leaders of sundry action groups. The programme called for high-quality public services, an attack on inequality, the creation of 'well-paid and rewarding jobs', and protection of the planet from the 'climate and emergency change already upon us'. This and other blueprints had to be put back on the shelf as two further waves of Covid-19 broke over the country.

More considered engagements with the future and how it might be informed by earlier regimes of social justice were composed whilst the pandemic was in full flood. Hilary Cooper and Simon Szreter's ambitious *After the Virus: Lessons from the Past for a Better Future*, which proposed 'universal social security and welfare as a legal entitlement of all citizens aimed at enhancing the positive freedoms of all those needing its support',[4] appeared in September 2021, before the Omicron variants prolonged the medical crisis. In March 2022, Peter Hennessy was able to take a perspective across two years of Covid-19. 'A true national emergency had taken hold,' he claimed in *A Duty of Care*. 'It was swiftly plain that life in After Covid Britain would be enduringly different from Before Covid Britain.'[5] 'Gradually,' he wrote, 'we all came to realize that a line had been scored across our shared history. There could be no going back to January 2020.'[6] *A Duty of Care* replaced the five 'giants' of the 1942 Beveridge Report with five shared 'tasks': 'social care, social housing, technical education, preparing our economy and our society for artificial intelligence, combating climate change'.[7] At the top of the list was the treatment of the dependent elderly. 'Putting social care right – in effect placing a national care service where it belongs alongside the NHS – is fundamental to any post-Covid duty of care. This, above all, we owe to those who have died in the care homes and to their families.'[8]

Hennessy looked to the creation of 'a new and productive consensus' to implement his reforms.[9] As a leading historian of post-war politics, he was well aware that his far-reaching proposals were at the mercy of short-term events. His book went to press immediately before the government was engulfed in the 'partygate' scandal. When it was published, inflation and the cost of living were succeeding Covid-19 as the principal threats to the wellbeing of the population.[10] Despite the change of premiership from Liz Truss to Rishi Sunak, the prospect of politics after Covid-19 being full of 'the spirit of strife and contention, slander and reproach' could scarcely be higher. Hennessy was perhaps prudent to identify 2045 as the distant target date for his persuasive manifesto.

The conception of the pandemic as a framed event that would generate particular solutions dissolved with remarkable speed. Amidst what Adam Tooze terms a 'polycrisis', it became increasingly difficult to view Covid-19 as a discrete historical moment.[11] This was partly due to the conjunction of events. In the case of the Spanish Flu, the pandemic succeeded a global military conflict. In 2022, the order was reversed. Putin's full-scale invasion of Ukraine, a major threat to the political, military, and economic world order, began, as it happened, on the very same day that the last lockdown controls were lifted in England.[12] The defenestration of the Johnson administration was partly caused by the failure to observe Covid-19 regulations within Number 10, but the installation by the party membership of a prime minister wedded to neoliberalism owed more to the long-term drama of Brexit within the party and the cumulative failure of twelve years of Conservative governments. The successor administration of Rishi Sunak was far more concerned to reverse the policies of the short-lived Truss experiment than to embrace radical learnings from the pandemic. As was argued in chapter 6, the worldwide lockdown had only a transient effect on climate change. There had been a short-lived vision of a prelapsarian nature, and the battle against coronavirus generated a new awareness of the threat of zoonotic infection caused by population growth and agricultural exploitation. In practical terms, however, when the history of global warming comes to be written, the early 2020s will merit little more than a footnote.

There were, in addition, three aspects of the long-term social history of the pandemic that contributed to the desire to return to what was conceived as normal living. The first of these was embedded in the experience of loss. About one in eight of all deaths in the two years from March 2020 were from Covid-19. Chapter 2 traced the consequences of the isolated process of dying in intensive care, and the loneliness of funerals and their aftermath. A critical element in any bereavement is the prior capacity to communicate with those embarked on their last journey. As Pauline

Boss has lately argued, there is no closure to be achieved, rather an evolving relation with the deceased, informed by discussion during the final months and days, brought into focus by the ritual of funerals and shared grief, sustained over time by reflection on the departed.[13] All of these practices, which had been enhanced in recent decades by reconsideration of dying in an increasingly secular society, were threatened by the abrupt restrictions on contact with care home residents and patients in hospital wards, and the severe limitations on the conduct of Covid-19 and non-Covid-19 funerals alike. There were an estimated 6.8 million people suffering bereavement in 2020 and 2021, three-quarters of a million more than the preceding five-year average would have predicted.[14] The emergency constraints on grieving imposed during the crisis, which largely continued during the sequence of lockdown and its relaxation, have contributed to a depth of psychological suffering that is likely to persist long after the pandemic has retreated to a manageable illness.

What may turn out to be the most profound long-term consequence of the pandemic is inherently retrospective.[15] Over two years after the first cases in the UK, it was estimated that two million people were still displaying symptoms more than four weeks after their first infection, some because of the experience of a ventilator, most because of the lingering effects of the disease itself, whether or not they had been seriously ill. One and a half a million of these reported that the condition was adversely affecting day-to-day activities, and nearly four hundred thousand were finding their ability to undertake their usual activities had been 'limited a lot'.[16] In the summer of 2022, it was estimated that at any one time 110,000 people were missing from work in the British labour market because of the condition.[17]

There are a host of neurological and physiological malfunctions, the most common of which are fatigue, post-exertional malaise, brain fog, and shortness of breath.[18] Further, there is growing evidence that Covid-19 creates an 'epidemiological aftershock', rendering sufferers more vulnerable to other serious conditions such as heart disease and diabetes.[19] The incidence of long Covid mirrors the initial exposure to the disease, with the elderly, the poor, those with pre-existing conditions, and those engaged in frontline occupations more at risk. Unlike the deaths from Covid-19, however, women seem more vulnerable than men. Urgent research is being undertaken to identify the causal processes, with particular attention being paid to damage to the brain, lungs, and immune systems, but whilst there is a pathway to the elimination of the infection itself through the roll-out of modified vaccines, there are no established treatments and remedies for those gripped by its aftermath, and few reliable prognoses for how long and in what form the suffering will continue.[20]

The short-term consequences vary. Not being able to taste some foods or walk as far as once was possible are misfortunes. Not being able to concentrate, to think clearly, to decipher print, are continuing disabilities for workers or students, obstructing their ability to earn a living or complete a programme of study. Long Covid may have contributed to the fall later in 2022 of those their fifties and sixties seeking employment.[21] It is evident that some of those whose organs have been most seriously damaged will never make a full recovery. For the remainder, there is no clear timetable for the journey back to whatever they once considered was their everyday health.

There are also long-term psychological conditions generated by the encounter with the lethal disease. At the beginning of the pandemic, a key indicator of success was the 50 per cent who survived ventilation in an ICU. As time passed, it became evident that as many as one in three of those who made an apparent recovery were suffering from post-traumatic stress disorders, displaying a range of symptoms including flashbacks.[22] Their difficulties were compounded by the underfunded condition of the mental health services, where little provision had been made for an increase in demand caused directly by the pandemic. As chapter 3 discussed, those who cared for patients in the intensely pressured Covid-19 wards were also discovered to be vulnerable to forms of PTSD, as were healthcare staff dealing with other aspects of the trauma of life and death.

At least in the short term, the millions of Covid-19 victims were not engaged in a mission to build back better. For those undone by stress, there was at least the goal of restoring the psychological mechanisms which once allowed them to deal with suffering and mortality on a routine basis. They were in search of the kind of equilibrium which had enabled them to negotiate the challenges of their working and private lives. For long Covid sufferers, the ambition was simply to return as nearly as possible to the health they once enjoyed. For those living from day to day following the sudden loss of a partner and a barren funeral, it was an enforced journey to an unknown future.[23]

The second inheritance from the past was the unequal distribution of resources. Major natural disasters have variable impacts on populations depending on circumstance and fortune. There was no standard experience of Covid-19. At the most basic level, some avoided infection or recovered unharmed, some died or experienced long-term ill-health. In Britain's pandemic, the comfortable middle class, who often suffered little more than a disruption of successive holiday plans and the dislocation of their social networks, had little in common with key workers exposed every day to infection, dreading above all that they would bring the contagion home to their families. Households whose economy improved because their income was secure and their outgoings restricted lived in a different world from those finding it increasingly difficult to spend what little they had as efficiently as once they could. There were employees forced towards a minimum wage by the furlough scheme, and enterprises profiting from the skewed demand for necessities or the careless contracting of a panicking government. There were individuals who just grew two years older, kept fit by daily exercise and shielded by lockdown from quotidian illnesses, and, by contrast, men and women, mostly but not always elderly, whose health suddenly declined from minor breathing problems to a ventilator and an unaccompanied death.

A line between those who could contemplate a return to a version of their former lives and those for whom this was a deeply unwelcome prospect was drawn by the distribution of resources before the medical crisis. Where, by reason of occupation, race, or gender, everyday existence was already a constant struggle to balance the weekly budget or gain access to essential services, Covid-19, as was argued in chapter 5, represented a further disempowerment. Micro strategies for spending efficiently were disrupted. Inherited debts increased. Domestic disadvantages such as too few rooms for the family, too small gardens, too limited access to digital communication devices, shifted existence from the difficult to the unbearable. Occupations which themselves delivered too small or uncertain an income represented an increased threat to health as they were clustered in the category of key workers unable to work safely at home. Coping with the pandemic was an endeavour calling for a wide range of adjustments to everyday living, together with sheer luck in avoiding the random threats to health. Success was a matter not of courage or choice, but rather of resources and leverage in a dangerous world.

The long-term momentum of increasing inequality tracked by Michael Marmot and other observers was only temporarily checked by the pandemic. Furlough (which successfully held down unemployment whilst the GDP contracted by just over a fifth between the last quarter of 2019 and the second quarter of 2020) and the £20 Universal Credit uplift demonstrated the instant effect the state could have on the security and living standards of the poor should it choose to do so.[24] The inability of the wealthy to buy their way to health in the intensive care wards and vaccination queues ensured a basic equality of experience in the frontline of the war against Covid-19. However, the cash payments were withdrawn at the earliest possibility, and the NHS emerged from the pandemic either under severe pressure or in a state of terminal collapse, depending on how close the observer was to the treatment of patients.[25] The House of Commons Public Affairs Committee reported in March 2022 that the long-term declines in referrals for suspected cancer, and in the provision of elective care where targets were last met in February 2016, were unlikely to be adequately addressed by the plans that had been announced.[26] The number of people on consultant-led elective care waiting lists rose from 4.25 million at the beginning of the pandemic to seven million by August 2022, and showed no sign of falling at the beginning of 2023.[27] There were in addition an unknown number who were yet to present their symptoms, or whose referrals had been cancelled.

The only post-Covid-19 certainty was that both private individuals and public institutions would have, in real terms, less money to spend on their requirements, however they were defined. Those who had prospered during the pandemic began to turn in growing numbers to private practice to deal with the postponed treatment of delayed diagnoses.[28] The mounting cost of living crisis, and the renewed decline of public services, ensured that the arc of deprivation would continue to worsen. The BAME community, which suffered more than any other section of society, saw its life-expectancy decline even further than the population as a whole. Covid-19 baked into British society and the economy the inequalities that it inherited.

This was apparent in the generation whose future was particularly affected by lockdown. As chapter 5 discussed, various forms of domestic deprivation, including the absence of adequate space and information technology, impacted on the periods of home schooling. When the classrooms re-opened, inspectors found the capacity of children to progress through the curriculum had been compromised. Ofsted summarized the position at the end of the 2021/2 school year:

> The pandemic has affected pupils' learning during the year. As we come to the end of the school year, some pupils are not as ready for the next stage as they would usually be. Children in Reception joined with a wider range of starting points. Despite much work from schools, some have not caught up to where they need to be as they move into key stage 1. Similarly, some Year 6 pupils are not ready for secondary school.[29]

The prospect of recovering lost time was undermined by the circumstances of home schooling. 'Covid-19-related disruption,' reported the Education Endowment Foundation in May 2022, 'has negatively impacted the attainment of all pupils, particularly those from disadvantaged backgrounds. There is evidence that the attainment gap between disadvantaged students and their classmates has grown.'[30] The deficiencies were widely recognized by teachers and various professional bodies. It is too soon to know how far the remedial actions now being undertaken, including a grant of £24 million by the Department for Education in October 2022 to rebuild literacy skills, will succeed in rectifying the damage caused by the pandemic.[31] Rather than progressing to a better future, cohorts of children face an uncertain journey back to the level they should already have reached.

Across the population, those experiencing difficulties with their mental health faced particular difficulties. The depressed and the anxious in the successive surveys were dominated by those who were already unable easily or safely to cope with their lives. They were by far the most vulnerable as stress increased and access to coping mechanisms was blocked. Here, as in many other areas, the threat was not the virus itself, but Covid-19 in conjunction with conditions which in earlier times were already serious constraints on everyday living. The long-term underfunding of support services, worsened by the diversion of resources into somatic medicine during the pandemic, made the clinical resolution of such pathologies more difficult to achieve. In these circumstances, lockdown did real and persisting harm. Face-to-face encounters in doctors' surgeries, where signs of growing difficulty might have been detected, ceased to occur, or had to be conducted through masks. The closure of schools for two prolonged periods meant that teachers were unable to pick up unreported problems in the home. How far virtual conversations by phone or video calls were able to compensate for these omissions remains a matter of debate.

The third inheritance from the past was the cluster of domestic practices that were mobilized ahead of the government's programme of containment. During the weeks before lockdown became official policy, households were paying heed to warnings in the press and had already begun to take actions to mitigate the threat to their health and to cope with the looming curtailment of their freedoms. They adjusted and readjusted their lives as Covid-19 followed its unpredictable course and quarantine regulations were constantly revised. In many contexts, it has been necessary to look backwards to preceding strategies for living in order to understand the issues of survival in the pandemic. If coronavirus was initially a new challenge to medical science, and mass quarantine unknown in late-modern Britain, managing locked-down households and closed workplaces and schools required far more adaptation than invention.

For politicians, shutting down much of the economy and confining the movement of the mass of the population in peacetime appeared almost inconceivable. In practice, they were able to undertake such actions because their electors had prepared the way. Despite the alarms of conspiracy theorists on both the left and the right, the new regime was imposed on a largely consensual population. 'Lockdown' was a euphemism coined for Covid-19. In public discourse it was a more modern and urgent term than 'quarantine', which had its roots in fourteenth-century Venice. It was, however, a literal misdescription of the event. The doors of British homes were only ever locked from the inside, and then perhaps less rigorously than usual given the sharp fall in burglary during the pandemic.[32] It was otherwise in totalitarian regimes. The Chinese government took to breaking into people's homes in search of Covid-19 contacts and locking residents in apartment buildings where cases had been detected.[33]

It mattered that the mass of the population had confidence in medical science and official statistics. The reports of the ONS and other government agencies were critical in resisting the claims of anti-vaccination campaigners and other conspiracy theorists that the infection was a hoax created to benefit avaricious big pharma or power-hungry governments. From first to last, however, the central question was confidence not so much in the state as in society's capacity to adapt established resources and behaviours to meet the threat of the coronavirus. Across Western Europe and the United States, consumers changed their patterns of behaviour ahead of controls imposed by government.[34]

By mid-February 2020, it was evident that a major international health crisis was looming, and households immediately began to rearrange their strategies for budget management. They ensured that where possible their debts were reduced or paid off, that kitchen shelves were adequately stocked, and that they had supplies of the domestic comforts and diversions that they would need to get through what was assumed would be an intense but short-lived period of confinement. Change can be measured in matters as weightless as the seeds that were purchased in unprecedented quantities for a spring that promised to be like no other in living memory. As we saw in chapter 8, the long history of the development of the private home as a location of comfort, recreation, and emotional support made it possible to conceive an existence temporarily shorn of the freedom to leave it.

Over the preceding century, a combination of demography, domestic architecture, rising living standards, and a responsive consumer market had generated a home-centred recreational culture that could be readily expanded when it ceased to be possible to go out. As chapter 7 discovered, whilst landlines and multiple forms of digital communication were not seen as adequate alternatives to physical contact and face-to-face conversation, for a limited time they could be sufficient to maintain social relations over distance. By 2020, the digital divide in the UK had significantly narrowed. Many users had to acquire new skills as they engaged with conferencing applications, and the cost of devices and connectivity remained a problem. The elderly faced the steepest learning curve but, helped by younger family members and spurred on by the evident gains of joining the digital universe, many were prepared to make the effort.

Had the pandemic struck a decade or more earlier, lockdown would have been a far more destructive and resisted experience. In the event, householders did more of what they had always done: cooking, watching television, reading, playing computer or card games, talking to each other, and pursuing a widening range of hobbies. The single most important asset for surviving lockdown was the fenced garden, a place of safety, recuperation, and diversion. The single most important regulation was the day's permitted exercise. The ancient, mostly unrecorded recreation of walking, with or without a dog, was critical to physical and mental wellbeing throughout the worst of times. Britain survived the pandemic by enhancing the normal.

Where there were extensions to established routines, it was in the increased time devoted to archiving memories and disposing of accumulated household clutter. A life foreshortened was on everyone's mind. With varying degrees of intensity, it accompanied the progress of each day, turning attention to past achievement and to interrogating what was unfinished when the pandemic struck. At the end of the first lockdown, the novelist Ian McEwan described an existence where, 'bleached of events, one day like another, time compresses and collapses in on itself'. The consequence has been 'an exponential growth in introspection, day-dreaming, mental drifting, especially about the past. We find ourselves tumbling backwards through time, achieving a new understanding of ourselves as we embrace without guilt a stillness in the midst of our days.'[35] Some locked-down householders with time on their hands took up long-held ambitions better to understand the trajectories of their families. There was a boom in the already flourishing online ancestry sites, which avoided the need to visit the now shuttered archives and registry offices.

Despite the continual postponement of the end, the pandemic society assumed that at some point it would be possible to return to pleasures as essential as freely choosing to connect with others without fear or constraint. If change was required, it was the necessary process of developing and confirming new relationships, or, conversely, escaping in a consensual manner those which were no longer working. What was lost, such as critical months in the development of a new grandchild or the comfort given to the dying or bereaved, could not be regained in any manifesto for change, however visionary. Equally, there was an expectation that the calendar of diversions which structured social time, whether regular visits to pubs, restaurants, and cinemas, or celebrations of birthdays and weddings, or holidays abroad, would be reactivated after two postponed years. An enhanced awareness of global warming was not sufficient to prevent an immediate surge in airline bookings as soon as testing and vaccine restrictions were lifted. Where acute deprivation had caused daily life to descend into chaos, there was no prospect of a return to established routines. But the bulk of the population were travelling through the pandemic back to everyday comforts with large meanings for themselves and their networks.

It is instructive that a significant inheritance of Covid-19 is in the level of homeworking. Whilst there has been some return to offices, there are indications that the new normal is likely to be closer to the period of widespread closures than to pre-pandemic routines.[36] A management survey of fifty thousand UK employees in June and July 2022 found on average they were going into their offices for 1.45 days of a working week.[37] Hybrid working is becoming more common, and more widely accepted, however reluctantly, by employers. In common with the entire experience of Covid-19, the privilege varies with income. The survey found that one in twelve of those earning under £15,000 were able to work some part of the week at home, compared with almost a third of those earning between £30,000 and £40,000. The principal reported motive of those making the change was an improved work–life balance. They had discovered new pleasures in old comforts.

Change

A natural disaster such as a pandemic has an ambiguous effect on radical visions of the future. In one perspective, the extension of collective action and the exposure of injustice create a fresh sense of the possible and the necessary. Rebecca Solnit draws inspiration from a literal or metaphorical flood:

> When a storm subsides, the air is washed clean of whatever particulate matter has been obscuring the view, and you can often see farther and more sharply than at any other time. When this storm clears, we may, as do people who have survived a serious illness or accident, see where we were and where we should go in a new light.[38]

A Mass Observation diarist is one of many Covid-19 witnesses who dreamt of a better world:

I want to believe that this pandemic will go down in history as a great turning point in our collective perception of and approach to wealth inequality, racism, right-wing politics, good leadership, community, climate change and the list could go on and on.[39]

Alternatively, the unexpected requirement to expand the role of the state and spend hitherto unimaginable sums on the welfare of the people is seen as a passing anomaly, with no implications for the long-term verities of low taxation and small government.[40] The sheer otherness of an essentially medieval event of plague and quarantine excludes it from the day-to-day conduct of a modern economy. Neoliberalism is not responsible for the mismanagement of a wet market in Wuhan and should not be diverted from its historical trajectory. In Britain, this view for the time being prevailed with the formation of a short-lived right-wing government under Liz Truss in September 2022, followed by the installation of the fiscally orthodox Rishi Sunak.

In the longer term, persisting anger at unnecessary Covid-19 deaths and the vast waste of money on purchasing equipment and commissioning services from the private sector, together with the exposure of multiple dimensions of inequality and a renewed commitment to public services, may yet lead to 'a great turning point'. A focus of change will be a fresh engagement with the idea of community. From the outset, the response to the constraints of lockdown and the threat of infection foregrounded the interdependence of individuals in the most basic social units.

The Covid-19 pandemic was a history of men and women taking precautions in order to reduce the risk to others.[41] Politicians saw a nation of individuals who needed to be lectured and, where necessary, policed in order to overcome their natural tendency to selfish behaviour. In practice, lockdown was largely observed, the day's exercise was undertaken, and masks were widely worn until the messaging about infection became diluted during 2021. Key workers, a much wider category of employees than was at first recognized, suffered at times unmanageable stress performing vital services whilst exposing their families to the risk of infection. The spirit of voluntary endeavour reached into the very heart of the medical intervention. The vaccination centres set up early in 2021 were staffed by local people giving up their time and expertise to secure the health of others. It was impossible to sustain the fears that once had been entertained about the imposition of injections in the face of the cheerful, almost celebratory atmosphere of the medical buildings, church halls, and other requisitioned and improvised sites where the efficient procedure took place.[42]

The instant surge of organized and more often unstructured help for those unable to manage their lives in the crisis took the government by surprise. Throughout the pandemic, the state and the centralized bureaucracy largely failed to understand the society they were managing, whereas those who were subjected to the modern form of quarantine, facing the prospect of death and bereavement on an unprecedented scale, displayed a far more accurate and responsive grasp of what they could do for themselves and each other.[43]

Some forms of association were forbidden, and others became more essential. Material deprivation and prior mental and physical health everywhere determined what was possible and bearable. Encounters in public places such as the school gates, coffee shops, entertainment venues, and a host of face-to-face organizations were halted or permitted in different forms. The domestic arena became a location of both enhanced interactions and new tensions as household members sought to balance the need both for company and for solitude. Rather than a single pattern of behaviour, there was a collective exploration by a stressed population of new ways of living with each other.

Lockdown was at its heart a spatial event. However distant the origins of Covid-19 and remote the instructions of government, the 'fatal Breath' resided in the few cubic metres of air surrounding an individual. The pandemic prevented all but key workers from stepping out of their homes except for their daily exercise, and, in its full form, from leaving the villages, suburbs, or inner cities where they lived. Twenty-first-century citizens suddenly found they enjoyed as much freedom to travel as medieval serfs. Whereas there were many elements of continuity in how home life was foregrounded, the basic prohibition on movement was a fundamental break with the modern era.

In the pandemic, community embraced a set of distinct meanings. At the outset, it was a locality of visible, effective kindness.[44] On the second anniversary of Covid-19, a journalist visiting Rugeley in the East Midlands, still in long-term recovery from closure of its heavy industry, encountered a new sense of interpersonal support. 'During lockdown,' she wrote, 'people were delivering letters offering to help each other picking up groceries and giving lifts to funerals.'[45] 'In my home area in north-east London,' writes Peter Hennessy, 'I was aware of the generosity of neighbours in offering to shop for others, volunteers who contacted the shielders (of whom I was one) or helped at larger vaccination sites and food banks.'[46] There were degrees of organization and varying levels of continuity with pre-pandemic activities. But now these personal, largely instinctive forms of support were noticed. As with so much of the response to Covid-19, they occurred immediately need arose, before any kind of national services could be arranged. Goodwill was adapted to need in ways which made a major difference to the lives of those suddenly cut off from other previous forms of support.

Community was more emphatically a physical entity, defined during the rigorous phases of lockdown by the ancient measure of how far someone could walk from their home and back on a daily basis. Transport revolutions since the eighteenth century and successive waves of information technology had increasingly weakened ties with a home address. As chapter 7 discussed, the internet displayed the hopes that had once been invested in it, playing a vital role in connecting isolated individuals and families. At the same time, daily life was bounded by particular buildings and thoroughfares. The unfamiliar was made familiar as individuals and families explored often for the first time the streets and open spaces in their neighbourhood. The renewed interest in gardening generated an awareness of specific soils and weather. The further destinations of trunk roads and railway lines for a time became irrelevant. It no longer mattered whether there was an airport within reach. With movement prohibited except for work or health, places were no longer on the way to somewhere larger or more important. They existed for themselves; the inhabitants came to know them as their own. Covid-19 made Britain local again.[47]

With the newly enhanced sense of locality, the knowledge people had of each other became more significant. Operational kindness required not just a generous spirit but also accurate information about the needs of a particular individual or household and how best they might be met. The centralized Test and Trace scheme failed because the government supposed that London-based call centres staffed by hastily trained operatives could generate detailed biographies of the people they were trying to help, and in turn that those they had rung would trust their advice. In practice, individuals with specific family commitments or ethnic loyalties, or with overriding work or financial constraints, were unwilling to cooperate with distant, uninformed instructions to stay at home. Conversely, calls from familiar telephone numbers, and physical visits to the home by public health officials or other trusted local figures, opened conversations that facilitated adjustments to the practical demands of quarantine.

Localities had renewed importance as a framework for effective communication networks. The long transition towards making connections independent of distance was at critical junctures thrown into reverse. This became especially important when there was a need to resist the anti-vaccination campaigns. The conspiracy theories flourished in a world of enclosed digital communities, where unorthodox truths were reinforced by exchange between tightly networked individuals. It became apparent around the beginning of 2021 that alongside national messaging, the most effective means of countering vaccine hesitancy was to ensure that those who were uncertain, or hostile, received accurate and relevant information from people they knew and respected in their neighbourhoods. The channels were not important. They might be posters, leaflets, street WhatsApp groups, ad hoc conversations, or public meetings. What mattered was who was connecting with whom. The sources could be religious leaders or other familiar, authoritative voices, conversing in a register and a language that was best understood by the listeners.

Finally, it was recognized that community action required public resources and control over how they were spent. Spontaneous goodwill was not sufficient to meet all the demands of a locked-down, infection-threatened society, nor were informal or organized neighbourhood charities, despite the labour and generosity of their supporters. After a decade of cuts to local government funding, essential services were barely able to meet statutory demands, let alone the sudden increase in Covid-19-related activity. Britain entered the pandemic with an overwhelmingly centralized economy. Local government controlled 1.6 per cent of GDP compared with 6 per cent in France and 11 per cent in Germany.[48] When the crisis broke, the state's instinctive reaction was to issue national contracts to private providers.

Over time, however, some learning occurred. Concessions were made to both the needs of devolved budgets and the capacity of elected officers and their bureaucracies to spend them effectively. After fierce argument, part of the Test and Trace budget was transferred to the network of public health officials to spend in their localities. Funding was given to vaccination campaigns mounted by community leaders. Charities based in towns and cities running telephone support lines for those threatened by domestic abuse or other forms of mental and physical hardship received grants. Scotland and Wales discovered more about their capacity to act independently of national government as they exercised responsibility for the management of their health services and quarantine regulations. Together, such initiatives helped Britain through the pandemic. Long-term action to reverse the centralizing instincts of the Treasury will, however, require a fundamental overhaul of the structures of democratic control and funding in the UK.

The reform of central/local relations is implicated in the cause of Scottish and Welsh devolution, which has been strengthened by their distinctive, more community-based response to the crisis. A wholesale revision of relations between Westminster and the nations, and, within each of these entities, the urban centres and the periphery, is long over-due, and was propelled forward by Covid-19. At the end of 2022, the Labour Party published a major constitutional review, chaired by the former prime minister Gordon Brown. It argued that 'the continuing over-concentration of power in Westminster and Whitehall is undermining our ability to deliver growth and prosperity for the whole country.'[49] Alongside devolution of funding to metro mayors and local government, the report proposed the replacement of the House of Lords by an elected Assembly of Regions and Nations. The reformed second chamber would have around two hundred members, about a quarter of the size of the current body, elected on a basis which is yet to be determined. In an accompanying newspaper article, Brown argued that 'the goal of an irreversible transfer of wealth, income and opportunity to working families across the United Kingdom is dependent upon the irreversible transfer of political power closer to the people. The two go together.'[50] Abolition of the House of Lords has been Labour Party policy throughout its existence, and it remains to be seen whether it finally fulfils this ambition after the next election.

Should a further coronavirus variant take hold that is either more infectious or more lethal or both, there is no reason to suppose that it will provoke more than a frustrated resignation. The risk the government took in dismantling all legal controls in February 2022, whilst infection and hospitalization rates were still high, was a reflection more of the strains on the economy than the limits set by the population at large.[51] There were in most households powerful ambitions to remake relationships and establish better ways of living, so far as resources and access to public services permitted. Hope was anchored to a sense of ending, however ragged that turned out to be. But as another Covid-19 spring took its course, the predominant sentiment was not anger, or rebellion, or relief, or despair, although all were present. Rather, it was one of a society wearied by stress and confinement. After two long years of fear, infection, and death, there was an overriding desire in every sense to breathe more freely.

Notes

Chapter 1 Writing the Pandemic

1 UK Commission on Bereavement, *2022 Summary Report: Bereavement is Everyone's Business* (2022), 4; Julia Samuel, *Grief Works: Stories of Life, Death and Surviving* (London: Penguin Life, 2017), xii; Ashton M. Verdery, Emily Smith-Greenaway, Rachel Margolis, and Jonathan Daw, 'Tracking the reach of COVID-19 kin loss with a bereavement multiplier applied to the United States', *Proceedings of the National Academy of Sciences of the United States*, 117, 30 (28 July 2020): 17695–701.

2 Jonathan Calvert and George Arbuthnott, *Failures of State: The Inside Story of Britain's Battle with Coronavirus* (London: Mudlark, 2021), 265.

3 *https://www.change.org/p/borisjohnson-hold-a-public-inquiry-into-the-government -s-handling-of-the-covid-19-pandemic-covid19*.

4 *Daily Mail*, 23 March 2021. See also *Guardian*, 12 June 2021.

5 GOV.UK, 'Commission established to shape UK commemoration for COVID-19' (21 July 2022).

6 On Defoe's narrative strategy, see Ernest R. Gilman, *Plague Writing in Early Modern England* (Chicago: University of Chicago Press, 2009), 229–43; Everett Zimmerman, 'H. F.'s Meditations: A Journal of the Plague Year', *PMLA: Publications of the Modern Language Association of America*, 87 (1 May 1972): 417–23.

7 *A Collection of Very Valuable and Scarce Pieces Relating to the Last Plague in the Year 1665* (London: J. Roberts, 1721), 14.

8 'An Account of the First Rise, Progress, Symptoms and Cure of the Plague: Being the substance of a Letter from Dr Hodges to a Person of Quality', in *A Collection of Very Valuable and Scarce Pieces*, 16.

9 Frank M. Snowden, *Epidemics and Society: From the Black Death to the Present* (New Haven: Yale University Press, 2019), 40; Paul Slack, *Plague: A Very Short Introduction* (Oxford: Oxford University Press, 2012), 11; William Rosen, *Justinian's Flea: Plague, Empire, and the Birth of Europe* (London: Viking, 2007), 247; Salvador Macip, *Modern Epidemics: From the Spanish Flu to Covid-19* (Cambridge: Polity, 2021), 38.

10 Daniel Defoe, *Due Preparations for the Plague, as well for Souls as Body. Being some seasonable Thoughts upon the visible approach of the present dreadful Contagion in France; the properest measures to prevent it, and the great work of submitting to it* (1722; New York: Harvard University Press, 1903), 10.

11 Slack, *Plague*, 11.

12 Defoe, *Due Preparations for the Plague*, 63.

13 Rosemary Horrox, trans. and ed., *The Black Death* (Manchester: Manchester University Press, 1994), 100.

14 Nicholas A. Christakis, *Apollo's Arrow: The Profound and Enduring Impact of Coronavirus on the Way We Live* (New York: Little, Brown Spark, 2020), 78; William H. McNeill, *Plagues and Peoples* (London: Penguin, 1979), 120.

15 Slack, *Plague*, 78.

16 Defoe, *A Journal of the Plague Year* (1722; London: Penguin, 2003), 45–6.

17 Laura Spinney, *Pale Rider: The Spanish Flu of 1918 and How It Changed the World* (London: Vintage, 2018), 96.

18 Zeynep Tufekci, 'Why did it take so long to accept the facts about Covid?', *New York Times*, 7 May 2021; Megan Molteni, 'The 60-year-old scientific screwup that helped Covid kill', *Wired*, 13 May 2021; Richard Horton, *The Covid-19 Catastrophe* (2nd edn, Cambridge: Polity, 2021), 212.

19 Cited in *Guardian*, 23 March 2020.

20 For an early critique of the prevailing orthodoxy, see Emanuel Goldman, 'Exaggerated risk of transmission of COVID-19 by fomites', *The Lancet: Infectious Diseases*, 20, 8 (3 July 2020): 892–3. See also Carl Zimmer and Jonathan Corum, 'The coronavirus in a tiny drop', *New York Times*, 1 December 2021; Peter Baldwin, *Fighting the First Wave: Why the Coronavirus was Tackled so Differently across the Globe* (Cambridge: Cambridge University Press, 2021), 163–4.

21 Trisha Greenhalgh et al., 'Ten scientific reasons in support of airborne transmission of SARS-CoV-2', *The Lancet*, 397, 10285 (1–7 May 2021): 1604. See also Ben Spencer, 'A year on, it could be time to wipe the slate clean on Covid hygiene policy', *Sunday Times*, 28 March 2021; Zimmer and Corum, 'The coronavirus in a tiny drop'.

22 Emma Smith, *Portable Magic: A History of Books and Their Readers* (London: Allen Lane, 2022), 167–8. See also Michael Greger, *How to Survive a Pandemic* (London: Bluebird, 2020), 284.

23 Calvert and Arbuthnott, *Failures of State*, 336. See also Stephen Reicher, 'Covid measures give us choice. They are not restrictions on British life', *Guardian*, 28 October 2021.

24 Defoe, *Journal of the Plague Year*, 194.

25 Thomas L. Friedman, 'Our new historical divide: B.C. and A.C. – the world before corona and the world after', *New York Times*, 17 March 2020.

26 Mark Honigsbaum, *The Pandemic Century: A History of Global Contagion from the Spanish Flu to Covid-19* (London: Penguin, 2020), 278.

27 Baldwin, *Fighting the First Wave*; Christakis, *Apollo's Arrow*; Macip, *Modern Epidemics*; Spinney, *Pale Rider*; Snowden, *Epidemics and Society*; Slavoj Žižek, *Pandemic! Covid-19 Shakes the World* (Cambridge: Polity, 2020); John M. Barry, *The Great Influenza* (London: Penguin, 2020).

28 Jonathan Calvert, George Arbuthnott, and Jonathan Leake, 'Coronavirus: 38 days when Britain sleepwalked into disaster', *Sunday Times*, 19 April 2020; Calvert and Arbuthnott, *Failures of State*. The authors claim that the exposé was 'the most popular online article in the history of *The Sunday Times* and *The Times*', reaching an audience of twenty-four million in Britain (*Failures of State*, 285).

29 Horton, *The Covid-19 Catastrophe*; Jeremy Farrar and Anjana Ahuja, *Spike: The Virus vs the People – the Inside Story* (London: Profile, 2021).

30 For instance, Dev Sridhar, *Preventable: How a Pandemic Changed the World and How to Stop the Next One* (London: Penguin Random House, 2022).

31 Comptroller and Auditor General, *Initial Learning from the Government's Response to the COVID-19 Pandemic*, Session 2021–2, 19 May 2021, HC66.

32 On the evolution of Mass Observation, see Nick Hubble, *Mass Observation and Everyday Life: Culture, History, Theory* (Basingstoke: Palgrave Macmillan, 2006).

33 On the value of Mass Observation as a source for studying the pandemic, see Marina Warner, 'Lockdown has created new forms of boredom – and not all of them are bad', *Guardian*, 9 March 2021.

34 Claire Langhamer, 'Mass observing the pandemic', seminar paper, *May 19: Learning to Live with Risk and Responsibility* (Mass Observation [hereafter MO], 19 May 2021).

35 MO, *12 May Diaries 2020*, 255.

36 MO, *Covid Diaries from Non-Mass Observers* [hereafter *Non-Mass Observers*], CV19 42, 30 June 2020. See also MO, *Spring Directive 2021*, A7000.

37 MO, *Non-Mass Observers*, CV19 17, 5 May 2020. See also MO, *Special Directives*, 29 March 2020, T7044.

38 *Covid Realities*, 'Aurora T.', 31 July 2021. See also 'Lexie G.', 28 July 2021; 'Lola P.', 27 March 2021.

39 *https://www.ft.com/coronavirusdiaries*; *https://www.mirror.co.uk/news/uk-news/coronavirus-mans-diary-lays-bare-21748565*; *https://www.marieclaire.co.uk/tag/covid-diaries*.

40 *Letters from Lockdown* (London: Chatto & Windus, 2020).

41 Franca Roeschert, '"Covid & Me" diaries: community voices', The Young Foundation, 3 May 2020; Joseph Rowntree Foundation, *COVID-19: The Key Worker Diaries* [hereafter JRF, *Key Worker Diaries*]; *https://theconversation.com/lockdown-diaries-the-everyday-voices-of-the-coronavirus-pandemic-138631*.

42 See for instance, *https://www.aberdeencity.gov.uk/sites/default/files/2020-05/Covid-19-Diary-Deposit-Guidance.pdf*; *https://plymouthculture.co.uk/covid-19/diaries/*.

43 David Barnett, '"Everyone's got a book in them": boom in memoir industry as ordinary people record their stories', *Guardian*, 24 September 2022. On the autobiographical tradition, see David Vincent, *Bread, Knowledge and Freedom* (London: Methuen, 1982).

44 John Naughton, *100 Not Out: A Lockdown Diary, March–June 2020* (privately published, 2020).

45 *https://covid2020diary.wordpress.com/*.

46 'Sam', a junior doctor, *https://www.nhs70.org.uk/story/nhs-72*.

47 Charles E. Rosenberg, 'What is an epidemic? AIDS in historical perspective', in *Explaining Epidemics and Other Studies in the History of Medicine* (Cambridge: Cambridge University Press, 1992), 279.

48 Horton, *The Covid-19 Catastrophe*, 56.

49 For a discussion of this usage, see MO, *Diaries 2nd Series. Covid Special 2020* [hereafter *Covid Special 2020*], B3227, 17 May 2020.

50 Owing to variations in definitions of Covid-19 mortality and in the thoroughness of national recording systems, the Johns Hopkins count is likely to represent a significant under-estimation of the global death toll. David Spiegelhalter and Anthony Masters, 'We can be confident there have been far more than 5 million global Covid deaths', *Guardian*, 7 November 2021.

51 Anna Gross, 'History shows pandemics rarely end neatly or with complete eradication', *Financial Times*, 13/14 March 2021.

52 McNeill, *Plagues and Peoples*, 120.

53 Helen Branswell, 'How the Covid pandemic ends: scientists look to the past to see the future', *Stat*, 19 May 2021.

54 Lord Sumption, 'Government by decree – Covid-19 and the Constitution', 2020 Cambridge Freshfields Lecture, 27 October 2020, reprinted in *Law in a Time of Crisis* (London: Profile, 2021), 218.

55 John Stuart Mill, *On Liberty* (London: Longmans, Green and Company, 1857), 6.

56 Sumption, *Law in a Time of Crisis*, 230. For a more cautious and balanced assessment of the legal issues generated by lockdown regulations, see Adam Wagner, *Emergency State* (London: The Bodley Head, 2022).

57 Daisy Fancourt, Feifei Bu, Hei Wan Mak, and Andrew Steptoe, *UCL COVID-19 Social Study 2020–2022*, UK Data Service, SN: 9001, *Results Release 1* (27 March 2020). Later the sample was increased to seventy thousand. For a full report of the two-year study, see Daisy Fancourt, Andrew Steptoe, and Alexandra Bradbury, *Tracking the Psychological and Social Consequences of the COVID-19 Pandemic across the UK Population: Findings, Impact, and Recommendations from the COVID-19 Social Study* (March 2020–April 2022) (UCL, September 2022).

58 Fancourt et al., *UCL COVID-19 Social Study: Results 5* (22 April 2020).

59 Adam Tooze, *Shutdown: How Covid Shook the World's Economy* (New York: Viking, 2021), 238.

60 John Richetti, *Daniel Defoe* (Boston: Twayne, 1987), 121.

61 Alice Kaplan and Laura Marris, *States of Plague: Reading Albert Camus in a Pandemic* (Chicago: University of Chicago Press, 2022).

62 John Richetti, 'Defoe as narrative innovator', in John Richetti, ed., *The Cambridge Companion to Daniel Defoe* (Cambridge: Cambridge University Press, 2009), 121–38.

63 Albert Camus, *The Plague* (1947; London: Penguin, 2013), 35–7, 102; Kaplan and Marris, *States of Plague*, 88–9.

64 Defoe, *Journal of the Plague Year*, 60.

65 Orhan Pamuk, *Nights of Plague* (London: Faber & Faber, 2022). For fictional treatments of aspects of the Covid-19 crisis, see, *inter alia*, Ali Smith, *Companion Piece* (London: Hamish Hamilton, 2022); and Gary Shteyngart, *Our Country Friends* (London: Allen & Unwin, 2022).

66 For a fuller discussion of this point, see David Vincent, 'The pandemic has raised fears about loneliness. History suggests we should worry about the opposite, too', *Time*, 7 July 2020; David Vincent, 'The epidemic and the pandemic: loneliness and Covid-19', in Corinna Guerra and Marco Piazza, eds, *Disruption of Habits during the Pandemic* (Rome: Mimesis International, 2022), 71–84.

67 Adam Tooze, 'In media res', *Chartbook on Shutdown*, 4 September 2021.

68 Rosen, *Justinian's Flea*, 3

69 Barry, *The Great Influenza*, 396–7; Honigsbaum, *The Pandemic Century*, 278 n. 51.

70 Johns Hopkins Coronavirus Resource Centre, 31 September 2022.

71 World Health Organization [hereafter WHO], '14.9 million excess deaths associated with the COVID-19 pandemic in 2020 and 2021' (5 May 2022).

72 Honigsbaum, *The Pandemic Century*, 28; Spinney, *Pale Rider*, 76.

73 Leo Benedictus, 'Covid-19: behind the death toll', Full Fact, 26 March 2021.

74 Simon Garfield, *The End of Innocence: Britain in the Time of AIDS* (rev. edn, London: Faber & Faber, 2021), 425.

75 Office for National Statistics [hereafter ONS], 'Weekly provisional figures on deaths registered where coronavirus (COVID-19) was mentioned on the death certificate in England and Wales, registered 17 April 2020' (January 2021).

76 ONS, 'Weekly provisional figures on death registrations involving Covid-19 in England and Wales by sex and age group, registered 25 March 2022' (5 April 2022).

77 'Sir David Spiegelhalter: When a politician says they follow the science, that's when I start screaming', *The Times*, 12 September 2020.

78 David Spiegelhalter and Anthony Masters, 'Covid by numbers: 10 key lessons separating fact from fiction', *Guardian*, 10 October 2021.

79 James S. Amelang, trans. and ed., *A Journal of the Plague Year: The Diary of the Barcelona Tanner Miquel Parets 1651* (New York: Oxford University Press, 1991), 59, 69–71.

80 Gladys Lewis had had chronic obstructive pulmonary disease, and a son had Down's syndrome and had been on life support with pneumonia earlier in the year. BBC Wales, 5 November 2020.

81 Steven Morris, 'Chef's parents and brother die from Covid within week after jab refusal', *Guardian*, 9 August 2021.

82 Bradley Jolly, 'Pensioner, 90, dies after refusing treatment when he found out Covid-19 had killed wife', *Daily Mirror*, 29 April 2020.

83 Slack, *Plague*, 115.

84 See, for instance, the magisterial review of the first year of the pandemic in Jonathan Freedland, 'The magnifying glass: how Covid revealed the truth about our world', *Guardian*, 11 December 2020. Also Devi Sridhar, 'Covid-19 has shown us that good health is not just down to biology', *Guardian*, 25 December 2020.

85 The distinguished former vice-chancellor of universities in South Africa and Britain, Brenda Gourley: 'In transition', *Covid2020diary*, 10 May 2020.

Chapter 2 Illness, Death, Bereavement

1 Tim Hayward, 'Covid and me: 10 days on life support', *Financial Times*, 22 January 2021. Used under licence from the *Financial Times*. All Rights Reserved.

2 Rachel Clarke, *Breath Taking: Inside the NHS in a Time of Pandemic* (London: Little, Brown, 2021), 198.

3 Nuffield Trust, 'End of life care' (27 March 2023).

4 Elisabeth Kübler-Ross, *On Death and Dying* (1969: New York: Touchstone, 1997), 21.

5 Atul Gawande, *Being Mortal* (London: Profile, 2015), 128.

6 Rachel Clarke, *Dear Life: A Doctor's Story of Love and Loss* (London: Little, Brown, 2020), 210.

7 Clarke, *Dear Life*, 207–8.

8 British Heart Foundation, *UK Factsheet* (April 2023).

9 Department for Transport, 'Reported road casualties in Great Britain, provisional estimates: year ending June 2021' (25 November 2021).

10 Kübler-Ross, *On Death and Dying*, 123.

11 The first purpose-built British hospice, St Christopher's Hospice, was opened by Cicely Saunders in 1967.

12 See for instance, Karen E. Steinhauser et al., 'Factors considered important at the end of life by patients, family, physicians, and other care providers', *JAMA*, 284 (2000): 2476–82.

13 Julia Samuel, *Grief Works: Stories of Life, Death and Surviving* (London: Penguin Life, 2017), 225.

14 ONS, 'Deaths in private homes, England and Wales (provisional): deaths registered from 28 December to 11 September 2020' (19 October 2020); Venna Raleigh, 'Deaths from Covid-19 (coronavirus): how are they counted and what do they show?' (The King's Fund, 23 April 2021).

15 V. H. Galbraith, ed., *The Anonimalle Chronicle* (Manchester: Manchester University Press, 1970), 30, cited in Horrox, trans. and ed., *The Black Death*, 65.

16 Tooze, *Shutdown*, 85.

17 The King's Fund, 'Was building the NHS Nightingale hospitals worth the money?', 5 May 2021.

18 Clarke, *Dear Life*, 127.

19 For a similar triage scheme in the USA, drawn up by the American College of Chest Physicians, see Greger, *How to Survive a Pandemic*, 272–3.

20 Calvert and Arbuthnott, *Failures of State*, 227–9, 242, 250, 257, 258–60. Also George Arbuthnott et al. 'Revealed: how elderly paid price of protecting NHS from Covid-19', *The Times*, 25 October 2020.

21 Sebastian Payne, 'The spectre of lonely care home deaths hangs over the government', *Financial Times*, 15 June 2020. See Matt Hancock's attempts to blame this tragedy variously on lack of PPE, the NHS, Public Health England, local authorities, and care home staff in Matt Hancock, with Isabel Oakeshott, *Pandemic Diaries* (London: Biteback, 2022), 128, 139, 157, 176, 215, 226, 231, 235.

22 Robert Booth, '"Three weeks of hell": the peak of Covid-19 at hard-hit UK care home', *Guardian*, 14 June 2020.

23 Figures for England and Wales. ONS, 'Deaths involving COVID-19 in the care sector, England and Wales: deaths registered between week ending 20 March

2020 and week ending 2 April 2021' (11 May 2021); Pamela Duncan, 'More care home residents died of Covid in second wave than first in England and Wales', *Guardian*, 11 May 2021.

24 Sirin Kale, '"They were withering away": why did Colin Harris and nine others die in a Skye care home?', *Guardian*, 8 September 2020.

25 See, for instance, Robert Booth, 'The East End care home where Covid stole the lives of 21 people', *Guardian*, 13 July 2022.

26 Naughton, *100 Not Out*, Day 49, 9 May 2020, 60; Phil Hammond ('MD'), *Dr Hammond's Covid Casebook* (London: Private Eye, 2021), 13–14.

27 Kale, '"They were withering away"'.

28 Calvert and Arbuthnott, *Failures of State*, 263.

29 Michael Rosen, *Many Different Kinds of Love: A Story of Life, Death and the NHS* (London: Ebury Press, 2021), 3–4.

30 For similar medical advice to deal with Covid-19 with paracetamol, see Sirin Kale, '"They were trying to resuscitate him as I watched": Rodolfo Silva died, aged 58, of Covid-19', *Guardian*, 30 December 2020.

31 Aamna Mohdin, '"Why do you ignore us?" The families trying to talk to Boris Johnson', *Guardian*, 2 September 2020 (Jade Foster-Jerrett).

32 Sarah Marsh, '"Covid has ripped the family apart": the lives lost in the UK's third wave', *Guardian*, 20 July 2021.

33 A reasonable doubt. One in ten cases in the first wave were caught in hospital.

34 Louella Vaughan, 'Where are the patients? The factors affecting the use of emergency care during Covid-19' (Nuffield Trust, 16 June 2020).

35 Rachel H. Mulholland et al., 'Impact of COVID-19 on accident and emergency attendances and emergency and planned hospital admissions in Scotland: an interrupted time-series analysis', *Journal of the Royal Society of Medicine*, 113, 11 (4 October 2020): 444–53.

36 NHS, 'Annual A&E Activity and Emergency Admissions statistics, NHS and independent sector organisations in England' (15 April 2021).

37 David Spiegelhalter and Anthony Masters, 'How is it possible that the number of deaths is now so low?', *Guardian*, 4 April 2021; Baldwin, *Fighting the First Wave*, 225.

38 Marie Curie, *Better End of Life 2021: Death, Dying and Bereavement during Covid-19, Research Report* (April 2021), 32.

39 Robin McKie, 'Interview. Neil Ferguson: "One year ago, I first realised how serious coronavirus was. Then it got worse. . .", *Guardian*, 14 March 2021.

40 According to the estimate by Michael Marmot. Ben Spencer, '"Racist" oxygen device may explain why Covid hit minorities so hard', *The Times*, 20 November 2021.

41 Clarke, *Breath Taking*, 6.

42 For a detailed description of the procedure, see Jim Down, *Life Support: Diary of an ICU Doctor on the Frontline of the Covid Crisis* (London: Penguin, 2021), 141–2.

43 Clarke, *Breath Taking*, 87.

44 MO, *12 May Diaries 2020*, 184.

45 Down, *Life Support*, 148.

46 Clarke, *Breath Taking*, 123.

47 Hannah Brady, 'Is Boris Johnson to blame for my dad's death? I hope the Covid inquiry will tell me', *Guardian*, 30 June 2022.

48 Down, *Life Support*, 163.

49 Samuel, *Grief Works*, 269.

50 Gawande, *Being Mortal*, 177.

51 Clarke, *Dear Life*, 211.

52 'Becky. Hospice care. 5 April 2020', in *Letters from Lockdown*, 119.

53 thebmjopinion, 'Personal protective equipment is sexist' (9 March 2021).

54 Rachel Clarke, '"This man knows he's dying as surely as I do": a doctor's dispatches from the NHS frontline', *Guardian*, 30 May 2020.

55 'James. They called us, and we went. 13 May 2020', in *Letters from Lockdown*, 95; Anna Torrens-Burton et al., '"It was brutal. It still is": a qualitative analysis of the challenges of bereavement during the COVID-19 pandemic reported in two national surveys', *Palliative Care & Social Practice*, 16 (2022): 7–8.

56 Naughton, *100 Not Out*, Day 60, 20 May 2020, 72.

57 Jim Down, 'My Covid diary: an ICU doctor reports from the front line', *The Times*, 24 March 2020.

58 'I'm an NHS consultant anaesthetist. I see the terror in my Covid patients' eyes', *Guardian*, 31 January 2021.

59 MO, *Special Directive*, N6725. Also Mohdin, '"Why do you ignore us?"' (Leshie Chandrapala).

60 Clarke, *Breath Taking*, 161–2. Also Rachel Clarke, 'Covid's cruellest blow? Keeping the dying from their loved ones', *Guardian*, 10 May 2021.

61 Peter Walker and Robert Booth, 'Hancock vows to give families "right to say goodbye" to loved ones', *Guardian*, 15 April 2020.

62 *The Art of Dying Well: Deathbed Etiquette Covid-19* (St Mary's University, Twickenham, 2021).

63 Cited in Rachael Healy, 'PTSD, long Covid and a paltry pay offer: three nurses on how the pandemic changed them', *Guardian*, 4 August 2021.

64 Down, *Life Support*, 149.

65 Roopa Farooki, *Everything is True: A Junior Doctor's Story of Life, Death and Grief in a Time of Pandemic* (London: Bloomsbury, 2022), 129.

66 Rosen, *Many Different Kinds of Love*, 163.

67 'Lisa. Through my phone. 24 April 2020', in *Letters from Lockdown*, 171–4.

68 Torrens-Burton et al., '"It was brutal. It still is"': 2.

69 Hayward, 'Covid and me'.

70 Alex Evans, Casper ter Kuile, and Ivor Williams, *This Too Shall Pass: Mourning Collective Loss in the Time of Covid-19* (The Collective Psychology Project, 2021), 8.

71 Rosen, *Many Different Kinds of Love*, 24–35.

72 Torrens-Burton et al., '"It was brutal. It still is"': 1–17. See also Pauline Boss, *Ambiguous Loss: Learning to Live with Unresolved Grief* (Cambridge, MA: Harvard University Press, 1999), 7–8; UK Commission on Bereavement, *2022 Summary Report*, 8.

73 Margaret Stroebe and Henk Schut, 'Bereavement in times of COVID-19: a review and theoretical framework', *OMEGA – Journal of Death and Dying*, 82, 3 (2021): 501.

74 The research is reported in Emily Harrop et al., *Supporting People Bereaved during Covid-19: Study Report 1* (Cardiff University and University of Bristol, 27 November 2020): 1–7; Emily Harrop et al., 'End of life and bereavement experiences during the COVID-19 pandemic: interim results from a national survey of bereaved people', *BMJ Supportive & Palliative Care*, 11: A3 (March 2021). See also L. E. Selman et al., 'Factors associated with higher levels of grief and support needs among people bereaved during the pandemic: results from a national online survey', *medRχiv* (8 February 2022): 1–14.

75 Peter Townsend, 'Isolation, desolation and loneliness', in Ethel Shanas et al., *Old People in Three Industrial Societies* (London: Routledge & Kegan Paul, 1968), 262.

76 Boss, *Ambiguous Loss*, 9–10.

77 See, for instance, Cruse, Marie Curie, Age UK, the National Bereavement Partnership, Grief Encounter, letstalkaboutloss.

78 Cruse Bereavement Care, 'Coronavirus: grief and trauma', *https://www.cruse.org.uk/coronavirus/trauma* (no longer available online).

79 Naughton, *100 Not Out*, Day 49, 9 May 2020, 60–1.

80 For a description of the process, from several personal experiences, see David Vincent, 'The technology of bereavement', *Covid2020diary*, 9 April 2021. See also Jonathan Freedland, 'History suggests we may forget the pandemic sooner than we think', *Guardian*, 29 January 2021.

81 Defoe, *A Journal of the Plague Year*, 42.

82 Harriet Sherwood, '"It's grief upon grief": the harsh reality of funerals in lockdown', *Guardian*, 14 April 2020.

83 Naughton, *100 Not Out*, Day 32, 22 April 2020, 42.

84 MO, *12 May Diaries 2020*, 101.

85 UK Commission on Bereavement, *2020 Summary Report*, 9. Also Co-op Funeralcare, *A Nation in Mourning Report: Is the UK Heading towards a Grief Pandemic?* (July 2020), 3; Torrens-Burton et al., '"It was brutal. It still is"': 8.

86 Church of England, 'Restricted funerals and their impact on grief'. Research conducted January 2021.

87 SunLife, *The Cost of Dying Report 2021* (2021), 18–22. SunLife claims to be the market leader in insuring the elderly and funerals.

88 SunLife, *The Cost of Dying*, 49.

89 Sarah Marsh, 'Epidemic of grief: the challenge of the UK's massive loss of life', *Guardian*, 13 January 2021.

90 *https://welldoing.org/article/covidspeakeasy-providing-support-bereaved-partners*.

91 Rachel Williams, '"I have grieved in a hidden limbo": losing a loved one in Covid's first wave', *Guardian*, 27 March 2021. See also Clarke, 'Covid's cruellest blow?'

92 Robert Booth, 'Families bereaved by Covid say UK plan to allow Christmas mixing is '"sheer madness"', *Guardian*, 25 November 2020.

93 MO, *12 May Diaries 2020*, 184. See also general comments about victim anger by Professor Lucy Selman, cited in Robert Booth, 'UK's Covid bereaved suffer heightened grief, finds study', *Guardian*, 27 November 2020.

94 Julia Samuel, cited in Emma Jacobs, 'Therapist Julia Samuel on how to manage anxiety and grief during coronavirus', *Financial Times*, 26 March 2020.

95 Simon Bray, 'Loved and lost: grief in the time of coronavirus – a photo essay', *Guardian*, 21 August 2020.

96 Rebecca Abrams and Cruse Clinical Director, Andy Langford, webinar, 5 May 2020.

97 Philip Williamson, 'State prayers, fasts and thanksgivings: public worship in Britain 1830–1897', *Past and Present*, 200, 1 (August 2008): 133, 155–8.

98 World Evangelical Alliance, 'WEA calls for global day of prayer & fasting on Sunday, March 29 – and prayer beyond!', 23 March 2020.

99 Harriet Sherwood, 'Easter, Passover, Ramadan . . . festivals test the faithful's resolve over lockdown', *Guardian*, 12 April 2020.

100 Robert Crampton, 'Tracking down the Covid winners and losers', *The Times*, 5 June 2021. See the equally critical assessment by the historian and novelist A. N. Wilson in the same paper: 'Church shepherds have lost their flocks. The

Archbishop of Wokeness, Welby, and the equally inept Nichols are not leaders that the faithful deserve', 25 December 2020.

101 Aina Khan, 'Amid the sorrow over cancelled Eid plans, British Muslims should feel let down too', *Guardian*, 31 July 2020.

102 MO, *2020 Summer COVID and Time*, B2710.

103 'Stephen. Closing the church doors. 30 March 2020', in *Letters from Lockdown*, 13.

104 'Penny. Goodbye old friend. 4 May 2020', in *Letters from Lockdown*, 222–3.

105 Laura Bear et al., *'A Good Death' during the Covid-19 Pandemic in the UK: A Report of Key Findings and Recommendations* (LSE, 2020), 10.

106 Ecclesiastical.com, 'Churches go digital to counter lockdown' (17 August 2020); Miriam Partington and Sebastian Shehadi, 'How coronavirus is leading to a religious revival', *New Statesman* (27 April 2020); Henry Mance, 'How the pandemic reinvigorated religion: from drive-through confessions to solitary funders, faith leaders are finding new ways to connect', *Financial Times*, 22 May 2020; Jessamin Birdsall, Bryony Loveless, and Tom Sefton, *Church in Action 2020–2021: A Survey of Churches' Community Response to the Pandemic* (London: The Church Urban Fund, The Church of England, 2021), 13.

107 'Stephen. Closing the church doors', 13.

108 MO, *Covid Special 2020*, D4736, 22 March 2020.

109 Reported in *The Times*, 10 June 2020.

110 Harriet Sherwood, 'Let us disobey. Churches defy lockdown with secret meetings', *Guardian*, 22 November 2020.

111 Usmaan Mufti, Zaynah Asad, Naira Abdelaal, and Ayman Benmati, *A Year of Lockdown: The Impact on Muslims* (Muslim Census, 6 April 2021).

112 Ahmed Al-Dawoody and Oran Finegan, 'COVID-19 and Islamic burial laws: safeguarding dignity of the dead' (30 April 2020) *https://blogs.icrc.org/law-and-policy/2020/04/30/covid-19-islamic-burial-laws/*; Sukaina Hirji, Arifali Hirji, and Edin Lakasing, 'The impact of Covid-19 on Islamic burial rites, *GM Journal*, 23 June 2020.

113 See, for instance, Northern Care Alliance, *Risk Management Covid-19 – Hospital Deaths Only – Muslim Patients* (October 2020).

114 Michael Marks, 'SARS-CoV-2 infection rate very high amongst UK strictly-Orthodox Jewish community', London School of Hygiene and Tropical Medicine, 2 February 2021; Katherine M. Gaskell et al., 'Extremely high SARS-CoV-2 seroprevalence in a strictly-Orthodox Jewish community in the UK', *BMJ Yale*, 1 February 2021. Harriet Sherwood, 'Large weddings, packed schools: concern as some Haredi Jews flout England lockdown', *Guardian*, 29 January 2021.

115 ONS, *Religion, England and Wales: Census 2021* (29 November 2022).

116 Hattie Williams, 'Financial crisis threatens Church's strategic plans', *Church Times*, 1 February 2021; Steve Bruce, *British Gods: Religion in Modern Britain* (Oxford: Oxford University Press, 2020), 150.

117 Kaya Burgess, 'Church of England spends millions but fails to convert cash into congregations', *The Times*, 20 September 2021.

118 Hannah Rich, 'Anglican churches in the UK are shrinking in size but not impact', *Christianity Today*, 24 November 2020.

119 Andrew Village and Leslie Francis, 'Shielding but not shielded', *Church Times*, 12 February 2021.

120 *https://www.churchofengland.org/news-and-media/news-releases/millions-join-worship-online-churches-bring-services-home-pandemic*.

121 Andrew Village and Leslie J. Francis, 'The Baptist experience of the first national lockdown', *Baptist Times*, 12 March 2021.

122 Birdsall et al., *Church in Action 2020–2021*, 16–17.

123 u3a, *u3a in the Time of Corona: Experiences of u3a Members during Lockdown* (London: Third Age Trust, 2020), 100.

124 Bruce, *British Gods*, 60–1.

125 Mufti et al., *A Year of Lockdown*.

126 Hattie Williams, 'Financial crisis threatens churches' strategic plans', *Church Times*, 5 February 2021.

127 Paul Bickley, 'Religious trends in a time of international crisis', Theos (11 August 2020).

128 Kaya Burgess, 'Archbishop of Canterbury: Churches celebrate Easter return of their flock', *The Times*, 22 April 2022.

129 The Catholic Church, Bishops' Conference of England and Wales, 'Returning to Mass at Pentecost' (9 May 2022).

130 Although the terms BME and BAME have recently been abandoned by the government, no alternative terminology has been proposed. Given that they are still widely used in discussions about race and equality, we have continued to employ them throughout this book.

131 Savanta: ComRes, 'RSA – Public Polling, March 2021'.

132 'Leaving a mark on the world' was bottom at 9 per cent. Bickley, 'Religious trends'.

133 Evans et al., *This Too Shall Pass*, 8.

Chapter 3 States of Mind

1 MO, *Non-Mass Observers*, CV 19 17, 10 May 2020.

2 MO, *Non-Mass Observers*, CV 19 17, 18 April 2020.

3 MO, *Non-Mass Observers*, CV 19 17, 28 April 2020.

4 MO, *Non-Mass Observers*, CV 19 17, 14 April 2020.

5 MO, *Non-Mass Observers*, CV 19 17, 7 May 2020.

6 MO, *Non-Mass Observers*, CV 19 17, 22 April 2020.

7 Farrar and Ahuja, *Spike*.

8 GOV.UK, *Covid-19: Mental Health and Wellbeing Surveillance Report* (12 April 2022), ch. 2.

9 ONS, *Opinions and Lifestyle Survey: Coronavirus and Depression in Adults, Great Britain January to March 2021* (5 May 2021); ONS, *Coronavirus and Depression in Adults, Great Britain: July to August 2021* (1 October 2021). No further reports were made.

10 ONS, *Opinions and Lifestyle Survey* (4 February 2021); ONS, *Coronavirus and the Social Impacts on Great Britain* (1 April 2022).

11 Fancourt et al., *UCL COVID-19 Social Study: Results 44* (7 April 2022) (final report).

12 ONS, 'Mapping loneliness during the coronavirus pandemic' (7 April 2021); Department for Digital, Culture, Media, and Sport, *Tackling Loneliness Annual Report February 2022: The Third Year* (15 February 2022).

13 Fancourt et al., *UCL COVID-19 Social Study: Results 44*, 14. Loneliness in the first lockdown is examined in Feifei Bu, Andrew Steptoe, and Daisy Fancourt, 'Loneliness during a strict lockdown: trajectories and predictors during the COVID-19 pandemic in 38,217 United Kingdom adults', *Social Science & Medicine* (November 2020): 1–6.

14 For a rare discussion of the absence of change in the emotion tables, see Tim Adams, 'Despite everything, we're no unhappier than we were a year ago', *Guardian*, 5 June 2021.

15 Farrar and Ahuja, *Spike*, 141–2. The calculation was made by the epidemiologist Neil Ferguson before the House of Commons Select Committee in June 2020.

16 Reviewed in David Vincent, *A History of Solitude* (Cambridge: Polity, 2020), 231–5.

17 Surgeon General under Barack Obama, fired by Donald Trump, reappointed by Joe Biden.

18 Vivek H. Murthy, *Together: Loneliness, Health and What Happens When We Find Connection* (London: Profile, 2020), 10.

19 Bianca DiJulio, Liz Hamel, Cailey Muñana, and Mollyann Brodie, *Loneliness and Social Isolation in the United States, the United Kingdom and Japan: An International Survey* (San Francisco: The Henry J. Kaiser Family Foundation, 20 August 2018), 3.

20 Kelly Rhea MacArthur, 'Treating loneliness in the aftermath of a pandemic:

threat or opportunity?', in J. Michael Ryan, ed., *Covid-19. Volume 1: Global Pandemic, Societal Responses, Ideological Solutions* (London: Routledge, 2021), 198. The study upon which these claims were made was the *Cigna US Loneliness Index* (2018), which based its finding on all the top three UCLA categories. For a similarly apocalyptic view of the impact of Covid-19 on loneliness, see Debanjan Banerjee and Mayank Rai, 'Social isolation in Covid-19: the impact of loneliness', *International Journal of Social Psychiatry*, 66, 6 (2020): 525–7.

21 Christina Victor, Ann Bowling, John Bond, and Sasha Scambler, 'Loneliness, social isolation, and living alone in later life', *Research Findings no. 17: Growing Older Programme* (Economic and Social Research Council, 2003); G. Clare Wenger, Richard Davies, Said Shahtahmasebi, and Anne Scott, 'Social isolation and loneliness in old age: review and model refinement', *Ageing and Society*, 16 (1996): 336. See also Vincent, *A History of Solitude*, 222.

22 Rowena Leary and Kathryn Asbury, 'Alone in the COVID-19 lockdown: an exploratory study', OSF Preprints, 30 June 2021: 13.

23 Martina Luchetti et al., 'The trajectory of loneliness in response to COVID-19', *The American Psychologist*, 75, 7 (2020): 902–4.

24 Luchetti et al., 'The trajectory of loneliness', 905.

25 Robert D. Putnam, *Bowling Alone: The Collapse and Revival of American Community* (New York: Simon & Schuster, 2000), 27.

26 The Jo Cox Commission on Loneliness, *Combatting Loneliness One Conversation at a Time: A Call to Action* (London, 2017).

27 HM Government, *A Connected Society: A Strategy for Tackling Loneliness – Laying the Foundations for Change* (Department for Digital, Culture, Media, and Sport, October 2018). For the background to the document, see Vincent, *A History of Solitude*, 220–1.

28 DCMS, *Loneliness Annual Report: The Third Year* (15 February 2022). For a survey of government policies on loneliness since 2017, see Philip Loft, *Tackling Loneliness* (House of Commons Briefing Paper, 22 February 2021).

29 Nicola Davis, 'UK's mental health has deteriorated during lockdown says Mind', *Guardian*, 20 June 2020.

30 Denis Campbell, 'UK lockdown causing "serious mental illness in first-time patients"', *Guardian*, 16 May 2020; Pamela Duncan and Patrick Butler, 'Depression in British adults doubles during coronavirus crisis', *Guardian*, 18 August 2020; Richard Bentall, 'Has the pandemic really caused a "tsunami" of mental health problems?', *Guardian*, 9 February 2021.

31 Charles E. Rosenberg, 'What is an epidemic? AIDS in historical perspective', in *Explaining Epidemics and Other Studies in the History of Medicine* (Cambridge: Cambridge University Press, 1992), 278–9.

32 Cited in Michael Savage, 'Poll reveals scale of "home alone" Christmas in the UK this year', *Guardian*, 5 December 2020. Also Emma Beddington, 'There is an epidemic of loneliness', *Guardian*, 22 March 2021; Dennis Campbell, 'Action needed to tackle post-Covid "loneliness emergency", MPs say', *Guardian*, 24 March 2021.

33 Daisy Fancourt, Andrew Steptoe, and Feifei Bu, 'Trajectories of anxiety and depressive symptoms during enforced isolation due to COVID-19 in England: a longitudinal observational study', *Lancet Psychiatry*, 8 (9 December 2020): 146.

34 Daisy Fancourt, Andrew Steptoe, and Liam Wright, 'The Cummings effect: politics, trust and behaviours during the COVID-19 pandemic', *The Lancet*, 396, 10249 (15 August 2020): 464–5.

35 MO, *12 May 2020 Diaries*, MT 2020 41.

36 MO, *12 May 2020 Diaries*, MT 2020 41.

37 Public Health England, *Alcohol Consumption and Harm during the COVID-19 Pandemic* (15 July 2021); Bukky Balogun, Rachael Harker, John Woodhouse, and Agnieszka Suchenia, *Alcohol Harm* (House of Commons Library, 24 November 2021).

38 Alcohol Change, 'Research: drinking in the UK during lockdown and beyond' (July 2020). See also Rob Davies, 'UK alcohol sales fall despite rise in home drinking', *Guardian*, 19 December 2020.

39 Sadie Boniface, '2021 alcohol consumption and harm: no signs of a "return to normal"' (Institute of Alcohol Studies, 26 January 2022).

40 ONS, 'Alcohol-specific deaths in the UK: registered in 2020' (7 December 2021), 2.

41 Public Health England, *Alcohol Consumption and Harm during the COVID-19 Pandemic* (15 July 2021).

42 Colin Angus, Maddy Henney, and Rob Pryce, 'Modelling the impact of changes in alcohol consumption during the COVID-19 pandemic on future alcohol-related harm in England' (University of Sheffield, April 2022): 2.

43 FMCG GURUS, 'Chocolate trends within the UK 2020' (2 November 2020); Sarah Butler, 'Chocolate sales soar as UK shoppers comfort eat at home amid Covid', *Guardian*, 31 October 2020; 'More than half of Brits snacked more in lockdown' (University of Sheffield, 23 June 2021).

44 MO, *12 May 2020 Diaries*, MT 2020 144.

45 MO, *12 May 2020 Diaries*, MT 2020 52.

46 u3a, *u3a in the Time of Corona*, 18.

47 MO, *12 May 2020 Diaries*, MT 2020 245.

48 MO, *12 May 2020 Diaries*, MT 2020 245. Spelling and punctuation in original.

49 *Covid Realities*, 'Victoria B.', 28 May 2021.

50 *Covid Realities*, 'Alex R.', 21 June 2021.

51 *Covid Realities*, 'Fiona T.', 17 May 2021.

52 Pauline Boss, *The Myth of Closure: Ambiguous Loss in a Time of Pandemic and Change* (New York: Norton, 2022), 8.

53 Fancourt et al., *Tracking the Psychological and Social Consequences of the COVID-19 Pandemic*, 24.

54 For a discussion of these dilemmas, see Sarah Boseley, 'Coronavirus shielding scheme to be eased in England from 6 July', *Guardian*, 22 June 2020.

55 *Covid Realities*, 'Eric J.', 21 May 2021.

56 MO, *Special Directive, 2020*, B7216.

57 MO, *Covid Special 2020*, B6900, 17 May 2020.

58 *Covid Realities*, 'Holly W.', 22 June 2020.

59 National Health Service, 'Main symptoms of coronavirus (COVID-19)' (22 July 2021).

60 MO, *Non-Mass Observers*, CV 19 42, 14 May 2020.

61 Naughton, *100 Not Out*, Day 32, 22 April 2020, 41–2.

62 u3a, *u3a in the Time of Corona*, 20.

63 Defoe, *Journal of the Plague Year*, 15.

64 NHS, *Delivery Plan for Tackling the COVID-19 Backlog of Elective Care* (February 2022), 10.

65 Fancourt et al., *UCL COVID-19 Social Study: Results 36* (22 July 2021).

66 After starting alongside each other, confidence in the Welsh and Scottish administrations was from May 2020 onwards consistently at least a point higher than in the English.

67 ONS, 'Compliance with coronavirus (Covid-19) guidelines' (12 April 2021).

68 Fancourt et al., *UCL COVID-19 Social Study: Results 36*.

69 Fancourt et al., *UCL COVID-19 Social Study: Results 44*.

70 ONS, 'Compliance with coronavirus (Covid-19) guidelines'.

71 Vincent, *A History of Solitude*, 223.

72 Fancourt et al., *UCL COVID-19 Social Study: Results 36*.

73 Defined as those with a 'self-reported long-standing illness, condition or impairment that reduces the ability to carry out day-to-day activities'.

74 ONS, 'Coronavirus and the social impacts on disabled people in Great Britain: 3 to 28 February 2021' (9 April 2021), table 7.

75 ONS, 'Coronavirus and the social impacts on disabled people in Great Britain, 27 March–6 April 2020' (24 April 2020), table 20.

76 Dustin Z. Nowaskie and Anna C. Roesler, 'The impact of COVID-19 on the LGBTQ+ community: comparisons between cisgender, heterosexual people,

cisgender sexual minority people, and gender minority people', *Psychiatry Research* (March 2022): 1–12; Victoria J. McGowan, Hayley J. Lowther, and Catherine Meads, 'Life under COVID-19 for LGBT+ people in the UK: systematic review of UK research on the impact of COVID-19 on sexual and gender minority populations', *BMJ Open*, 11 (2021): e050092.

77 Jessica Fields, James K. Gibb, and Sarah A. Williams, 'Queer people's experiences during the pandemic include new possibilities and connections', *The Conversation*, 27 June 2021.

78 *Covid Realities*. 'Eric J.', 2 March 2021.

79 The new-found confidence of the anxious introvert was discussed by Jon Ronson on BBC's *Newsnight*, 20 March 2020: *https://www.youtube.com/watch?v=DNOi -UnDzlk*.

80 Cited in Jonathan Freedland, 'Adjust your clocks: lockdown is bending time completely out of shape', *Guardian*, 24 April 2020.

81 u3a, *u3a in the Time of Corona*, 91.

82 Alzheimer's Society, *Worst Hit: Dementia during Coronavirus* (September 2020), 12.

83 Andrew Gregory, 'Dementia killing more women than Covid-19', *The Times*, 8 August 2021.

84 ONS, 'Deaths involving COVID-19, England and Wales: deaths occurring in June 2020' (17 July 2020); Alzheimer's Society, *Worst Hit*, 4, 15.

85 Alzheimer's Society, *Worst Hit*, 4, 15

86 Cited in Amelia Hill, 'Eight in 10 people living alone with dementia completely isolated since March', *Guardian*, 14 July 2020.

87 Age UK, *The Impact of COVID-19 to Date on Older People's Mental and Physical Health* (2020), 5.

88 Alzheimer's Society, *Worst Hit*, 31.

89 Alzheimer's Society, *Worst Hit*, 25.

90 u3a, *u3a in the Time of Corona*, 92.

91 Gavin Francis, *Intensive Care: A GP, a Community and Covid-19* (London: Profile Books and Wellcome Collection, 2021), 90.

92 Pamela Duncan and Sarah Marsh, 'Antidepressant use in England soars as pandemic cuts counselling access', *Guardian*, 1 January 2021.

93 Cited in Duncan and Marsh, 'Antidepressant use in England soars.'

94 On the increase in people seeking mental health advice, see Rethink Mental Illness, 'Demand for mental health advice soars in year after first lockdown' (23 March 2021).

95 MIND, *Trying to Connect: The Importance of Choice in Remote Mental Health Services* (2021), 54–6. Figures for September–November 2019 and 2020. Data

for children and young people was published by NHS Digital. In the absence of equivalent data for adults, MIND collected figures from individual mental health trusts via a Freedom of Information request.

96 Lloyds Bank, *Lloyds Bank UK Consumer Digital Index 2021* (2021), 17.

97 MIND, *Trying to Connect*, 54–6.

98 MIND, *Trying to Connect*, 13.

99 *Letters from Lockdown*, 186.

100 See, for instance, Vera Baird on women, cited in Owen Bowcott and Jamie Grierson, 'Refuges from domestic violence running out of space, MPs hear', *Guardian*, 28 April 2020; Sajid Javid on children, cited in Jess Staufenberg, 'Sharp increase in UK child sexual abuse during pandemic', *Guardian*, 8 July.

101 Eleni Romanou and Emma Belton, *Isolated and Struggling: Social Isolation and the Risk of Child Maltreatment, in the Lockdown and Beyond* (NSPCC Evidence Team, June 2020), 3, 8, 10.

102 Yvonne Roberts, 'Hunger, violence, cramped housing: lockdown life for the poorest children', *Observer*, 21 June 2020.

103 Romanou and Belton, *Isolated and Struggling*, 3–4.

104 Jamie Grierson, 'Physical abuse of older children soared during lockdown, says NSPCC', *Guardian*, 25 August 2020.

105 Ofsted, *The Annual Report of Her Majesty's Chief Inspector of Education, Children's Services and Skills 2019/20* (1 December 2020).

106 PA Media, 'Number of children needing foster care soars during pandemic, says Barnardo's', *Guardian*, 23 June 2020.

107 Ria Ivandić, Tom Kirchmaier, and Ben Linton, 'Changing patterns of domestic abuse during Covid-19 lockdown', *Centre for Economic Performance, Discussion Paper*, 1729, December 2020: 1–50; Ria Ivandić and Tom Kirchmaier, 'Domestic abuse in times of quarantine' (Centrepiece, Summer 2020).

108 *Covid Realities*, 'Danni M.', 25 January 2021.

109 Tirion Havard, 'Domestic abuse and Covid-19: a year into the pandemic' (House of Commons Library, 11 May 2021).

110 ONS, 'Domestic abuse during the coronavirus (Covid-19) pandemic, England and Wales: November 2020' (25 November 2020).

111 Havard, 'Domestic abuse and Covid-19'. Elsewhere it was reported that calls to the Perpetrator Helpline almost doubled. Savannah Dawsey-Hewitt et al., *Shadow Pandemic – Shining a Light on Domestic Abuse during Covid* (Women's Aid, 2021).

112 Henry McDonald, 'Domestic abuse surged during lockdown, Panorama investigation finds', *Guardian*, 17 August 2020.

113 Refuge, 'Refuge's National Domestic Abuse Helpline: a year on from lockdown', 23 March 2021; Jane Grierson, 'Calls to domestic abuse hotline in England up by 60% over past year', *Guardian*, 23 March 2021; Mark Townsend, 'Domestic abuse cases soar as lockdown takes its toll', *Guardian*, 4 April 2020.

114 Ivandić et al., 'Changing patterns of domestic abuse during Covid-19'.

115 David Vincent, *Privacy: A Short History* (Cambridge: Polity, 2016), 52–66.

116 ONS, 'Domestic abuse and the criminal justice system, England and Wales: November 2021' (24 November 2021).

117 The first Commissioner is Nicole Jacobs, who was the former Chief Executive Officer at the charity Standing Together Against Domestic Violence.

118 Jessica Murray, 'Government failing to tackle violence against women, says Jess Phillips', *Guardian*, 28 December 2021.

119 ONS, 'Deaths from suicide that occurred in England and Wales: April to July 2020' (2 September 2021); ONS, 'Deaths from suicide that occurred in England and Wales: April to December 2020' (14 April 2022); ONS, 'Coronavirus (COVID-19) latest insights: deaths' (23 September 2022).

120 ONS, 'Coronavirus (COVID-19) latest insights: deaths'.

121 Jane Pirkis et al., 'Suicide trends in the early months of the COVID-19 pandemic: an interrupted time-series analysis of preliminary data from 21 countries', *Lancet Psychiatry*, 8, 7 (13 April 2021): 579–88.

122 ONS, 'Deaths from suicide that occurred in England and Wales: April to December 2020'.

123 Samaritans, *One Year On: How the Coronavirus Pandemic Has Affected Wellbeing and Suicidality* (June 2021), 5.

124 Loring Jones, Margaret Hughes, and Ulrike Unterstaller, 'Post-traumatic stress disorder (PTSD) in victims of domestic violence: a review of the research', *Trauma, Violence and Abuse*, 2, 2 (April 2001): 99–119.

125 NHS, *Overview – Post-Traumatic Stress Disorder* (27 September 2018).

126 Dirk Richter and Lucy Foulkes, 'Yes, lockdown was bad for mental health. Not to do it would have been worse', *Guardian*, 5 July 2021.

127 Chris Thomas and Harry Quilter-Pinner, *Care Fit for Carers: Ensuring the Safety and Welfare of NHS and Social Care Workers during and after Covid-19* (IPPR, April 2020), 12. Findings based on a YouGov poll of a thousand health workers.

128 Samaritans, *One Year On*, 5.

129 YouGov online survey of 1,008 NHS employees in the UK, carried out between 12 and 17 August 2021, reported in NHS Charities Together, '60,000 NHS staff living with post-traumatic stress following pandemic' (13 May 2022).

130 Clarke, *Breath Taking*, 128.

131 Anonymous, 'We care workers face a terrible decision: risk people's lives or go

without pay', *Guardian*, 8 May 2020. See, more generally, Healy, 'PTSD, long Covid and a paltry pay offer'.

132 Royal College of Physicians, 'What are we learning from the workforce about the impacts of COVID-19?' (18 May 2020).

133 Down, *Life Support*, 111. Also Clarke, *Breath Taking*, 143, 175; 'James. They called us, and we went. 13 May 2020'.

134 Farooki, *Everything is True*, 50.

135 Farooki, *Everything is True*, 69.

136 Anna Bawden and Denis Campbell, 'More than 77,000 NHS staff in England have caught Covid, shows research', *Guardian*, 25 May 2021.

137 Tim Cook, Emira Kursumovic, and Simon Lennane, 'Exclusive: deaths of NHS staff from Covid-19', *Health Service Journal*, 22 April 2020.

138 Luke Haynes, 'Hancock denies PPE shortages caused any of 1,500 NHS staff deaths from Covid-19', *GPOnline*, 10 June 2021.

139 JRF, *Key Worker Diaries*, 'Kayleigh', 8 April 2020.

140 Neil Greenberg et al., 'Mental health of staff working in intensive care during Covid-19', *Occupational Medicine*, 71, 2 (March 2021): 65. See also Nathalie Grover, 'Nearly half of NHS critical care staff report PTSD, depression or anxiety', *Guardian*, 13 January 2021; Rhiannon Lucy Cosslett, '"They were freaking out": meet the people treating NHS workers for trauma', *Guardian*, 23 January 2021.

141 Royal College of Psychiatrists, '230,000 new PTSD referrals forecast as a result of the pandemic' (3 December 2021).

142 Denis Campbell, 'NHS sets up mental health hubs for staff traumatised by Covid', *Guardian*, 22 February 2021.

Chapter 4 Connections

1 On websites and in other media it was often shortened to 'Clap for Carers'.

2 u3a, *u3a in the Time of Corona*, 101.

3 MO, *Special Directives*, M6815(2).

4 u3a, *u3a in the Time of Corona*, 101.

5 MO, *Non-Mass Observers*, CV 19 42, 2 April 2020.

6 u3a, Mandy, Islington, in *Living History Diary Part 2*, 27 March 2020.

7 See, for instance, Rachel Clarke, 'Not one of my NHS colleagues believes the NHS as we know it can survive much longer', *The Times*, 25 July 2021.

8 Twitter, 9 April 2020. Also a similar sentiment on Twitter, 23 April 2020.

9 Farooki, *Everything is True*, 41.

10 Sophie Harris et al., '"It's been ugly": a large-scale qualitative study into the difficulties frontline doctors faced across two waves of the COVID-19 pan-

demic', *International Journal of Environmental Research and Public Health*, 18, 13067 (10 December 2021): 7.

11 Rachel Clarke, 'What price human life? Overworked NHS staff have to answer this every day', *Guardian*, 26 October 2021.

12 'Violent incidents at GP practices double in five years, BMJ investigation finds', *BMJ*, 31 May 2022.

13 DCMS, 'Enabling safe and effective volunteering during coronavirus (COVID-19)' (13 November 2020 and subsequent updates).

14 Cited in *Our Chance to Connect: Final Report of the Talk/Together Project* (March 2021), 35.

15 *Our Chance to Connect*, 36.

16 The Policy Institute, King's College London, *Life under Lockdown: Coronavirus in the UK* (9 April 2020), 4, 40. See also Sarah Young, 'Coronavirus: social distancing measures are bringing communities together, study finds', *Independent*, 23 March 2020. See also the survey reported in *Property Reporter*, 26 May 2020.

17 ONS, *Opinion and Lifestyle Survey (Covid-19 Module), 9–20 April: Coronavirus and the Social Impacts on Great Britain* (30 April 2020).

18 ONS, *Coronavirus and the Social Impacts on Older People in Great Britain: 3 April to 10 May 2020. Indicators from the Opinions and Lifestyle Survey on the Social Impact of the Coronavirus (COVID-19) Pandemic on Older People in Great Britain* (22 June 2020), figs 11 and 12.

19 *Our Chance to Connect*, 37.

20 Oliver Wright, 'Our sense of community restored by Covid pandemic', *The Times*, 1 January 2021.

21 Fancourt et al., *UCL COVID-19 Social Study: Results 39* (7 October 2021), 59–62.

22 Fancourt et al., *Tracking the Psychological and Social Consequences of the COVID-19 Pandemic*, 45.

23 MO, *12 May 2020 Diaries*, 181.

24 Val, Wales, in u3a, *Living History Diary*, 31 May 2020.

25 MO, *Non-Mass Observers*, CV 19 45, 9 April 2020.

26 MO, *12 May 2020 Diaries*, 284.

27 MO, *12 May 2020 Diaries*, 284.

28 Cited in Esther Addley, 'Making up with the Joneses: how Covid-19 has brought neighbours closer', *Guardian*, 5 June 2020.

29 MO, *Covid Special 2020*, A6788, 18 March 2020.

30 MO, *Covid Special 2020*, B6560, 20 March 2020.

31 Cited in Jonathan Watts, 'Britain beyond lockdown: what we learned from two weeks on the road', *Guardian*, 6 July 2020.

32 Fancourt et al., *Tracking the Psychological and Social Consequences of the COVID-19 Pandemic*, 45.

33 'Peter. Memories of Liverpool. 4 May 2020', in *Letters from Lockdown*, 267.

34 MO, *Special Directives*, L4071.

35 Whilst preparing this book, the author was twice rung by an employee of Shropshire County Council to enquire if there was anything they could do for me as a shielded resident. The answer was no, but it was good to be asked.

36 Simon Jenkins, 'If the Church of England worships online, how can its historic buildings survive?', *Guardian*, 26 December 2020.

37 Mufti et al., *A Year of Lockdown*.

38 Steven Vass, 'From the temple to the street: how Sikh kitchens are becoming the new food banks', *The Conversation*, 22 July 2015; Jim Reed, 'Coronavirus: the Sikh community kitchen feeding thousands', BBC News, 9 June 2020.

39 Chris Baranuik, 'Sharing apps are booming but will the kindness continue?', BBC News, 10 August 2021.

40 MO, *Special Directives*, T7044.

41 On the balance between increase and decrease in volunteering, see Fancourt et al., *Tracking the Psychological and Social Consequences of the COVID-19 Pandemic*, 10, 45.

42 MO, *12 May 2020 Diaries*, 417. Also, MO, *12 May 2020 Diaries*, 154.

43 The Trussell Trust, *Trussell Trust Data Briefing on End-of-Year Statistics Relating to Use of Food Banks: April 2020–March 2021* (April 2021), 7–8.

44 MO, *Special Directives*, W7394.

45 Hancock, *Pandemic Diaries*, 120.

46 JRF, *Key Worker Diaries*, 'Charlotte', 17 April 2020.

47 See multiple media stories, including *Mirror*, 31 March 2020; *The Sun*, 31 March 2020; *St Helens Star*, 27 March 2020.

48 MO, *12 May 2020 Diaries*, 398.

49 MO, *12 May 2020 Diaries*, 294.

50 The Trussell Trust, *End of Year Statistics* (22 April 2021).

51 Sabine Goodwin, *Independent Food Bank Emergency Food Parcel Distribution in the UK, February to November 2019 and 2020* (22 December 2020).

52 The Trussell Trust, *Trussell Trust Data Briefing*, 3.

53 *Covid Realities*, 'Nellie K.', 3 April 2021.

54 The Trussell Trust, *End of Year Statistics*.

55 The Trussell Trust, *State of Hunger: Building the Evidence on Poverty, Destitution, and Food Insecurity in the UK. Year Two Main Report* (May 2021), 90.

56 *Covid Realities*. 'Danni M.', 1 January 2021.

57 *Covid Realities*. 'Victoria B.', 12 January 2021.

58 Vikram Dodd, 'UK police receive 194,000 calls from lockdown "snitches"', *Guardian*, 30 April 2020; Jenni Russell, 'Lockdown is turning us into a nation of spies', *The Times*, 13 May 2020.

59 Dodd, 'UK police receive 194,000 calls from lockdown "snitches"'.

60 Alex Evans, 'Police see surge in neighbours snitching on lockdown flouters in West Yorkshire', *Wakefield Express*, 17 April 2020.

61 Aitor Hernández-Morales, 'Corona-snitches thrive in lockdown Europe', *Politico*, 7 April 2020. For a similarly overwhelmed Staffordshire police force, see MO, *Diaries 2nd Series, Covid Special 2020*, B3227.

62 Josh Halliday and Nazia Parveen, 'Tool to report lockdown rule-breakers "risks fuelling social division"', *Guardian*, 9 April 2020.

63 See Ministry of Housing, Communities and Local Government, 'Guidance to support local authority compliance and enforcement activity, including Covid-19 secure marshals or equivalent', 10 May 2020 [withdrawn 19 July 2021].

64 Cabinet Office, 'Coronavirus (COVID-19): what has changed – 9 September' (9 September 2020).

65 Cabinet Office, 'Coronavirus (COVID-19): what has changed – 22 September' (22 September 2020).

66 The fines in Scotland started at a lower level but had the same maximum. Those in Wales began with a fixed penalty of £60 but had no maximum.

67 Cabinet Office, 'Coronavirus (COVID-19): What has changed – 22 September'.

68 Fiona Hamilton, '"Rule of Six" informants swamp police coronavirus line', *The Times*, 22 September 2020.

69 Martin Bentham, 'Outcry over Covid "Stasi snoop" as Kit Malthouse says home-owners should snitch on neighbours', *Evening Standard*, 14 September 2020.

70 Cited in John Humphrys, 'Rule of Six: should we snitch on our neighbours?', YouGov (27 September 2020).

71 Clea Skopeliti, 'Boris Johnson contradicts ministers and says only snitch on neighbours if they are having "Animal House" parties', *Independent*, 17 September 2020.

72 Cited in Natasha Hinde, 'The psychology of snitching on neighbours in the age of Covid', *HuffPost*, 29 September 2020.

73 Humphrys, 'Rule of Six'.

74 Cited in Joy Lo Dico, 'My very British revolt against the "Rule of Six"', *Financial Times*, 18 September 2020.

75 Vincent, *Privacy*, 107–9.

76 Cited in Humphrys, 'Rule of Six'.

NOTES TO PP. 107–11

77 John Drury, Stephen Reicher, and Clifford Stott, 'COVID-19 in context: why do people die in emergencies? It's probably not because of collective psychology', *British Journal of Psychology*, 59, 3 (July 2020): 692. Also Nicola Davis, 'Don't blame public for Covid-19 spread says UK scientist', *Guardian*, 16 June 2020.

78 Hinde, 'The psychology of snitching on neighbours'.

79 The conclusion of Stephen Reicher's research programme at St Andrews, summarized in Stephen Reicher, 'In pretending that Covid is over, the UK government is playing a dangerous game', *Guardian*, 5 July 2022.

80 Humphrys, 'Rule of Six'.

81 E. Wight Bakke, *The Unemployed Man: A Social Study* (London: Nisbet, 1933), 94; Alan Deacon, *In Search of the Scrounger* (London: Bell, 1976), 59.

82 George Orwell, *The Road to Wigan Pier* (1937; London: Penguin, 1989), 72.

83 David Vincent, *Poor Citizens* (London: Longman, 1991), 86.

84 Joel Golby, 'These lockdowns reveal the UK's true character: we are a nation of snitches', *Guardian*, 13 January 2021.

85 Huan Tong et al., 'Increases in noise complaints during the COVID-19 lockdown in spring 2020: a case study in Greater London, UK', *Science of the Total Environment*, 785, 147213 (1 September 2021).

86 Fiona Hamilton, '"Rule of Six" informants swamp police coronavirus line', *The Times*, 22 September 2020.

87 Anna Mikhailova, Christopher Hope, Michael Gillard, and Louisa Wells, 'Exclusive. Government scientist Neil Ferguson resigns after breaking lockdown rules to meet his married lover', *Daily Telegraph*, 5 May 2020.

88 Cited in Oliver Wright, 'Virus adviser Neil Ferguson "right to resign after breaking lockdown", says Hancock', *The Times*, 6 May 2020.

89 Hancock, *Pandemic Diaries*, 534.

90 Fancourt et al., *UCL COVID-19 Social Study: Results 20* (10 September 2020), 4; Results 38 (10 September 2021), 4.

91 Fancourt et al., *UCL COVID-19 Social Study: Results 17* (30 July 2020), 44.

92 For summaries of the research on which this finding is based, see Stephen Reicher, 'Most of us are sticking to the lockdown rules, so why do we blame one another?', *Guardian*, 15 January 2021; Reicher, 'In pretending that Covid is over'.

93 Zoe Williams, 'Would you shop your neighbour? The Rule of Six will expose everyone's true nature', *Guardian*, 21 September 2020.

94 Defoe, *Journal of the Plague Year*, 41.

95 Defoe, *Journal of the Plague Year*, 190.

96 Cited in Calvert and Arbuthnott, *Failures of State*, 152.

97 The quote is from *The Dick Cavett Show*, 18 October 1979. (Mary McCarthy was herself orphaned by the 1918 flu epidemic.)

98 SAGE, 'Summary of the effectiveness and harms of different non-pharmaceutical interventions' (21 September 2020).

99 Public Health England, *The Report on Exercise Alice. MERS-CoV* (2016), 9.

100 Robert Booth, 'Coronavirus report warned of impact on UK four years before pandemic', *Guardian*, 7 October 2021.

101 Cited in David Pegg, 'What was Exercise Cygnus and what did it find?', *Guardian*, 7 May 2020. See also Sridhar, *Preventable*, 138.

102 National Audit Office, *The Government's Preparedness for the COVID-19 Pandemic: Lessons for Government on Risk Management* (HC 735, Session 2021–22, 19 November 2021), 10.

103 Rosie Collington and Mariana Mazzucato, 'The love affair with consultants', *Guardian*, 20 September 2021.

104 Boston Consulting and Deloitte websites.

105 Rowena Mason, 'Government admits 50 firms were in VIP lane for Test and Trace contracts', *Guardian*, 7 September 2022.

106 Public Accounts Committee, *Covid-19: Test, Track and Trace (Part 1)* (10 March 2021). See also House of Commons Committee of Public Accounts, *Twenty-Third Report of Session 2021–22 Report, Test and Trace update* (HC 182, 27 October 2021), 7.

107 Adam Briggs, Deborah Jenkins. and Caroline Fraser, *NHS Test and Trace: The Journey So Far* (The Health Foundation, 23 September 2020).

108 On the cost of NHSTT, see Public Accounts Committee, *Covid-19: Test, Track and Trace (Part 1)*.

109 Billy Kember and Chris Smyth, 'Test and Trace: where did it all go wrong?', *The Times*, 11 November 2020.

110 Cited in, Sophie Charara, 'England's contact tracers are unprepared, confused and bored', *Wired*, 25 August 2020.

111 Kember and Smyth, 'Test and Trace'; Robert Booth 'What has gone wrong with England's Covid test-and-trace system?', *Guardian*, 13 August 2020.

112 MO, *Summer 2021: Covid Testing Stories*, C3603.

113 Scottish Government, 'Various questions regarding coronavirus contact tracing strategy: FOI release' (29 June 2020).

114 The Scottish approach is described in Sridhar, *Preventable*, 151.

115 Scottish Government, 'Coronavirus (COVID-19): Scotland's route map – supporting evidence for the 30 July Review' (5 August 2020).

116 Welsh Government, 'Test Trace Protect. Our strategy for testing the general public and tracing the spread of coronavirus in Wales' (4 June 2020).

117 Northern Ireland Department of Health, 'Covid-19 Test, Trace, Protect, Support Strategy' (28 May 2020).

118 MO, *2020 Summer COVID and Time*, H5845.

119 Public Accounts Committee, *Covid-19: Test, Track and Trace (Part 1)*.

120 Kember and Smyth, 'Test and Trace'.

121 Public Health England, 'Directors of Public Health in England' (updated 7 September 2021).

122 Department of Health and Social Care, Public Health England, *Directors of Public Health in Local Government. Roles, Responsibilities and Context* (January 2020).

123 'Memorandum to Matt Hancock and Dido Harding from the leaders of Barnsley, Wakefield, Bradford, Kirklees, Sheffield, Calderdale and Rotherham Councils' (7 August 2020).

124 On the problems with the 0300 code, see, Kember and Smyth, 'Test and Trace'

125 'Memorandum to Matt Hancock and Dido Harding'.

126 Cited in Josh Halliday, 'Four key failings of England's Covid-19 Test and Trace system', *Guardian*, 4 August 2020. The failings of the centralized system are repeatedly addressed in Hammond, *Dr Hammond's Covid Casebook*, 73, 85, 100, 194.

127 Timothy M. Lenton, Chris A. Bolton, and Marten Scheffer, 'Resilience of countries to COVID-19 correlated with trust', *Scientific Reports*, 12, 75 (2022): 1–15.

128 See, for instance, Stephen Reicher, 'Offering twice-weekly Covid tests is futile without proper support for self-isolators', *Guardian*, 6 April 2021.

129 'Memorandum to Matt Hancock and Dido Harding'.

130 'Memorandum to Matt Hancock and Dido Harding'.

131 The 80 per cent target was calculated as early as February 2020 and became the standard measure adopted by SAGE. Joel Hellewell et al., 'Feasibility of controlling COVID-19 outbreaks by isolation of cases and contacts,' *Lancet Global Health*, 8, 4 (April 2020): e488–96; SAGE, 'Thirty-second SAGE meeting on Covid-19' (1 May 2020).

132 Department of Health and Social Care, 'NHS Test and Trace service to strengthen regional contact tracing' (10 August 2020).

133 Department of Health and Social Care, 'Local authorities across England receive funding to support new Test and Trace service' (11 June 2020).

134 Caroline Fraser and Adam Briggs, 'What have we learned from a year of NHS Test and Trace?' (The Health Foundation, 3 June 2021).

135 Halliday, 'Four key failings'. On the need to support 'the most economically disadvantaged' who were required to isolate, see Christina J. Atchison et

al., 'Perceptions and behavioural responses of the general public during the COVID-19 pandemic: a cross-sectional survey of UK adults', *BMJ Open*, 11 (2021): e043577.

136 Fraser and Briggs, 'What have we learned'.

137 Deborah Harkins, 'How local tracing partnerships are supporting NHS Test and Trace' (Public Health England, 19 October 2020).

138 Harkins, 'How local tracing partnerships are supporting NHS Test and Trace'.

139 See, for instance, online advertisement: 'Covid-19 Response – Call Handler 10 p/h Temporary Office based, Kingston-upon-Thames, start date 9 August 2021.'

Chapter 5 Getting and Spending

1 Michael Marmot, *Fair Society, Healthy Lives: The Marmot Review* (2010).

2 Michael Marmot et al., *Health Equity in England: The Marmot Review 10 Years On* (The Health Foundation, February 2020), 5.

3 Marmot et al., *Health Equity in England*, 5. For similar findings, see Veena Raleigh, 'How much longer and further are health inequalities set to rise?' (The King's Fund, 10 October 2021).

4 Suzanne Fitzpatrick et al., *Destitution in the UK 2020* (Joseph Rowntree Foundation, December 2020).

5 Jonathan Cribb, Thomas Wernham, and Xiaowei Xu, 'Pre-pandemic relative poverty rate for children of lone parents almost double that for children living with two parents' (IFS, 4 July 2022); Jonathan Cribb, Tom Waters, Thomas Wernham, and Xiaowei Xu, 'Living standards, poverty and inequality in the UK: 2022' (IFS, 14 July 2022).

6 Adam Corlett, Felicia Odamtten, and Lalitha Try, *The Living Standards Audit 2022* (Resolution Foundation, 4 July 2022), 5.

7 According to Calvert and Arbuthnott's blow-by-blow account, Johnson finally took an interest in the subject three days later, on 28 February. *Failures of State*, 147.

8 Michael Marmot et al., *Build Back Fairer: The Covid-19 Marmot Review. The Pandemic, Socioeconomic and Health Inequalities in England* (Institute of Health Equity, 2020), 5.

9 ONS, 'Coronavirus (Covid-19): 2020 in charts' (18 December 2020). Figure relates to birth certificates mentioning Covid-19 up to 4 December.

10 Marmot et al., *Build Back Fairer*, 5; also 14.

11 Marmot et al., *Build Back Fairer*, 7.

12 Marmot et al., *Build Back Fairer*, 5.

13 The figure was reduced to 70 per cent from 1 July 2021.

14 Andrew Powell and Brigid Francis-Devine, *Coronavirus: Impact on the Labour Market* (House of Commons Library, 20 September 2021), 13.

15 Valentina Romei and Chris Giles, 'UK suffers biggest drop in economic output in 300 years', *Financial Times*, 12 February 2021.

16 On pessimistic forecasts, see Richard Partington, 'The UK's Covid-19 unemployment crisis in six charts', *Guardian*, 3 February 2021.

17 ONS, 'Employment in the UK: April 2022' (12 April 2022).

18 On the relative value of the JRS and Universal Credit, see Karl Handscomb, Cara Pacitti, Hannah Slaughter, and Dan Tomlinson, 'Back to the furlough: U-turn to retain furlough scheme in closed sectors paves way for fresh lockdowns' (Resolution Foundation, 9 October 2020).

19 Torsten Bell and Mike Brewer, *The 12-Month Stretch: Where the Government Has Delivered – and Where It Has Failed – during the Covid-19 Crisis* (Resolution Foundation, 18 March 2021), 5; Cribb et al., 'Living standards, poverty and inequality in the UK'.

20 On the sector-specific nature of the economic consequences of lockdown, see Nye Cominetti et al., *Long Covid in the Labour Market: The Impact on the Labour Market of Covid-19 a Year into the Crisis, and How to Secure a Strong Recovery* (Resolution Foundation, 17 February 2021), 6.

21 Richard Blundell, Robert Joyce, Monica Costa Dias, and Xiaowei Xu, *Covid-19: The Impacts of the Pandemic on Inequality* (IFS, 11 June 2020), 8–9. Also, Laura Gardiner et al., *An Intergenerational Audit for the UK 2020* (Resolution Foundation, October 2020), 9; Nye Cominetti and Hannah Slaughter, *Low Pay Britain 2020* (Resolution Foundation, September 2020), 5; Mike Brewer et al., *The Living Standards Audit 2020* (Resolution Foundation, July 2020), 5.

22 Torsten Bell and Lindsay Judge, *Lockdown Lessons: What 2020 Has to Teach Us about the Difficult Weeks Ahead* (Resolution Foundation, January 2021), fig. 4.

23 Bell and Brewer, *The 12-Month Stretch*, 7; Cominetti et al., *Long Covid in the Labour Market*, 8.

24 Mike Brewer and Karl Handscomb, *All Together Now?: The Impacts of the Government's Coronavirus Income Support Schemes across the Age Distribution* (Resolution Foundation, September 2020), 3.

25 ONS, 'An overview of workers who were furloughed in the UK: October 2021' (1 October 2021).

26 Kathleen Henehan, *Uneven Steps: Changes in Youth Unemployment and Study since the Onset of Covid-19* (Resolution Foundation, 14 April 2021); Partington, 'The UK's Covid-19 unemployment crisis in six charts'.

27 Defoe, *Journal of the Plague Year*, 87; also 201. See also MO, *Covid Special 2020*, B3227, 5 May 2020, for a discussion of the relevance to the pandemic of this observation.

28 Devi Sridhar, 'Covid-19 has shown us that good health is not just down to biology', *Guardian*, 25 December 2020.

29 For an exploration of this issue, see Bruno Latour, *After the Lockdown: A Metamorphosis*, trans. Julie Rose (Cambridge: Polity, 2021), 35.

30 JRF, *Key Worker Diaries*, 'Kayleigh', 7 April 2020.

31 Naughton, *100 Not Out*, Day 15, 5 April 2020, 23.

32 The Health Foundation, *Covid-19 Impact Inquiry* (July 2021); The Health Foundation, *Technical Supplement 1 for the COVID-19 Impact Inquiry Report: COVID-19 Health Outcomes* (July 2021); The Health Foundation, *The Continuing Impact of COVID-19 on Health and Inequalities: A Year on from Our COVID-19 Impact Inquiry* (24 August 2022); Veena Raleigh, *Deaths from Covid-19 (Coronavirus)* (The King's Fund, 23 August 2022).

33 The Health Foundation, *Better Housing is Crucial for Our Health and the Covid-19 Recovery* (28 December 2020).

34 ONS, 'Coronavirus (COVID-19) related deaths by occupation, England and Wales: deaths registered between 9 March and 28 December 2020 (25 January 2021).

35 ONS, 'Updating ethnic contrasts in deaths involving the coronavirus (COVID-19), England: 24 January 2020 to 31 March 2021' (26 May 2021); Public Health England, *COVID-19: Review of Disparities in Risks and Outcomes* (9 June 2020, updated 11 August 2020).

36 ONS, 'Updating ethnic contrasts in deaths involving the coronavirus (COVID-19), England: 10 January 2022 to 16 February 2022' (7 April 2022).

37 UK Research and Innovation, *Ethnicity and Covid-19* (10 December 2021).

38 Ben Humberstone, Deputy Director of Health and Life Events, ONS, cited in Nicola Davis, 'Higher Covid deaths among BAME people "not driven by health issues"', *Guardian*, 16 October 2020.

39 Social Metrics Commission, *Measuring Poverty in 2020* (July 2020), 11. 'Persistent' poverty was where the family was in poverty this year and for two of the three preceding years.

40 Lindsay Judge and Fahmida Rahman, *Lockdown Living: Housing Quality across the Generations* (Nuffield Foundation, July 2020), 10.

41 BMA, 'COVID-19: the risk to BAME doctors' (24 August 2021).

42 'Independent review into the deaths of London bus drivers from Covid-19 suggests earlier lockdown would have saved lives' (Institute of Health Equity, 27 July 2020).

43 Aamna Mohdin, '"A hero on the frontline": five London bus drivers who were killed by coronavirus', *Guardian*, 27 July 2020.

44 Peter Goldblatt and Joana Morrison, *Initial Assessment of London Bus Driver Mortality from Covid-19* (UCL Institute of Health Equity, 2020); Peter Goldblatt and Joana Morrison, *Report of the Second Stage of a Study of London Bus Driver Mortality from Covid-19* (UCL Institute of Health Equity, 2021).

45 Cited in Sirin Kale, '"Bus drivers were forced to play Russian roulette" – the shocking truth about the death of Mervyn Kennedy', *Guardian*, 15 September 2020.

46 Kale, '"Bus drivers were forced to play Russian roulette"'.

47 Frances Ryan, 'Remote working has been life-changing for disabled people, don't take it away now', *Guardian*, 2 June 2021.

48 ONS, 'Homeworking hours, rewards and opportunities in the UK: 2011 to 2020' (19 April 2021).

49 JRF, *Key Worker Diaries*, 'Owiya', 16 April 2020.

50 JRF, *Key Worker Diaries*, 'Owiya', 7 April 2020.

51 Vincent, *Poor Citizens*, 51–159.

52 Bell and Judge, *Lockdown Lessons*, 3.

53 Ofqual, *Learning during the Pandemic: Review of Research from England* (12 July 2021); Bell and Judge, *Lockdown Lessons*, 3.

54 *Covid Realities*, 'Eric J.', 19 June 2021. Also *Covid Realities*, 'Howie P.', 17 February 2021.

55 JRF, *Key Worker Diaries*, 'Charlotte', 6 April 2020.

56 *Covid Realities*, 'Alex R.', 14 February 2021.

57 *Covid Realities*, 'Alex R.', 28 November 2020.

58 *Covid Realities*, 'Lexie G.', 30 March 2021.

59 *Covid Realities*, 'Roisin G.', 22 June 2020.

60 *Covid Realities*, 'Gracie H.', 2 November 2020.

61 *Covid Realities*, 'Zara R.', 15 June 2020.

62 Waitrose's online sales increased by 182 per cent during 2020, and Ocado's by 35 per cent.

63 *Covid Realities*, 'Meg. T.', 20 November 2020.

64 MO, *12 May Diaries 2020*, 418.

65 *Covid Realities*, 'Dorothy T.', 9 November 2020.

66 The contents of the box delivered weekly by administrative error to this book's author, and passed on to a local food bank until, after several requests, the service was stopped. See also MO, *2020 Summer COVID and Time*, A6936.

67 LocalGov.uk, 'Shielding package FAQs pack: local authorities'.

68 Department for Food, Environment and Rural Affairs, 'Coronavirus (COVID-19): apply for the Food Charities Grant Fund' (17 June 2020).

69 FSA, *Covid-19 Consumer Tracker Survey: Annual Summary Report (Waves 1–12)* (May 2021), 13–14. The figures refer to England, Wales, and Northern Ireland.

70 FSA, *Covid-19 Consumer Tracker Survey*, 15.

71 FSA, *Covid-19 Consumer Tracker Survey*, 11.

72 JRF, *Key Worker Diaries*, 'Charlotte', 9 April 2020.

73 *Covid Realities*, 'Eric J.', 1 May 2021.

74 *Covid Realities*, 'Victoria B.', 24 July 2020.

75 Defoe, *Journal of the Plague Year*, 9.

76 Ministry of Housing, Communities and Local Government, 'English Housing Survey 2018–2019: second homes – fact sheet' (9 July 2020); Scottish Government, 'Housing statistics quarterly update: December 2020' (15 December 2020); Welsh Government, 'Research on second homes: evidence review summary' (13 July 2021).

77 *East Anglia Daily Times*, 19 March 2020. See also William Humphries, Charlotte Ware, and Sean O'Neill, 'Rural communities fear influx from coronavirus-stricken cities', *The Times*, 20 March 2020; Anoosh Chekelian, 'How second home owners expose locals to coronavirus and endanger Britain', *New Statesman*, 8 April 2020.

78 MO, *Covid Special 2020*, A6788, 20 March 2020.

79 Nick Gallent, 'COVID-19 and the flight to second homes', *Town and Country Planning* (April/May 2020): 141–4.

80 'Statement from Transport Scotland on restrictions on non-essential ferry travel' (24 March 2020).

81 Severin Carrell, 'How Outer Hebrides were perfectly primed to tackle coronavirus', *Guardian*, 24 April 2020.

82 Steven Morris, 'Police may be asked to stop England residents escaping to Wales to avoid lockdown', *Guardian*, 2 November 2020. It is doubtful whether the endlessly contested Welsh Marches had ever been effectively closed to travellers.

83 Hamptons, 'Londoners spend a record £54.9bn on property outside the Capital' (2022). Also *Which*, 1 August 2021.

84 Sarah Marsh, 'Escape to the country: how Covid is driving an exodus from Britain's cities', *Guardian*, 26 September 2020.

85 Rupert Neate, 'Super-rich buying up "Downton Abbey estates" to escape pandemic', *Guardian*, 14 November 2020.

86 Rupert Neate, 'Private jet bookings soar as wealthy flee second England lockdown', *Guardian*, 3 November 2020.

87 Niko Kommenda, 'Wealthy UK flyers opt for private jets to evade Covid lockdowns', *Guardian*, 21 January 2021.

88 NetJets, 'Flying during COVID-19 pandemic: frequently asked questions'; Jyoti Mann, 'Private jet business Air Partner reaps benefit from Covid-wary passengers', *Financial Times*, 27 August 2021; Tooze, *Shutdown*, 97.

89 Knightsbridge Circle website.

90 Eilidh Hargreaves, 'Private members club vaccinating clients abroad is "proud" to offer the service', *Daily Telegraph*, 12 January 2021. See also Samuel Osborne, '£25,000-a-year private club flying members to UAE and India to get Covid vaccinations', *Independent*, 13 January 2021.

91 Kate Wills, 'Meet the super-rich skipping the queue for a vaccine vacation', *Evening Standard*, 25 February 2021.

92 Hargreaves, 'Private members club vaccinating clients abroad is "proud" to offer the service'.

93 Amelia Tait, 'Covid clinics: hope and high prices on the long road to recovery', *Guardian*, 2 January 2022.

94 Andrew Murphy and Valentin Simon, *Private Jets: Can the Super Rich Supercharge Zero-Emission Aviation?* (Transport & Environment, May 2021), 3.

95 Martin-Brehm Christensen et al., *Survival of the Richest: How We Must Tax the Super-Rich Now to Fight Inequality* (Oxfam International, January 2023), 7.

96 Robert Watts, 'Rich List 2021: how the Covid pandemic spawned more billionaires than ever', *The Times*, 21 May 2021. Globally, the Forbes List to 6 April 2021 also reported the largest ever rise in the total wealth of billionaires. Ruchir Sharma, 'The billionaire boom: how the super-rich soaked up Covid cash', *Financial Times*, 14 May 2021.

97 Michael Sainato, 'Billionaires add $1tn to net worth during pandemic as their workers struggle', *Guardian*, 15 January 2021.

98 Knight Frank, *The Wealth Report* (2022), Wealth Sizing Model.

99 Alistair Gray, 'More than 5 million people become millionaires despite pandemic', *Financial Times*, 23 June 2021.

100 Torsten Müller-Ötvös, cited in Rob Davies, 'Rolls-Royce: Covid has spurred record sales of our cars', *Guardian*, 10 January 2022.

101 Cited in Hilary Rose, 'How the pandemic changed the super-rich', *The Times*, 15 November 2021.

102 Cited in Archie Bland, 'Sailing away: superyacht industry booms during Covid pandemic', *Guardian*, 12 December 2021.

103 Dominic Rushe, 'Netflix loses subscribers for first time in 10 years – and considers advertisements', *Guardian*, 19 April 2022; Kari Paul, 'Netflix's slump

continues as company loses 1 million users in second quarter', *Guardian*, 19 July 2022; John Naughton, 'Have the tech giants finally had their bubble burst? I'd hate to speculate', *Guardian*, 6 August 2022.

104 Sharma, 'The billionaire boom'.

105 Jack Leslie and Krishan Shah, *(Wealth) Gap Year: The Impact of the Coronavirus Crisis on UK Household Wealth* (Resolution Foundation and Standard Life Foundation, 12 July 2021), 34–5.

106 ONS, 'Travel trends 2019' (22 May 2020), fig. 4. The International Passenger Survey was suspended on 16 March 2020, making it impossible to generate comparable figures for 2020.

107 MO, *Covid Special 2020*, D4736, 6 April 2020.

108 Bank of England, *Money and Credit – December 2020* (1 February 2021).

109 Brigid Francis-Devine, *Coronavirus: Impact on Household Savings and Debt* (House of Commons Briefing Paper 9060, 6 July 2021). The household savings ratio measures household savings as a proportion of household disposable income.

110 ONS, 'Households (S.14): households' saving ratio (per cent): current price: £m: SA' (31 March 2022).

111 Bank of England, *Money and Credit*, monthly reports March 2020 to November 2021.

112 ONS, *Family Spending Workbook 2: Expenditure by Income* (16 March 2021), table A8: 'Household expenditure as a percentage of total expenditure by disposable income decile group'.

113 Cited in Mike Brewer and Ruth Patrick, *Pandemic Pressures: Why Families on a Low Income are Spending More during Covid-19* (Resolution Foundation, 11 January 2021).

114 Michael Savage and Toby Helm, 'Universal Credit cut will push 800,000 people into poverty, Boris Johnson is warned', *Guardian*, 19 September 2020.

115 Tom Waters and Thomas Wernham, 'The expiry of the Universal Credit uplift: impacts and policy options' (Institute for Fiscal Studies, 15 July 2021).

116 *Covid Realities*, 'Lexie G.', 27 July 2021.

117 Department of Work and Pensions, press release, 'Government launches £500m support for vulnerable households over winter' (30 September 2021).

118 Karl Handscomb and Lindsay Judge, *Caught in a (Covid) Trap: Incomes, Savings and Spending through the Coronavirus Crisis* (Resolution Foundation, November 2020), 11.

119 *Covid Realities*, 'Lexie G.', 29 April 2020.

120 FCA, *Financial Lives 2020 Survey: The Impact of Coronavirus* (11 February 2021). See also Corlett et al., *The Living Standards Audit 2022*, 5–6.

121 Mike Brewer and Karl Handscomb, *The Debts That Divide Us* (Resolution Foundation, 7 February 2021).

122 Citizens Advice, *Lockdown Debts: Estimating the Size of Lockdown Arrears* (30 October 2020).

123 Citizens Advice, *Excess Debts – Who Has Fallen Behind on Their Household Bills due to Coronavirus?* (8 September 2020).

124 Citizens Advice, *Delivering Debt Advice during a Pandemic: Debt Impact Report 2020/21* (March 2021). On the government subsidy to advice services, see Citizens Advice, 'Citizens Advice welcomes new funding for debt advice' (9 June 2020). Also *StepChange Policy Research: Debt Advice Client Insights 2021* (StepChange, 2021).

125 JRF, 'Nearly two thirds of families on Universal Credit forced into lockdown debt "nightmare"' (17 June 2020).

126 ONS, 'Personal and economic well-being in Great Britain: January 2021' (21 January 2021); Francis-Devine, *Coronavirus: Impact on Household Savings and Debt*, 13–14.

127 Handscomb and Judge, *Caught in a (Covid) Trap*, 4.

128 Bank of England, *Money and Credit – July 2021* (31 August 2021).

Chapter 6 Nature

1 MO, *12 May Diaries 2020*, 253.

2 Cabinet Office, 'Guidance. Staying at home and away from others (social distancing)' (1 May 2020); Jennifer Brown and Esme Kirk-Wade, *Coronavirus: A History of English Lockdown Laws* (House of Commons Library, 30 April 2021), 4–6.

3 The one attempt to examine the long-run history of walking amongst the lower orders, Morris Marples's pioneering *Shanks's Pony: A Study of Walking* (London: J. M. Dent, 1959), is now over sixty years old. See also Miles Jebb, *Walkers* (London: Constable, 1986), 84–5. The more recent, sophisticated histories of walking have largely been confined to the activities and writings of literary pedestrians. See, for instance, Rebecca Solnit, *Wanderlust: A History of Walking* (London: Verso, 2001); Anne D. Wallace, *Walking, Literature, and English Culture: The Origins and Uses of Peripatetic in the Nineteenth Century* (Oxford: Clarendon Press, 1993). On the significance of everyday pedestrian relaxation, see Vincent, *A History of Solitude*, 32–70.

4 [W. Thom], *Pedestrianism; or, An Account of The Performances of celebrated Pedestrians during the Last And Present Century; with a full narrative of Captain Barclay's Public and Private Matches* (Aberdeen: Brown and Frost, 1813); Robert

W. Malcolmson, *Popular Recreations in English Society 1700–1850* (Cambridge: Cambridge University Press, 1973), 43.

5   For a recent survey, see Roderick Floud, *An Economic History of the English Garden* (London: Allen Lane, 2019).

6   Niamh McIntyre and Damien Gayle, 'Poorest areas of England have less than third of garden space enjoyed by richest', *Guardian*, 26 February 2022.

7   ONS, 'One in eight British households has no garden' (14 May 2021).

8   MO, *2020 Summer COVID and Time*, A6936.

9   MO, *2020 Summer COVID and Time*, B7084.

10 William Wordsworth, *A Guide through the District of the Lakes in the North of England* (Kendall: Hudson and Nicholson, 1835), 60.

11 Joe Stone, '"Fresh air is medicine": British ramblers on the joy of their daily walk', *Guardian*, 27 February 2021.

12 Matthew Beaumont, 'As cities enter new lockdowns, it's time to rediscover the joys of walking', *Guardian*, 17 October 2020.

13 Amy Fleming, 'Walk this way! How to optimise your stride and focus your mind to get the most from your daily stroll', *Guardian*, 28 May 2020.

14 'Alison. Wildlife is not in lockdown. 6 May 2020', in *Letters from Lockdown*, 182.

15 MO, *Special Directives*, 17 March 2020, M6815.

16 Stone, '"Fresh air is medicine"'. Also MO, *2020 Summer COVID and Time*, B725; MO, *2020 Summer COVID and Time*, C7297.

17 Josh Halliday, 'Lake District mountain rescue warning after "chaotic" festive period', *Guardian*, 4 January 2022.

18 Helen Pidd, '"The litter was a shock": 2020's Covid-driven rush on UK national parks', *Guardian*, 1 January 2021.

19 Isabel Hardman, *The Natural Health Service: How Nature Can Mend Your Mind* (London: Atlantic Books, 2021), ix–x.

20 Pidd, '"The litter was a shock"'.

21 Rhys Blakely, 'Antisocial visitors to national parks face "Asbo orders"', *The Times*, 15 January 2022.

22 Beaumont, 'As cities enter new lockdowns, it's time to rediscover the joys of walking'.

23 Cited in Rachel Dixon, '"I feel alive and free": the joy of lockdown running', *Guardian*, 19 March 2021.

24 MO, *12 May 2020 Diaries*, 227.

25 Steven Lovatt, *Birdsong in a Time of Silence* (London: Particular Books, 2021), 2.

26 Stephen Moss, 'Birdsong has risen like a tide of hope from our silenced cities. Is it here to stay?', *Guardian*, 2 May 2020.

27 Lovatt, *Birdsong in a Time of Silence*, 3.

28 *https://www.museumoflondon.org.uk/discover/recording-london-soundscapes-past -present*. The modern London recordings were made on behalf of the Museum by Will Cohen of 'String and Tins'. I am grateful to Emily Brazee, Media Officer, Museum of London, for information about these recordings.

29 MO, *12 May 2020 Diaries*, 185.

30 MO, *Non-Mass Observers*, 31 March 2020, CV19 49.

31 Feifei Bu et al., 'Longitudinal changes in physical activity during and after the first national lockdown due to the COVID-19 pandemic in England', *Scientific Reports*, 11 (2021), art. 17723.

32 Department for Transport, 'Official statistics. The impact of the coronavirus pandemic on walking and cycling statistics, England: 2020' (22 September 2021).

33 Tom Edwards, 'Covid: data shows rise in Londoners walking, running and cycling in lockdown', BBC, 26 March 2021.

34 Laura Laker, 'Big rise in UK weekend cycling amid calls for more investment', *Guardian*, 22 July 2021.

35 Travis Elborough, 'Parks are our national lifeblood', *The Oldie*, 25 March 2020.

36 RSPB, *Recovering Together: A Report on Public Opinion on the Role and Importance of Nature during and in Our Recovery from the Coronavirus Crisis in England* (January 2021).

37 Bird Guides.com, 'Huge uptake in Garden BirdWatch during lockdown' (17 May 2020).

38 RSPB, *Recovering Together*.

39 Rachel Cooke, 'Like Dickens, we're learning the value of plodding through our frigid streets', *Guardian*, 2 January 2021. The function of walking in Dickens's life and work is examined in David Vincent, 'Social reform', in Robert L. Patten, John O. Jordan, and Catherine Waters, eds, *The Oxford Handbook of Charles Dickens* (Oxford: Oxford University Press, 2018), 428–9. See also Claire Tomalin, *Charles Dickens: A Life* (London: Viking, 2011), 45, 309, 320, 375.

40 For recent surveys, see Sue Stuart-Smith, *The Well Gardened Mind: Rediscovering Nature in the Modern World* (London: William Collins, 2020); Hardman, *The Natural Health Service*, 6–28, 123–44.

41 See, *inter alia*, Hugh O'Donovan, *Mindful Walking: Walk Your Way to Mental and Physical Well-Being* (Dublin: Hachette Books, 2015); Claire Thompson, *Mindfulness and the Natural World: Bringing Our Awareness Back to Nature* (London: Leaping Hare Press, 2018).

42 Michel Roux Jr, 'Wherever I go in the world, I take my trainers and a pair of shorts', *Guardian*, 19 March 2021.

43 Rachel Ann Cullen: 'Running has saved my mental health', *Guardian*, 19 March 2021. See also Rachel Ann Cullen, *Running for My Life* (London: Blink Publishing, 2018).

44 Emine Saner, 'Kate Humble on walking – and how to improve it: "The rhythm is really good for your brain"', *Guardian*, 24 February 2021.

45 Stone, '"Fresh air is medicine"'.

46 Hardman, *The Natural Health Service*, 82.

47 Summarized in Shane O'Mara, *In Praise of Walking* (London: Vintage, 2019), 128.

48 Hardman, *The Natural Health Service*, 229.

49 Monica Heisey, 'A joyless trudge? No, thanks: why I am utterly sick of "going for a walk"', *Guardian*, 27 February 2021.

50 MO, *12 May Diaries 2020*, 276. Also MO, *Special Directives*, N6622.

51 Defoe, *Journal of the Plague Year*, 118.

52 Camus, *The Plague*, 86.

53 Brian Harrison, 'Animals and the state in nineteenth-century England', *The English Historical Review*, 88, 349 (October 1973): 786; John K. Walton, 'Mad dogs and Englishmen: the conflict over rabies in late Victorian England', *Journal of Social History*, 13, 2 (1979): 221.

54 Daniel Thomas, 'UK faces puppy shortage as demand for lockdown companions soars', *Financial Times*, 22 May 2020.

55 Pet Food Manufacturers Association, *https//www.pfma.org.uk/statistics*.

56 For instance, Simon Usborne, 'Hot dogs: what soaring puppy thefts tell us about Britain today', *Guardian*, 30 July 2020; Nicola Davis, 'Pet buyers should report dodgy sellers, says UK's top vet', *Guardian*, 18 November 2021.

57 Lucy Campbell, 'UK taskforce to tackle rising number of pet thefts', *Guardian*, 8 May 2021.

58 MO, *2020 Summer COVID and Time*, A7000.

59 MO, *12 May Diaries*, 124.

60 Lucy Campbell, 'Owners offload dogs bought in lockdown by pretending they are strays', *Guardian*, 23 October 2021; Sam Wollaston, 'Rescue me: why Britain's beautiful lockdown pets are being abandoned', *Guardian*, 1 December 2021; Jessica Murray, 'RSPCA shelters "drowning" in animals amid cost of living crisis', *Guardian*, 25 August 2022; Ali Mitib, 'Families give up their pets as cost of living bites', *The Times*, 15 August 2022.

61 Floud, *An Economic History of the English Garden*, 240–6.

62 MO, *12 May Diaries 2020*, 415. Also MO, *Covid Special 2020*, B6900, 1 April 2020.

63 Jane Perrone, 'How coronavirus changed gardening forever', *Financial Times*, 11 September 2020.

64 Rachel Mead, 'Nature and nurture', *The New Yorker*, 24 August 2020, 20–4.

65 On new gardeners, see Guy Barter, chief horticulturalist of the RHS, cited in Sarah Marsh, 'Flower power: Covid restrictions fuel boom in plant and bulb sales', *Guardian*, 31 October 2020. On flower sales, see Perrone, 'How coronavirus changed gardening forever'.

66 Cited in Jane Dudman, '"A silver lining to the big, black cloud": allotments during lockdown', *Guardian*, 2 September 2020.

67 *Small Holdings and Allotments Act*, 1908, Section 23. See also S. Martin Gaskell, 'Gardens for the working class: Victorian practical pleasure', *Victorian Studies*, 23, 4 (1980): 484–7.

68 Siân de Bell et al., 'Spending time in the garden is positively associated with health and wellbeing: results from a national survey in England', *Landscape and Urban Planning*, 200 (2020): 7.

69 Stuart-Smith, *The Well Gardened Mind*, 13.

70 Stuart-Smith, *The Well Gardened Mind*, 7. See also Rebecca Nicholson, 'Cultivating calm: how gardening helps me find peace', *Guardian*, 4 January 2022.

71 MO, *Special Directives*, 7145.

72 MO, *Special Directives*, N6622.

73 Cited in Dudman, '"A silver lining to the big, black cloud"', *Guardian*, 2 September 2020.

74 Interviewed in Mead, 'Nature and nurture', 24.

75 MO, *12 May Diaries 2020*, 383.

76 Lucy Bannerman, 'Coronavirus: gardening gives hope, says TV presenter Kate Garraway', *The Times*, 9 October 2020. She found a similar resource in walking in nature: Carol Midgley, 'Walking With . . . Kate Garraway review – holding on to the "hope of a miracle" in nature', *The Times*, 11 November 2021.

77 Guardian readers, '"I've seen a heron, deer, a hare . . .": Guardian readers' lockdown garden transformations', *Guardian*, 20 June 2021.

78 Cited in Dudman, '"A silver lining to the big, black cloud"'.

79 *Register of Bishop Ralph of Shrewsbury*, Somerset Record Society X (1896), 555–6, cited in Horrox, trans. and ed., *The Black Death*, 112. Ralph, formerly Chancellor of the University of Oxford, is described by the *Dictionary of National Biography* as 'a wise and industrious bishop, learned and extremely liberal'.

80 David Wilkins, *Concilia Magnae Britanniae et Hiberniae* (1739), vol. II, 738, cited in Horrox, trans. and ed., *Black Death*, 113.

81 See also the response of the city of Florence when the plague arrived in 1399. Iris Origo, *The Merchant of Prato* (London: Penguin, 1963), 311–29.

82 Amelang, trans. and ed., *A Journal of the Plague Year*, 44.

83 Amelang, *A Journal of the Plague Year*, 45.

84 Amelang, *A Journal of the Plague Year*, 48.

85 Pope Francis, in conversation with Austen Ivereigh, *Let Us Dream: The Path to a Better Future* (London: Simon & Schuster, 2020), 35.

86 Wilkins, *Concilia*, III, 100-1, cited in Horrox, trans. and ed., *Black Death*, 120.

87 *https://www.churchofengland.org/about/policy-and-thinking/our-views/environment-and-climate-change/why-you-should-act*

88 Mark Harrison, *Disease and the Modern World: 1500 to the Present Day* (Cambridge: Polity, 2004), 189. Also Honigsbaum, *The Pandemic Century*, xiv–xv, 280.

89 For a balanced account of the likely origins of Covid-19 in the wet market in Wuhan, see Michael Worobey et al., 'The Huanan Seafood Wholesale Market in Wuhan was the early epicenter of the COVID-19 pandemic', *Science*, 337, 3609 (26 July 2022): 951–9. Also Laura Spinney, 'Angela Rasmussen on Covid-19: "This origins discussion is the worst thing about Twitter"', *Guardian*, 13 August 2022.

90 Sarah Gilbert, *44th BBC Dimbleby Lecture*, BBC Radio 4, 6 December 2021.

91 Richard Hatchett, 'G7 summit: an opportunity to conquer the pandemic' (Coalition for Epidemic Preparedness, 11 June 2021).

92 Laura Spinney, 'Regardless of where the virus came from, there's a growing risk of another Covid-like phenomenon occurring', *Guardian*, 27 August 2021.

93 Tobias Rees, 'From the Anthropocene to the Microbioscene. The novel coronavirus compels us to rethink the modern concept of the political,' *NOĒMA*, 10 June 2020.

94 Lauri Myllyvirta, '11,000 air pollution-related deaths avoided in Europe as coal, oil consumption plummet' (Centre for Research on Energy and Clean Air, 30 April 2020).

95 See, *inter alia*, Jonathan Watts, 'Coronavirus may prove boost for UK's bees and rare wildflowers', *Guardian*, 9 April 2020; Stephen Moss, 'Birdsong has risen like a tide of hope from our silenced cities. Is it here to stay?', *Guardian*, 2 May 2020; Kaya Burgess, 'Britain's wildlife flourishes during Covid-19 lockdown', *The Times*, 28 December 2020.

96 Sarah Marsh, 'Rail commuting in Great Britain at less than half pre-pandemic level', *Guardian*, 30 October 2021. The guidance was withdrawn in England

on 19 July 2021, and reintroduced as from 13 December 2021, due to the Omicron wave of infection.

97 Valentine Quinio and Kathrin Enenkel, 'How have the Covid pandemic and lockdown affected air quality in cities?' (Centre for Cities, 10 December 2020).

98 Sandra Laville, 'Manchester becomes latest UK city to delay clean air zone', *Guardian*, 21 May 2020.

99 Patrick Greenfield and Peter Muiruri, 'Conservation in crisis: ecotourism collapse threatens communities and wildlife', *Guardian*, 5 May 2020.

100 UN News, 'Carbon dioxide levels hit new record; COVID impact "a tiny blip", WMO says' (United Nations, 23 November 2020).

101 Naughton, *100 Not Out*, Day 26, 16 April 2020, 36.

102 MO, 12 May 2020, 417.

Chapter 7 Communication

1 David Sanderson, 'Sales of plague novels soar amid coronavirus lockdown', *The Times*, 23 April 2020.

2 A third novel in the series, *The Bullet That Missed*, was published in September 2022.

3 Richard Osman, *The Thursday Murder Club* (London: Penguin, 2021), 18.

4 Osman, *The Thursday Murder Club*, 13–14.

5 Osman, *The Thursday Murder Club*, 42.

6 Osman, *The Thursday Murder Club*, 89.

7 Oliver Telling, 'Bloomsbury Publishing to "materially" beat profit guidance amid reading boom', *Financial Times*, 26 January 2022. Also Alison Flood, 'UK book sales in 2021 highest in a decade', *Guardian*, 11 January 2022.

8 Alison Flood, 'UK book sales soared in 2020 despite pandemic', *Guardian*, 27 April 2021.

9 World Economic Forum, 'Book sales are up: this is what we've been reading during the pandemic' (26 May 2021).

10 Flood, 'UK book sales in 2021 highest in a decade'.

11 Publishers Association, *Publishing in 2020* (2021).

12 Publishers Association, 'Audiobooks soar during pandemic' (26 November 2021).

13 Alison Flood, 'Crime fiction boom as book sales rocket past 2019 levels', *Guardian*, 7 July 2020.

14 On this market, see Claire Armistead, 'Why we're falling in love with romance novels all over again', *Guardian*, 16 January 2022.

15 Cited in Flood, 'UK book sales soared in 2020 despite pandemic'.

16 Stephen Lotinga, chief executive of the Publishers Association, citing industry records, in *Guardian Review Section,* 14 November 2020.

17 Figure from Nielsen BookScan, reported in Flood, 'UK book sales in 2021 highest in a decade'.

18 It changed its title from *The Guinness Book of Records* at the end of the twentieth century.

19 Respectively of Bob Mortimer and Billy Connolly.

20 On the performance of Bloomsbury, see Telling, 'Bloomsbury Publishing to "materially" beat profit guidance amid reading boom'.

21 Cited in Kalyeena Makortoff, 'Harry Potter publisher Bloomsbury reports record sales amid reading boom', *Guardian*, 15 June 2022.

22 John Naughton, *From Gutenberg to Zuckerberg: What You Really Need to Know about the Internet* (London: Quercus, 2012), 138. See, for instance, Ben Anderson and Karina Tracey's study of how the early embrace of the internet added to rather than displaced existing patterns of communication: 'Digital living: the impact (or otherwise) of the internet on everyday British life', in Barry Wellman and Caroline Haythornthwaite, eds, *The Internet in Everyday Life* (Oxford: Blackwell, 2002), 149.

23 Susan Whyman, *The Pen and the People: English Letter-Writers 1660–1800* (Oxford: Oxford University Press, 2009), 9; David Vincent, *Literacy and Popular Culture: England 1750–1914* (Cambridge: Cambridge University Press, 1989), 21–52.

24 Statista, 'Total addressed letter volume in the United Kingdom between 2011 and 2021' (9 December 2021).

25 Ofcom, *Annual Monitoring Update for Postal Services Financial Year 2020–21* (9 December 2021), 3. Figure for six months up to September 2021. On a 17 per cent rise in letter writing in the United States in the lockdown, see Tanya Basu, 'Letter writing staved off lockdown loneliness. Now it's getting out the vote', *MIT Technology Review*, 18 September 2020.

26 National Literacy Trust, 'Children and young people's letter writing in 2021' (20 October 2021).

27 First class next-day delivery times fell to almost twenty points below the official target of 93 per cent. Lorna Booth and Gloria Tyler, *Performance of Royal Mail* (House of Commons Library, 16 June 2021), 2–4.

28 ONS, *Social Trends, No. 41* (2011), 'Lifestyles and social participation', 3. Answers to the question: 'How often . . . do you contact a close friend, relative or someone else close to you (apart from your spouse or partner) about how you're feeling or just to catch up?'

29 MO, *Special Directives*, 17 March 2020, M6815.

30 MO, *Non-Mass Observers*, CV19 17.

31 Gaby Hinsliff, 'Walking therapy: how lockdown intensified friendship', *Guardian*, 12 February 2021.

32 'Diana. Lockdown play partner. 13 June 2020', in *Letters from Lockdown*, 236–7.

33 David Maughan Brown, *Covid2020diary*, 29 March 2020.

34 MO, *Special Directives*, L7310.

35 MO, *12 May Diaries 2020*, 413.

36 MO, *12 May Diaries 2020*, 149.

37 The popularity of quizzes during the pandemic is explored in Philip Coggan, 'Why the British love quizzes', *Financial Times,* 13 February 2022.

38 MO, *2020 Summer COVID and Time*, B725.

39 MO, *12 May Diaries 2020*, 375.

40 Ofcom, *Online Nation. 2021 Report* (9 June 2021), 3.

41 MO, *12 May Diaries 2020*, 365. Amongst the video games, Fortnite boomed in the pandemic. See Devon Pendleton and Alexander Sazonov, 'Fortnite, rappers and the billion-dollar pandemic gaming boom', *Bloomberg UK* (19 May 2020).

42 MO, *12 May Diaries 2020*, 165.

43 On an unsatisfactory attempt to keep a choir of thirty-five voices functioning online, see MO, *12 May Diaries 2020*, 188.

44 Latour, *After the Lockdown*, 29.

45 The Digital Entertainment and Retail Association, 'Lockdown streaming drives entertainment sales to £9bn' (8 January 2021).

46 Val, Wales, in u3a, *Living History Diary*, 31 May 2020.

47 Karen Hao and Tanya Basu, 'Why does it suddenly feel like 1999 on the internet?', *MIT Technology Review*, 3 April 2020.

48 Lloyds Bank, *UK Consumer Digital Index 2021* (May 2021), 17, fig. 10.

49 Elise Taylor, 'What makes a food go viral? Inside the explosive popularity of TikTok's feta pasta', *Vogue*, 1 March 2021; Waitrose and Partners, *Food and Drink Report 2021–22* (2021), 17.

50 MO, *Non-Mass Observers*, CV19 7.

51 See the activities featured in the organization's video, *u3a Life in Lockdown* (YouTube).

52 It was launched by myself in my capacity as a Pro Vice Chancellor of the Open University, on the basis of a grant of $10 million from the William and Flora Hewlett Foundation.

53 Open University, 'OpenLearn's response to the pandemic' (13 July 2021).

54 Open University, 'Inside Track' (18 August 2022).

55 Ofcom, *Online Nation*, 3.

56 Offcom, *Online Nation*, 3, 9.

57 ONS, 'Internet users, UK: 2020. Internet use in the UK; annual estimates by age, sex, disability and geographical location' (6 April 2021). The Lloyds Bank 2020 survey found a similar level of 7 per cent of the population 'almost completely offline'. Lloyds Bank, *UK Consumer Digital Index 2020* (May 2020), 11.

58 Ofcom, *Online Nation*, 12.

59 Centre for Ageing Better, *Covid-19 and the Digital Divide* (July 2021).

60 ONS, 'Internet users, UK: 2020'.

61 Lloyds Bank, *UK Consumer Digital Index 2021*, 13.

62 Amelia Hill '"Computers are marvellous!": older people embrace internet in lockdown', *Guardian*, 10 March 2021. 'Probus' is a network of clubs for the retired or semi-retired.

63 'Xenia. A birthday in lockdown. 3 April 2020', in *Letters from Lockdown*.

64 For instance, Farooki, *Everything is True*, 103.

65 Naughton, *100 Not Out*, Day 42, 2 May 2020, 53–4. See also David Vincent, 'Screen life', *Covid2020diary*, 30 April 2020.

66 Kate Murphy, 'Why Zoom is terrible', *New York Times*, 29 April 2020.

67 Ross Barkan, 'This year proved once and for all: screens are no substitute for real life', *Guardian*, 30 December 2020.

68 Statista, 'Daily active users (DAU) of the Zoom app on android and iOS devices in the United Kingdom (UK) from January to November 2020' (November 2020).

69 MO, *Special Directives 2020*, B7287.

70 For a discussion of this difficulty during the expansion of postal communication before the Penny Post, see Bruce Redford, *The Converse of the Pen: Acts of Intimacy in the Eighteenth-Century Familiar Letter* (Chicago: University of Chicago Press, 1986), 2; James Daybell, *The Material Letter in Early Modern England: Manuscript Letters and the Culture and Practices of Letter-Writing, 1512–1625* (London: Palgrave Macmillan, 2012), 148–74.

71 Lauren Berlant, 'Intimacy: A Special Issue', in *Intimacy*, edited by Lauren Berlant (Chicago: University of Chicago Press, 2000), 6.

72 On the first public controversy about postal espionage, see David Vincent, *The Culture of Secrecy: Britain 1832–1998* (Oxford: Oxford University Press, 1998), 1–9; Howard Robinson, *Britain's Post Office* (London: Oxford University Press, 1953), 47, 55, 91–2.

73 See, for instance, Jerry M. Rosenberg, *The Death of Privacy* (New York: Random House, 1969); Myron Brenton, *The Privacy Invaders* (New York: Coward-McCann, 1964); Vance Packard, *The Naked Society* (London: Longmans, 1964).

74 Lloyds Bank, *UK Consumer Digital Index 2020*, 21, fig. 16; Lloyds Bank, *UK Consumer Digital Index 2021*, 28, fig. 20.

75 Pilita Clark, 'Year in a word: Zoom', *Financial Times*, 21 December 2020; Naughton, *100 Not Out*, Day 91, 20 June 2020, 107.

76 Lloyds Bank, *UK Consumer Digital Index 2021*, 29, fig. 21.

77 Ross Barkan, 'This year proved once and for all: screens are no substitute for real life', *Guardian*, 30 December 2020.

78 Hao and Basu, 'Why does it suddenly feel like 1999 on the internet?'

79 See, in particular, John Naughton, *A Brief History of the Future: The Origins of the Internet* (London: Phoenix, 2000); Naughton, *From Gutenberg to Zuckerberg*; and his weekly column on the technology of communication in the *Observer*.

80 Naughton, *100 Not Out*, Day 3, 24 March 2020, 11.

81 Naughton, *100 Not Out*, Day 12, 2 April 2020, 21.

82 William Cobbett, *Cobbett's Advice to Young Men, and (incidentally) to Young Women, in the Middle and Higher Ranks of Life. In a Series of Letters, Addressed to a Youth, a Bachelor, a Lover, a Husband, a Father, a Citizen, or a Subject* (London: W. Cobbett, 1829), Letter V, 'To a Father', para. 61.

83 See, for instance, William Cobbett, 'William Cobbett's advice to a father on vaccination', in *Vaccination Tracts: Opinions of Statesmen, Politicians, Publicists, Statisticians, and Sanitarians, No. 1* (London: William Young, 1879). On the campaign more generally, see Michael Bennett, *The War against Smallpox: Edward Jenner and the Global Spread of Vaccination* (Cambridge: Cambridge University Press, 2020).

84 Shoshana Zuboff, *The Age of Surveillance Capitalism: The Fight for the Future at the New Frontier of Power* (London: Profile Books, 2019).

85 Reported in John Zarocostas, 'How to fight an infodemic', *The Lancet*, 395 (29 February 2020).

86 See, for instance, WHO, 'Coronavirus disease (COVID-19) advice for the public: Mythbusters' (19 January 2022).

87 Cited in Charles Arthur, *Social Warming: The Dangerous and Polarising Effects of Social Media* (London: Oneworld, 2021), 275–6.

88 Hancock. *Pandemic Diaries*, 217.

89 GOV.UK, 'Coronavirus (COVID-19) in the UK. About the coronavirus (COVID-19) in the UK dashboard' (29 September 2022).

90 David Vincent, 'Sadly', *Covid2020diary*, 24 February 2021.

91 See, for instance, ONS, 'Coronavirus (COVID-19) latest insights. A live roundup of the latest data and trends about the coronavirus (COVID-19) pandemic from the ONS and other sources (18 February 2022).

92 David Spiegelhalter and Anthony Masters, *Covid by Numbers: Making Sense of the Pandemic with Data* (London: Pelican Books, 2021), 11–12.

93 David Spiegelhalter and Anthony Masters, 'Can you capture the complex reality of the pandemic with numbers? Well, we tried. . .', *Guardian*, 2 January 2022.

94 Stephen Reicher, 'The weakest link in fighting Covid is not the public, it's the UK government', *Guardian*, 13 December 2021.

95 Gideon Skinner, Jayesh Navin Shah, and Cameron Garrett, *Trust in Science. UKRI Research: How Has Covid-19 Affected Trust in Scientists?* (Ipsos, 22 September 2020), 8–9.

96 *One Year with Covid-19: How Institutions Fared* (Ipsos, 2021), 2. The surveyed countries were Australia, Canada, Germany, the United States, Russia, France, Japan, and the UK.

97 Ben Goldacre, *Bad Science* (London: Fourth Estate, 2008), 246–70.

98 Holly Else and Richard Van Noorden, 'The fight against fake-paper factories that churn out sham science', *Nature*, 23 March 2021.

99 Nadja Durbach, '"They might as well brand us": working-class resistance to compulsory vaccination in Victorian England', *Social History of Medicine*, 13, 1 (April 2000): 47.

100 On the scale of the attack in the United States, see James K. Meeker, 'The political nightmare of the plague: the ironic resistance of the anti-quarantine protesters', in J. Michael Ryan, ed., *Covid-19. Volume II: Social Consequences and Cultural Adaptations* (London: Routledge, 2021), 109–21.

101 Devi Sridhar, 'I've been lied about and others get death threats. Covid has shown the power of misinformation', *Guardian*, 1 January 2022.

102 See also Sridhar's discussion of the suicide after prolonged harassment of an Australian scientist. Devi Sridhar, 'A scientist in the public eye has taken her own life. This has to be a wake-up call', *Guardian*, 12 August 2022.

103 Frank Swain@SciencePunk. The summary circulated widely on the internet.

104 The British Medical Association, *Secret Remedies* (London, 1909), vii, cited in Vincent, *Literacy and Popular Culture*, 168.

105 Shaun Callaghan, Martin Lösch, Anna Pione, and Warren Teichner, 'Feeling good: the future of the $1.5 trillion wellness market' (McKinsey, 8 April 2021).

106 Julia Fellowes, 'Pfizer accused of pandemic profiteering as profits double', *Guardian*, 8 February 2022.

107 Centre for Countering Digital Hate, *The Disinformation Dozen* (24 March 2021); Centre for Countering Digital Hate, *Disinformation Dozen, The Sequel* (28 April 2021).

108 Jasper Jackson and Alexandra Heal, *Misinformation Market: The Money-Making Tools Facebook Hands to Covid Cranks* (The Bureau of Investigative Journalism, 21 January 2021).

109 Jasper Jackson, Alexandra Heal, and Tim Wall, 'Facebook "still too slow to act on groups profiting from Covid conspiracy theories"', *Guardian*, 11 April 2021.

110 Jackson and Heal, *Misinformation Market*.

111 Arthur, *Social Warming*, 280.

112 Neil F. Johnson et al., 'The online competition between pro- and anti-vaccination views', *Nature*, 582 (11 June 2020): 230–4.

113 Ofcom, 'Covid-19 news and information: summary of views about misinformation' (7 July 2020).

114 Hannah Al-Othman, 'Bradford's Covid vaccine ambassadors to inoculate against conspiracy theories', *Sunday Times*, 29 November 2020.

115 Jon Roozenbeek et al., 'Susceptibility to misinformation about COVID-19 around the world', *Royal Society, Open Science*, 7 (2020): 1–15. The countries studied were the UK, Ireland, the United States, Spain, Mexico.

116 Samanth Subramanian, The deep conspiracy roots of Europe's strange wave of cell-tower fires', *Politico*, 18 May 2020.

117 Al-Othman, 'Bradford's Covid vaccine ambassadors to inoculate against conspiracy theories'.

118 It was defined as 'delaying acceptance or refusal of vaccination despite availability of vaccination'.

119 The Royal Society and the British Academy, *COVID-19 Vaccine Deployment: Behaviour, Ethics, Misinformation and Policy Strategies* (21 October 2020), 1; The British Academy, 'Vaccine hesitancy threatens to undermine vaccine response' (10 November 2020).

120 The Royal Society and the British Academy, *COVID-19 Vaccine Deployment*, 1.

121 YouGov/CCDH Survey Results. Fieldwork 24–5 June 2020. Also Alex Hern, 'Nearly one in six Britons would refuse Covid-19 vaccine – survey', *Guardian*, 7 July 2020.

122 Steven Lloyd Wilson and Charles Wiysonge, 'Social media and vaccine hesitancy', *BMJ Global Health*, 5 (23 October 2020).

123 Elaine Robertson et al., *Predictors of Covid-19 Vaccine Hesitancy in the UK. Household Longitudinal Study* (2 January 2021). Also Linda Geddes, 'Covid vaccine: 72% of black people unlikely to have jab, UK survey finds', *Guardian*, 16 January 2021; Nazia Parveen, Aamna Mohdin, and Niamh McIntyre, 'Call to prioritise minority ethnic groups for Covid vaccines', *Guardian*, 18 January 2021.

124 Laura Spinney, 'Could understanding the history of anti-vaccine sentiment help us to overcome it?', *Guardian*, 26 January 2021, table 16.

125 ONS, 'Coronavirus and vaccine sentiment, 9 August 2021', *Opinions and Lifestyle Survey (Covid-19)*, 23 June–18 July 2021, table 16.

126 ONS, 'Coronavirus and vaccine sentiment, 9 August 2021', table 1a.

127 ONS, 'Coronavirus and vaccine sentiment, 9 August 2021', table 18.

128 NHS, 'Covid-19 monthly announced vaccinations' (15 April 2021). Period: 8 December 2020–7 April 2021. Population aged fifty+, first dose.

129 Clea Skopeliti, 'Coronavirus vaccine: councils to get £23m to encourage high-risk groups to have jab', *Guardian*, 25 January 2021; Nazia Parveen and Caelainn Barr, 'Black over-80s in England half as likely as white people to have had Covid jab', *Guardian*, 4 February 2021. Also Aamna Mohdin, 'BAME groups urged to have Covid vaccine in UK TV ad campaign', *Guardian*, 18 February 2021; Aamna Mohdin and Caelainn Barr, 'One in four elderly black people in England still not vaccinated', *Guardian*, 5 June 2021; NHS, 'Bridging the uptake gap: COVID-19 vaccination toolkit for Black African and Black African Caribbean communities' (June 2021).

130 NHS, 'Covid-19 monthly announced vaccinations' (8 July 2021). Period: 8 December 2020–30 June 2021. NHS, 'Covid-19 monthly announced vaccinations' (13 January 2022). Period: 8 December 2020–31 December 2021. Population aged fifty+, first dose; ONS, 'Black Caribbean ethnic group: facts and figures' (27 June 2019).

131 ONS, 'Coronavirus (COVID-19) latest insights: vaccines' (23 February 2022).

132 Population aged fifty+, first dose.

133 Cited in Parveen and Barr, 'Black over-80s in England half as likely as white people to have had Covid jab'. See also James Hitchings-Hales, 'How is institutional racism causing COVID-19 hesitancy in Britain?', *Global Citizen*, 4 May 2021.

134 Fancourt et al., *Tracking the Psychological and Social Consequences of the COVID-19 Pandemic*, 13.

135 Joint Committee on Human Rights, House of Commons and the House of Lords, 2020, *Black People, Racism and Human Rights*, Eleventh Report of Session 2019, cited in Rochelle Ann Burgess et al., 'The COVID-19 vaccines rush: participatory community engagement matters more than ever', *The Lancet*, 10 December 2020: 8.

136 Robert Booth, Niamh McIntyre, and Tobi Thomas, 'Millions of unjabbed a key concern as England scrambles to vaccinate', *Guardian*, 15 December 2021.

137 Spiegelhalter and Masters, *Covid by Numbers*, 196.

138 The balance of scientific opinion, however, increasingly supported the view that the origin was in the fish market not the laboratory. Michael Worobey et al., 'The Huanan market was the epicenter of SARS-CoV-2 emergence', *Zenodo*, 26 February 2022; Jonathan E. Pekar, 'SARS-CoV-2 emergence very likely resulted from at least two zoonotic events', *Zenodo*, 26 February 2022.

139 Justin McCarthy, 'Big pharma sinks to the bottom of US industry rankings' (Gallup, 3 September 2019). 'Education' was seventeenth in the table.

140 Connor Ibbotson, 'Where do people believe in conspiracy theories?' (YouGov, 18 January 2021).

141 MO, *Special Directives 2021*, B3227.

142 MO, *Special Directives 2021*, B7012. Also MO, *Special Directives 2021*, E7024; MO, *Special Directives*, H417.

143 Roozenbeek et al., 'Susceptibility to misinformation about COVID-19 around the world': 10.

144 WHO, *Conducting Community Engagement for COVID-19 Vaccines: Interim Guidance* (31 January 2021).

145 Cited in Mark Townsend, 'Vaccine hesitancy wanes despite thousands joining "Freedom March"', *Guardian*, 26 June 2021.

146 Sridhar, 'I've been lied about and others get death threats'.

147 Burgess et al., 'The COVID-19 vaccines rush'.

148 Burgess et al., 'The COVID-19 vaccines rush'.

149 Helen Pidd, 'Inspiring confidence: Liverpool GPs tackle the vaccine race gap', *Guardian*, 4 February 2021. On the successful use of mobile vaccine buses more generally, see Chris Smyth, 'UK in final vaccine push amid rising minority uptake', *The Times*, 24 June 2021.

150 Sadiq Khan and Nadhim Zahawi, 'The vaccines are safe. We would urge all minority groups to get one', *Guardian*, 31 January 2021.

151 *Final Report of the Royal Commission Appointed to Inquire into the Subject of Vaccination* (London: HMSO, 1896), 137.

152 *Final Report . . . into the Subject of Vaccination*, 138.

Chapter 8 Home

1 Waitrose and Partners, *Food and Drink Report 2021–22*, 3. The report was based on a national survey of 2,000 people together with information from Waitrose and John Lewis stores.

2 Waitrose and Partners, *Food and Drink Report 2021–22*, 7.

3 Prime Minister's Office, 'Prime Minister's statement on coronavirus (COVID-19): 23 March 2020'.

4 ONS, 'Coronavirus and the economic impacts on the UK' (22 October 2020, 19 November 2020); Larry Elliott, 'Working from home is proving to be a revolution in our way of life', *Guardian*, 26 October 2020; 'The Guardian view on empty offices: goodbye to all that?', *Guardian*, 4 August 2020.

5 Cited in Eleni Courea, Graham Paton, and Jonathan Ames, 'Coronavirus: reluctant office staff defy government call to commute', *The Times*, 31 August 2020.

6 ONS, *Coronavirus and the Social Impacts on Great Britain, 16–27 March 2022* (1 April 2022), table 6, Working from Home.

7 Naughton, *100 Not Out*, Day 11, 1 April 2020, 21.

8 Torsten Bell, 'Work', in 'Life after Covid, will our world ever be the same?', *Guardian*, 20 November 2020.

9 Ivana Isailović, 'The "new normal" privatization of the workplace', *Law and Political Economy*, 20 July 2020.

10 Prime Minister's Office, 'Prime Minister's statement on coronavirus'.

11 A further 1.5 million were advised to shield on the basis of a Covid-19 population risk assessment.

12 Vincent, *Privacy*, 10–11, 56–7, 83–4, 118–22.

13 Margery Spring Rice, *Working-Class Wives: Their Health and Conditions* (1939; 2nd edn, London: Virago, 1981), 129.

14 *Report of the Committee on Privacy* (1972), p. 26, para. 78.

15 Edwin Heathcote, *The Meaning of Home* (London: Francis Lincoln, 2012), 25.

16 Waitrose and Partners, *Food and Drink Report 2021–22*, 8.

17 Twitter, 31 March 2020.

18 Despite her political career, she had published at least eighteen novels by this point. She was subsequently promoted to the Cabinet post of secretary of state for Digital, Culture, Media, and Sport.

19 A. Aassve et al., 'The COVID-19 pandemic and human fertility', *Science*, 369, 6502 (24 July 2020): 370–1.

20 ONS, 'Provisional births in England and Wales: 2020 and Quarter 1 (Jan. to Mar.) 2021' (24 June 2021); Maja Gustafsson and David Willetts, 'A return to boom and bust (in births). How birth cycles will affect public spending pressures over the coming decade' (Resolution Foundation, 15 October 2021). In this sense, the prime minister and his wife bucked the trend by conceiving a daughter in the middle of the third Covid-19 outbreak,

21 Frederica Cocco, 'Baby bust: economic stimulus helps births rebound from pandemic', *Financial Times*, 18 April 2022.

22 Alison Flood, 'Research finds reading books has surged in lockdown', *Guardian*, 15 May 2020.

23 Reading Agency, 'Reading connects a world in self-isolation' (2 April 2020).

24 Ofcom, *Media Nations 2020* (3 November 2020).

25 Hancock, *Pandemic Diaries*, 89.

26 MO, *Non-Mass Observers*, CV19 42, 21 March 2020.

27 MO, *Special Directives*, C5381.

28 Rebecca Smithers, 'How Britain's Covid-19 panic buyers triggered a tinned food renaissance', *Guardian*, 23 August 2020.

29 MO, *Non-Mass Observers*, CV19 45, 7 April 2020. Also MO, *Special Directives*, P3924(1).

30 MO, *Special Directives*, L4071.

31 Naughton, *100 Not Out*, Day 13, 3 April 2020, 22–3.

32 David Vincent, 'Log-stack', *Covid2020diary*, 24 September 2020. My own supplier, 'Logalog' of Newport, Shropshire, experienced a similar boom.

33 Kelza Pilkington, in 'Coronavirus Diaries: an engineering CEO and a supermarket assistant on working during lockdown', *Financial Times*, 28 April 2020. See also MO, *Special Directives*, S5866.

34 Steven Taylor, 'Understanding and managing pandemic-related panic buying', *Journal of Anxiety Disorders*, 78 (2021): 1.

35 See, for instance, the reasoned account of the practice in MO, *Covid Special 2020*, D4736, 16 March 2020.

36 Kantar Consulting report based on a sample of thirty thousand households, reported in *More or Less*, BBC Radio 4, 15 April 2020.

37 On the culpable delays at this time, see Calvert and Arbuthnott, *Failures of State*, 102 and *passim*. On the excessive costs of emergency purchasing, see Hammond, *Dr Hammond's Casebook*, 165

38 George Grylls, 'Storage of unused PPE costs the taxpayer £700,000 a day', *The Times*, 8 August 2022.

39 MO, *12 May Diaries 2020*, 221. On the social media post, see my 20 April 2020 entry in *Covid2020diary*: 'I have measured out my life with coffee spoons': 'After listening to the activities of our grandchildren on a Zoom call, our daughter returns our enquiry: "So, what have you two been doing?" We both of us realised that we really had no answer to that question.'

40 MO, *Non-Mass Observers*, CV19 49, 2 May 2020.

41 MO, *Special Directives*, H7124.

42 MO, *12 May Diaries 2020*, 190.

43 It was published as a Kindle edition, *100 Not Out: A Lockdown Diary* (23 November 2020). He continued his Memex1.1 daily blog, but its focus was far from confined to the pandemic.

44 Marina Warner, 'Lockdown has created new forms of boredom – and not all of them are bad', *Guardian*, 14 April 2021.

45 Jonathan Freedland, 'Adjust your clocks: lockdown is bending time completely out of shape', *Guardian*, 24 April 2020.

46 MO, *2020 Summer COVID and Time*, 03436a.

47 MO, *2020 Summer COVID and Time*, B7496; 'Karl. A different time. 3 July 2020', in *Letters from Lockdown*, 220.

48 *Covid Realities*, 'Connie G.', 6 October 2020. See also MO, *2020 Summer COVID and Time*, C7557.

49 Naughton, *100 Not Out*, Day 20, 10 April 2020, 30.

50 Natalia Martinelle et al., 'Time and emotion during lockdown and the Covid-19 epidemic: determinants of our experience of time?', *Frontiers in Psychology* (6 January 2021): 1.

51 Moya Sarner, 'Brain fog: how trauma, uncertainty and isolation have affected our minds and memory', *Guardian*, 14 April 2021.

52 'Josh Cohen in conversation with Akshi Singh', *Solitudes Past and Present*, 7 January 2022, *https://solitudes.qmul.ac.uk/blog/josh-cohen-in-conversation-with-akshi-singh*.

53 MO, *Non-Mass Observers*, CV19 42, 2 April 2020; u3a, *Living History Diary*, 'Pam, Essex, 16 March 2020'.

54 MO, *Non-Mass Observers*, CV19 46, 3 May 2020; MO, *Special Directives*, F7035(3).

55 MO, *12 May Diaries 2020*, 108.

56 MO, *12 May Diaries 2020*, 189.

57 Cited in Naughton, *100 Not Out*, Day 16, 6 April 2020, 26.

58 Andrew Ellson, 'Coronavirus: now we're all working from home on an egg', *The Times*, 7 May 2020.

59 Waitrose and Partners, *Food and Drink Report 2021–22*, 21.

60 For similar patterns across Europe see EIT Food, *COVID-19 Impact on Consumer Food Behaviours in Europe* (Aarhus: Aarhus University, Denmark, December 2021).

61 MO, *Special Directives*, H7124.

62 Waitrose and Partners, *Food and Drink Report 2021–22*, 7.

63 MO, *12 May Diaries 2020*, 196.

64 Ian Johnson, 'Kingfisher bets DIY boom to continue as it makes record profits', *Financial Times*, 22 March 2022.

65 Miles Brignall, 'Hobbycraft reports 200% boom in online sales since start of pandemic', *Guardian*, 3 August 2020.

66 Cited in Anna Turns, 'How hobbies helped people stay positive during lockdown', *Positive News*, 25 June 2020.

67 MO, *12 May Diaries 2020*, 234.

68 MO, *12 May Diaries 2020*, 46.

69 Rupert Jones, 'Puppy power: the costs and pitfalls of buying a dog', *Guardian*, 10 October 2020.

70 Naughton, *100 Not Out*, Day 16, 6 April 2020, 26. Also Annie and Freya Lawrie, 'We rescued him but in the end I think he rescued us', in Jenny Stevens, '"Our rescue cat rescued us": how pets provided unconditional love in lockdown', *Guardian*, 3 March 2021.

71 Cited in Zoe Wood, 'Going for gold: pet firm reports resurgence in fishkeeping', *Guardian*, 27 November 2020.

72 The court case was examined in David Vincent, 'Follow the tortoise', *Covid2020diary*, 28 April 2020.

73 MO, *2020 Summer COVID and Time*, C2310.

74 MO, *12 May Diaries 2020*, 395.

75 JRF, *Key Worker Diaries*, 'Kayleigh', 6 April 2020.

76 Yetunde James, *Marie Claire Covid-19 Global Diaries*, 8 June 2020.

77 JRF, *Key Worker Diaries*, 'Owiya', 11 April 2020.

78 MO, *12 May Diaries 2020*, 193.

79 'Marcus. My unexpected second paternity leave. 4 May 2020', in *Letters from Lockdown*, 261.

80 ONS, 'Coronavirus and how people spent their time under lockdown' (27 May 2020). See also Alexandra Topping, 'Pandemic could lead to profound shift in parenting roles, say experts', *Guardian*, 19 November 2020.

81 Mark Sweney, 'Digital detox and post-pandemic catch-ups fuel board game boom', *Guardian*, 15 November 2021.

82 Zoe Wood, 'UK jigsaw puzzle sales hit £100m as "people find a balance in their lives"', *Guardian*, 1 February 2021. For similar increases in the United States, see James Doubek and Art Silverman, 'With people stuck at home, jigsaw puzzle sales soar' (NPR, 13 April 2020).

83 Tom Tyler, *British Jigsaw Puzzles of the Twentieth Century* (Shepton Beauchamp, Somerset: Richard Dennis, 1997), 9–10; Chris McCann, *Master Pieces: The Art History of Jigsaw Puzzles* (Portland, OR: Collector's Press, 1998), 7–8.

84 James Tapper, 'We are railing: Britain embraces the joys of the humble train set', *Guardian*, 25 October 2020. On the history of the company, see Anthony McReavy, *The Toy Story: The Life of Times of Inventor Frank Hornby* (London: Ebury Press, 2002).

85 'The LEGO Group delivers strong growth in 2020' (Licensing International, 10 March 2021); 'The LEGO Group achieves strong growth while investing to build for the future' (LEGO.com, 8 March 2022).

86 For a survey of these changes since the beginning of the twentieth century, see Vincent, *A History of Solitude*, 153–81.

87 Ministry of Housing and Local Government, *Homes for Today & Tomorrow* (London: Her Majesty's Stationery Office, 1961), 15. Also John Burnett, *A Social History of Housing* (London: Methuen, 1986), 304–8.

88 ONS, 'Internet sales as a percentage of total retail sales (ratio) (%)' (22 April 2022).

89 Waitrose and Partners, *Food and Drink Report 2021–22*.

90 EIT Food, *COVID-19 Impact on Consumer Food Behaviours in Europe*, 13.

91 MO, *12 May Diaries* 2020, 255.

92 Rebecca Smithers, 'Quesadillas or cashew stir-fry? Meal kits boom as UK seeks inspiration', *Guardian*, 19 August 2020.

93 JRF, *Key Worker Diaries*, 'Justyna', 19 April 2020.

94 'Valerie. Going grombre (with style). 22 June 2020', in *Letters from Lockdown*, 276–7.

95 MO, *Covid Special 2020*, B3227, 16 June 2020.

96 The range of emotions is reported in Paul Campbell and *Guardian* Readers, 'Locksdown: readers share their home haircut adventures', *Guardian*, 24 April 2020.

97 MO, *Non-Mass Observers*, CV19 45, 15 April 2020.

98 MO, *Non-Mass Observers*, CV 19 42, 30 April 2020, 6 May 2020.

99 Catherine H. Mercer et al., 'Impacts of COVID-19 on sexual behaviour in Britain: findings from a large, quasi-representative survey (Natsal-COVID)', *BMJ, Sexually Transmitted Infections*, 98 (2022): 471.

100 See, for instance, Zoe Williams, '"I feel a bit rusty": has Covid killed our sex lives?', *Guardian*, 25 September 2021.

101 Mercer et al., 'Impacts of COVID-19 on sexual behaviour in Britain'.

102 Pam Sonnenberg et al., 'Intimate physical contact between people from different households during the COVID-19 pandemic: a mixed-methods study from a large, quasi-representative survey (Natsal-Covid)', *BMJ Open*, 12 (2021): e055284.

103 Alexandra Jones, 'The new summer of love: "People are desperate to have sex – it's been a long year"', *Guardian*, 5 June 2021.

104 UK Health Security Agency, 'New STI diagnoses and rates in England, by gender, 2012 to 2021' (4 October 2022).

105 Public Health England, 'The impact of the COVID-19 pandemic on prevention, testing, diagnosis and care for sexually transmitted infections, HIV and viral hepatitis in England. Provisional data, January to September 2020' (December 2020): 1–38; Emily Dema et al., 'Initial impacts of the COVID-

19 pandemic on sexual and reproductive health service use and unmet need in Britain: findings from a quasi-representative survey (Natsal-COVID)', *Lancet Public Health* 7 (2022): e36–47.

106 He subsequently received a police fine for his attendance at the party.

107 See for instance MO, *Non-Mass Observers*, CV19 37, 11 May 2020.

108 MO, *Special Directives*, F7074(2). Also MO, *Special Directives*, G7129(2).

109 MO, *Special Directives*, Spring 2021, B1752.

110 Jasmin Dhillon, in 'Coronavirus Diaries: NHS respiratory doctor and an expectant mother on facing the virus', *Financial Times*, 23 April 2020.

111 'Nishma. Untouched dresses in the drawer. 3 April 2020', in *Letters from Lockdown*, 22–3.

112 'Nishma. Untouched dresses in the drawer', 23–4.

113 JRF, *Key Worker Diaries*, 'Kayleigh', 8 April 2020.

114 Fancourt et al., *UCL COVID-19 Social Study: Results 8* (3 May 2020); *Results 31* (24 February 2021), fig. 27.

115 ONS, 'Mapping loneliness during the coronavirus pandemic'.

116 The age bands were 18–29, 30–59, 60+.

117 Stig Abell, 'Stig Abell on . . . loneliness', *Sunday Times*, 19 April 2020.

118 Chitra Ramaswamy, 'Losing my mum in lockdown was a brutal lesson in the abject loneliness of grief', *Guardian*, 21 December 2020.

119 MO, *2020 Summer COVID and Time*, C2310.

120 MO, *2020 Summer COVID and Time*, B3635.

121 'Josh Cohen in conversation with Akshi Singh'.

122 On the pressure of people as a cause of loneliness, see Ryan Hammond et al., 'Lonely in a crowd: investigating the association between overcrowding and loneliness using smartphone technologies', *Scientific Reports*, 11, 24134 (December 2021).

123 *Covid Realities*, 'Rosie K.', 2 March 2021.

124 Vincent, *A History of Solitude*, 153–81.

125 *Covid Realities*, 'Claire M.', 26 November 2020.

126 *Covid Realities*, 'Alex R.', 24 April 2021. Also *Covid Realities*, 'Erik J.', 17 July 2021.

127 Neil Smith, Isabel Taylor, and Valerija Kolbas, *Working from Home and Mental Health during the COVID-19 Pandemic* (National Centre for Social Research, July 2021). Also Michael Savage, 'Revealed: rise in stress among those working from home', *Guardian*, 4 July 2021.

128 *Covid Realities*, 'Syeda F.', 24 November 2020.

129 Fred Cooper, 'Family carers, loneliness, and COVID-19: preliminary findings

from "Caring Through Coronavirus"', Pathologies of Solitude Zoom Seminar, 16 February 2021.

130 For an examination of the interaction between underfunding and loneliness in the welfare system, see Alison Stenning and Sarah Marie Hall, 'On the frontline: loneliness and the politics of austerity', *Discover Society*, 6 November 2018.

131 Johann Zimmermann, *Solitude Considered with Respect to Its Dangerous Influence upon the Mind and Heart* (London: C. Dilly, 1798), 21.

Chapter 9 Aftermath

1 Defoe, *Journal of the Plague Year*, 219–20.

2 Defoe, *Journal of the Plague Year*, 225.

3 New Economics Foundation, press release, 29 June 2020.

4 Hilary Cooper and Simon Szreter, *After the Virus: Lessons from the Past for a Better Future* (Cambridge: Cambridge University Press, 2021), 281.

5 Peter Hennessy, *A Duty of Care: Britain before and after Covid* (London: Allen Lane, 2022), 115.

6 Hennessy, *A Duty of Care*, 120.

7 Hennessy, *A Duty of Care*, 132.

8 Hennessy, *A Duty of Care*, 137.

9 Hennessy, *A Duty of Care*, 132.

10 Michael Marmot, 'Studying health inequalities has been my life's work. What's about to happen in the UK is unprecedented', *Guardian*, 8 April 2022.

11 Adam Tooze, 'Crisis Pictures (Krisenbilder) – mapping the polycrisis', *Chartbook #73* (21 January 2022). On a similar fading of the historical frame of the pandemic in the USA, see Ross Barkan, 'For better or worse, the pandemic seems slated to fade from our collective memory', *Guardian*, 9 January 2023.

12 On 24 February, the legal requirement to self-isolate following a positive test was removed together with routine contact tracing and the legal requirement for close contacts who are not fully vaccinated to self-isolate.

13 Pauline Boss, *The Myth of Closure: Ambiguous Loss in a Time of Pandemic and Change* (New York: Norton, 2022).

14 UK Commission on Bereavement, *2022 Summary Report* (2022), 4.

15 On the scale of the global threat posed by long Covid in the autumn of 2022, see the comments of the head of the WHO: Tedros Adhanom Ghebreyesus, 'The data is clear: long Covid is devastating people's lives and livelihoods', *Guardian*, 12 October 2022.

16 ONS, 'Prevalence of ongoing symptoms following coronavirus (COVID-

19) infection in the UK: 1 September 2022' (1 September 2022); ONS, 'Coronavirus (COVID-19) latest insights: infections' (10 February 2023). A parallel WHO study using a twelve-week delay found that at least seventeen million people in Europe were suffering from long Covid. Nicola Davies, 'Covid can cause ongoing damage to heart, lungs and kidneys, study finds', *Guardian*, 23 May 2022; Jamie Smyth, 'At least 17m people in Europe have had long Covid, says WHO', *Financial Times*, 13 September 2022.

17 Tom Waters and Thomas Wernham, 'Long COVID and the labour market' (Institute for Fiscal Studies Briefing Note BN246, 27 July 2022), 2.

18 Alvin Chang, 'The astounding impact and reach of long Covid, in numbers and charts', *Guardian*, 12 October 2022.

19 Sarah Neville, 'The growing evidence that Covid-19 is making us all sicker', *Financial Times*, 30 August 2022.

20 On current research, see, for instance, Gwenaëlle Douaud et al., 'SARS-CoV-2 is associated with changes in brain structure in UK Biobank', *Nature*, 7 March 2022; Hannah E. Davis et al., 'Characterizing long COVID in an international cohort: 7 months of symptoms and their impact', *eClinical Medicine*, 15 July 2021; Zeynep Tufekci, 'If you're suffering after being sick with Covid, it's not just in your head', *New York Times*, 25 August 2022.

21 Camilla Cavendish, 'Britain's jobs "miracle" hides some uncomfortable truths', *Financial Times*, 16 September 2022.

22 Samuel R. Chamberlain et al., 'Post-traumatic stress disorder symptoms in COVID-19 survivors: online population survey', *BJPsych Open*, 9 February 2021; Sarah Marsh, 'One in three survivors of severe Covid diagnosed with mental health condition', *Guardian*, 7 April 2021.

23 Steven Taylor, 'I wrote the book on pandemic psychology. Post-Covid will take some getting used to', *Guardian*, 24 February 2022.

24 Jonathan Cribb, Tom Waters, Thomas Wernham, and Xiaowei Xu, 'Material living standards held up surprisingly well through the pandemic on average – but the self-employed, low-income working families, and people from ethnic minority groups suffered increased deprivation' (Institute for Fiscal Studies, 8 July 2021).

25 On the worst case, see, for instance, the views of Rachel Clarke: 'The claim that the NHS "coped" with Covid is not true – it's drowning and damaged', *Guardian*, 23 March 2022.

26 House of Commons Committee of Public Accounts, *NHS Backlogs and Waiting Times in England* (7 March 2022).

27 BMA, 'NHS backlog data analysis' (October 2022); Max Warner and Ben

Zaranko, 'NHS waiting lists unlikely to fall significantly in 2023' (Institute for Fiscal Studies, 8 February 2023).

28 IPPR, 'Revealed: a third of adults struggled to access NHS during pandemic, driving many to private healthcare' (2 March 2022).

29 Ofsted, 'Education recovery in schools: summer 2022' (20 July 2022).

30 Alison Andrew et al., 'Inequalities in children's experiences of home learning during the COVID-19 lockdown in England', *Fiscal Studies*, 41, 3 (12 July 2021): 653–83; Education Endowment Foundation, *The Impact of COVID-19 on Learning: A Review of the Evidence* (May 2022), 3.

31 Department for Education, 'Bumper £24 million to boost children's literacy' (9 October 2022).

32 Tom Kirchmaier, Carmen Villa-Llera, and Shubhangi Agrawal, 'Burglaries and robberies fell during COVID – but in the poorest parts of Britain, violent crime is up' (LSE, 18 March 2022).

33 Associated Press, 'Anger in China after officials break into homes in hunt for Covid contacts', *Guardian*, 20 July 2022.

34 Tooze, *Shutdown*, 95–7.

35 BBC Radio 4, *The Today Programme*, 19 May 2020. See also David Vincent, 'Lessons in time', *Covid2020diary*, 20 May 2020.

36 ONS, 'Is hybrid working here to stay?' (23 May 2022); ONS, 'How people spent their time after coronavirus restrictions were lifted, UK: March 2022' (9 August 2022).

37 Reported in *Global Business Outlook*, 'UK citizens do 1.45 days' work from the office', 25 August 2022.

38 Rebecca Solnit, 'The impossible has already happened. What coronavirus can teach us about hope', *Guardian*, 6 April 2020. For a more extended discussion of this argument, see Rebecca Solnit, *A Paradise Built in Hell: The Extraordinary Communities that Arise in Disaster* (rev. edn, London: Penguin, 2020).

39 MO, *Special Directives*, B6895.

40 Tooze, *Shutdown*, 132

41 Stephen Reicher and Linda Bauld, 'From the "fragile rationalist" to "collective resilience": what human psychology has taught us about the Covid-19 pandemic and what the Covid-19 pandemic has taught us about human psychology', *Journal of the Royal College of Physicians of Edinburgh*, 51, 1 (December 2021), S12–18. See also Jonathan Jackson et al., 'The lockdown and social norms: why the UK is complying by consent rather than compulsion' (LSE, 27 April 2020). At an international level, see, Tooze, *Lockdown*, 86, 96.

42 In my own case, my second vaccination was in a marquee on Ludlow Racecourse.

My wife and I emerged in time to watch the twelve o'clock race, although there was no opportunity to bet on the outcome. My friend and colleague Brenda Gourley reported a similar experience at Brighton Racecourse.

43 Jolanda Jetten, Stephen D. Reicher, S. Alexander Haslam, and Tegan Cruwys, *Together Apart: The Psychology of Covid-19* (London: SAGE, 2020), xiii.

44 On community support networks and their importance on the eve of Covid-19, see Hilary Cottam, *Radical Help: How We Can Remake the Relationships between Us and Revolutionise the Welfare State* (London: Virago, 2019), 205–6.

45 Sarah O'Connor, 'Return to Rugeley', *FT Weekend Magazine*, 19/20 March 2022, 28.

46 Hennessy, *A Duty of Care*, 126.

47 Discussed further in Vincent, 'Going local', *Covid2020diary*, 30 March 2020.

48 Peter Macfadyen, *Flatpack Democracy 2.0: Power Tools for Reclaiming Local Politics* (Bath: eco-logicbooks, 2019).

49 The Labour Party, *A New Britain: Renewing Our Democracy and Rebuilding Our Economy. Report of the Commission on the UK's Future* (Newcastle-upon-Tyne, December 2022), 2.

50 Gordon Brown, 'Think our plan to fix British politics is a pipe dream? Think again', *Guardian*, 6 December 2022.

51 In mid-March 2022, Covid-19 infection rates were rising in all the nations except Northern Ireland, where they had for the time being levelled. ONS, 'Coronavirus (COVID-19) Infection Survey, UK: 18 March 2022'.

Index

A and E departments *see* Accident and
Emergency departments
abuse
  child 18, 82–4
  domestic, women 18, 84–7
Accident and Emergency departments
  34–36
adoption, child 84
adultery 207
AIDS 12, 21, 66, 172
alcohol consumption 21, 36, 68–9, 76, 191,
  217, 225
Alzheimer's Society 79
ambulances 25, 30, 33, 34, 35, 38, 40, 91,
  155
anti-vax, *see* vaccines, vaccine hesitancy,
  anti-vaxxers
anxiety, stress 22, 23, 44, 62, 63, 67–9, 70–3,
  77–8, 79, 81, 82, 87, 115, 130–3, 138,
  146–7, 158–61, 168–70, 220, 228, 239,
  242, 248, 263
  see also Post-Traumatic-Stress Disorder
Archbishop of Canterbury, Justin Welby 2,
  52, 53, 56, 122, 171, 235–6
autobiography 11

BAME groups *see* ethnicity, minority ethnic
  groups
Barnardo's 84
Beaumont, Matthew 153, 155
bereavement 1–2, 18, 23, 44–58, 61, 230, 232,
  237–9, 245
birds, birdsong 91, 151–6, 158–9, 173
birth rate 209–10
Bishop Ralph of Shrewsbury 170
board games 181, 221, 223

book clubs 182
books *see* reading
Boss, Pauline 71, 237–8
Boston Consulting 113
British Psychological Society 81
Brown, Gordon 251
buses, bus drivers 131–2
  see also transport, public

Camus, Albert 17, 18, 162, 176
cancer 18, 33, 45–6, 50–1, 74, 88, 241
care homes, workers, social care 8, 28, 31–3,
  36, 50, 65, 78–81, 90, 128–31, 176–7,
  233–4, 236, 238
Catholic Church 58
charity, giving 94–104, 247–50
childbirth, infancy 227–8
chocolate, consumption of 68–9, 76, 89
Church of England 49, 51–2, 53–4, 56, 57,
  58, 98
cinema 16, 76, 145, 182, 245
Citizens Advice 148
'Clap for Our Carers' 91–4, 107, 129
Clarke, Rachel 28–9, 37, 38, 39, 41, 88
Clean Air Act (1956) 173
climate change, global warming 13, 157,
  171–5, 206–7, 236, 237, 245–6
'clinically extremely vulnerable' (shielded)
  21, 71, 96, 98, 100, 120, 137, 207,
  214
Cobbett, William 190
Cohen, Josh 231
community, neighbourhood 92–3, 94–104,
  110, 117, 118–21, 122, 153, 199–200,
  202–3, 248–51
Cooke, Rachel 159

312